IMPROVING
TEACHING-LEARNING
PROCESSES

IMPROVING
TEACHING-LEARNING
PROCESSES

RAY H. SIMPSON

PROFESSOR OF EDUCATIONAL PSYCHOLOGY
UNIVERSITY OF ILLINOIS

1953

LONGMANS, GREEN AND CO.
NEW YORK · LONDON · TORONTO

LONGMANS, GREEN AND CO., INC.
55 FIFTH AVENUE, NEW YORK 3

LONGMANS, GREEN AND CO. LTD.
6 & 7 CLIFFORD STREET, LONDON W 1

LONGMANS, GREEN AND CO.
215 VICTORIA STREET, TORONTO 1

IMPROVING TEACHING-LEARNING PROCESSES

FIRST EDITION

LIBRARY OF CONGRESS CATALOG CARD NUMBER 52-13684

Printed in the United States of America
VAN REES PRESS • NEW YORK

CONTENTS

learner problem identification be pointed?—Developing learner identification of problems through departmental changes—School-wide attack on questions related to problem identification—Operating principles for developing problem-identification abilities—Bibliography

5. ABILITY TO SELECT APPROPRIATE PROBLEMS
   FOR STUDY   97

Evaluative questions on problem selection—Problem-selection ladder—What are possible bases upon which to decide what to study?—What are criteria to be considered in actual selection of problems for study?—Could the teacher do a better job of selecting problems than the learner?—Will not cooperative problem selection cause much time to be wasted?—Should in-class and out-of-class work on problems be individual or group?—How will texts or courses of study be covered in problem approach? — Moving from teacher-dominated assignments toward learner-teacher selected problems—What are some responses to learner self-evaluation of problem-selection ability?—Operating principles for developing problem-selection abilities—Bibliography

6. PROBLEM SOLUTION FOR EFFECTIVE LEARNING 140

Evaluative questions related to learning problem-solution processes—What attitudes and points of view contribute to effective learning of problem-solution processes?—Problem-solution practice ladder—Proposed solution try-out ladder—Helping the learner recognize the need for solutions to his problems—Keeping solution attempts on the right track—An example of individualized problem-solution operation—What are signs of success in problem-solution activities? — How long should a single problem be worked on? Who should decide when a change is to be made? On what basis should a decision be made?—How teacher can help bring work to a close on a particular problem in a profitable way—An example of students' evaluation of one aspect of problem-solving processes — Operating principles and suggestions for problem-solution practice—Bibliography

systematic self-evaluation of his own educational record-keeping?—How may learners help one another through a reciprocal study and evaluation of each other's records?—What kind of learner records can constitute one part of reports for parents?—Operating principles for the development of effective learner record-keeping—Bibliography types of reading goals?—How may in-school reading goals be related to out-of-school behavior?—Some uses of goals and measurements—What changes in reading emphasis are probable with increasing use of process approaches?—Operating principles for developing functional reading for problem attack—Bibliography

Part Four: LABELED TEACHING METHODS AND PROCESS-RELATED PROBLEMS

Part Five: RESEARCH EVIDENCE

Part Six: THE CHALLENGE OF THE FUTURE

Part One

INTRODUCTION AND METHOD
ASSUMPTIONS

1

INTRODUCTION

THIS BOOK is designed primarily to meet the teaching and learning needs of those concerned with more effectively meeting teaching-learning situations in junior and senior high schools. In most schools of education or teachers' colleges, this volume would be suitable as a text in the methods course. In educational psychology courses, where much emphasis is placed upon translating psychological principles into educational practices, this book will help the teacher and student think through key psychological problems related to efficient operation in teaching and learning situations.

Let us examine the situation that faces Jim Snider and Jane Williams, both college juniors, who are preparing to teach in either junior or senior high school. In their methods courses their teachers may encourage them only to study what they will do when they actually become teachers. This is the conventional approach to methods courses and can be useful as far as it goes. In addition, the teacher can also help Jim and Jane face the fact that here and now they are in a realistic teaching-learning situation, the methods course, which can be used as a laboratory for gaining a better understanding of and facility in dealing with teaching-learning processes. A distinguishing feature of this text is its emphasis both upon (1) a study of what the student will do when he later is a teacher, and (2) a study of the present teaching-learning situation in which he plays a key role as a learner.

Because of the dual emphasis just mentioned, most of the illustrations used in the text come from high-school classes and from college teacher-training situations. The examples of practices from high schools will aid the student in visualizing and dealing with situations he will later face when his primary role becomes that of teacher.

3

Illustrations drawn from college teacher-training classes will help the student analyze and study the teaching-learning processes of which he is, while taking the course, most intimately a part. There is an implicit underlying assumption here that one of the best ways of aiding the learner in understanding concepts and processes involved in teaching-learning situations is to help him experience, study, and plan different kinds of learning and teaching in his own experience as a student. It should be emphasized also that Jack Snider and Jane Williams, the prospective teachers, are likely to become better teachers if they see the close relationship between their roles as teachers and their roles as perennial learners. The good teacher must continue to be or become a good learner.

This book has grown largely out of the writer's work and study in trying to teach learners democratically and effectively on levels ranging from the first grade through the graduate level. It developed from a realization that a study of teaching methods alone is not enough. For effective leadership in modern schools, the teacher must concern himself with both teaching and learning processes. Since these are very frequently woven together, our study essentially becomes one of teaching-learning processes.

During the first half of the twentieth century, educators and prospective educators have recognized individual differences in intelligence, personality, motivation, and other characteristics, which are very important in teaching-learning processes. Since psychologists and others have objectively shown the range of individual differences, many methods have been proposed to handle them in mass education. Some of these, homogeneous grouping for example, have been largely attempts to meet the problem by dividing those in a particular grade or class into two or more groups, usually on the basis of either intelligence or achievement or a combination of these two. While this procedure cuts down, at least temporarily, the spread of individual differences *in terms of some aspects of ability, the spread in individual purposes and goals and in some other key factors in learning is about as wide as before.*

Other attempts to handle individual differences, such as the contract plan, do to some extent adjust the *speed* of the work to the individual. Here again, however, little or no attention is given to differences in the individual goals and purposes of the learner. Unfortunately, the problem of how individual differences can be taken care of effectively in mass education is far from solved. In some

teachers and prospective teachers, the knowledge of individual differences has caused a feeling of frustration. Many have said in effect,
"Yes, I recognize individual differences but one just cannot take care
of them in classes of twenty-five to fifty students."

Any successful method of meeting individual differences in mass
education must give great attention to the goals and purposes of the
individual learner. This means that the learner must participate more
and more in decisions affecting him. Many of these decisions will
revolve around what, when, and how he will study.

In his annual report published in October 1941, President Sey-
mour of Yale wrote: "The educated man is the one who has learned
to educate himself." The University of Michigan's Carrothers states:
"The greatest need of the hour in education is the discovery of ways
to shift work from teachers to pupils." [1] We can do a much better
job of education if we keep constantly before us the goal of producing self-starting learners who will be able to teach themselves.
In working toward this goal we shall constantly strive to help the
learner assume more and more responsibility in improving the basic
steps in his learning processes.

Primary goals of the high-school teacher who believes in teaching
the learner to teach himself, self-education, will include at least the
following: first, to develop in the student the *continuing* desire to
acquire those learnings that he needs most for happy living and
learning; second, to help the learner develop these skills necessary
for identifying and selecting wisely those problems he will work on
during learning; third, to help the learner to practice the abilities
needed in solving the problems he ought to meet. If these goals are
really accepted by the educator, a first major step will have been
taken toward visualizing the problem of individualizing instruction.

If the learner is to develop the abilities necessary to teach himself, it is important that we clearly recognize the steps of the learning
process in which he must gain competence.

Since life is made up of one problem after another, the major part
of basic learning processes revolves around problems, their identification, selection, and solution, together with service learnings that
must be given attention. These, then, will be our major concern.
Before launching into a preliminary discussion of them, let us examine some key premises of the book.

[1] G. E. Carrothers, "Size of Job and Growth of Worker," *School and Society*,
65 (May 31, 1947), 406.

This book is based on several premises. The first is that *it is virtually impossible for the teacher to go very far in adequately meeting the challenge of individual differences as long as he tries to manage for each learner all of the learning processes over which many teachers now hold a virtual monopoly.* If a teacher alone tries to make each assignment for every learner, diagnose the strengths and weaknesses of each learner, select all materials to be used by each learner, decide when each resource will be used by each learner, make every test for each learner, and do all the other steps in effective learning that teachers have traditionally tried to handle *for* the learner, the teacher in mass education is in an impossible situation insofar as reaching a solution to teaching-learning problems related to individual differences is concerned. Attempts designed to cope with individual differences must not saddle the teacher with undesirable overloads.

The second major assumption is that *basic teaching-learning processes* and *psychological principles related to these processes are fundamentally similar regardless of the age of those with whom we are working.* An attempt is made in this text to emphasize this premise. For example, some high-school teachers contend that high-school students are too immature to be expected to think. Evidence is presented later to show that even elementary and preschool children can and do think. How effectively they think depends largely upon the teacher guidance they get.

The third premise is that *learning problems connected with varied individual needs, abilities, and attitudes can be optimistically attacked if the teacher is willing to relinquish gradually some of his monopolistic control of certain steps in teaching-learning processes and consciously build up in each learner the ability to handle for himself, with appropriate guidance, all steps in learning processes.* This process may be called the developing of self-education in each learner. It should be recognized that mere acceptance of this premise will not help the educator unless he is willing to go through a period of rethinking his teaching and learning concepts. Effective use of the concept will also involve building up techniques and procedures that are likely to be somewhat different from those now used by most educators.

A fourth premise is based on the idea that *the best teacher is the one who teaches the learner how to teach himself.* If one of our major goals is to train the learner to be able to carry on systematic learning when he leaves school and to be able to meet effectively the problems he faces, then, even if it were economically feasible to have a teacher for every two or three learners, it would probably be unsound psychologically. This would certainly be true if the teacher alone selected all materials, made all evaluations, decided exactly what was to be studied, and appropriated for himself practice in the other procedures necessary for effective independent learning.

A fifth premise underlying this material is that *it is particularly important that professional courses for educators and future educators be laboratories for studying and improving procedures in meeting individual differences in an effective and democratic fashion.* It would seem to be true, for example, that a course in educational psychology would not be very effective if the principles which are taught in precept are daily violated in practice. Teachers and administrators are likely to work with others the way they as learners have been handled. Thus, one problem of the professional educator becomes that of showing learners that he is trying to practice what he preaches.

The premises that have just been stated will become clearer as other chapters in the book are developed. A preview of subsequent chapters will now be given.

ASSUMPTIONS UNDERLYING TEACHING

Consciously or unconsciously, every teacher is basing the decisions he is continually making upon a set of assumptions. The actual assumptions being made are frequently unrecognized by either the teacher or the learners whom they affect. For example, when a history or science teacher decides to assign pages 281-295 of a text for study by all students or when a mathematics teacher tells all students to do problems 1 through 10 on page 87 of a text, each is making a large number of assumptions about learner needs, the role of the teacher, the most efficient role of the learner, interpersonal relations, and individual differences, to mention only a few. In Chapter 2 some possible assumptions are described in seven major areas. The reader is also given a picture of the assumptions the writer believes to be most sound psychologically. These are used as an underlying basis for the remainder of the book.

THREE FUNDAMENTAL STEPS IN LEARNING PROCESSES

The primary problem the high-school teacher faces is one of helping students do a better job of meeting current and future problems.

Identifying problems, a first major step. Regardless of what subject is being taught, a first and fundamental phase of the learning process is that of identifying possible problems upon which it might be desirable for the learner to work. This step and possible methods of developing learners along this line will be discussed in Chapters 3 and 4. Training the learner to recognize his present and probable future needs will not only free the teacher somewhat for other tasks but will also give the learner practice in getting the learning process under way.

Should learners help set up the course structure? If we accept the idea that learners should practice planning their own learning activities, what are some of the possible methods of helping them to determine their needs and problems? Does the learner's practice in planning his work in a course make it unnecessary for the teacher to preplan course activities? Can an individual teacher emphasize process learnings in his courses if others in the school are using approaches with basically different assumptions? How may school departments or school staffs make a broader attack on questions related to problem identification? These and other problems are attacked in the two chapters devoted to problem identification in an attempt to clarify the need for practice in this process on the part of the learners, and also in an attempt to suggest some specific ways that teachers may go about helping learners develop basic motivation for their course procedures and general school activities.

Key points suggested with respect to problem identification include the following: (1) Learning the processes involved in problem identification should be considered a paramount goal for both teachers and learners. (2) Adequate problem identification is a process that is probably as difficult as problem solution, and the former needs much consideration because in most classes it has been neglected in the past. (3) In moving from non-learner identification of problems to be studied we must expect a certain amount of bewilderment on the part of the learner and in many cases on the part of the teacher also. (4) Reshaping course activities to give the learner and the teacher practice in problem identification will involve considerable changes in goals and procedures insofar as the typical teacher is concerned.

Selecting appropriate problems for study. After a learner has gained some practice in identifying problems of importance to him, he, with the help of the teacher, faces the major task of deciding on which of the identified problems at a particular time it is likely to be most profitable for him to work. This second major step is discussed in Chapter 5. What are the possible bases upon which one might decide what to study? Would it not be possible for the teacher to do a better job of selecting the problems than the learner? If the answer to this question is yes, how is the learner to get practice in this phase of the learning process for later use? How will prearranged courses of study or class setups or texts be covered in an approach with emphasis on learning processes? How does one move from the conventionally practiced teacher-dominated assignments toward teacher-learner selected problems? These and other problems are considered in the chapter related to problem selection.

Some ideas of key importance gleaned from the discussion of problem-selection abilities are the following: Teacher dictation of assignments may seem to get quick results. However, since the learner is being deprived of an opportunity to get his own learning under way, systematic learning after the teacher is no longer around is not very probable. Thus, a goal of paramount importance is that of having the student work on problems in such a way that he will carry over his learnings into out-of-school situations. Instead of teaching what, when, and how subject matter will be learned, the teacher's main purpose becomes one of helping the student in this connection to learn how to take the initiative in getting his own learning started.

Effective progress in teaching problem-selection abilities frequently starts with the teacher analyzing and improving his own selection of personal and professional problems for systematic study and may start when the teacher asks himself such a question as, "How can I effectively know and improve *my own skill* in selecting the professional or personal problems which I need to study so that I may teach more happily and more effectively?"

Of key importance is the fact that to learn wisely how to select problems the learner must have actual experience and practice in selecting problems. One test of learner and teacher effectiveness in the matter of problem selection is the extent to which the learner himself has improved in the ability to decide wisely what he should study at any particular time. It must be recognized that old ideas, attitudes, and habits relating to the question of what constitutes education and schooling tend to change slowly, if at all. In like fashion, ideas, attitudes, and habits relating to the question, "Who should select problems for study?", will probably take considerable time to change. Difficulty in producing change should be anticipated by the alert teacher or prospective teacher. It should be recognized also that a high degree of democracy in guided problem selection by learners involves the use of techniques and skills on the part of the teacher and the learner that take considerable time to develop.

Problem solution for effective learning. In Chapter 6, which deals with this problem, some of the issues considered are these: What points of view contribute to desirable learning of problem-solution processes? Should the in-class and the out-of-class work of problem solution usually be individual or group? How could we help the learner recognize the need for solutions to his key problems? How can we keep problem solution on the right track and what are some of the signs of success in such activities? How do we know when the work on a particular problem should be stopped at least temporarily and an attack made on a different problem?

Here are some of the key ideas about problem-solution practice: Learning the process of problem-solving is of more importance to the learner in science or history than the memorizing of solutions or conclusions already held by the teacher or textbook writer. A goal in problem-solving in English or social studies classes should usually be to get a variety of possible solutions rather than to get "the solution." If the teacher's goal, regardless of the subject he is teaching, is to guide learners into solving problems more intelligently, then he should, above all, attempt to use the scientific method of problem solution in meeting his own personal and professional problems.

One of the most profitable aspects of developing the solution to a particular problem should be the improvement of problem-solving techniques for attacking other problems. In fact, in an educational situation, the primary goal in solving problems would not be simply to get the best solution to the problems being studied at a particular time, but rather to learn better ways of arriving at solutions to these and *to other problems to be encountered later as well.* The learner needs aid in finding and improving methods of working out his own solutions to his problems. It should be emphasized also that learning "by copying down a lecture or memorizing for a test" is likely to *discourage* the development of a problem-solving attitude by leading the learner to believe that education is primarily copying, memorizing, and testing, followed by more copying, more memorizing, and more testing. Only what is practiced is learned and the digestion of ideas obtained from various resources and their organized assimilation into the ideas already held on the problems being studied are primary requisites for effective and economical learning. In general, in a class where the learners are acquiring ability connected with problem solution, it is much more important for the teacher to suggest possible approaches and possible techniques than to try to give a pat answer ("the right answer," "the Gospel") to every controversial issue that develops.

SERVICE LEARNING PROCESSES

To gain needed facility in handling the three main steps in the learning processes, it is necessary for the high-school student (also for the teacher as a learner) to acquire skill in at least five "service" learning processes. The term "service" is used since these processes essentially serve and support the key processes of problem identification, selection, and solution. The service processes briefly discussed below include: (1) evaluation, including self-diagnosis; (2) personal educational record-keeping; (3) obtaining, selecting, and using appropriate resources; (4) democratic interpersonal relations; (5) purposeful reading.

Evaluation. In Chapter 7, devoted to "Basic considerations related to developing evaluative abilities," such questions as the following are considered: What are the differing concepts of evaluation and how are these related to self-evaluation? What is the relation of evaluation to diagnosis? To testing? To critical thinking? To marking? What are the advantages and disadvantages of attempted teacher monopoly of evaluation as opposed to having both the teacher and the learner participate in a systematic evaluation of learning? How old should learners be to start self-evaluation? Is learner self-evaluation likely to eliminate the need for teacher evaluation?

Some of the key operating principles that are developed for evaluation are the following: A primary purpose of evaluation should be to help the learner see where and how he can become more efficient in learning. In general, of course, the fundamental purposes of evaluation are to make living better and happier. The learner should have many guided evaluating experiences so that he can evaluate with greater efficiency in school, and, even more important, be able to carry on wise evaluation after he gets out of school. Since evaluation should be thought of largely as a beginning rather than an end process, it is important that evaluation begin as soon as work is started; thereafter, frequent opportunities should be provided for the student to judge the worth of his work. A teacher's evaluation in connection with a specific course should begin with his preplanning of course activity.

Learning to evaluate better may be one purpose of evaluating in a particular learning situation. In addition to individual evaluations, it should be kept in mind that evaluation of group goals, procedures, and resources is frequently a worth-while procedure.

Marking can result from evaluation. It is important to remember, however, that while evaluation is a key phase of efficient learning, marking may or may not accompany such evaluation. Marking in a sense is an appendage to evaluative processes.

The evaluation-orientation in this book frankly places considerable emphasis upon developing self-evaluative abilities in the learner. In Chapter 8, devoted primarily to self-evaluation, such questions as the following are considered: What suggestions may be made for encouraging self-evaluation by the learner? What tools are available that may be used in helping the learner in self-evaluation? What suggestions involve the construction and use of self-evaluative resources? What are illustrations of learner self-evaluation?

It is assumed in Chapter 8 that one of the primary goals in learning improvement is that of developing self-evaluative abilities. A major goal in self-evaluation is to improve the quality of motivation in the learner. Interest and motivation are likely to be stimulated if the learner himself is taught how to diagnose his needs, strengths, weaknesses, and to set up plans in line with this diagnosis. It is emphasized that learning self-evaluation is a long-time problem that takes much time and effort and cannot be achieved overnight or even in a month, a semester, or a year. Self-evaluation should involve frequent examination of goals and procedures and should be a continuous process that goes on concurrently with other major parts of the learning process. An important part of evaluation is to set up or plan specific behavior changes that will be put into effect to improve self-efficiency. Unless evaluation results in present and future improvement, it is to be considered of doubtful value. In self-evaluation, the learner should be encouraged to develop a critical attitude toward his own efficiency. The development of the ability of the student to evaluate aspects of his own efficiency so that he may intelligently go about improving his work, is at least as important as the development of the ability to memorize an assignment given by the teacher.

Educational record-keeping by the individual learner. In order that the learner, with the guidance of the teacher, may have a systematic basis for moving ahead on problem identification and problem attack, it would seem desirable if not absolutely necessary that a rather comprehensive record of learning activities be kept by the student. Chapter 9 is devoted to the problem of "developing ability to keep personal education records for effective learning." Questions of the following types are considered: What are the possible purposes the learner may have in keeping personal educational records? What suggestions may the teachers give the learners to help them improve in record-keeping for learning purposes? How may the instructor and other students help the learner evaluate his work through a periodic examination or evaluation of the learner's record? How may the learner help himself through a systematic self-evaluation of his own educational record-keeping, which reflects the processes and the products of his own learning? How can learner records constitute one part of the reports for parents? Some students who have used this material in mimeographed form suggest that a brief study of record-keeping before a study of other parts of the book is made would give useful orientation for initial improvement in record-keeping. Some teachers and students may want to use Chapter 9 in the first part of the course for this reason.

The following are a few of the operating principles that seem to be sound for the development of effective learner record-keeping: The possible purposes for keeping educational records are many, but getting practice in keeping effective records, stimulating motivation, having sound bases for evaluation, and helping the learner identify his own strengths and weaknesses would seem to be some of the major purposes for which educational records should be kept.

In general, materials included in the record should be those that are most meaningful and helpful to the learner in his work on his assignments or problems. It is important that the record be not merely a compilation of ideas derived from various resources. Rather it should also contain the student's own reactions to the ideas gleaned and his criticisms of them, in terms of situations that he feels he is likely to face, is facing, or he has actually faced.

The organization of a record should ordinarily be in terms of a tentative outline of problems that the learner has set up and that he is attacking. This tends to make records individual and original, with no two learners keeping exactly the same kind of record. Different parts of the record should be set up in a flexible fashion so that ideas can be added to different parts without the necessity of recopying parts that have already been organized. Thus, the ideas in the educational record should be put into the learner's outline rather than the outline of the person who wrote the book, article, or lecture, from which the ideas are taken. It is pointed out that learners can improve in record-keeping through systematic study of their own records and those of others. Such improvement is likely to facilitate other key activities in the learning process.[2]

Obtaining, selecting, and using resources effectively. In conventional teaching-learning situations where the process emphasis is not used, attention is generally given to the use of reading resources, but little or no attention is placed on giving learners practice in obtaining and intelligently selecting resources for effective learning. Chapter 10 gives attention to some resource problems, examples of which are the following: What are some of the tools that may be used for measuring abilities related to acquiring, selecting, and using printed resources? How is improved learning practice connected with resources that make use of texts? What changes might be suggested in the text or resource acquisition setup that would improve it from the problem standpoint? What are some suggestions regarding the improvement of the acquisition of resources needed in learning situations? How may we develop the ability to select resources critically and effectively? How may learnings connected with the use of resources be improved?

The operating principles developed in the chapter on resources emphasize that resources for learning purposes should be got and used as much as possible in a purposeful fashion, purposeful particu-

---

[2] Students in the methods course are encouraged to practice record-keeping themselves for two main purposes: (1) to facilitate their learning in the methods course, and (2) to give them a better basis for the later training of high-school students in efficient record-keeping.

larly from the standpoint of the learner. The learner should not only see why he is using them, but should also participate in the setting up of the purposes that dictated their use. Purposeful gathering of ideas from resources should replace overemphasis on mere absorption of ideas. The primary questions the learner should have in mind about any resource should be: Is this resource likely to give me help on problems I should study, and will my use of resources be likely to improve from contact with it?

The professional learner should be systematically building up a personal file of resources he can use to improve his teaching and other professional activities. These should, of course, be organized for easy use. Improving the use of the book as a resource will generally involve getting greater value from the frequently "neglected" parts of the book: table of contents, preface, first and last paragraphs of chapters (for initial orientation), index, front thesis (if any), title page, reference sections, pictures, charts, and diagrams. Resources should be used not only to help the learner get possible answers to problems, but also to help him get his bearings, identify the problems upon which he should work, and evaluate his activities.

Of key importance is the fact that resources that are very appropriate for one learner in the class may be thoroughly inappropriate for another learner in the same class. Some contributing factors to this situation are individual differences in needs, attitudes, skills, and basic abilities, and in each learner's feeling of just what is a significant problem to him.

Developing desirable group learnings. An important combination of learning processes clusters around the individual learner's connections with group activities. Chapter 11 is devoted to the problem of developing desirable group learnings. Some of the questions considered are the following: What is the importance of studying group behavior? What are the possible ways in which individuals, classes, and small groups may evaluate their effectiveness in group discussion situations? What difficulties are likely to be encountered in attempting to improve any type of group work in school? To what extent should the student participate in the setting up of groups in which he is a learner? What are the roles that a teacher should take in developing effective learner participation in groups? What are the roles in which students need practice if they are to become effective participants in a discussion?

Among the key operating principles developed in the chapter on group functioning are the following: The goals and purposes of learning groups should both reflect and develop the common member goals and purposes. Thus, the primary purpose of the discussion group is to help members identify, select, and solve common problems. The skills necessary for effective group behavior can be learned and, therefore, such learning constitutes a legitimate goal of group operation.

Perhaps the outstanding weakness of our society today is shown by the striking inability of many of its members to work cooperatively with each other in meeting mutual problems. Such a weakness should challenge educators to revise, perhaps radically, the conventional patterns of teacher-dominated group discussions.

Decisions affecting class groupings and sub-groupings should generally be decided by the teacher and learners cooperatively. The purposes for which a class or group is set up should be major factors in determining who belongs to the particular class or group.

The teacher as the major class leader is in a key position for gearing group activities to democratic values and procedures. A democratic teacher is able to take upon himself a great variety of group roles. In any particular situation he attempts to assume that role which will most likely be of value to the learners.

Class members should be helped to see that the large and small group discussions provide opportunities in which they may practice group skills in situations where failure is not tragic or at least of considerable significance, as it might be outside of school. A major change must take place in the current attitude, which is all too common, that the teacher is almost solely responsible for class or small group success. The teacher and learners need cooperatively and continuously to evaluate and plan improvement in group goals and group operations as well as in individual behaviors in a group situation.

Developing reading abilities needed for problem-process attack. As has been indicated in Chapters 3 through 6, we will be concerned primarily with the three basic parts of problem-process learnings: identifying problems, selecting possible problems for study, and solving problems. In Chapters 7 through 11 we will discuss four types of supporting or service learnings: evaluating; keeping educational records; getting, selecting, and using resources;

and developing desirable group behaviors. A fifth type of group of service learnings is discussed in Chapter 12, learnings related to developing reading abilities needed for identifying and attacking problems.

In the discussion in Chapter 12 of reading learnings for problem-process attack, such problems as the following are considered: What changes in in-school and out-of-school reading are needed if we are to develop desirable reading attitudes and skills? What role do individual differences play in the selection and use of reading resources? Who should determine the reading goals of the learner? What are the types of reading goals and how are these related to out-of-school reading behaviors? With increasing use being given to teaching-learning processes, what changes in reading emphases are likely?

These are a few of the key operating principles drawn from the discussion of reading: Immense ranges of reading ability, interest, and purpose among learners of a particular class are not only to be expected but are probably desirable if each learner's functional reading abilities are being developed in terms of his individual needs and capacities. It is unsound to think, as is conventionally done, of reading retardation in terms of some average standard. Rather, retardation in reading, as in other areas, must be considered on an individual basis—where is this learner in terms of *his* capacities and needs? The individual learner must participate to a greater extent in setting up his reading goals. Such participation will not only improve motivation and make the reading more meaningful while he is in school, but will help him build up the attitudes and skills he needs if he is to continue reading systematically and most profitably after he gets out of school.

The *uses* of reading should be taught concomitantly with the *how* of reading. Teachers at all levels and in practically all subjects can improve the learning of their students if they give attention to the learners' attitudes and skills related to reading.

Finally, and perhaps most important of all, the conclusion is reached that many student difficulties in reading can be traced to reading disabilities in teachers and administrators. The teacher or administrator who makes little or no systematic use of reading for identifying and solving his professional problems is not only setting a poor example for his students, but is contributing to his own professional stagnation. Continuous and systematic professional reading by the educator will aid his students and can also help make teaching a more challenging and satisfying experience.

The foregoing discussion on key learning processes and service learnings may be represented by the following diagram:

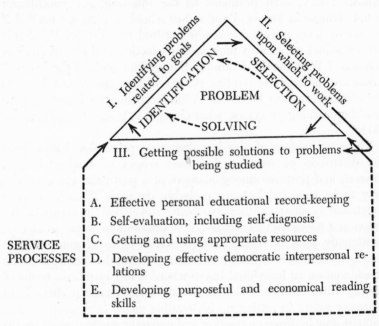

Although problem identification tends to precede problem selection and problem solution, it should be noted that there is frequently no clear-cut sequence of the steps that are followed by the high-school or college learner. Rather, two or more of the eight processes that have been mentioned are typically carried on concurrently. Thus, for example, in attempting to solve a group of problems the learner usually identifies new problems and practices record-keeping at the same time. At any particular time, however, the main emphasis for learning purposes should probably be upon practicing one or a limited number of the processes.

TEACHING METHODS AND PROCESS-RELATED PROBLEMS

An analysis of labeled teaching methods. "Name" methods analyzed in Chapter 13 include three main categories:

1. *Those where the primary goal is to convey subject matter,* including the daily-assignment method, the Morrison plan, the Dalton system, and the subject-matter core or subject-matter common learnings approaches.

2. *Those methods designed to give primary weight to learners' purposes,* including the activity approach, the project method, and the experience unit.

3. *A method planned to teach solutions to problems that the school has identified,* the core and common learnings approaches that have problem emphasis.

In the discussion of each of the methods a picture has been given of its purposes, characteristics, and limitations or weaknesses.

Process-related problems. Five illustrative problems and the relation of each to learning processes are discussed in Chapter 14. The five problems are considered to show something of the range of problems that the teacher faces and to show some sample ways of approaching such problems. Problems discussed include:

What is desirable discipline and how can it be developed?

How can we develop favorable attitudes and appreciations?

What cautions need to be observed in interpreting standard test results?

What are the possible uses and dangers of marking?

What difficulties confront the teacher who attempts to improve class interpersonal relations?

Research evidence on traditional vs. newer methods. When students, teachers, administrators, and supervisors consider ways of improving teaching-learning processes, all too little attention is usually given to experimental or research evidence on the efficiency of proposed newer practices. In Chapter 15 three research studies are considered and an extensive bibliography is given of several dozen others.

The challenge the teacher faces. In the final chapter the challenge facing the teacher who seriously tries to improve teaching-learning processes is briefly considered.

2

ASSUMPTIONS THAT MAY UNDERLIE

COURSE APPROACHES

Problems for consideration

What are some alternate assumptions that might be considered in planning teaching and learning behavior in a high-school or college course?

What differences in what is done by students and teacher are likely to result if one pattern of assumptions is accepted rather than another?

What are the assumptions that are conducive to basic improvement in teaching-learning processes?

ASSUMPTIONS THAT MAY BE MADE IN MEETING
TEACHING-LEARNING PROBLEMS

Teaching is essentially a continuous round of decision-making in problem situations. This is true both in the class in which this text is being used and in all high-school classes. In what main areas do these decisions fall? On what assumptions should such decisions be made?

As the teacher or prospective teacher considers the problems he is likely to face, and as he actually faces these problems, he finds that the decisions he must make are largely dependent upon the basic assumptions which he implicitly or explicitly accepts concerning teaching-learning goals and processes. It is the primary purpose of this chapter to help the reader visualize some of the possible fundamental assumptions upon which teachers and learners may operate.

Three types of teachers

As a basis for our discussion let us take a brief look at some characteristic activities of three types of teachers.

Edward Smith, a social studies teacher, selects a single history text before classes start. Assignments are determined entirely by him and are given to students on a day-to-day basis. The tests, given periodically, reflect the primary goal of Mr. Smith; to have learners know common information, particularly that in the text, and be able to answer questions on this information. Class time is largely devoted to a discussion of the information contained in the text and to additional information the teacher or students possess. The general approach being used by this teacher has been labeled the "Common information pattern." Assumptions underlying the type of approach used by Mr. Smith will be developed later in this chapter.

Elaine Jenkins, an English teacher, starts the school year with a set pattern of units, which her high-school sophomores will study during their course in English. One of the five units Miss Jenkins selects for the year is "humor." Teacher-established objectives in this unit, which is studied by all students during November and the first part of December, include (1) the enjoyment and appreciation of humor, (2) the stimulation for participation in discussion, reading, and writing, and (3) the development of a discriminating taste for humor. Miss Jenkins has decided what units will be studied and how much time will be devoted to each. The students may have a large share in deciding exactly what books, pictures, and other resources will be used and what will be studied *within* the prescribed unit. Such choices may be made by individuals or by groups. The tests used in the course typically include more than the amount of information learned. Attempts are made by Miss Jenkins to test for attitudes toward different types of humor. The assumptions underlying the type of teaching generally represented by Miss Jenkins will be analyzed under the heading of the "Common units pattern."

Jack Fitzpatrick, a mathematics teacher, represents the third general approach to teaching and learning to be analyzed in this chapter. Before his course in general mathematics for ninth-grade students begins, he engages in the following representative types of activities: (1) an analysis of the types of problems on which individual learners had found it profitable to work during the preceding year (these constitute a reservoir of possible problems for students), (2) a study of teaching and learning difficulties encountered in the preceding year, (3) a re-examination of diagnostic tests and other resources the teacher should have at hand at the beginning of the year, and (4) a study of possible ways of improving student leadership of learning activities. After the course starts, Mr. Fitzpatrick encourages learners to spend the first few weeks in a consideration of present and possible future problems and needs related to mathematics. Individual learners are encouraged to identify their present abilities and the situations they face, and in the light of such an analysis to set up, with Mr. Fitzpatrick's guidance, individual and group activities in mathematics. The course curriculum for individuals will differ in terms of such factors as their present abilities, their current or probable future needs, and their attitudes toward mathematics. Most of the latter three-fourths of the course will be devoted to improving techniques for identifying and solving mathematical problems significant to the learner. The assumptions underlying the approach that Mr. Fitzpatrick is using will be analyzed under the heading of the "Common process pattern."

Three patterns of assumptions

As we consider conflicting assumptions related to teaching and learning, it appears that at least three patterns of assumptions emerge. These patterns, about each of which a group of assumptions seems to cluster, have been labeled (1) common information pattern, (2) common units pattern, and (3) common process pattern. The fundamental differences between the assumptions supporting different patterns will become apparent as the assumptions are described. An attempt will also be made to show some of the significant differences in teacher and student behavior that tend to result from the use of conflicting assumptions.

Although many more areas might have been selected for illustrative purposes, we have chosen to consider assumptions related to (1) goals and purposes, (2) the nature of learner needs and abilities, (3) the nature of transfer of training, (4) the nature of learner record-keeping, (5) the basis for motivation, (6) the responsibilities of the learner and the teacher, and (7) the procedures and behaviors to be practiced in the teaching-learning situation.

Common information pattern

Where the common information pattern is explicitly or implicitly accepted by the teacher (as in the case of Edward Smith) or by the learner, these assumptions tend to be made: the goals for the course or class should be teacher-determined; students should take the goals and purposes on the authority of the teacher. The primary objective of the work in history, English, or science, for example, is to acquire a body of content or information. It is further assumed that in the time available in a class or course it is possible and desirable for the student to learn practically all of the body of information that will be needed later on. And finally, the assumption is made that a class of students should come out of a particular course or curriculum with a common set of theory or a particular body of subject matter known.

Where these assumptions, which Mr. Smith implicitly accepted, prevail concerning desirable goals and purposes, the teacher plans in detail, even before seeing the students, the specific information to be studied. Decisions about what should be studied are based exclusively on teacher and/or expert authority. The goals and purposes of all learners in a particular class are assumed to be almost uniform insofar as the work of that course is concerned. Goals and purposes are supposed to be handed from the teacher to the learner.

Common units pattern

With this pattern the assumptions that tend to be accepted by such a teacher as Miss Jenkins are the following: Problem or unit areas should be teacher-determined, but within each of these problem or unit areas, such as "humor," the student should be given some leeway in deciding what he will do. Here the primary goal of the work is to learn how to attack the problems in unit or problem areas designated by the teacher. It is further assumed that, during the course, it is necessary and desirable for the learner to face and to solve practically all of the important problems that he will encounter after he leaves school. Learners should come out of a particular course with the ability to attack a group of common problems studied in the course.

We note here that learner goals and purposes are given considerable weight within the unit area designated by the teacher. However, under this teaching-learning setup the instructor or teaching group still exclusively makes the decisions about what units or what problems should be studied and also decides in what sequence they should be studied. Thus, individual learner goals and purposes are not considered in the over-all patterning of the course or curriculum.

Here, primary goals, purposes, and problems to be studied are teacher-determined, and the assumption is made that at any particular time all the learners in the class should work on the same unit.

Common process pattern.[1]

In this pattern, subscribed to by Mr. Fitzpatrick, the mathematics teacher, the following assumptions hold: *The learner should have a major share in setting up his individual goals in line with his purposes in a particular course or a particular curriculum. Since individual learner goals and purposes are also of fundamental importance at any particular stage of the learning process, the individual learner should help decide the problem areas upon which he as an individual will work.*

The primary purpose of the work is to learn the processes and attitudes necessary for identifying and attacking the realistic new problems that the learner will be likely to face during and after he leaves school. It is considered impossible for the learner, while in school, either to acquire all the facts and information he will need, or to learn the solutions to all the problems he will face. But it is possible, and is highly desirable, for him to emphasize and to learn the processes of problem approach. In practicing these processes the learner will use many facts and much information when problems are vehicles for learning the important processes involved in attacking new problems.

Finally, the learners should come out of a course or curriculum with improved ability to attack, with varying degrees of success, realistic problems with elements of uniqueness which the individual learner in each case is likely to face.

Using this pattern of assumptions, neither the curriculum nor the course work for a particular learner can, or should be, rigidly structured in advance. It differs from the units approach in that at

---

[1] To emphasize the assumptions the writer believes are basic to improved teaching-learning processes, these assumptions have been italicized.

any particular time the individual learners in a class may be working on quite different problems. The learner's goals and purposes are used to a considerable degree in structuring his curriculum and his course work.

Giving much weight to the goals and purposes of the student in making the decision about what he will work on at any particular time means that different learners in the same class are likely to be working on quite different problems. Administratively, this is quite upsetting to some teachers and administrators who like to have a course prepatterned on a logical basis, even if that sacrifices what is a sound psychological basis for the individual learner.

ASSUMPTIONS RELATED TO THE NATURE OF LEARNER NEEDS AND ABILITIES

Common information pattern

With the common information pattern, assumptions would include the following: The culture in which the school is operating is a nearly constant one, with the importance of particular facts remaining reasonably constant. Thus, most of the facts a student needs after he gets out of school he should learn while he is in school.

All learners in a particular class are interested in now, or should be interested in, and will eventually use, the same body of knowledge, and the needs of all learners in the class are approximately the same. The individual student either does not know what he wants or, if he does, this should be largely disregarded in any particular course content.

Lack of experience and ability on the part of the students in such processes as getting appropriate resources, evaluating adequately, and identifying problems of importance is sufficient reason for keeping learners from practicing these processes. Learning should be thought of primarily as understanding or acquiring the end product of someone else's thinking. Thus, the learner should participate almost exclusively in information acquisition processes.

Where this pattern of assumptions is followed, we tend to have a teaching-learning situation where the main function of the learner is to acquire the facts, information, and theories that are laid out for him in the text or by the teacher. A single text, with perhaps some supplementary material, is considered sufficient for class purposes. A common set of information and concepts is thought most necessary for satisfactory communication among members of a democratic society. In the measurement of the results of a course, that learner has learned most and best who has learned the most facts.

Common units pattern

This pattern is likely to depend on the following assumptions: The school is serving a society in which the specific problem solutions and units of information needed remain fairly constant. This being the case, the learner can acquire the solutions to the problems he needs to attack while in school, and thus be prepared to face these problems after he gets out of school. All students are interested in now, or should be interested in, and will eventually face, almost the same problem situations. Learning should be thought of primarily as a process of getting possible solutions to problems that someone else has selected.

The needs in the area to be studied are approximately the same for each learner in a class. Since the learner does not know what problem should be studied, information or problem areas should be indicated to him by the teachers. However, within these problem areas, the student should be given some discretion about what particular part of them he will study. The teacher, department, or school should not only identify the units or problems to be studied, but should supply almost all resources necessary for effective practice in problem identification and solution.

Systematic learning is largely a process that goes on in school with quite limited improvement after school is over. The ability to meet certain specific problems is most necessary for adequate relationships among members of a democratic society. In the evaluation of a course, that learner has learned most and best who can solve the problems that were taken up in the course.

In courses where these assumptions are accepted, all the students in a class study the same units in teacher-determined sequence, since their needs are assumed to be common to that degree. Within the unit an attempt is made to meet individual differences in needs and abilities by having different learners use varied resources and work on problems of a complexity suitable to the achievement level of the individual student. For example, in a general mathematics class where a unit on insurance is being studied, one student of limited ability might work on comparing the cost and benefits from car insurance as set up by two companies, another student of greater ability might attempt to compare the relative benefits and costs of term insurance, annuities, and straight life and to determine for what kinds of needs each is probably best.

Common process proponents, while heartily favoring this movement in the direction of taking care of individual differences, feel that insufficient attention is given to student purposes and learner needs in such areas as self-evaluation, problem identification, and over-all structuring of learning activities.

Common process pattern

The assumptions that follow are basic in this pattern. *The culture served by the school is a very dynamic one and many of the solutions learned in school may not be very appropriate outside of school, or, more specifically, the learner has an important need to know how to make adjustments to new, sometimes radically new, situations. Thus, all students are interested in now, or should be interested in, and will eventually use, similar learning processes in systematically attacking problems outside the school. The learner should actually practice in school all the processes he will later need in systematically identifying and attacking novel problem situations.*

Each individual is uniquely different, and the best way to help the learner is to aid him in learning a way to help himself. If the student does not now know how to decide wisely what to study, then he should learn with guidance to make increasingly better decisions concerning the identification of problems. Also, lack of learner ability in such processes—self-evaluation, appropriate record-keeping, interpersonal relations, and other types of learning—is good and sufficient reason for helping learners to develop in these fields and is not a valid reason for keeping learners from practicing in these areas. Experiences that take place in initiating systematic learning and in arriving at the end products of learning are extremely important.

A common democratic technique of problem attack is most necessary for satisfactory communication in a democracy.

Systematic learning should be thought of primarily as made up of processes that should be improved in school in such ways that similar behaviors will be continued after the learner leaves school. In the evaluation of the work, that learner has learned most and best who is most able to identify and attack new problems, related to the course, which he is likely to face after the course is over and who has the attitudes necessary to carry his skills into action. This will necessarily involve continued learning because of the unique nature of new problems.

When the common process pattern of assumptions is followed, information is acquired and problems are solved, but the basic concern of the teacher is to help the learner become more proficient in meeting ever-changing situations. To do this, the learner works on acquiring facility in teaching himself to learn. In other words, the learner is building up procedures and attitudes he can use in analyzing and solving new problem situations, which always have novel elements or combinations of elements.

The reader will remember that in our illustration near the beginning of this chapter we used a social studies teacher, an English teacher, and a mathematics teacher to introduce these assumptions. It should be pointed out here that none of the three patterns is particularly tied up with any subject field. Any one of the three patterns of assumptions may be used with any subject field. Combinations of assumptions are also possible, of course, with some coming from one pattern and some coming from another or others.

ASSUMPTIONS RELATED TO THE NATURE OF TRANSFER OF TRAINING

Common information pattern

Assumptions in this pattern include the following: If people know the facts or body of information in a particular area, they will use these facts or information at appropriate times. Transfer is best if a good supply of facts or information is stored for later use. If a subject is "covered" by the use of a text and lectures, the student will learn the material, retain it, and carry it over to meet problem situations outside the school in which such information could presumably be of value. That information learned will be used when a problem situation presents itself in which such information might be needed.

Where the assumptions in the preceding paragraph about the

nature of transfer of training are accepted, the emphasis obviously will be upon the acquisition of a wealth of ideas which have been organized by someone else, usually the teacher or the author of a text. Those who oppose this pattern of assumptions cite evidence that indicates the rapid forgetting of facts, particularly if they are learned out of the problem context in which they are supposedly to be used. A further objection is keynoted by the question: Even if the facts are remembered for test purposes, are they likely to be pulled out for use in a problem situation in which their use might be appropriate?

Common units pattern

Proponents of this approach to teaching-learning situations are likely to make these assumptions: Learners not only need to know the facts, but they need to learn them in specific problem situations. Transfer is best if the answers to specific problems, which the school has identified, are studied by the student. If certain problems or problem areas or units are attacked and mastered with some success, the learner will be ready to meet successfully the problems he will face outside of school. Common problems change relatively little—thus solutions learned in school will last the pupil throughout most of his life.

The common units pattern of assumptions is designed to promote better transfer of training through helping the learner to acquire his facts in the problem situations where these facts are to be used. It is argued that in realistic problem situations the learner is likely to remember and to use more information if that information has been organized and learned in the problem situations for which it is intended. In both the common information pattern and in the common units pattern, information is learned, but in the former it is likely to be learned only in an information context, while in the common unit pattern it is learned more in pertinent problem organization.

One of the major objections that may be raised to this approach revolves around these questions: Should not learners also get practice in identifying the units and problem areas that will be studied? Unless practice is given in these and other processes covered almost exclusively by the teacher, will not the learner be crippled in trying to transfer problem attacks to situations where the teacher is no longer present?

Common process pattern

In this pattern these assumptions are accepted. *Students not only need to know facts and the solutions to particular problems, but they also need to have techniques that will help them more effectively to meet new problems as they are encountered.*

Transfer is best if the learner participates in all of the processes, including problem identification and self-evaluation, that he will need to attack effectively the new problems he will meet after he leaves school. If the learner acquires certain specific processes of a dynamic sort for more effectively attacking new problems, he will be in a better position to meet a changing world, with all its changing problems.

Since the learner's problems will be ever-changing, a dynamically improving method is the most lasting key to learning.

If this pattern of assumptions were utilized, students would acquire facts and study problems, but the primary area of commonality in a particular course would be a common concern with and a common practice of those learning processes considered necessary for continued learning and effective problem attack after the learner is no longer under the tutelage of the teacher. More specifically, different learners in the same class would acquire somewhat different bodies of subject matter; they would work on different problems; but all would be concerned with practice and improvement in such key learning processes as identifying problems desirable to study, self-evaluating, getting the resources needed for meeting problems, and working with others in group situations.

If courses were set up along subject lines, mathematics for example, the student would, with the help of the teacher, select pertinent problems in the area of mathematics upon which it would be profitable for him to work. The primary emphases would be upon learning how to continue learning in the area after the support of the teacher is withdrawn.

At this point the reader is encouraged to consider a particular course he has been in and attempt to decide which pattern or what combination of patterns was used.

Common information pattern

The primary assumption in this pattern would be that record-keeping on the part of the student is largely a matter of recording the organization of a lecture or of printed material.

Organization of what is written is almost entirely borrowed from the text or the teacher. The record of the learner reflects little, if any, of his thinking or critical analysis of what he sees or hears. Records are supposed to be similar for all.

Common units pattern

In this pattern the assumption is that student record-keeping should be largely a matter of recording possible answers and useful information for solving a list of problems which the teacher has decided are important for study.

The student is encouraged to get and to organize ideas within the unit framework. At any particular time, the learner records would all probably be on the same unit, but within that unit the ideas and their organization might vary considerably. More attention is likely to be given to possible ways of keeping a record than is the case in the information pattern.

Common process pattern

Here the assumption is made that the individual should be encouraged to develop his record-keeping ability and to use different approaches and procedures as aids in identifying, selecting, and solving problems.

Emphasis is put on the desirability of recording the needs, problems, possible solutions, and learner reactions to ideas gleaned from various sources and resources. The records of different learners in the same class will probably show greatly differing content for at least three reasons. In the first place, different learners are likely to be working on widely divergent problems. In the second place, even if some of the sub-problems being attacked are similar for two students, it is quite probable that the resources used will differ, at least in part. In the third place, the individual learner's reactions to the ideas gleaned from common resources will show his individuality and developing point of view. Considerable attention in the student's record would be given to getting practice in keeping records for the different learning purposes he might have in different situations.

ASSUMPTIONS RELATED TO THE BASIS FOR MOTIVATION

Common information pattern

In this pattern it is assumed that motivation will be satisfactory if the teacher and text indicate and thoroughly explain the subject matter to be learned.

An attempt is not made to use, or even to determine, the differing motivations of the individual students. If the learner is assigned to the class, the teacher operates on the assumption that what is good motivation for one in the class should be good motivation for all others in the class.

Common units pattern

Here the assumption is that motivation is likely to be satisfactory if the learner is made aware of certain important problems or problem areas that the school has decided he should attack, and then is given an opportunity to work primarily on these problems.

More attention is given to individual motives in this pattern than in the common information pattern. However, from a psychological standpoint the question may well be raised: Are individual motives given sufficient attention when all are expected to work on the same problem or unit at the same time?

Common process pattern

Motivation is best when the learner has participated in all phases of the decision about the specific problems on which he as an individual learner will work, including those on which he as a member of a group will work.

The preceding assumption presupposes that the learner will, generally speaking, work more aggressively and more profitably if he has shared in a real way in decisions that affect what he will study, when he will study, and how he will study. It is argued that in those decisions where he is not given a share he is being trained in teacher-dependence, since that is what he is practicing.

In the common process pattern it is assumed that motivation, to be most successful, must prepare the learner to be self-motivating in his work after he leaves school. Hence, it is necessary to wean the learner from teacher-dependent motivation before he leaves school.

ASSUMPTIONS RELATED TO THE RESPONSIBILITIES OF THE LEARNER AND THE TEACHER

Common information pattern

In this teaching-learning pattern it is assumed that the teacher's primary responsibility is to know the subject matter and present it in an organized manner. The responsibility of the learner is primarily to grasp the information the teacher says he should learn. It is assumed that pupils should be *given* the best possible organization of material. Evaluating on a systematic basis is the exclusive job of the teacher. Approximately the same amount of teacher control of the learning processes should be maintained during the whole period of work in a course.

Where the assumptions in the preceding paragraph are accepted, teacher-pupil planning has no place. Teacher-made plans are given to the learners in such forms as: text to be studied, dictated assignments, questions asked in class, and test questions given. Learner responsibilities are primarily those of attending class and of preparing to pass, by whatever means seem most expeditious, the periodic tests given by the teacher, primarily for marking purposes.

Common units pattern

In this pattern the teacher's primary responsibility is to identify and to organize the important units in an area, to present these to the students, to help them work out an understanding of each and get possible solutions to each. The responsibility for setting the problem or informational areas to be attacked is that of the teacher or someone other than the learner. The responsibility of the learner is to get and to organize information or to attack problems in the area selected by the teacher. The student should be given the best possible organization of information or problems to be studied, within which organization he is encouraged to do some structuring. Evaluating is primarily the job of the teacher, but may be done to a limited extent by the learner within the problem or unit area set up by the teacher. It is assumed that decisions regarding the problem areas to be studied should be retained by the teacher, although the learner may be permitted increasing responsibility within a particular problem area.

Courses operating along the lines indicated by the assumptions in the preceding paragraph give the teacher almost exclusive responsibility for and control of somewhat fewer decision areas than in the information pattern. This means learner responsibilities and opportunities for decision practice are greater in the common units pattern than in the information pattern. However, the teacher or teacher-group still is likely to have a monopoly on over-all course structuring, including decisions relating to the conclusion that all learners at any particular time shall be studying the same unit.

Common process pattern

In this pattern it is assumed that the teacher's primary responsibility is to help the learner to identify some of the important problems he faces or may face, and to improve the learning processes needed in such identification as well as in the eventual solution and behavior activities connected with such problems.

The learner has a responsibility not only for helping to get the facts and principles he will use in his attack on problems, as he may in the common units pattern, but he should also help to decide what problems to attack and what processes to use at any particular time.

The learner, with guidance, should be encouraged to work out an organization of ideas, principles, and procedures that may be of use to him in learning how to identify and attack the problems of the course more successfully.

Systematic evaluation is extremely important for improving the over-all learning processes. The individual learner should practice it by himself and in cooperation with the teacher and the student learning group.

Teacher assistance to the learner should be given only when needed at any particular time in a course, and should be withheld as much as possible so that the learner may achieve and maintain desirable independence.

Where the common process pattern of assumptions prevails, an attempt is made to help the student assume an increasing *share* of the responsibility for handling successfully key parts of the learning process. The effect of this upon former teacher responsibilities is to make most, if not all, of them shared rather than exclusive. One additional responsibility to which the teacher gives attention is that of eventually weaning the learner from dependence upon the teacher. This weaning is necessary if the learner is to continue systematic learning after he is no longer under the guidance of the teacher.

**ASSUMPTIONS RELATED TO THE PROCEDURES AND
BEHAVIORS TO BE PRACTICED**

Common information pattern

It is assumed in this pattern that the behaviors that most need practice are those involved in having someone give the learner some information that he must reproduce or identify on a test. It is further assumed that there is a certain fixed amount of subject matter that can and should be covered by all learners.

Repetition of subject matter is to be avoided, but continuous repetition of the same learning processes is standard operating procedure. It is usually assumed that all members of a class can read with profit and understanding material suited to about the average level of that class, and that at any particular time all learners in a class should be studying about the same information.

The assumptions indicated in the two preceding paragraphs are likely to result in a learner's repeating over and over again a sequence similar to this: Listen to the text assignment, study the assigned material to be prepared to pass a test, listen to a lecture or discussion on the same or related material as that assigned, repeat the preceding three steps several times, take a test. This behavior pattern, with few, if any, modifications, is repeated time and time again. Information is acquired but new learning processes and patterns are given very little attention.

Common units pattern

In this pattern it is assumed that the behaviors most needed are those of gathering information and/or problem solutions in areas designated by the teacher or the school. It is also assumed that everyone has the same or very similar problems and the solutions to these should be gathered in the course.

Repetition of study of the same problems is to be avoided, it is supposed, except where done in cycles; but repetition of similar learning processes is considered all right.

Practicing the use of a variety of resources within a particular unit area is assumed to be better for meeting individual differences in ability than is the use of a single text for the class.

In courses where this patterning is followed students are likely to have more varied practice in learning processes than is true in the information pattern. A fairly typical description of the behaviors practiced is difficult to draw because of this greater variability in what is practiced. However, the following sequence is sometimes representative: the learner listens to the teacher's statement of what the next unit will be, why it is important, and perhaps a description of some of the possible ways of approaching it. The teacher may have the unit rather highly structured, in which case the behaviors practiced may closely approximate those on the information pattern. However, the learner will probably help set up some group or committee work. He may get practice in organizing a problem or project himself. He will probably get some experience in gathering printed resources and may get practice in using human resources. Some evaluation for learning purposes may be made involving systematically setting up unit goals, diagnosing individual strengths and weaknesses, and checking up on improvements that have been made.

Perhaps the main objection the common-process-pattern advocates would have to this approach is that, while it is a big improvement over the information pattern, it does not go far enough.

Common process pattern

Underlying assumptions in this pattern include these: The behaviors that need the most guided practice are those (1) *of identifying problems of importance,* (2) *of selecting problems for study,* (3) *of getting possible solutions to be practiced through these problems,* (4) *of actually trying out proposed solutions, and* (5) *of "service learnings" (such as record-keeping, self-evaluation, resource-getting) that support the first four on this list.*

Everyone uses similar learning processes in attacking life problems, but in an educational situation different learners in the same course can and should use different problems and different facts as vehicles for acquiring these processes and using them most effectively. At any particular time all the learners in a class may be practicing similar functional learning processes.

Continuous repetition of the same learning behaviors in almost exactly the same form (such as memorizing for test purposes) is considered as undesirable as the unnecessary repetition of problems or information. Since different students are likely to be attacking different problems and seeking different information, a great variety of resources must be used.

In classes where the assumptions mentioned in the three preceding paragraphs are accepted, at least as much attention is given to improvement in such learning processes as self-evaluation, problem identification, and purposeful reading, as is given to information acquisition and problem-solving.

These assumptions are tied up with giving the learner a major *share* in deciding what he will study, when he will study, and how he will study. They are also closely related to the assumption that learner purpose is of paramount importance in efficient learning. Where considerable weight is given to learner purpose and learner decision, the activities each student will practice in a particular class are likely to be quite different from those of his fellow students, at least in terms of the specific ideas and problems being studied. However, all the problems may be in a similar area (social studies, for example) and the learning processes being emphasized may be quite similar.

At this point the reader is encouraged to try to decide which pattern of assumptions he thinks would probably be the best for his learning purposes in some course he is taking.

Part Two

DEVELOPING ABILITIES IN BASIC
LEARNING STEPS

3

IDENTIFYING PROBLEMS OF

IMPORTANCE

Some problems to consider

Why does the learner need to learn how to identify his problems himself rather than depend on the teacher to do it for him?

What questions should the learner continually ask himself if he is to develop the ability to recognize his problems?

How should the curriculum for an individual learner be developed?

How may the teacher encourage the learner to identify his own needs and problems?

What preplanning should the teacher do in preparation for a course largely set upon a cooperative teacher-student planning basis?

Introduction. As has already been indicated, a first major step in getting the learning process under way is to identify intelligently some of the learner's present and prospective problems. This is an ability that takes much practice if one is to do it economically and effectively. The ability on the part of the learner to take this step successfully will be of paramount importance in determining whether he will be intrinsically motivated and whether he will actively help carry on the learning because he sees its probable benefit to him. If the teacher or someone else attempts to take this step for the learner the latter is not likely to accept responsibility for his learning in a wholehearted fashion. Rather, he is likely to learn systematically only as long as the teacher is around and then in a rather passive manner.

As a basis for considering some of the factors involved in learning problem identification, the following evaluative questions are offered, each stated as the learner might ask it of himself.[1]

EVALUATIVE QUESTIONS RELATED TO PROBLEM
IDENTIFICATION

Origin and motivation of learning activity

1. To what degree is my systematic learning becoming self-starting?

2. Am I usually a learner who simply does what he is told by the teacher *or* a student who goes ahead on his own getting guidance from the instructor but not dictation?

3. Has my motivation been primarily based on recognized needs or on external pressures?

4. Am I trying to work up to my capacity or just to get by?

Use of writing in learning to identify problems

5. Have I made a written diagnosis of my present needs and of my prospective needs?

6. Have I written down a large number of specific goals toward which I need to work?

Communication in problem identification

7. Are the goals and purposes of those people with whom I am working understood by me? (This might involve an instructor, an administrator, a supervisor, or colleagues.)

8. Does it appear that my goals and purposes are understood by those with whom I work?

The problems identified

9. Have the problems I have identified been quite varied or have they been only in a narrow field?

10. As I carry on my systematic study, do newly recognized problems frequently emerge as being significant ones for me to study?

---

[1] These questions are primarily phrased for individual diagnosis by the student in teacher-training courses where learning methods are studied. It is also suggested that high-school students can and should be trained to ask themselves similar questions.

As the learner considers the questions above, it is not expected that he will be able to answer all or even most of them with the best possible answers. If he were, he would seem already to have developed to a high degree his ability to identify his problems successfully. It is anticipated that even the "best learners" will have to answer some of the questions in a way that indicates a need for improvement. The questions are designed to suggest to the student and to the teacher areas that need additional consideration in this seminal part of the whole learning process. The questions may be thought of as diagnostic tools to help set the stage for improvement.

LEARNING-MOTIVATION LADDER

Do independently set up own goals and problems and face them wisely with a minimum of help from others.

With necessary guidance, have set up well-thought-out goals and suitable problems and have started to meet them.

See purposes of instructor, accept them as important, and work to carry them out without having any share in forming them.

Understand purposes of instructor directing work, largely reject them, but work to get extrinsic rewards.

Work for extrinsic rewards (credits, marks, etc.) without understanding purposes of instructor.

Learning based on fear.

READ UP ⟶

In my class, or classes, at what level of motivation on the ladder above do I operate?

What can I do to move higher on the ladder?

SHOULD THE LEARNER PARTICIPATE IN DETERMINING COURSE CONTENT AND IN THE MAKING OF ASSIGNMENTS?

As has been suggested in the evaluation questions, problem identification is one of the key learning processes in which the high-school teacher needs to encourage his students to have practice. The Learning Motivation Ladder also emphasizes that if motivation is to be high the student must have a major share in helping to set up his own goals and purposes. In most classes the goals and purposes, particularly of the teacher, are specifically indicated by the assignments. Learner goals and purposes may be reflected in the ways he works on these assignments. In any case, both student motivation and problem identification are closely related to assignment-making. This makes the issue of *who* should participate in assignment-making of key importance.

Should the learner participate in assignment-making? Most elementary teachers and some high-school teachers would probably answer "Yes, of course," to this question; most college teachers and some high-school teachers would probably be as strongly convinced that the making of assignments is the exclusive job of the teacher in an efficiently run school. Below are given in the form of an imaginary dialogue some of the major arguments related to the teacher-determined assignment vs. the cooperatively-determined assignment controversy.

ADVOCATE OF TEACHER-DETERMINED ASSIGNMENTS: I do not have any faith in having the pupils make their own assignments. I tried it one day and the pupils just looked at me when I said, "You make your own assignments today." Another day, when I did not have time to prepare an assignment, I told each pupil to assign something for himself to do and none of them did much of anything for the next day. I know pupils cannot make their own assignments because I have tried it.

ADVOCATE OF COOPERATIVELY-DETERMINED ASSIGNMENTS: You are implying that, if the teacher does not dictate the assignment, the pupil makes his own without help. I am as much opposed to having untrained pupils make their own assignments without guidance and direction in *how* to do it as you are, but I do think there is a great difference between having the pupils *help* to plan assignments and just turning the pupils loose to shift for themselves. The former is educational, but the latter has little if any educational value, it seems to me.

TEACHER-DETERMINED ADVOCATE: Yes, but since the teacher has much more experience and background he should make the assignments. Why have somebody who doesn't know anything about it making assignments when the teacher is there to do it?

COOPERATIVELY-DETERMINED ADVOCATE: If I want to teach someone the skill of driving a car, I try to give him some practice in driving a car; otherwise, how will he really learn to get where he wants to go in a car when another driver is not around? In the same way, since I want the pupil to learn how to plan his own work, it seems to me that it is necessary to give him some practice in planning while it can be done with guidance. Of course, if he is to have a teacher or some other person with him throughout life to plan every step for him, I suppose learning how to plan his own activities wisely is unnecessary. However, I am interested in teaching him how to help himself.

TEACHER-DETERMINED ADVOCATE: Yes, but that takes too much time. It is much quicker to dictate what is to be done than it is to waste time fooling around with the pupils' ideas regarding what should be studied.

COOPERATIVELY-DETERMINED ADVOCATE: You have raised a very important and difficult problem. In the first place, we may raise this question: Is head-of-department dictatorship, course-of-study dictatorship, or administrator dictatorship desirable? I agree that sometimes, even if we do feel that it is undesirable, it frequently exists and we have to make the best of a bad situation. However, the limitations of the situation can be explained to those with whom we work and teachers and learners will try to operate as wisely as possible within the existing framework, not forgetting to try to change an undesirable framework.

TEACHER-DETERMINED ADVOCATE: I know, but it is too much trouble to spend time with the opinions of all the pupils. They won't all agree anyhow. Some will want to do one thing and some another and I will know that something else is best. Then what will I do?

COOPERATIVELY-DETERMINED ADVOCATE: I think disagreement is desirable and necessary in the early stages of planning. The reasons for various points of view can be explained and listed. It may, and, in fact, it usually will be found that everyone should not have the same assignment since the needs of different pupils are likely to be different. I'll admit that it is much more "trouble" for the teacher to try to meet the needs of the learner than it is for the teacher simply to dictate a "canned" assignment, with the food for everyone coming out of the same tins, but I feel that even from my standpoint the "extra trouble" is desirable because of the added satisfaction I get out of helping pupils learn how to help themselves.

Recapitulation on who should make assignments. Obviously, the answer to the question that has been raised is tied up with many problems, some of which are of the following types. Do we want to produce a learner who can teach himself or one who is continually dependent upon having someone to dictate to him what he should do next? Do we think that functional democracy in the classroom is worth the trouble? Is a teacher justified in taking the great amount of time and thought necessary to change from teacher-determined assignments to cooperatively-determined assignments? How will administrators and parents regard democratic as opposed to autocratic classrooms? Is acquiring the ability to plan wisely the steps to take in learning as important as memorizing information? Is teacher-pupil planning "harder" than "mass assignment" only because the former has been little practiced?

Experimental evidence tends strongly to support the teacher who favors having the learner *help* plan what, when, and how he is to study. (See the bibliography at the end of Chapter 15 for evidence.) The following sections give specific suggestions for understanding and developing the abilities related to such activities.

WHAT ARE THE POSSIBLE METHODS OF HELPING LEARNERS TO DETERMINE THEIR NEEDS AND PROBLEMS?

Problem identification can be learned. Many and perhaps most of the learners in our schools at the present time have had little or no systematic practice in recognizing their present and prospective needs or problems, or in learning how to plan their own study wisely. This being the case, some educators say that since the learners cannot do it well ("I tried it one day!" said one teacher), they should have no part in this first major step of efficient learning. The obvious and perfectly sound answer to this reaction is that if they could identify their problems easily, there would be little need from an educational standpoint to give much attention to this skill. The very fact that learners are in most cases pathetically weak in effectively getting under way the first major step in the thinking and learning process, selecting real needs, and preparing to meet them, is all the more reason for taking weeks, months, and even years to develop skill in this primary step in the thought process. Unless our school products have had sufficient practice in selecting and effectively meeting realistic problems while in school, it is scarcely to be expected that this will be done outside of school except as it is learned through other educational media.

Why learn to identify problems? As has been suggested before, developing the ability to identify needs and developing skill in deciding wisely what to study constitute important goals for the learner. These abilities are of primary importance from at least two standpoints. *First,* the learner is much more likely to be able to work effectively if he has had a share in developing the problems upon which he is working. When he has finished a task, he will be able to say with sincerity that the problems upon which he has worked were of vital importance to him. The *second* important reason for developing these abilities is that the learner will need to use them on his own after he leaves school. If the teacher has had a monopoly in attempting to determine learner needs and learner problems, the student may do a pretty fair job of mastering certain aspects of the learning process as long as the teacher is with him. But when the teacher is gone, as he will be after the individual leaves school, the learner is likely to be at a loss to know how to proceed with systematic learning unless the teacher has given him guided practice in this vitally important step of the learning process.

The teacher's role. As has been suggested in the preceding paragraph, the primary role of the teacher is one of guidance rather than dictatorship. The teacher will attempt to develop a democratic teacher-learner relationship. The teacher will constantly recognize that learning, to be effective, must take place from within and cannot be imposed from without.

A learner needs to be able to get his own learning under way. To be such a self-starter he must have had guided experience in this first step of the learning process—in determining the needs and problems on which it is desirable for him to consider working. It must be recognized that a certain amount of "puzzlement" is inevitable in getting this process under way, and the teacher should not be too much disturbed if learners do not seem to be moving along as rapidly as might be hoped. It is always easier for the learner to move rapidly ahead on something upon which he needs little or no practice, such as memorizing information from a textbook to be reproduced on an examination paper, than to go through the amount of "mental upset" necessary for effective learning.

The following suggested methods of helping the student identify many of the problems he should consider studying are not all-inclusive but are given to help teachers, and the learners themselves, who wish to promote democratic, functional learning through student participation in the identification of problems and needs. In a high-school course situation, the teacher and his learners will have to decide whether a particular problem is appropriate for study on the specific course the students are taking. It is also recommended that the teacher use methods similar to those suggested below in diagnosing *his own* problems and needs.

I. *Methods of utilizing printed materials as aids in determining basic problems and real needs*

Problem lists. Many schools have found the use of *problem lists,* such as that suggested by Mooney (8), to be useful. These problem lists may be administered at the beginning of the year; they form one basis for helping the English and social studies teachers, particularly, to decide the types of problems and units that will be studied during the school year. Obviously, using problem lists is only a first step in bringing into the open for the benefit of both learners and teachers some of the conflicts and vaguely felt needs upon which the learners should consider working.

Tests, inventories, and questionnaires. Frequently, it is advisable for a teacher or a group of teachers to obtain sample copies from publishers of standardized inventories, questionnaires, and tests of hobbies, adjustment, personality, character, social development, interest, needs, and problems. These may be used in a variety of ways. One use, obviously, is to help the teacher and/or the learners to decide whether additional copies of the instrument should be acquired for mass use in the school. The sample copies will also suggest probable problem areas to which the teacher and the learner should give consideration. They will also frequently suggest types of questions that the teacher and/or the learners might consider using in constructing informal classroom tools for diagnosing needs and problems. Usually sample sets of tests include a manual and keys and all can be obtained at a nominal cost from the publishers. Studies of the manuals themselves will sometimes provide worth-while stimulation to the teacher. Such scales and inventories can also be of value in giving educational and vocational guidance to the students.

Professional resources. Perhaps the most significant and readily available type of printed material that teachers and pupils have is contained in professional references that describe the ways in which other teachers and pupils have identified significant problems. References such as those by Giles (7), Wittkop (13), and Barnes (2) have been found useful by numbers of teachers. For practically every problem that teachers and learners face in a particular classroom, a description of a similar one and how it was met can be found in the wealth of professional resources currently available. One major source for discovering such useful resources is, of course, the *Education Index.*

The published lists of problems in various areas, which other learners have found it profitable to attack, will frequently suggest significant problems that have not been recognized by particular learners or teachers up to the present time. For example, see the material by H. H. Giles in *Teacher-Pupil Planning,* pages 241 to 251 (7). Students in teacher-training classes have found lists such as those given by Woodruff (15) to be of considerable value.

Agencies and institutions. The published materials of agencies and organized institutions dealing directly with basic individual and community problems are frequently a fertile source of help in discovering important types of problems upon which to work. For example, some high-school groups have studied the printed materials on problems put out by juvenile courts and labor organizations. While the study was being made, the major problems faced by these organizations were listed. Examination of the printed material in many cases has been supplemented by direct contacts with the organizations concerned.

Orientation. An orientation study of available materials in various areas can be made in an effort to determine some of the problems that others have felt to be significant. The teacher and learners may inspect the many pertinent magazines, books, pamphlets, tests, newspapers, and other appropriate materials which, under optimum conditions, should be brought to the classroom. During the early stages of problem identification and problem selection, broad reading for background and orientation constitutes a significant prerequisite for intelligent identification and selection of specific problems for study.

Much use can well be made of tables of contents, prefaces, and chapter summaries in texts in determining the types of problems that writers feel to be of importance. The desirability of identifying a great variety of problems to which consideration might be given should be made before a particular problem or group of problems is selected for study.

II. *Methods of promoting discussions that will help each learner to discover his basic problems and needs*

Uses of discussion. It is important for the teacher and the learner to remember that acquiring abilities connected with recognizing important problems for study is in itself a problem of first-rate importance, and one is therefore justified in spending considerable time and effort in learning how to do this more effectively. Since this initial step in the sound learning process has been sadly neglected in the past, it will probably be desirable at first to spend what may seem to be a disproportionate amount of time on it in class. To learn how to plan one's activity wisely is not a waste of time and is worthy of considerable classroom discussion. For example, students in an American history class at the beginning of the school year spent two or three class periods raising questions concerned with their purposes in studying history. Questions such as the following were asked: Is our only purpose to study this information to pass a pencil-and-paper test? Is it our purpose to learn how to get along better with other individuals? Do we want to learn how to solve community problems? Is the solution of our personal problems one of the purposes in studying American history?

Closely related to the questions raised in the preceding paragraph is the issue of raising questions within oneself and with class members about the fundamental purposes of the school and activities connected with it. It is frequently desirable to have some individual and group soul-searching. The following questions are frequently productive of worth-while thought and discussion: What do I think are the basic purposes of education? What do I think would be of most value for me to study in this class? Who should decide what should be studied in school? Why? What would I like to be able to do well at the end of the term that I do rather poorly at the present time? What have been my aims and goals in the courses from which I have received the most value? Upon what problems did I work in my most valuable courses? Whom do I consider to be the best-educated people? What would I need to do to become like them? (Also, see the evaluative questions in the section that deals with problem selection on pages 97-99.)

Enlisting the help of learners. As early as possible the teacher should enlist the help and cooperation of the learners themselves in raising and answering the questions relating to what should be studied. In most groups, if the learners are skillfully led, a wealth of valuable ideas can be pulled from the combined thinking of the individuals in the group. The following procedure has sometimes been found desirable. First, each individual attempts to list the problems related to the class which he feels are most important to him. Second, small groups of those who seem to have similar problems can be organized and each individual in the group can suggest the problems he sees as important. This will frequently suggest problems that other learners in the group had not heretofore considered. Thus, the learner can enlarge his initial list of recognized problems. Third, the class as a whole can list on the board, or elsewhere, all of the problems that have been identified by different individuals in the group. This procedure will frequently help the class identify problems that are of common interest to a major number in a group. Such problems can later form the basis for class attack and discussion. The procedure will also suggest to individual members of the class additional problems that may not have been considered before. This will make the selection of problems for individual study a more soundly based process.

Studying strengths and weaknesses. Another approach to problem identification is to encourage learners to study carefully and critically the strengths and weaknesses of various aspects of the classroom activity and the organization and procedures of the whole school. Before this is done, areas of study and the purposes of the school, the classes, and the teachers should usually be discussed with the learners. Care needs to be taken that the students are led to go about this in a constructive way rather than in an attempt to decry everything that is happening in the school. Areas appropriate for study might include such problems as: What are the weaknesses in our student government and how might we go about eliminating them? At what points in our school life should we pupils assume greater responsibility? Are there aspects of our noon-hour activity that need to be improved? What can be done about improving the participation in extracurricular activities?

Mistakes. In this whole process it is extremely important to recognize and help others appreciate the fact that, inevitably and even necessarily, mistakes will be made if the activity carried on is really to be a fruitful, educational one. If no mistakes are made, it is questionable that what was done was very desirable educationally, since the learner was already apparently a master of the process. This is important in considering the probable value of discussions related to problem identification. Some mistakes are the price of learning how to improve in the process of soundly identifying problems for study.

Individual or group problems? Another issue that sometimes needs discussion is tied up with questions relating to the kinds of problems that can best be attacked individually and the kinds of problems that can best be attacked by the group. Generally speaking, those problems that are most common to the group as a whole would form the basis for class attack; those problems about which a large number are concerned, but not nearly the whole class, can form the basis for small group attack; and, those problems which are rather individual in nature at the time of study may be attacked individually by concerned learners. If the decision is made that a particular problem is of small or large group interest, the question may profitably be raised concerning what would be the advantages of a large vs. a small group for this particular problem? Discussion of the *what* and *when* of the study will clarify points of view on the purpose of study.

Learners' future plans. Another approach to problem identification through discussion is to lead each learner to think more about his own tentative plans for future activities and to discuss with others his reasons for them. Ideas about how such discussion can be promoted and led can be gleaned by the teacher through observation and utilization of casual conversations before and after regular class periods or in the homeroom. Such questions as the following on occupational activity are frequently productive: What occupations should I consider entering? Which of these are occupations for which it now appears too many students are preparing? For which are too few now preparing? What problems and situations do I anticipate that I would be facing in each of these occupations? For which of these types of situations do I feel I am now largely unprepared? How might a course of this sort help me on some of these problems? The same type of questions may be raised in connection with social, home, financial, and educational problems, and problems in other areas.

Criteria-making. Discussions can be used to help learners set up criteria to be kept in mind while trying to decide wisely what to study. This problem is more fully discussed in Chapter 5 (pp. 104-112) under the heading, "What are the criteria to be considered in the actual selection of a problem for study?" An actual list the writer worked out with his students is given for illustrative purposes. Discussion of such criteria will sometimes give a different slant or point of view on problems that learners have, but have not recognized to any great extent.

Encouragement should be given for frequent and critical examination of the worth of the study now being carried on in the class in comparison to the probable worth of the study of another problem or group of problems. Through discussion, learners can be helped to recognize that studying the best ways of working individually, and as a group, is frequently a more important problem for consideration than any other. Analyzing effective procedures is too frequently neglected in the typical classroom.

Getting problem-identification materials. The teacher and the learners may consider the problem of getting needed materials for aid in problem identification itself as a practical and educational one upon which to work. Outside of school the learner will need to know how to face it, and he is not likely to get guided practice in doing so unless he gets it in school. Some of the materials that might be discussed as potentially helpful in problem identification are magazines, pamphlets, newspapers, free materials from commercial companies, books, tests, and inventories.

Keeping parents and taxpayers informed on what is being done in school, and why, is a problem that may be discussed with the students. This type of discussion is of value in raising with learners the question of interpersonal relations and influencing people.

III. *Methods of using writing or composition as a tool in helping the learner discover basic problems and needs*

Diaries and autobiographies. Teachers have frequently found it desirable to encourage each learner to keep a diary of the problems he faces each day, the difficulties he encountered in meeting them, the successes he achieved, the interests his problems aroused in him, and the needs and weaknesses he has been able to recognize in himself. If the teacher and pupils feel it to be wise, a certain time during the regular class period can be taken each day for one or more weeks to put these things into writing. Then an individual or group analysis of the results can be made. To avoid any personal embarrassment, writeups can be anonymous at least when used for analytical purposes if it seems wise.

The teacher may sometimes encourage the writing of confidential autobiographies that stress past and present problems related to such areas as the school, the home, friends of the same sex, friends of the opposite sex, personal problems, fears, recognized weaknesses, ambitions.

Listing the advantages and disadvantages of each problem. It is usually desirable to provide considerable flexibility and choice to the learner in the initial selection of individual and group problems for study, but the learner should be constantly encouraged to consider *and list* the probable advantages and disadvantages of studying each problem. This will tend to provide some insurance against snap judgments based on little or no thinking and will frequently suggest additional problems that the student had not clearly formulated.

Record of discussion answers. Sometimes teachers find it advisable to encourage each learner to keep a record of the answers he has received to questions relating to suitable problems upon which to work. These questions may have been asked of employers, parents, brothers and sisters, or other students. A record should also be kept of group discussions and ideas. Unless such a record is kept many ideas will inevitably be lost through the forgetting process.

Constructing questions. Pupils may set up simple questionnaires and formulate systematic lists of questions that will be used to determine what characteristics and abilities employers particularly want from school graduates. The questions can also attempt to get at the types and qualities or abilities in which employers think school graduates are rather weak. For example, a group of high-school English students under the direction of their teacher set up a check list of skills and abilities that were related to English. This list was sent to a variety of employers in a community and each employer was asked to respond to such questions as: Do you feel that the graduates of_____High School are strong, moderately strong, or weak in spelling ability? The results of the questions were analyzed by the class and they formed the basis for learner emphasis during the year. The teacher was surprised at the strength that was given to motivation through this procedure. The construction of questions can provide the basis for identifying many problems that would otherwise not be scrutinized.

Problems of other learners. Learners and teachers can make considerable use of lists of problems built up from year to year by other students in the school. Such lists are also useful as guides for the teacher who wishes to add through the year, and during the summer particularly, to her stock of newspaper, magazine, pamphlet, test, and book resources which will help solve more effectively the problems students face. Such a procedure gives the teacher a basis for selecting functional resources.

Thumbnail sketch. Since the teacher needs to know about the learner as an individual in order to give him appropriate guidance, it is frequently desirable to keep a chart or a place for a thumbnail sketch upon which are jotted notes and observations on the behavior of each learner. Behavior is particularly significant when the individual involved is "off his guard." These notes frequently suggest learner problems or needs. One teacher's notes included such items as "shy," "cocksure," "too quick to generalize," "lonesome," "has difficulty hearing," "talks too loudly," "too conscientious," "depends too much on teacher," "is a watcher and not a doer," "looks unhealthy." If it seems advisable in a particular school, this thumbnail sketch may become part of the permanent record of the pupil with all the teachers adding to it so that changing needs may be noted and needs recognized by one teacher and not by another may be called to the attention of the latter.

Listing plans and needs. When an orientation study of available material is being made, each learner should keep a list of problems in various areas that seem important for him to study. This may be done by encouraging each learner (*a*) to list the types of activities he is likely to engage in during the next few years and (*b*) to try to identify those situations for which he is relatively ill-prepared. The lists may then be pooled with profit on the blackboard. Such pooling should be accompanied by a discussion of the possible advantages, disadvantages, and dangers involved in studying each problem. Such a discussion will frequently lead students to recognize the importance of problems that had seemed relatively unimportant to them before. Another diagnostic written approach is used to help the learner set up, either individually or with the group, a test to investigate weaknesses and abilities in the selection of appropriate problems for study. If we agree that learner problem selection is an important skill, then it would seem to merit some diagnostic testing. Such a test might include items like the following: What points should a learner consider in trying to decide what is best for him to study? Why is it important for the learner to participate in a decision about what he will study? What are the questions we should ask ourselves about a problem before deciding to start to study it intensively? How would a student know that he is progressing in the ability to decide wisely what is best for him to study?

IV. *Methods of utilizing resources that are different from those already mentioned in ferreting out the basic problems and needs of the learners*

Community resources. One may lead the learner to utilize others in the community more extensively in helping to identify problems now faced but unrecognized and problems likely to be encountered later on. We may encourage each pupil to ask systematically such questions as: What problems that you now face has your schooling been of little help to you in meeting? For example, what do you now think you should have got out of your English work while you were in school? We may encourage the learner particularly to question, tactfully, of course, those people in activities, such as those of a housewife, or occupations into which he might go. Learners may survey the needs and interests of adults in the community—poor housing, unsanitary living conditions, need for dental care, need for medical care, unproductive agricultural practices, inadequate recreational facilities.

Teachers and learners should use planned first-hand experiences and observations such as visits, excursions, trips to places where students may participate in an occupational process, or at least see what is going on under normal circumstances. Road-making, bridge-building, shoe-repairing, house construction, lawmaking, merchandising, newspaper editing and printing are examples of such activities. A systematically thought-through list of questions made before the trip, which are to be answered by the observations, will usually make the activity more profitable than unplanned visits.

Learners and teachers may consult on problems with local administrative officers such as the principal or supervisor, the state or university consultants, and with colleagues. They may also be greatly helped by non-school agencies interested in improving community life. These would include such organizations as the farm security administration, the health department, the department of public welfare, Boy Scouts, 4-H Clubs, F.F.A. Clubs, farm bureaus, Y.M.C.A.'s, Y.W.C.A.'s, and churches. Closely related to this approach is having groups of adults in the community help work out the types of problems that need to be attacked. These would include such matters as unwise expenditures of public money in the community, and what can be done about them. This can sometimes be used as the lever in revitalizing such an organization as the parent-teachers association. Service clubs can also be of help in determining basic community religious, leisure-time, social, and economic needs.

Student Council and free periods. The school should develop and use a really functioning student council as an approach to isolating important pupil and school problems. For example, in one school attention was focused on these problems through the student council: How can we eliminate interruptions in classes due to announcements? How can we improve the conditions of our halls? What can be done about the noise, confusion, and dirt in the cafeteria? How may leisure time during the lunch hour be more profitably used?

The teacher can frequently identify a significant number of learner problems through observing learners in their free periods when they engage in activities of their own choice. For this approach to be successful it is desirable for the schoolroom to have a variety of materials of various kinds and for the teacher to have some systematic way of taking down significant observations about individual pupils. The free reading period, where developed, has been found a most useful time to get information on individual problems and needs.

Closely related to the approach suggested in the preceding paragraph is that of inviting learners to bring their toys or other recreational materials to school. These, or their lack, are frequently significant and may suggest the need for making materials in the school for leisure-time activities in the home.

Using school visitors. Visitors to the school should be encouraged to talk with learners and to lead them to ask questions concerning their prospective needs, both recreational and leisure-time. This discussion should, of course, be tied up with helping the learners to see how what is being done in school is actually benefiting them now and/or is likely to be of benefit in the future.

Learner self-diagnosis. Teachers should encourage each learner to carry on with teacher guidance a *continuous* diagnostic program. The results of diagnostic checks (tests, inventories, and questionnaires) of abilities, needs, attitudes, interests, should be utilized in helping the learners to set up needed "assignments." This individualized diagnosis should start in the first week of school and continue through to the end of the year. Otherwise, teacher-pupil planning is not likely to be rooted as soundly as it should be.

Additional problems. Below are some additional questions or problems for the teacher, or prospective teacher, which may be utilized in analyzing and using the points given in the preceding paragraphs:

Which of the methods suggested under each of the four main sections—I, II, III, IV—have you actually tried or seen tried?

Which of the methods suggested under each of the four main sections do you feel would be the most difficult for you to use? Tell why in each case. Would this indicate they should not be tried at all? Explain.

What additional methods could you add under each of the main sections?

Indicate the grade level in which you are most interested. Rank the suggestions under each group or section in the order of their probable usefulness at this grade level.

DESIRABLE PREPLANNING FOR A COURSE BY THE TEACHER

Need for preplanning. The teacher who expects to give his learners practice in the initial step of the learning process, problem identification, should consider taking certain steps before the class meets the first time to ensure the most profitable learning.

Preplanning is an area sadly neglected and yet it is of paramount importance to the "cooperatively-determined" teacher. To many, preschool planning means outlining the material to be covered so that the course is done up in a neat "package" before the students are even seen. To some, preschool planning means dividing the number of times the class is to meet into the number of pages of the text so that a given number of pages can be covered each meeting and the text "effectively" studied before the end of the term.

The treatment suggested below indicates that the community is the source of orientation for the teacher's planning and that the teacher essentially goes through similar steps to those that the learner will be encouraged to use.

Investigating learner needs. An effort should be made by the teacher to determine the most pressing personal and community problems, needs, and tensions related to the field in which he is teaching. It is quite probable that these are the problems that learners will see some importance in studying if given adequate opportunities to help identify what is to be studied. In other words, the *teacher essentially goes through* steps similar to those that the learners may be encouraged to use in identifying problems. For example, Sayward (11, pp. 272-74) was concerned about the fact that the traditional courses in mathematics required of students in high schools have served largely as preparation for advanced work in mathematics or related fields even though this did not seem to be what all or even the majority of high-school students would need most. Working on this assumption, Sayward and those with whom she worked made a specific study of what mathematics a woman needs in actual life outside the school. As a result, a functional course in mathematics developed *which produced well-motivated students who were themselves suggesting realistic problems related to mathematics which they would like to study,* such as, "How do you figure out a tax on real estate with a tax rate expressed in so many different ways?" Teacher preplanning pays off.

Planning method. The preplanning teacher will do well to consider in detail some changes in *method.* One way to proceed is to write down the key procedures that were used the preceding year and then to list specific changes that might be considered in moving in the direction of greater learner participation in problem identification. Flexibility, rather than rigidity, should characterize the plans so that they can take into account the developing needs and problems of individual learners.

Getting resources. Resources appropriate in helping to identify and solve problems likely to be raised should be accumulated by the teacher in anticipation of the demand for such materials as soon as the course gets under way. Of course many additional resources will be added by the teacher and learners, working cooperatively during the course, but an initial supply helps avoid discouragement in the use of a new method.

Self-diagnosis by the teacher. Many teachers have found it profitable to attack this problem of assignments and what to study by critically examining and studying the ways of improving various phases of their own professional learning, particularly the phase of problem identification. Numerous teachers brought up under an educational regime where they had little or no chance to participate in the planning of their own study have never learned how to do this effectively for themselves. When this is the case, it is doubtful whether these same teachers will teach effective and functional planning to those with whom they work without considerable effort. A teacher with whom the writer is acquainted started out by not merely thinking about but by actually listing the main professional problems she was facing. This, she found, was not easy since she had had little previous practice in it. Then she attempted to break down these problems into sub-problems, which would be more susceptible to systematic study. The sub-problems, she found, could be more pointedly stated in the form of questions. At this point she actually began to study and list the resources available for suggesting solutions and began to try out those solutions that seemed the most promising. She found that not only was she identifying and meeting her own problems in a much more satisfying way than previously, but in addition she was actually beginning to appreciate better the methods she should be using to help her students make their learning really function in their lives.

Preview. In the next chapter are some descriptions of how individual teachers, departments, and school faculties have given learners direct practice in identifying their own problems.

BIBLIOGRAPHY

1. Association for Supervision and Curriculum Development. *Toward Better Teaching.* Washington, D.C.: The Association, 1949.
2. BARNES, R. A. "Discovering Student Needs." *Journal of Higher Education,* 12:469-72; December 1941.
3. CODIGNOLA, E. "A School Which Is a City." *New Era,* 29:184-86; September 1948.
4. DOANE, D. C. *Needs of Youth.* New York: Bureau of Publications, Teachers College, Columbia University, 1942.
5. EVANS, H. M. "The Ubiquitous Problem of Objectives in Youth Education." *Teachers College Record,* 52:481-89; May 1951.

6. GATES, A. I., *et al. Educational Psychology.* New York: The Macmillan Co., 1948. pp. 446-84, 652-55.
7. GILES, H. H. *Teacher Pupil Planning.* New York: Harper and Bros., 1941.
8. MOONEY, R. L. "Surveying High School Students' Problems by Means of a Problem Checklist." *Educational Research Bulletin,* 21:57-69; March 1942.
9. MORRISON, GEORGE W. "Adult Education in Simcoe County. *Canadian Forum,* 28:125; September 1948.
10. MURSELL, J. L. *Successful Teaching.* New York: McGraw-Hill Book Co., Inc., 1946. pp. 51-52, 86-89.
11. SAYWARD, R. K. "Mathematics Breaks with Tradition." *High School Journal,* 22:272-74; November 1939.
12. WATTENBERG, W. W. "Real Needs Focus Learning." *High School Journal,* 35:11-16; October 1951.
13. WITTKOP, N. L. "My Pupils Make Their Own Assignments." *The Clearing House,* 15:414-415; March 1941.
14. WOODRUFF, A. D. "An Exploratory Evaluation of Teacher Education." *Educational Administration and Supervision,* 32:1-18; January 1946.
15. WOODRUFF, A. D. *The Psychology of Teaching.* New York: Longmans, Green and Co., 1948. pp. 100-107.

4

PROBLEM IDENTIFICATION THROUGH TEACHERS, DEPARTMENTS, AND SCHOOL STAFFS [1]

Some problems to consider

With whom and when should the learner experiment with developing problem identification?

How may the individual teacher in a traditional, conservative setup move from teacher-dictated assignments toward assignments that are learner-planned with teacher guidance?

How can school departments revise the "what" and "how" of instruction to include problem identification?

What can faculties do on a school-wide basis to develop problem identification in learners?

Introduction. In some situations the individual teacher may find it difficult, at least initially, to get school faculty or even departmental interest in training students in problem identification. It is with this type of situation that the descriptions in the first part of this chapter are concerned. It should be noted that in even the most hidebound educational framework, it is still possible for the alert and developing individual teacher to make fundamental improvements *in his own classroom.* Such improvements are frequently contagious.

---

[1] This chapter and other chapters in the book are addressed primarily to the teacher or prospective teacher of high-school students. However, it is recognized that these professional students of teaching and learning will frequently be in college or graduate classes. Hence, the high-school teacher's role as a student is given considerable emphasis in discussions and illustrations.

In other schools only one or two departments may be concerned with improving problem identification processes in students. The middle part of this chapter contains descriptions of some changes such departments have made.

The last portion of this chapter describes situations in which school-wide attention is given to problem identification activities.

WITH WHOM AND WHEN SHOULD THE LEARNER EXPERIMENT WITH DEVELOPING PROBLEM IDENTIFICATION?

Single-class approach. Some teachers may wish to develop their techniques in improving learner identification of problems in all their classes. Other instructors may wish to start out on a more tentative basis and work with only a single class, probably the smallest one the teacher has. When the latter method is followed, recognition is made of the fact that learning how to plan work with the learners is for a different purpose from that behind the traditional assignment. The former process involves displacing many attitudes and habits that have become thoroughly ingrained in the teacher who may have had actual experience only with the teacher-dominated type of assignment. The change also involves building up many new democratic techniques and approaches to take the place of the old. All of this not only takes time, but also takes some effort on the part of the teacher. A social science teacher, for example, took his smallest class and attempted to apply democracy in planning the work of the class. He explained his goals to the high-school group with which he was working. He frankly admitted that he was not as yet very skilled at doing it and would need their thinking and cooperation if they were to get the most out of the work. The group finally decided they should try to identify some of the social science problems they faced in their classroom, school, and community. Through this approach the pupils learned that social science was not simply learning a lot of facts for the inevitable test, but rather it was identifying and studying better ways of meeting the problems they needed to face constructively. The teacher learned that democracy in planning and assignment-making can work if it is given a fair trial.

One-day-a-week initial approach. Some teachers have found it desirable to start out by sticking to familiar methods of making assignments on four days a week, and then on the fifth to experiment with the newer methods of problem identification and pupil-teacher planning. For instance, one English teacher stuck to familiar teacher-dictated assignments in the classics except on Friday of each week, the day that usually was the most difficult for her. On Friday the teacher decided to help the pupils try to find their own basic reading needs and interests and to help them meet these. She found that usually the needs and interests of each pupil were different from those of every other pupil. She attempted to start with each pupil where he was and to try to get him a little higher in skill and interest. This approach worked out so well that the program was expanded to include Thursday as well as Friday. English gradually changed, for most of the learners, from a forced and teacher-purposed activity to a pleasurable and profitable learner-purposed experience with teacher guidance. Eventually, all school days became "Fridays" in that English class. More work was done than had been done under the old method. The work for teacher and pupils changed from largely a routine and a bore to a satisfying experience in living. Incidentally, the level of appreciation, as indicated by the reading the pupils did in their free time, began to move upward because there was no longer the unbridgeable gap between what the teacher was calling English and what the pupils were able to work on with a substantial degree of understanding.

Sometimes the questions of "When?" and "With whom?" should newer methods of problem identification be tried are answered by fortuitous circumstances. Blitch (4, p. 131) relates: "On one occasion while the teacher [of an eighth-grade class] was ill for four days, she wrote suggestions for class procedure. On the fifth day she came back to school unexpected by the class. When she arrived the class was already in progress. The chairman and class paused long enough to say they were glad she was back, but straightway returned to their work, not even asking her to 'take over.' . . ." It should be noted that this teacher had already moved some distance toward learner participation in planning before her enforced absence, but the latter did demonstrate how much initiative, independence of action, and dependability her learners could assume.[2]

It is not recommended that eighth-grade pupils spend too much of their time unsupervised until our schools do a better job of

[2] This illustration is designed to help the teacher visualize the types of self-responsibility he is trying to develop.

training them. There is evidence, however, to show that they can do a lot more than we frequently give them credit for being able to do.

HOW MAY THE TEACHER HELP THE STUDENT LEARN THE PROCESS OF PROBLEM IDENTIFICATION?

As with most questions regarding method there is no single best answer to the one just posed. Rather, the developing teacher should be familiar with various ways of meeting the problem. Brief descriptions of some possible answers to the problem will be helpful.

Using learner life experiences. Let us begin with an actual description of how a science teacher, Leftwich (14, pp. 472-74), started off his class scheduled for physics. After deciding to use life experiences in which the youngsters were concerned as a starting point the teacher and the individual students began free reading periods and discussions that would give the learners some background to aid them in the identification and selection of worthwhile problems. Preceding this step, however, the teacher had done some preliminary investigation of problems related to physics upon which the students might work. A survey was made by the class of machines and appliances in the community and some students began to suggest school, home, and community problems. These problems were defined in class discussions and tentative plans for their solution were set up.

A refrigerator, a victrola, an electric fan, a radio, a pump, engines, and other machines and appliances were placed in the classroom. A variety of books and other materials were gathered together and made readily available to the learners. A weak battery that would not turn over the automobile motor started the work on a series of problems including how to care for and use storage batteries, motors, generators, how to use a hydrometer and voltmeter for testing and other problems related to specific gravity, pressure in electricity, and the chemical nature of a battery. The automobile motor was finally started but not before many problems related to physics had been investigated.

Representative of other functional activities that developed from orientation reading and the exploring of machines are the following: Several car generators and a victrola were repaired; a public-address system for the school was studied and planned; circulars on good radio programs were put out; a gasoline engine was repaired by making a gas tank, installing piston rings, grinding valves, retiming, and painting. Many other practical problems in heating, plumbing, lighting, and electricity were also attacked. The class provided stimulating and self-generating learning for both the teacher and the students.

Cooperatively setting up goals and purposes. A second major approach to developing learner identification of problems is that of encouraging the learner to record his own needs, plans, purposes, and goals insofar as he is able to do this. Blitch (4), a high-school teacher of civics, English, and Latin, believed that helping the pupils share in selecting the purposes and goals of the year's work had two apparent advantages: first (p. 125), it "contributed to their feeling that the work would be of value to them and to the security that comes from knowing 'where we're going'"; second, "The purposes and goals decided upon together were readily accepted by the pupils as standards in terms of which their progress throughout the year could be measured."

Part of the time during the first four or five days of the school year was spent in cooperatively setting up goals and purposes. *The remaining time was spent in having regularly* assigned *lessons in spelling and literature* similar to those with which the learners were familiar.

Blitch (4, p. 126) gives the following description of procedure: "In this planning with the pupils the purposes and goals were concerned with both subject matter to be explored and with certain traits that would help them to live more effectively in school and out of school. The selection of these traits grew out of a discussion of the ideals of the school and how to get the greatest possible good out of school life. In order to make sure the traits discussed were not empty-sounding terms the teacher and class further defined them by listing behaviors that would characterize a person possessing them. The students wrote in their notebooks the behaviors characteristic of each of these traits—initiative and independence of action, dependability, poise, the wise use of freedom, and the ability to work well with others,—and agreed to put themselves to the test of seeing to what extent they measured up to the objectives decided upon by the group. These objectives were used as a basis of reference throughout the year when, sometimes as a group and sometimes as individuals, the class checked back to see in what respects they were attaining or failing to attain them. Sometimes these checking periods took the form of group discussions, sometimes they were individual conferences, and at times they were written evaluations by individual pupils.

"Near the end of the year there was a final period of rechecking these aims to determine the progress of individuals and that of the group as a whole. In the case of the written individual evaluations the pupils were asked to be very frank in expressing their opinions. They were assured the papers would not be graded and urged not to make their comments with an eye to pleasing the teacher. These pupil evaluations were used as one type of evidence concerning the achievement of the educational objectives toward which the teacher and class were working. [See reference 4, pp. 134-37 for pupil self-appraisals related to acquiring initiative and independence of action.]

"These goals also served as a basis for reports to parents. Before narrative comments were reported on their report cards, each of the pupil's teachers had a conference with him concerning his growth in regard to these and other objectives. Both pupil and teacher voiced their opinions in these conferences and the narrative comments developed reflected both opinions."

Excerpts of Blitch's report (4, p. 126) are significant in that they show how situations were arranged through which the pupils learned to use resources that were available in a high school.

"During the planning periods held near the first of the year, the pupils expressed the need for becoming acquainted with their schedule, the school regulations and equipment and the location of the library and other parts of the building. In addition they expressed their need for becoming acquainted with their teachers and with each other. Ways of meeting these needs were discussed, and the teacher and class set about participating in activities which would accomplish these ends.

"As a means of becoming acquainted with the school, excursions were taken through the building and to points on the campus ... pupils took turns in doing errands that took them to different parts of the building. The schedule was posted and discussed, regulations were explained .., school ideals were presented and the school song and pledge learned." During the first few days the schedule was shortened and pupils remained in the homeroom getting acquainted with each other and their homeroom teacher. Guided experience was given in finding information on various types of problems. Activities such as note-taking, organizing material, and report-making were participated in by pupils.

Raising realistic questions. A third approach to the task of learning and teaching problem identification is to raise questions and more questions in order to stimulate the pupils to think about problems. Willets (22, pp. 360-64), recognizing among other things that most ninth-grade pupils of average and below average mental ability will not be scientists, technicians, or engineers, but will need to develop a relatively few simple and specific mathematical skills, decided the first step in the course was helping pupils recognize problem situations. To aid in this process he raised questions such as the following: "How is the idea of fire insurance a solution to a problem?" and "Why does the Bell Telephone Company run advertisements showing a graph distribution of long distance telephone calls through an average day showing peaks at 10:30 A.M., 2 P.M., and 7 P.M.? What problem is it seeking a solution to?" (Willets reports 37% saw no problem, and of the 63% who recognized some problem 12% thought the idea was to have more people make calls at peak times, and only 40% recognized the true problem. This is one commentary on the lack of attention most of our schools have given to problem identification.)

Obourn and Montgomery (16, pp. 72-80) used the question raising approach in science teaching by posing this one: What claims of manufacturers for their products cannot be substantiated by scientific experimentation? For example, can the claims for what Vitamin B_1 tablets would do to plants be substantiated? (Not only did this question-raising approach to the study that followed give the learners practice in identifying, selecting for study, and solving problems, but it also encouraged them to have a healthy skepticism regarding advertisers' claims.)

Using human resources. A fourth way of developing functional problem-identification ability is to encourage learners to make use of human resources in the community. Classes in almost any subject can set up specific questions about the needs and weaknesses in the area to ask of parents, employers, recent graduates of the school, professional groups, and others in the community in order to help identify problems that might be considered for study. For example, an English high-school class decided to interview employers in the community regarding what they felt were the major weaknesses in the writing and speech of the high-school graduates whom they had employed. In many cases the students were much impressed by the specific writing and speaking standards that employers indicated were helpful in getting and holding a job. Motivating interest in oral and written composition disappeared as a problem for the teacher. The students had begun to learn how to motivate themselves.

Greene (10, p. 455) and students in a college preparatory English course found freshmen college students visiting in town very glad to discuss the problems they had experienced in college. Some even came to school and led discussions of freshmen college work. These students found problems by talking with those who had actually met them in their more advanced schoolwork.

Using diagnostic tools. A fifth approach to problem identification involves the use of diagnostic tools such as tests, inventories, and questionnaires on abilities, attitudes, interests, or needs. Since the primary purpose of using these tools is to raise problems in the mind of the learner, he himself may be guided in scoring his paper and in drawing some implications and conclusions from the results. This is another way of moving responsibility for individual learning from teacher to learner where it eventually belongs.

Tests, inventories, or questionnaires used for the purpose mentioned in the preceding paragraph may be teacher or teacher-learner constructed or they may be standardized tests purchased from a publisher. An example of the use of the former type is that described by McAllister (15, p. 48) who gave a test of citizenship in the intermediate and grammar grades which was for use in learner self-evaluation, a phase of problem identification. The objective questions used were grouped under: neatness (6 questions); work habits (8); sportsmanship (5); and courtesy (10). Illustrative questions are the following: "Do I help to keep the floor neat by helping to pick up papers or chalk and by cleaning my shoes before I come in?" "Do I follow instructions exactly, not trying to 'get by'?" "Am I a good loser?" and "Can I take jokes and teasing without answering crossly?" McAllister suggests that to eliminate any temptation to cheat, the teacher explains to the students that the results will not in any way affect their regular grades but that the purpose of the test is to help each one check up on himself. This precaution is particularly important in schools where pupils are very grade conscious.

Having more traditional goals, Greene (10, pp. 455-57) early in the school year used tests that included writing a theme, doing oral work, taking standardized tests on reading, vocabulary, and general English (including punctuation, pronunciation, capitalization, grammar usage). Learners were helped to see the primary purpose of the tests, that of diagnosing needs.

Writing letters. A sixth approach to problem identification lies in encouraging learners to write letters to those who will be likely to have a share in deciding what will be expected of the student later on. The interviewing of employers has already been suggested. Letters to employers or class-constructed questionnaires sent to employers will frequently produce equally stimulating motivation and can also give functional practice in composition.

In a college preparatory high-school English class Greene (10, pp. 453-55) promoted letter-writing to colleges. After discussing various types of colleges that class decided it would be well to ascertain the exact requirements in English for college entrance and to find out the nature of freshmen college English. To do this the class composed letters and sent them to fifteen colleges. Not only was this good communication experience using functional composition, but it was felt that if the pupils could get a clear picture of what might be expected of them they would do more intelligently purposeful work in English.

The answers obtained from the letters were very helpful in indicating to the students the skills stressed by the various colleges and universities. Many specific weaknesses or deficiencies, which colleges had found prevalent in high-school graduates, were also noted in the answers. The points made in the letters were grouped and tabulated. These provided the basis for setting up individual goals.

Sharing problems. A seventh approach, which can frequently be taken after some of the other approaches already suggested have been used, involves taking the results of individual learner researches or small group identification of problems and combining these on the board or on paper for every member of the group to see. The importance of each problem so identified can be emphasized by having the individual or group who uncovered it state why the problem seems significant. Through this process more problems are likely to take on added significance to each learner and his motivation for study will thus be enhanced.

Small individual problems out of a big group one. In an eighth approach the teacher and learners together decide on a single big problem or unit on which all will start to work. As the work proceeds the individual pupil is encouraged to investigate the areas of the big problem that seem most important to him. As the project develops it is very possible that fewer and fewer will be working on the same parts of it.

It is important to have each learner keep a developing list of problems he has identified as important for him. This provides a basis both for intelligent problem selection and for help in deciding when it is desirable to postpone work on an old problem and start work on a new one.

TOWARD WHAT KINDS OF PROBLEMS SHOULD LEARNER PROBLEM IDENTIFICATION BE POINTED?

Keeping problems familiar and not too complex at first. If the learner has had little or no experience in problem identification or selection, it is usually well to encourage him to try to identify problems that directly concern him. These may be, for example, vocational, social, personal, or educational problems. It is usually unsound to start out with faraway (in the mind of the learner) problems with which it is hard for the learner to come to grips initially. For example, large national and international questions are not likely to be as appropriate for initial study as these: How can we promote safety in our community? Is it desirable to control loan companies? What factories are contaminating our stream or river and what should be done about it? The big problems are unquestionably important, but if students learn how to identify and solve personal and community problems they are getting excellent training for tackling larger problems later. It is unfortunate that we have students trying to study federal social-security legislation before they are able wisely to handle a simple problem like "How should we go about eliminating a tree that might fall down in high wind on the school grounds and probably damage life and property?" Encouragement should be given to the identification of problems that have real significance to students and that are adapted to their present level of problem-solving ability.

While the aspect of student interest in problems can be overworked, it is frequently well to encourage each learner to suggest topics or problems for discussion or study in which he is particularly interested. This usually at least helps him to identify more clearly some of his own interests. Sometimes sound motivation can be developed by combining this approach with other approaches.

Learner self-rating. Another type of approach is to encourage the learner to diagnose his own strengths and weaknesses so that something may be done about the latter. This self-evaluation approach may be made from other angles also. For example, the learner may be asked to rate or rank himself in relation to a designated group of students, perhaps his own class, on certain factors or abilities that can be measured and are important to him, such as intelligence, achievement in various learning areas, and interests. Then he can be allowed to compare his own ratings with those he gets on tests measuring these abilities. Teachers who have tried this have found great individual variation in ability to estimate one's own status accurately. This is an indication that our schools have neglected this phase of learner development. For sound adjustment and reasonable "aspiration level" Socrates' dictum, "Know thyself" cannot be ignored.

Arsenian (1, p. 302) found that students who grossly over estimated or underestimated their abilities, knowledges, and adjustment are on the average somewhat less intelligent and less well-adjusted. It is quite probable that better adjustment would be promoted if teachers gave more attention to helping the learner appraise his own abilities and limitations. We need to help the learner understand what is inside him as well as what is outside him.

From group to individual problems. Waters (21), in a significant study of learner participation in problem identification and teacher-learner planning, shows how a group apparently without much initial skill in problem identification or selection started off with all the class working on the same problem. As questions were being identified for a new problem, an interesting conclusion was reached by the students in Waters' class (21, p. 41): "During the development of these questions it became evident that some of the pupils with previous knowledge of magnetism were not challenged by some of the more elementary questions included in the above outline [of questions]. These pupils objected to group study of each question because 'we already know the answer to some of them.' *All seemed to agree that group study of each question was probably not the best plan to follow.* [Italics mine.] Consequently a plan was developed which permitted each pupil to study any questions he chose with guidance to select from the outline." This report suggests the possibilities of having questions pointed out from an initial study of a problem by all in a class.

DEVELOPING LEARNER IDENTIFICATION OF PROBLEMS THROUGH DEPARTMENTAL CHANGES

While there are very significant improvements an individual teacher can make in promoting sound motivation for learning through attempting to help learners identify their own problems, even more significant progress can be made where those in a department jointly plan improvements. Getting improvement will necessarily involve making changes, it should be remembered. Some illustrations of modifications on a departmental level are described below.

Examination of assumptions and purposes. The changes in a particular field, mathematics, as shown by Espy (8, p. 319-20), suggest a re-examination of the basic assumptions and purposes for which the courses are taught. She was teaching in a school where geometry was taught by teachers who felt there was great virtue in being able to write out and glibly recite the proof of the theorem, "The Square of the hypotenuse of a right triangle is equal to the sum of the squares of the other two sides"; where the study of both algebra and geometry meant many hours of boredom for pupils who were "compelled to sit quietly and appear interested in explanations of the board work of other students." The basic purposes in teaching mathematics had been given little if any consideration by most of the mathematics teachers. Traditional mathematics was taught in a traditional manner regardless of learner reaction.

The asking of questions, such as, "What good will this do me?" by intelligent learners helped to raise doubts in the minds of some teachers about the real value of the mathematics courses as they were then taught.

After a period of years of "soul-searching" and thinking, the faculty developed the philosophy that each learner should be treated as an individual who has present and prospective problems that he needs to learn to solve in a better fashion. In the field of mathematics this resulted in the development and use of these assumptions: (1) that most eighth-grade pupils are too young to profit from a formal algebra course and that they would get more value out of a well-taught general mathematics course; (2) that pupils not planning to go to college need much more training in everyday mathematics than they are now getting; (3) that geometry, if traditionally taught, is painful to fully half the pupils, promptly forgotten by most of them, and hence is of little value; (4) that the pupils planning to go to college should be given the formal mathematics needed for admission to the college of their choice; and (5) that boys and girls today need to know the fundamentals of mathematics now more than ever before. It should be pointed out that these assumptions did not arise full-grown but gradually grew out of the thinking and study of faculty members. It should also be emphasized that the teachers did not take the easy way out and say: "The way it is, is the way I was hired to teach it. It's too bad if the math now being taught is not very valuable to the pupils." Teachers can change a sterile learning situation even in a traditional setup *if they really want* to do so.

Espy (8, pp. 321-23) goes on to indicate two factors that were responsible for a number of changes in course offerings. First was a survey made by faculty members (students might well have participated in this type of survey) in which businessmen in the community told them that boys and girls applying for jobs did not know enough arithmetic. It appeared that most pupils were not having any practical arithmetic training after they were old enough to appreciate its significance.

Second was the realization on the part of the pupils and teachers that most of the formal algebra learned in the ninth grade was forgotten before they entered the eleventh-grade algebra classes. The staff attempted to make appropriate changes in course offerings and in the methods to meet learner needs.

Changes in problems and methods. In the general mathematics courses, such problems as the following were studied (in place of theorems, equations, and the formal, traditional type of exercise previously taught): real problems with which some of the pupils and graduates were confronted on their jobs in local stores, problems of percentage, how to measure land, how to operate a budget and spend wisely, how to figure interest, how to figure taxes, how the utilities bills are computed. Some of the problems were suggested by the learners.

Realistic practice in problem-solving was given by such problems as, "Mr. Smith's wife and two daughters wish to go to Atlanta. Considering the transportation alone, which will be the cheapest way for them to go: by train, by bus, or in the family car?" A study was made of the information needed and the ways to go about getting it. Groups worked independently and then results were compared. Interest in insurance was aroused, problems related to car insurance rates were considered. "If you borrowed a car, and while driving it ran over and hurt someone, who would be liable for a damage suit, your father or the one who owns the car?" is illustrative of the additional questions raised. Some insurance problems in textbooks were raised and pupils learned the meaning of such terms as premiums, beneficiary, annuity, endowment, cash surrender value, and special benefits.

Another problem-learning situation described by Espy is that of working through the financial problems likely to be faced by a young couple planning to get married on John's $50 a week. Housing, food costs, loans, budgets, and related questions raised a multitude of mathematical problems for which the pupils really wished to learn some possible solutions.

Key questions raised in functional courses by all concerned are: "Is it worth while?" "Is it a problem we are facing or are likely to face?" Flexibility is very important and the variability of individual needs must constantly be kept in mind. This means that different learners in the same class will frequently be working on very different problems.

A second departmental illustration of reorientation in decisions on what to study is provided by Smyth (17, p. 248) who, after studying the social studies offerings in the high school in which she taught, concluded that they (1) had excessive compartmentalization, (2) were not meeting the needs or interests of youth, (3) were not challenging pupils to accept individual responsibility, and (4) were taught to try to put subject matter across rather than to help learners better identify and meet the social problems they were going to have to face. Smyth and her colleagues decided to do something about the situation and gradually evolved "the new curriculum." While the pattern worked out in each individual school should vary according to the learner needs in that school, a study of some of the key characteristics of this new individualized social studies curriculum should be of value to all teachers.

Some of the characteristics of the curriculum developed by Smyth (17, pp. 248-50) and her colleagues are:

Courses in history, economics, sociology, and civics, as such, were abandoned. In their place were built units, at first teacher-constructed, "for the purpose of aiding pupils to realize the essential elements of society and its problems, and to challenge them to desire ways and means for the solution of such problems." Gradually, the pupils themselves assumed more and more responsibility in deciding what should be studied. This evolved into a pattern of pupil-teacher planning of the curriculum for the class or for groups of pupils in the class. This step gradually evolved for some teachers into "the stage of the individual pupil planning with his teacher the problem which seems best to meet his needs and interests. The philosophy that the needs of the individual are basic in the teaching process is fast gaining adherents" and some teachers were willing to accept the challenge by building up the teaching and learning techniques necessary to implement this philosophy.

An organizational scheme was tried which permitted each teacher to keep the same pupils for at least four semesters.

Instead of being presented with the expected textbook of ancient history and an assignment to take home, the sophomore pupil was encouraged to consider, largely through classroom discussions, the meaning and function of high-school education. He was further encouraged through similar means to make plans for his own high-school career and even beyond in some cases. Discussions were carried on to help him discover his personal needs and interests and to see what contributions the school offered to help him carry out his plans. In individual cases where this approach was met with antagonism (usually encouraged at home) a partial return was made to more formal assignments.

"First, for the class or group and later for the individual, ways and means of evaluating the choice of a problem are determined through pupil-teacher solution of the problem. From time to time as the need arises the following responsibilities are realized and accepted by each individual:

(1) Working out tentative plans for the problem to be studied.
(2) Collecting and caring for materials.
(3) Estimating and determining time needed.
(4) Sifting data, organizing and drawing conclusions, listing references.
(5) Improving English skills.
(6) Building class reference files.

(7) Contributing to department vertical files.
(8) Sharing with others—family, class, community,—the values derived.
(9) Evaluating references, learning practical applications, growth in the development of skills, work habits, and sense of responsibility and ability to solve problems."

Grouping by needs. A third description of modifications in the problem-identification area is reported by Hicks (12, pp. 63-65). He pictures departmental changes that originally grew out of a revision of the entire high-school curriculum. The revision represented an attempt to take better care of the needs, interests, and concerns of children. "The science department," says Hicks, "came to recognize and serve three groups of students: first, those who had some special interest along scientific lines, or who were interested in working on some special science project; second, those who were interested in science, but recognized no special problems; third, those who were planning to enter college."

The first group, those who had already identified some science problems of importance to them, were encouraged to make their own plans with appropriate guidance for solving their problems. They were given help in defining and analyzing problems, in securing information, and in planning methods of attacking the problems. As plans were carried out, the instructor gave needed help and guidance.

The second group made up of those who were interested in science, but had not proceeded to the point of identifying problems for study, discussed their work in other departments and their interests outside of school. Possible problems for study were suggested by the instructor and each learner identified some problem on which it appeared important for him to work. After definite selection of a problem the learner worked on it in a fashion similar to that used with the first group. Some of the work was individual and some of it was in groups. An attempt was made to have the work done in groups wherever it seemed that group work would be of most value to those concerned. Otherwise, most of the work was individually pursued most of the time with reciprocal help being given in the getting and using of resources, in evaluation, and in record-keeping.

With the group going to college, who saw a need for special courses, a more conventional pattern was followed. Textbooks, more definite assignments, checkups (frequently), and the doing of traditional experiments characterized the work of this group in school. In other schools a technique more similar to that used with the first two groups has been found successful.

The list given by Hicks (12, p. 64) of problems being worked on in science by high-school students in a typical period of work, for any one day, is illuminating. (The numbers in parentheses after each problem indicate the number of students working on it.)

"Working on a loud speaker for a radio which is to be used in their speech work. (2)

Building a pocket radio. (1)

Testing water from their homes in connection with a health unit of their homeroom. (3)

Making a study of vitamins, also related to a health unit in their homeroom. (3)

Doing chemistry experiments which have been assigned in connection with their textbook work in chemistry. (3)

Planning how to make an electric score board for the gymnasium. (3)

Taking a textbook course in senior science. (7)

Working problems of their physics course. (5)

Stuffing an owl. (2)

Taking junior science course. (4)"

During the time students were working on the problems indicated above, the instructor moved among the different groups, discussing, offering suggestions, and checking on progress. Students "taking a course" met in small groups and got help from the instructor as it was needed. Conferences with individuals and with small groups characterized much of the activity of the instructor.

Since the work was highly individualized, conventional checkups were not appropriate. One check sheet (12, p. 65) worked out by the students themselves included the following items:

"1. Present or absent [(a) absent from school, (b) absent from class, (c) absent from class but not excused].

2. On time.

3. Begins work promptly.
4. Continues work throughout period.
5. Works quietly.
6. Sticks to one problem until finished.
7. Reports when working elsewhere.
8. Hands in reports on time.
9. Considers others.
10. Works on science work.
11. Shows interest in work.
12. Finds own problems to work on.
13. Plans work well day by day.
14. Finds experimental work to do in connection with problem.
15. Considers all angles of a problem.
16. Draws conclusions from experiments.
17. Thinks on his own.
18. Does no complaining.
19. Is careful with materials."

Short weekly reports were also turned in by each student. At the end of each nine weeks the instructor gave a narrative report, along with reports from other teachers, to the parents.

Difficulties in individualizing work. Difficulties encountered in individualizing work, as given by Hicks (12, p. 65) are: "(1) getting students to recognize a science problem as a personal problem; (2) helping students to realize that in the home and community they are constantly meeting science problems; (3) knowing just how much planning to do with certain students; (4) locating and securing sufficient material in the form of books, pamphlets and so on to satisfy special student interests."

Advantages indicated by Hicks are: (1) Work becomes more purposeful. (2) Work can be tied up with other areas such as home economics, art, music, speech, and shop departments. (3) A student develops a method of work that is helpful in other fields. (4) More opportunities present themselves for developing responsibility. (5) Opportunities for training in self-evaluation are given. (6) The learner works on his own problems. (7) The learner can better see the relationship of science to other things.

In addition to discussing aspects of problem identification in our three departmental illustrations, we have attempted to give enough of that which followed learner and teacher-learner problem identification to put the reader in a better position to tie up the first main step in the learning process with subsequent steps.

SCHOOL-WIDE ATTACK ON QUESTIONS RELATED TO PROBLEM IDENTIFICATION

Some surprising things are likely to happen in the schools of a community when the staff becomes sufficiently concerned about education to re-examine the purposes of the schools and the methods currently being used to achieve these purposes. If such a re-examination is intensive and sincere, fundamental improvements are likely to result.

From blueprint to needs. For example, Dotson (7, pp. 489-90) and his staff made a study of their high-school offerings, in terms of individual needs, with the following conclusions: "We realized that our setup was not doing all that it could. We were, in a sense, drawing a hop-scotch for each student and directing him to hop into certain squares and attempting to give guidance toward the end of our job with him from accumulated records. We wondered how it would be to rub out the ones in the squares and try to help a student find himself day by day. If this could be done, guidance would become a continuous process. We realized the difficulty of this, and that extreme care must be taken to see that the student was progressing continually while working at the things which seemed important to him, and to his teachers. It was evident to us in the early stages of our planning that we could not find how to do this by studying what others have done and forming a new or modified plan, by selecting what, in our judgment, was good from various plans. Our program then was to begin with the child rather than a plan of action." However, ideas and suggestions from what others had done would be very helpful as the work of the staff and students progressed.

Improving life in the community. The problem of bettering the life of those served by the school should be of major concern to all educators. Waters (20, pp. 10-11) has given the following descriptions quoted from an earlier report, of some procedures directed toward the improvement of the social-economic factors operative in some schools and communities.

"1. Because of a consideration of health needs in the community, a number of activities have been set up through the cooperative work of teachers and pupils. The following are typical projects resulting from such study: (a) every child was examined for intestinal parasites, and treatment was given to those found infested; (b) children of families receiving any aid from the federal government were given dental examinations and necessary dental work was done; (c) our school helped to organize a parish society for crippled children. This organization, through the cooperation of pupils and teachers, cited cases of disability. These were brought to a parish clinic or taken to New Orleans where they received the attention of a specialist; (d) every child suspected of having tuberculosis was given a test and, if this was positive, further observation and treatment was provided; (e) about 30,000 free lunches were served to needy children. It was found that this not only improved their general health but had a favorable effect on class work and attendance.

"2. As a result of a study of conditions in the community, a district-wide recreational program, centered at the high school, was inaugurated for adults and students. A camp in the mountains was leased to provide 'outings' for the underprivileged children. The home economics teachers worked with the community on a program of home beautification. Students in biology classes grew many shrubs and plants for distribution in the community. These activities resulted from classroom work.

"3. As a result of studying the economic conditions in the community, the following things were accomplished: a hay baler was bought cooperatively so that more food might be stored for winter use; a garden and poultry club was organized with membership open to all high school students; over 200 dozen eggs and 90 pounds of poultry were marketed cooperatively; a night class in agriculture was organized for out of school boys.

"4. The economic life of the community was improved by the establishment of a canning plant, a refrigeration and meat curing plant, a community hatchery, the planting of thousands of trees and the terracing of land. Pupils did not formerly engage in such activities since no effort was made to adapt the work of the school to community needs."

Practical problems are closely related to certain aspects of home life, nutrition, gardening, child training, interior decoration, clothing, money management, health, renovation of furniture, family relationships, landscaping yards.

How to go about having the school have a direct effect on the homes and the community is an important problem. Some approaches used by one school are described by Templeton (18, pp. 22-23), as follows:

The school offers "the community such services as facilities and supervision for recreation, forums for discussion of community-wide problems, an opportunity to hear good music and participate in dramatics, to try their [patrons] hand with arts and crafts, and assistance with any individual problems."

The home-economics department, "working with the state department of education and specialists in the fields of music, recreation, and dramatics, acts on an advisory capacity. One full time teacher of home economics helped to coordinate adult and day school programs."

Assistance is given on such individual problems as those represented by the child who would not ask his friends into his home because "The homes of my friends are are so much nicer than mine. They have better furniture. I can't ask them here." This situation bothered the mother and made her realize her home needed to be improved. The high school offered to help her and a few slip covers "made with the assistance of high school girls, new curtains, and a different arrangement gave that home the 'new look' the boy envied in friends' homes."

Personal-relations aspects of solving problems are considered. It was found that: (a) The first conference often results in planning what should be done. (b) "If money is involved it is suggested that the money be saved over a period of time or that one thing be done at a time—one chair recovered one week, curtains made later."

Making a sharp break with tradition. In many schools attempting to take better care of individual differences it will probably seem wise, at least at first, to keep the present organizational setup. In other schools the faculty may feel that a definite break with tradition is needed. Part of the action of a school of the latter type is described by Chreitzberg (6, pp. 469-70).

"After several members of the Holtville faculty had attended the workshop at Vanderbilt last summer, they were more certain than ever that there was a need for a change in the type of education being offered to the boys and girls in the Holtville community. There were several reasons for feeling the need for this change. . . .

"First, there was a feeling on the part of our staff that the children were being taught that textbooks, subject matter, units, college entrance requirements, and similar imposed ideas from the child's point of view are the chief ends of education. The members of the staff, however, feel that personality growth and development, health and physical development, economic well-being, the ability to solve the many commonplace problems around the school, in the home, and the community, and similar problems should be the real aims of education. Second, there was the feeling that the principal and teachers have been directing and dominating the child's thinking by choosing the textbook which he studies, by giving him definite assignments in this textbook and requiring that he learn these assignments regardless of whether or not he believes in the ideas expressed in them, and by choosing the activities and experiences which he is to have, regardless of the child's interests or his ability to help in choosing these things for himself. He has been given little opportunity to develop initiative, to take responsibility or to think through his own problems. Third, there was a feeling that the child had been given little opportunity to study his environment in the school, the home and the community and, in turn, to work on this environment to improve it. Fourth, there was the fact that the textbooks and other reading material which the child has been required to learn has been written by men in other sections of the country who know little of the pressing social and economic problems of the rural South. On account of these and other reasons, the staff felt that the boys and girls in the Holtville community needed a different kind of education from that being offered in our school, which was more or less typical of the rural schools in this section. The above required a rather radical change in procedure and organization.

"After several meetings of the Holtville faculty, and after much informal discussion among the teachers, it was decided to organize the senior high school on a different basis. There are approximately 175 students in the senior high school division. These students were divided alphabetically into five sections disregarding grade or age lines. It was arranged to have two teachers present in each of these five sections. Each section elected a secretary from among the students and a representative to the planning committee. The secretary kept rather careful notes of the proceedings of each meeting. These sections met the first two hours of each day and discussed problems of interest to the child, the teacher keeping in the background. The main purpose of these discussions was to find the child's interests, and to bring his attention to some of the immediate problems of his environment. At the close of each day the secretaries and the members of the planning committees met with some members of the staff and made reports on the discussions for that day. As soon as it was found that a certain number of students were interested along some particular line, these students were encouraged to organize in a group on the interest basis." From a psychological standpoint one may question whether too much emphasis was placed on interests and not enough on needs. However, from visits to the Holtville school, the writer is convinced that the students are encouraged to investigate individual needs and so to develop intelligent interests.

Chreitzberg continues (6, pp. 470-71): "At the close of two weeks of discussions of this kind the senior high school students had divided themselves into about fifteen interest groups. The planning committee asked each group to set up objectives for the group and to outline plans for carrying out these objectives. These objectives and plans were referred back to the planning committee for approval before the group was made a permanent organization. I shall name a few of these groups and explain briefly how they work.

"One of the largest groups we had was interested in recreation. This group chose the two members of the staff who have charge of physical education to advise them. Since the group was rather large it was divided into four sections. One section took up the problem of equipping a recreation room for the school and the community. It has a collection of something over fifty games, which are checked out to students and homes similar to the method of checking books out in a library. Several thousand people have played in the recreation room since it was established. On Wednesday nights it is open to the community. Another section on recreation took the problem of building a bowling alley and equipping it. This sport has been quite popular in this school and community. A third section built a rifle range for a group of boys who formed a rifle club. A fourth section built an archery range. When these problems were completed, some members of the recreation group went into other groups or formed new ones. Some members remained in the recreation group and began plans and work for a school and community park.

"Another group of students took up the problem of conservation of soils, forests, and wild life. They ordered bulletins, books and other materials from various sources in the United States. They had specialists in their fields to visit the school and talk to the group. They made a number of trips to such places as the agricultural college, the State Department of Game and Fisheries in Montgomery, the bird farm near Prattville, Alabama, the power company near Thorsby, etc. . . . These boys bought five terracing machines; they have terraced for farmers several hundred acres of land. They have persuaded farmers to plant around 60,000 pine trees on land not suited for cultivation. They have influenced farmers to plant about sixty acres of kudzu, a soil-building crop. They are making plans to have three bird reservations in the area served by the school.

"Another group, which took the name of the personal service group, is working to improve the personal appearance of the students and people in the community. They have ordered much material and they are making a serious study of the proper way to care for the hair and skin. In connection with the science department they are making tests of all kinds of cosmetics used by students, toward learning which products are most economical and which give best results.

"We also have groups studying community canning, health, shopwork, practical bookkeeping, practical electricity, etc. . . . No grades or marks are given in this work. The child at various intervals writes up a report of the work done over a period of time and sends this to his parents.

"We have encountered some difficulties in our program thus far. We, as teachers, have not been trained to teach this type of program. We have difficulty in sensing situations and in seeing the many commonplace problems which the child faces every day in the school and community. Sometimes a teacher will have four or five groups working under him; he is inclined to like the work of one group and to give too much time to this group at the expense of other groups. Where teachers have not been able to help with groups, in some cases, we have been able to find a person or persons in the community who could help with their problems. This is especially true in the cases of the printing press group, the electricians' group, and the pottery group."

In summary, Chreitzberg says: "When teachers and pupils have had more experience in working on many school and community problems, the staff feels that the program is going to work very effectively in improving living in the school, the home, and the community."

Some results of break with tradition. To give a picture of the situation in the Holtville High School some years later we quote from Wallace, *et al* (19, pp. 15-20): "As we now work, during the first week of school the teachers meet with the students in groups and discuss the opening of school and the possibilities for the coming year. The grouping on the first day is usually tentative, without special regard for students' getting with the teacher with whom they hope to work most. After a day or two, as students begin to make plans for work, they shift from one group to another until each student has selected some teacher as a permanent adviser, known as his 'major teacher.' Usually the students are in home rooms under teachers who supervise the work in which they are primarily interested. For example, boys who expect to farm are in the agriculture teacher's group; students expecting to become bankers, stenographers, and so on choose the commercial teacher. Sometimes a student does not choose a group in which he is most interested, but the one that he believes can do him the most good. A girl who does not particularly like homemaking but who needs it rather badly may go to a home economics group in order to try to learn that kind of work. Other things considered in major grouping are the student's choice of a teacher, parents' wishes, location of friends, and recommendations of teachers. This grouping applies mostly to the upper four grades. The seventh and eighth grades are in junior high groups, some years combined and then divided into two groups, some years in separate groups according to grades. Both groups, however, work along similar lines and do not have the specialization in their program that characterizes the senior groups.

"A student's major teacher does far more for him than just check his attendance throughout the year. She helps him make his first plans of the year and then supervises his work, advising with him all year, in fact, she is responsible for him in every way; and though, of course, he goes to other teachers for various kinds of help, she must keep track of him and help him carry out his plans.

"At the present time, the major group period includes instruction in the field the teacher supervises, and in some years the time has been devoted to daily planning. Though the specific plans vary, throughout our trials of various methods in the last few years the major group idea has persisted as one of our most successful ways of working. Students like to feel that they have a special teacher to whom they may go with anything, and usually the students and their home room teacher are fast friends.

"... 'After major teachers are selected, what then?' ...

"During the opening days in September, all the pupils start by making definite plans concerning what they expect to do during the year and how they can go about meeting their needs and achieving their ambitions. Most of them have already had several conferences with teachers during the preceding spring on the work they are to do next year, and have talked it over with parents and friends and received their suggestions. What they will do in school depends on what they expect to do after finishing, what their parents expect of them, what they can do now to make living better, what they like to do for fun, what they can do well or have talent in, and what they need to do for self-improvement. After preliminary group discussions, the teachers talk to students individually. They try to make them see reasons for coming to school that are greater than just the wish to graduate. They help them set goals and purposes toward which they would like to work. Then they help them plan things that they can do in school and out that will help them reach their goals. They try to explore many possibilities, so that each student can find and take part in the things he needs or wants most. Usually a student finds something he likes unusually well and goes further in that than in anything else, and the teachers try to help each one 'find himself' by helping open up many different avenues of interest and work.

"Sometimes it is hard for a youngster to realize that he can have a share in deciding what he will make of himself and planning how to accomplish his purposes. He may be inclined to sit back and wait for the teacher to tell him what to do. Formerly we decided these things for students, but we have come to believe that to do so requires very little thinking on the student's part, and that if he is to amount to very much, he must use his intelligence in solving problems as they arise. We therefore try to help each one find out for himself what things he needs to do to become a successful person, and help him make plans to get these things done. This does not mean that the teachers let the students do anything they want to all year or even all day; in fact, it means just the opposite. It means that the teachers take time to work with each student, until together they decide what his needs, goals, and ambitions are and what he must do to achieve them. Then teachers and pupil together plan his school day to include all the things that seem to be good for him. Thus, instead of requiring him to take certain subjects such as American history, mathematics, and English, we require him first to use his own intelligence to help figure out what is best for him and then to do what is necessary to reach his goals.

"For example, a boy wants to be a salesman when he finishes school. He also wants to be a good citizen, one who is genuinely interested in making life better, and this he can be now as well as after he graduates. First, with the help of his teachers he makes a careful study of the vocation chosen and decides what it is about a person that makes him fail or succeed in the business of selling. He decides what sort of person he needs to become in order to be successful. He may decide he needs to know how to meet the public, how to speak correctly and with ease, how to figure, both on paper and mentally. He needs to be a good conversationalist along many lines. He should have courage and perseverance. He should be honest, dependable, prompt. He should know how to dress appropriately and should have the habit of being neat and clean at all times. He wants a strong, healthy body, and wants to know how to keep it that way. Next, in order to be a good citizen, he should know what is going on in the world and should do all he can for the service of his country. He should be interested in his government and exercise his voting privilege when the time comes and other privileges as they come now and later. He should take an active part in community affairs and have a genuine desire to make life better for himself and for others.

"With such purposes as these in mind, the boy with his teachers' help sets out to plan a program of work that will meet his needs. To become qualified as a salesman, he will study business arithmetic, English, manners, and social relationships. This does not necessarily mean he meets daily classes in all these subjects. He may learn arithmetic by auditing the bank books or helping keep records for some department in the school, in addition to working in a mathematics book. His English may come from making chapel talks or writing newspaper articles, as well as from studying textbooks and working exercises that his teacher recommends. He may learn correct manners and how to carry on a good conversation by guiding visitors, reading good books, and observing other people. But whatever his day's work consists of, he plans it with his own purposes in mind.

"In addition to these things, he may plan to get practical experience in selling, as well as training in such things as dependability and promptness, by working in the school store or selling advertising for the school paper or tickets for the senior play. To have and keep a healthy body, he may work with a group studying health and make a study of his own or his family's needs. In order to be an informed citizen, he plans to read a daily paper and to study the history and background of our country. He will also take advantage of every opportunity to be a good school citizen, helping keep things clean, cooperating with teachers and fellow-pupils, and obeying regulations. He may join a group of boys and girls doing something just for fun—playing basketball or ping-pong, working with clay or leather, making things from wood or other material. Sometimes the articles he makes are useful or ornamental in the home or can be sold for profit.

"In all of these activities, it is easy to see how he is serving his school—working in the school store, writing for the paper, guiding visitors, practicing good citizenship. He may also make definite plans for serving at home—he may add a little to the family income by working on Saturdays at the neighborhood store, or by selling any one of a number of articles that have a market in door-to-door selling. If the article he sells is a time- or labor-saving device or something equally useful, he will soon see that he is helping his neighbors as well as himself. He may make plans for serving in his community, church, or club. In fact, the teachers try to help the student plan to do whatever it is that he needs to do to achieve his own personal ambitions and to help him and others live a better and happier life; and all of these things become his program of work, his course of study in school. . . .

"We believe that this way of working together—teacher with pupil—gets better results than teacher or pupil working separately. Students cannot see all their own needs well enough to do their planning themselves. They must have help and guidance in selecting things to work on. They are often too immature and inexperienced to see very far ahead, and if unguided may be governed at times by personal likes and dislikes rather than by good judgment. On the other hand, the teachers from many years' experience have found that they cannot do a good job of planning all the things that students are to do, for they need to know what the students expect to do later, what their parents want for them, what they need and want to learn, and what their purposes are for coming to school. This is true because no two students are alike in background and past accomplishments, personal qualities and needs, ambitions, home needs, talents, and preferences. Besides, a boy or girl does his work, even when it is unpleasant, much more willingly if he has had a share in planning it and can see for himself the reasons for doing it; and the more willingly he works, the more he gets out of what he does.

"Teacher-pupil planning also has to its advantage the fact that each pupil is allowed to take as much responsibility as he can handle, his share gradually being increased as he grows in judgment and maturity. For example, a seventh-grade boy naturally likes to play. But there are other things he needs to do, whether he likes them or not, and he is not too young to have the reasons for doing these things pointed out to him and to be given a share in saying how he can do them. We can help him see that he needs to form health habits so he can keep a strong body, read the newspapers so he will be informed about what is going on, and learn to read, write, and figure rapidly and correctly because he will need these things in making a living. If we explain these things simply, it is not hard for him to see the importance of them; and if he understands why he is doing them, and if he helps plan how he will do them, he does them better than if the teacher merely states that his year's schedule will include reading, writing, arithmetic, health, current history, and physical education. In addition, he is getting valuable experience in making decisions and planning for himself. With patience and perseverance, a teacher can see that a youngster learns by doing things that interest him and help other people; and she will go over with him again and again the importance of doing worthwhile things, until finally he reaches the point where he sees his own needs, makes plans and decisions, and uses his time wisely, of his own accord, and does not need to have his teachers point out every little detail of the work he must do. This, of course, is the goal we want each student to reach before graduating, for we know that most students when they finish school are faced with the problem of working and living and making their own decisions.

"This way of working with children, trying to get them to think for themselves, sometimes seems slow and tedious. Students often plan unwisely and cannot see their needs. Teachers have to work long and patiently helping them, and often the quick and easy thing to do would be for the teacher to tell the student what to do and how; but this slower method is the only way we have found to teach boys and girls to use the intelligence they have in planning their own lives."

Conditions for school-wide change. In order for such a program of problem identification as that suggested above to succeed on a school-wide basis it is desirable that the following conditions be met: (1) Administrators concerned should not only know what is being attempted but should provide help and democratic leadership to staff and students. (2) A significant number of teachers on the staff must be concerned about doing a really good job and be willing to put forth some effort over and above what is needed to "get by." (3) Staff planning is of key importance and such planning will be done in the summer, in preschool planning conferences, and throughout the year. (4) All available resources should be tapped including trained professional personnel, which may be brought in from outside educational institutions. (5) The people of the community must be kept posted on developments and their help welcomed in setting up school plans and policies. The confidence of a majority of the people in the community must be maintained through proper public relations.

OPERATING PRINCIPLES FOR DEVELOPING PROBLEM-IDENTIFICATION ABILITIES

I. *Learning the process of intelligent problem identification should be a paramount goal for both teachers and learners*

    A. Too great haste makes for waste in getting the learning process under way. Complete teacher identification of problems is simpler, easier, and quicker than developing learner ability to identify problems. However, if teachers monopolize this process of identifying problems, the learner is thereby deprived of needed opportunities to practice such identification. Without practice the learner will not know how properly to identify his real problems when he needs to do so out of school. Guided practice in problem identification can serve as a means whereby the learner gains facility in doing this in many other situations.

B. The need for developing sound intrinsic motivation for learning work in later steps of the learning process is a basic reason for encouraging the learner to participate in the early steps. The learning process then becomes *his* rather than something imposed on him or on which he has been asked to work in a very limited capacity with all the important decisions made by someone else. Sometimes it is well to encourage the learner to make a thorough analysis of his purposes in studying.

II. *Steps to keep in mind in effective problem identification*

A. The identification of many problems by each learner should be encouraged before one problem is definitely selected for study.

B. At first, it is frequently well to guide the learner in identifying relatively simple problems, since the easier ones are those with which he is most likely to be able to cope best until he becomes fairly proficient in the whole learning process.

C. Before students in a particular situation attempt to identify their basic needs and problems it is frequently well for the teacher and learners to list the means or resources that have been found useful by others in identifying problems. Such a procedure will tend to encourage the learner to use and learn how to use resources he otherwise would probably not have used.

D. Problem identification is a phase of the learning process that should continue during the processes of problem selection and problem solution. Such additional problems as are identified should be listed as they are recognized as significant.

E. The teacher in cooperation with his class should attempt to set up diagnostic or evaluative checks of the learner's ability to identify problems. If the student participates in the construction of such tools, he is more likely to understand his strengths and weaknesses in this field.

F. The major share of the responsibility for problem identification should as rapidly as possible be shifted from the teacher to the learner. Unless this is done the learner is likely to leave school without being qualified in this key initial step of the learning process.

G. In working on problem identification it is very desirable for the learner to keep a comprehensive record of the problems identified. A note on the source of each problem for the learner is often helpful in improving the process by facilitating later analysis and evaluation.

III. *Difficulties to be expected*

A. A certain amount of bewilderment on the part of the learner (and perhaps the teacher) should be considered a normal aspect of the healthy use of the learning process. Unless the learner has some difficulty in problem identification, it is questionable whether this is a phase of the process upon which he needs to practice.

B. Some "mistakes" in problem identification are to be expected as a necessary concomitant to learning. The learner in tennis is, while learning, expected to make some mistakes in serving and, in a similar way, the learner in problem identification may not be expected to be perfect until some guided practice in this process is given. Mistakes are less costly during schooling than after graduation.

C. In schools or school systems where the emphasis has been largely upon the memorization of subject matter for passing examinations or where the teacher has assumed practically all the responsibility for deciding what will be studied, the learner's concept of his role in the educative process will have to be changed. The advantage of the greater mental maturity of older learners, high school or college, is frequently offset by their long adherence to a teacher-dominated pattern of education which they come to think of as the *only* pattern for education.

IV. *Steps the teacher needs to consider taking*

A. Sound teacher identification of his own professional problems constitutes an important goal for the instructor. Effective teaching progress often starts with producing changes in one's own ability in problem identification. It is healthy for the teacher to ask himself the question, How can I effectively improve my own skill in identifying the personal and professional problems I need to study in order to teach more happily and effectively?

B. A high degree of democracy in developing problem-identification ability involves skills and techniques on the part of the teacher that take years to learn. The added satisfaction the teacher gains through the use of more democratic procedures more than compensates for the additional effort the teacher may put in. Guided democratic problem identification becomes a challenge to both teacher and learners and produces sharp contrasts to the air of boredom frequently noted in teacher-monopolized problem identification.

C. An important phase of teacher preplanning is the gathering together of materials that suggest problems that are likely to be important for learners at least to face and consider in the process of problem identification.

BIBLIOGRAPHY

1. ARSENIAN, SETH. "Own Estimate and Objective Measurement." *Journal of Educational Psychology*, 33:291-302; April 1942.
   Pictures need for training in self-evaluations and suggests changed emphasis in guidance and teaching.
2. Association for Supervision and Curriculum Development. *Organizing the Elementary School for Living and Learning.* Washington, D.C.: The Association, 1947.
3. Association for Supervision and Curriculum Development. *Toward Better Teaching.* Washington, D.C.: The Association, 1949.
4. BLITCH, L. W. "Achieving Certain Educational Objectives through Work with Eighth-Grade Pupils." *High School Journal,* 26:123-37; May 1943.
   Pictures a teacher's attempt to help learners develop initiative, independence, dependability, poise, cooperativeness, social sensitivity, and problem-solving ability.
5. CARY, M. E. "The Fight Over Common Learnings in Minneapolis." *The Education Digest,* 17:1-4; October 1951.
   Describes what may happen when school-wide or system-wide improvements are attempted.

6. CHREITZBERG, JAMES. "A Rural School and Its Community." *The Southern Association Quarterly*, 3:469-71; August 1939.
   Ways of attacking learner and community needs are pictured by high-school principal. Some difficulties are noted.

7. DOTSON, JOHN A., *et al.* "The Benham, Kentucky, High School at Work." Parts I, II, III, IV. *The Southern Association Quarterly*, 4:486-500; August 1940.
   Pictures general setup. Also shows what some individual students are doing in a typical day in an individualized educational program.

8. ESPY, GLADYS. "A Description of Attempts To Meet the Mathematical Needs of High-school Pupils." *The Southern Association Quarterly*, 7:319-30; August 1943.
   Fine illustrations and descriptions of change from traditional practices.

9. EVANS, HUBERT M. "Objectives for Youth Education: Some Methodological Problems." *Teachers College Record*, 53:32-38; October 1951.
   Stresses methodological difficulties involved in reconstructing the general process for guiding and controlling the selection and structuring of appropriate educational objectives for today's youth.

10. GREENE, MARY. "Attempts To Meet the English Needs of College Preparatory Seniors in Waynesboro High School." *The Southern Association Quarterly*, 7:453-60; November 1943.

11. GWYNN, J. "Minor Bibliography on Secondary Education and the Needs of Adolescents." *High School Journal*, 35:27-30; October 1951.
    Lists helpful starting points for study.

12. HICKS, LEON. "A Program for Individualizing High-School Science." *High School Journal*, 24:63-65; February 1941.
    Changes in science courses are shown which are attempts to meet learner needs. Some difficulties encountered are listed.

13. KREMEN, BENJAMIN G. "An Evaluation of the Guidance Services in the High Schools of Fresno County." *California Journal of Secondary Education*, 27:41-46; January 1952.
    Describes criteria for diagnosis of school needs and indicates some of the main findings.

14. LEFTWICH, J. B. "Science in General Education." *The Southern Association Quarterly*, 3:472-74; August 1939.
    Brief, but excellent, picture of a science class attacking realistic problems.

15. McALLASTER, ELVA. "Am I a Good School Citizen?" *The Grade Teacher*, 59:48; May 1942.

Gives self-test questions through which the learner may check himself on neatness, work habits, sportsmanship, and courtesy.

16. OBOURN, E. S. AND MONTGOMERY, G. C. "Classroom Procedures for Developing the Elements of Problem Solving." *Science Education*, 25:72-80; February 1941.

Controlled experiments on real problems of interest and importance to learners are described.

17. SMYTH, TEXIE. "Making the Social Studies an Adventure in Individualized Teaching." *The Social Studies*, 32:247-50; October 1941.

Pictures evolution from formalized, subject-matter social studies to a plan designed to help meet the needs of individual learners.

18. TEMPLETON, M. G. "Home Economics: Parker Girls Serve the Community." *The Clearing House*, 16:22-23; September 1941.

A democratic home economics department helps students and housewives in realistic homemaking problems.

19. WALLACE, W., CHREITZBERG, J., AND SIMS, V. M. *The Story of Holtville*. Deatsville, Alabama: Holtville High School 1944.

Gives vivid picture of a developing high school in action together with some description of the origins of what is happening.

20. WATERS, E. A. "Science Instruction in Schools in the Southern Association Study in Secondary Schools and Colleges." *Science Education*, 27:6-11; February 1943.

Describes work of science teacher in total school setting. Shows procedures used by science teacher in seeking to improve his teaching and the total program of his school.

21. WATERS, E. A. *Study of the Application of an Educational Theory to Science Instruction*. New York: Bureau of Publications, Teachers College, Columbia University, 1942.

Excellent description of how science classes were individualized. Graphic description is given of procedures actually used. Also gives educational theory on which the classes were based. This is a contribution to Education 864.

22. WILLITS, WILLIAM. "New Objectives for Ninth Grade Mathematics." *Mathematics Teacher*, 35:360-64; December 1942.

Shows change from textbook mathematics to learning functional problem-solving.

5

ABILITY TO SELECT APPROPRIATE
PROBLEMS FOR STUDY

Some problems to consider

How does *problem selection* differ from problem identification? In what ways are they related?

What are questionable bases upon which decisions about what to teach a particular learner have frequently been made?

What are sound criteria for deciding what to teach?

How are criteria for deciding what to teach related to criteria for deciding what to study?

Who should select problems for study?

What effect is unsound selection of problems to teach or to study likely to have on problem solution?

How should texts and courses of study be used in individualized work on functional problems?

Introduction. The second key step in problem learning has been designated "Problem Selection." After the learner with appropriate guidance has identified a number of problems which it appears he should consider studying, he is quickly faced with the question, Which of these problems that I, with help, have identified is it best for me to work on at this time? An initial picture of some of the factors involved in making such a decision is presented below by means of questions the learner might well be encouraged to ask himself repeatedly.

EVALUATIVE QUESTIONS ON PROBLEM SELECTION

Writing down of goals and criteria for problem selection

1. Have I listed the specific immediate goals toward which I am working?

2. Have I listed the long-time goals toward which I am working?

3. Have I written down the specific criteria which I have thought through to aid me in deciding what to study? (For example, am I following immediate interests too much and not giving sufficient attention to basic needs?)

Defining problem

4. Have I sufficiently narrowed the problem area selected for study so that I can make appreciable progress?

Timeliness of problems

5. How closely are the problems I am studying related to_____
_____(name of course being taken)? What is my attitude toward studying what seems most valuable as against something entirely in the area designated by the course when the two seem to differ?

6. Have I written a diagnosis of what my problems involve and isolated the subproblems that need most immediate attention?

7. Do I recognize appropriate times to change to new problems?

8. Am I working on a problem that seems most pressing at this time?

Rethinking value of problems being studied

9. Am I continuously rethinking the probable value of problems being studied?

10. Do I see how working on the problems to which I am now giving time will help me reach both my immediate and long-time goals?

11. What has been the percentage of my work that has had sensible purposes as opposed to the percentage that has been "busy work"?

12. Am I planning work that really seems valuable to me or work done to meet some external requirement?

Changing to new problems

13. When my interests and needs have been at variance, have I followed the former too much?

14. Have I listed for each of at least three problems the probable advantages and disadvantages of studying it now?

15. Do I think well in planning far ahead?

PROBLEM-SELECTION LADDER

Learner on own initiative attempts to *select for study the problem that on the basis of sound criteria it seems best for him to study. Guidance is solicited from others as needed and teacher checks occasionally to see that this is done.

Learner and teacher together select problems for study on an individual basis.

Teacher and *learners* together select problems for study on a group basis.

Teacher selects area of problems for study but gives learner some leeway in selecting problems within area.

Teacher selects problems for study with some consideration for needs of individual learner who is to study problems.

Teacher selects problems for study with some consideration for needs of *group* being taught.

All problems to be studied are selected for the learner by someone outside the immediate classroom or because they happen to be in a particular text.

READ UP ⟶

In my classes which of the above alternatives most nearly describes the situation under which I am operating? What significance may this have in affecting the quality of my learning? What can I do to move higher on the ladder?

WHAT ARE THE POSSIBLE BASES UPON WHICH TO DECIDE WHAT TO STUDY?

The teacher and the prospective teacher as well as the high-school student should recognize the great variety of possible bases upon which the decision about what shall be taught and what shall be studied may be made. Probably no teacher uses any one basis exclusively. Many of the decisions teachers make regarding what to teach are arrived at with little or no conscious consideration of just *why* a particular thing is taught. Under these circumstances, tradition and what the teacher himself was taught are likely to be the determining bases. It should also be recognized that one group of bases, if adopted, may frequently lead to the teacher's emphasizing entirely different ideas and processes from those that will be considered of primary importance if other bases for deciding what to teach are adopted. In the following list are: (1) some bases the writer feels are of very minor importance; (2) one or two bases the writer believes are sometimes dangerous if much weight is given to them; and (3) some bases that are of paramount importance; however, each should be given careful consideration, and it is suggested that the reader decide in each case in which of the three groups he thinks the particular basis would be best placed. Some possible bases upon which it may be decided what is to be studied are:

What the teacher knows how to teach. If the teacher knows how to teach political history and does not know how to teach economic or social history, it is probable that his course in American history will consist chiefly of the history of political life in the United States.

How the teacher is prepared to teach. If the teacher is only prepared to teach everyone in his classes the same thing at the same time in the same way, it is unlikely that he will readily adapt his material to the individual abilities, interests, and basic needs of each learner.

What the parents want taught. If this basis for deciding what is taught is used exclusively and, for example, most of the parents in the community do not want the principles of evolution explained even in an advanced science class, then the principles of evolution are not taught in that community.

The identified or predicted problems that each learner in the community is now facing, or is likely to face in the future. These problems might include: How can I get along better with people? What are the techniques it might be advisable for me to use in deciding what it is most profitable for me to study? How may I prepare myself to be a good sales clerk? What should I learn how to do in school so that I may be successful in meeting the problems that arise in the home? What is the best preparation I can make to be successful in my college work?

That which it will be most pleasant to study. Using this basis exclusively would involve trying to decide the types of approaches that learners would like best without any particular training in "liking wisely." Although "progressive education" leaders never advocated this, some uninformed teachers and laymen thought this was the outstanding thing in "progressive education."

That which will be most rigorous and "disciplinary." This basis is almost the opposite in many cases of the preceding one and is heartily subscribed to by formal discipline advocates among educators. These educators think of education primarily as a hardening process made up of doing a long series of unpleasant tasks.

That which can be learned most easily. Those who put faith in this base think it is relatively unimportant *what* is learned as long as learning proceeds apace. Rapid learning is the goal with the kind of learning considered relatively unimportant.

That which the average pupil in the group usually needs most. Many courses and school curricula give certain materials that are to be studied by every pupil in a particular course or curriculum regardless of other considerations. No attention is given to individual differences in needs, abilities, interests, and attitudes.

That which is indicated in the state or city course of study. While courses of study will sometimes provide some help for the immature teacher, they frequently recommend study materials and procedures that are wholly inappropriate for a particular group. At best, such recommendations, if followed slavishly, will be of little or no value and may be even positively dangerous, particularly to attitudes and study habits, to many in a school group.

What appears to be best on the basis of experimental evidence. For instance, if scientific studies lend weight to the theory that formal arithmetic is taught too early, then the teaching of formal arithmetic will be postponed for a time by those who accept the experimental evidence.

That which integrates with other subjects being studied. Where this becomes the chief base one course essentially becomes an appendage or adjunct to one or more other courses.

One key idea that someone has thought good. The writer knows of a college dean who advocated teaching the History of United States Education solely to emphasize the idea that the public school runs from the kindergarten *through* the university.

Things of interest to the learners. Some teachers are so happy to see the pupils work hard regardless of what they are working on that their chief and almost only concern is to present what is interesting. Obviously, using this base alone will frequently encourage the learner to escape from the real problems he should be facing.

That which traditionally has been taught. The most conspicuous place where this has happened is probably in many high schools today where what is taught is very similar to what was taught in secondary schools two or three decades ago when the high-school population was very different from what it now is.

Materials and problems that are within, or just a little above, the present skills and abilities of the learner. If this criterion were applied more freely, much of what is now being taught in high-school English and mathematics would be eliminated for most high-school pupils. This basis gives recognition to the psychologically sound principle of starting with the learner where he is rather than trying to start with him where we think he and all other learners in a particular grade should be.

That for which there are enough materials available so that each pupil can have a copy. The only justification some high-school English teachers can give for forcing *King Lear* on their immature pupils is that "there is a plentiful supply of the books in the closet." If a plentiful supply of poison were available, would it also be used? This is not a facetious question, since *King Lear* is intellectual poison to the minds of a large percentage of high-school pupils who are far from ready for it.

That indicated as best after all of those most concerned with the learning activities have given some careful consideration to the various possibilities, the advantages and disadvantages of each in the light of present and probable future learner needs and problems. This would necessarily involve taking into account most if not all of the bases named in the preceding items and any others which the immediate situation led those most involved to consider important.

Additional issues on criteria. Additional issues which instructors and students should raise in trying to determine which bases it is desirable to give most weight to in a particular situation are:

What ways of selecting what is to be taught are the pupils, teachers, and community most accustomed to seeing used?

What are the present potentialities and developed skills of the teachers and pupils in the matter of wisely helping to decide what it is best to study?

What seem to be the limitations of the educational framework within which the teachers and the pupils operate? Does the course of study, for example, "force" one to teach or study something which it seems unnecessary or undesirable to study?

Is a gradual change from present bases of deciding what is to be studied likely to be more permanent than rapid, but forced, change? Can a compromise between these two possibilities be effected?

Rank the "possible bases" suggested in the preceding list in order of the importance of each insofar as you are able to judge this at the present time. Why do you place the first three at the top of the list?

Do you feel that any of the "possible bases" should usually be disregarded entirely? Why?

Which of the "possible bases" do you feel have been given entirely too much weight in the schools that you have attended? Give reasons for your answer.

Which of the "possible bases" if used may be a hindrance to the desirable pursuit of learning?

What would be your answer to this question: How should a teacher go about deciding what he will teach in a particular course? How should a learner go about deciding what he will try to learn in a particular course? Would your answer differ in different courses? Explain. Would it differ for different learners? Explain your answer.

If the course of study indicates you are expected to teach one thing to a group of seventh-grade pupils and you are convinced after studying them very carefully that to teach them this might do more harm than good and that what they need is something very different, which thing should you teach them, what the course of study indicates, or what you are convinced is best for them? Why?

WHAT ARE THE CRITERIA TO BE CONSIDERED IN THE ACTUAL SELECTION OF PROBLEMS FOR STUDY?

So far in this chapter we have presented (1) evaluative questions related to problem selection, (2) a picture of various levels of problem-selection practice, (3) some of the possible bases that *might* be used in deciding what to study (or to teach), and (4) some issues related to the criteria for deciding what to study. To make these ideas more specific a particular group of criteria will be presented and discussed.

The material in this section represents a summary of some of the ideas drawn up by the writer in cooperation with students in several of his classes. Since other teachers, regardless of field or level of instruction, and other students also face the problem of trying to decide intelligently what to study, this summary is presented here. The writer wishes to emphasize that little value is likely to be derived from these criteria by the teacher, or the student, if they are read and accepted uncritically. Rather, it is strongly felt that it is vitally important that each teacher, and his students, think through and work out their own set of criteria for deciding what problems they will study at a particular time. It is hoped that the points suggested here will direct thought and attention to some of the problems involved.

In the subsequent paragraphs are given some *suggestive* answers to the following questions: Why is there a need for teachers and students in all fields and at all levels to give attention to the question of what is *best* to study at a particular time and in a particular place? What are some criteria that may be worth while to apply when a student is trying to decide with the help of the teacher what is best for him to study? What are some suggestions and cautions teachers should keep in mind while attempting to guide the learner in developing the ability to select wisely what to study?

Reasons for considering problem selection. Some reasons for giving attention to the development of the ability to decide wisely what to study are indicated in the following paragraphs.

The deciding of what to study constitutes the first main step in efficient learning after a goodly list of possible problems for study have been identified. When this decision is made wholly, or almost wholly, by the teacher, the learner is getting little or no experience or practice in taking this essential step in getting the learning process under way. It is now recognized by psychologists, and many others, that unless the learner has an intrinsic purpose in studying his work, while it may be done as directed, it is likely to have as little effect on his behavior as the work of the boy in the classic example of forced learning who made the mistake of writing "I have went." He was kept in after school and directed to write, "I have gone," one hundred times. He stayed in, wrote "I have gone" one hundred times, and then left this note to the teacher who was out of the room at the time: "Teacher, I done what you told me to do and I have went home." Thus it is, too frequently, if the learner has not been consulted when the decisions are made about what, when, and how he shall study.

With many schools and teachers attempting to put decreasing emphasis upon marks, credits, and simply sitting in class, other and more basic types of motivation need to be brought into play if better learning is to result. One of the best motivators, unquestionably, is to have the learner participate in the decision about what he shall attempt to study. Certainly this does not mean that he shall, or should be permitted to, decide alone what he shall study, at least not until he has had much guided experience. It does mean that instead of the teacher dictatorially making this decision, the learner plays a gradually increasing part in making decisions that affect his own welfare.

There is an increasing recognition on the part of wide-awake teachers that our present educational setup is not adequately meeting individual educational needs. This is coupled with the realization that it is impossible to meet these needs as long as teachers reserve almost exclusively for themselves the responsibility of making all assignments and evaluations for every learner, of deciding what it is "best" for every learner to study, of selecting the materials for every learner to study, and even of deciding almost when and how the learner should study what the teacher has picked out for him. Not only do time limitations make this an impossible job for the teacher but *such a procedure also takes away from the learner the chance to develop in the ability to carry on these activities wisely.* Mass education can take care of individual needs *if* teachers will help the student develop the ability to decide intelligently (a) what it is best for him to study, (b) what resources should be used in studying these problems, and (c) how to evaluate what he has done so that he will do a better job of learning in the future.

The truth and significance of the statement, "The educated man is the one who has learned to educate himself," is increasingly becoming recognized by wide-awake teachers and administrators. If the activities carried on during formal schooling do not lead to organized education in the several areas after school, then the education has been distinctly limited in value. To make the years of formal schooling just the beginning of the learner's education rather than both the beginning and the end, and to give the learner a happier and better life, it is vitally important that he should have much practice in selecting the problems it is best for him to work on.

Mere recognition on the part of the teacher of the need for aiding students in learning how to decide wisely what to study is far from sufficient insurance that a teacher will do a good job of this. To lead learners properly in developing this ability is an art that requires years of study on the part of the teacher. Most teachers now trying to teach learners the abilities being discussed here are frequently frank to admit they are rather baffled. One teacher expressed it this way: "I know each learner should gain more independence in wisely deciding what he should study, but I don't know how to go about developing it."

If there is to be a gradual transition from the present situation in most classrooms, where the teacher assumes almost all the responsibility for deciding what should be studied, to a situation where the learners are given increasing responsibility for such decisions, the teacher must work out with the learners the best way of doing this in a particular situation. Unless the pupils are properly approached, they are likely to become disillusioned rapidly and feel that it is not worth the trouble.

The spreading of the "core" curriculum movement and common-learnings programs makes it imperative that the teacher and learner give additional consideration to reliable bases upon which to decide what it is best to study. In many of our better elementary schools we have, of course, had the core curriculum in essence, for a long time.

Functional democracy in education implies that the learner shall share in the making of decisions to the extent to which he is capable of sharing and in which he needs practice. This is much more vital to most learners than just reading *about* democracy.

Suggested criteria for problem selection. What criteria may be suggested for application to the selection of an appropriate problem for study? As was indicated in an earlier paragraph teachers or students are *not* encouraged simply to take this list and apply it to possible problems for study. Rather, teachers and prospective teachers *are* encouraged to study these suggested criteria and then to try to encourage students to develop a set of standards consonant with their degree of ability and maturity. It should be remembered that if criteria are to be basically meaningful, those who use them should have a share in developing them. Individuals in elementary, high-school, and college groups with whom the writer has worked have found the following questions helpful in intelligently arriving at sound problems for study.

1. Can I see how working on this problem is likely to help me meet one of my present needs or prepare me better to meet prospective needs in one or more of the following:

   a) An occupational situation? This should lead to (1) a consideration of several types of work in which the learner is most likely to engage, in view of his intelligence, financial backing, occupational desire, etc., and (2) a consideration of the types of problems he is likely to face in such occupations. Obviously, it is impossible to predict with certainty what the learner will actually be doing ten years from now but the approach suggested is likely to lead him to work harder and make him more thoughtful about his future problems.

   b) A social situation? For example, what types of speaking knowledges and skills are likely to be required for success or at least to be decided assets in a conversational group? In a discussion group? In an office situation? In a courting situation?

   c) A recreational or leisure-time situation? For instance, the ability to engage in certain types of games or other activities of a group or individual nature is likely to be an asset. Name some of these activities. How should I go about developing skill in them?

   d) A parental situation? What types of things do happy parents know? What skills related to raising children take some time and guidance to develop properly?

e) A situation involving work in making my community a better place in which to live? For example, do I have the training necessary to present a playground problem to leaders in the community, or do I know how to go about voting intelligently? If not, would studying this problem probably help me to prepare for this type of situation so important in a democratic community?

If the answers to any or all of the questions given about is "yes," then the questions given in succeeding paragraphs should be considered.

2. Is this a problem that I have already studied in an organized fashion? If so, are there other problems that would be more valuable for me to study? Do I need additional work experience before giving more time to an intensive study of this problem?

3. What might be the advantages of studying the problem at a later date? What would probably be the disadvantages of postponing the study of the problem?

4. Is my realization of the need for a study of this problem great enough to keep me working on it for a reasonable length of time? If not, perhaps it would be well to search further for a more appropriate problem. Do I appreciate the basic importance of the problem for me?

5. Does it seem likely that I will learn better how to *select* or solve problems through a serious consideration of this problem now proposed for study?

6. Is it likely that there will be a sufficient number of available sources, human and otherwise, to facilitate and justify my study of this problem at this time and in this place? (The possibility of using non-printed sources of help such as other learners, teachers, observations, letters, workers in various occupational fields, interviews with parents, should constantly be kept in mind. Also, magazine, newspaper, and pamphlet sources are often more usable than book sources. Always, the advisability of planning and using informal experimentation should be kept in mind.)

7. In view of my limited experience in problem-solving, is the problem under consideration simple enough for me to attack without getting swamped in complex ramifications? For example, the study of "What is a desirable method of national

price control?" is likely to be less appropriate from this standpoint for most students than is a study of "How can I learn to buy more wisely?" or "How should I make and use a budget?". A closely related problem for consideration is: Does the study of this problem promise some measure of tangible success to me so that I will not be discouraged in learning?

8. Am I seeing this problem sufficiently in relation to larger and more complex problems of which it is a part? For instance, if the learner is considering the study of "How can I become a wiser buyer and consumer?" does he consider the relationship of this problem to such organizations as Consumers Research, Consumers Union, and to governmental control of buying and selling?

9. Could work on this problem be related to work being done in other courses? Is this desirable or undesirable? Why do I think so?

10. Is the problem specific enough for me to get practical answers to my questions? Will such answers actually improve my way of living and tend to increase my happiness? The mere study of health is not as likely to meet this criterion as "What can and should I do to improve my own and others' health in this community?"

11. In what way might work on this problem be related to the fundamental skills generally considered a part of the work of a course of this sort? For instance, could the problem of "How can we go about actually raising a school garden?" be related or be part of the work in an English course? (One answer might be that this would provide many opportunities for practical and functional writing, speaking, and reading under guidance, which might be more useful than formalized English exercises.)

12. Should my needs be considered more important than the traditional concept of what should be done in a course? For instance, if the traditional way to start a ninth-grade class in American history is to give each learner a ninth-grade text and start him studying the first chapter, should this be done in preference to a study of keeping an efficient personal educational history, if the latter seems to be more needed by me as a learner? What reasons might be advanced for my answer?

13. How are parents, school officials, and others in the community likely to regard my study of a problem of this sort? If they are

likely to oppose it, but otherwise it seems like a "good" problem to study, how might I best approach this difficulty? For instance, a study of "What are the probable advantages and disadvantages of strikes and how should I regard a strike in the local mill" might be thought undesirable by certain groups in the community. In other communities race relations problems or problems related to evolution might be considered unfavorably. Public opinion should be weighed as one factor when decisions are being made about what to study.

14. With the help of the teacher have I sufficiently investigated, or am I going to investigate several problems before starting to work on any single problem? To work on the *best* problem implied that more than two problems have been considered, and then one of the possibilities has been picked out.

Additional criteria. Another set of suggestive criteria for deciding worth-while problems, particularly ones for group attack on discussion is presented by Raths (9, p. 7). The problems are ones arising from (1) everyday activities of children, (2) personal conflicts of individual children, or (3) disagreements among members of groups, as well as (4) subject matter learners were studying.

"1. Is the problem one that arose from within the group?
2. Is it a problem that needs to be solved?
    a) Is it important to the teacher?
    b) Is it important to the child?
    c) Does it affect many children?
    d) May it recur often?
    e) Is it an important community problem?
3. Does the problem call for reflective thinking?
    a) Has it more than one answer—not simply yes or no?
    b) Can it lead to other important issues?
4. Will the solving of this problem help in the solution of future problems that may arise?
5. Is the problem within the range of the group's experiences?
6. Does the teacher feel competent to guide the discussion of the problem?
7. Will the group benefit by the discussion of the problem?"

Although it is improbable that the learner or group of learners should be encouraged to set up and go through a list of criteria for problem selection every time a new problem is being considered, it is very desirable that each learner gradually build up a sound basis for developing his own functional criteria for problem selection. To do this he must have much practice in studying and using sound criteria. Individual needs can be met to a high degree in mass education if the learner is trained to play a major role in deciding what it is best for him to study at any particular time.

COULD THE TEACHER DO A BETTER JOB OF SELECTING PROBLEMS THAN THE LEARNER?

Learning only through practice. In many cases the teacher could probably make the "best" selection of problems to be studied. However, the basic issue involved goes much deeper. Let us use an illustration mentioned earlier which dealt with learning to drive a car. Suppose Mr. Smith is teaching his daughter Jane to drive a car and he says, "Now I can drive better than you can so you stay out of the driver's seat and let me teach you to drive that way. Since you cannot drive I do not want to take a chance on letting you get behind the wheel." Obviously, Jane will never learn to drive a car until she gets a chance *to practice* learning to drive a car. And it is just as true that the learner of social studies, or English, will never learn how to plan what he will study unless he is given a chance to practice this skill.

The question as it is usually stated implies that it is an either-or proposition: Either the learner *or* the teacher must alone make the selection. Actually, few if any educational leaders would advocate such a procedure, at least not during the learning-teaching situation, just as they would not expect Jane to learn to drive the car without some guidance.

All that has been said implies that the actual decision about what to study is not any more important, and in some cases may not even be as important, as is the practical experience the learner has in practicing under guidance the complex skill of rationally deciding what is to be studied. In the case of Jane learning to drive the car it is not so vitally important that she get to the shopping district of town in a minimum amount of time as it is that she have practice in the skill of driving the car so that she can get there again at some later date when her father does not happen to be around. Learning the process is frequently more important than the end point; thus, learning the process of wisely deciding what to study is frequently more important than the immediate decision about what is to be studied.

Mistakes are the price of learning. We should expect that pupils will do very poorly in helping to plan their work the first time they try it. One does not expect a boy or girl to stay on a bicycle the first time he gets on. We even expect that he may get some rather hard knocks in the process of learning. However, if the roadway is reasonably smooth and conditions are propitious, we have faith that he will eventually come through all right. Can we not have the same kind of faith in the case of planning, which is also a process that needs to be learned, always remembering that acquiring facility in planning the type of work it is best to do is a much longer and infinitely more complicated task than that of learning the skill of riding a bicycle? A careful study of transitional steps to be taken in moving from the teacher-dominated toward the teacher-learner cooperative school is extremely important and is discussed elsewhere in this and other chapters.

WILL NOT COOPERATIVE PROBLEM SELECTION CAUSE MUCH TIME TO BE WASTED?

It is said that Benjamin Franklin while a boy was frequently accused of wasting much time. When asked what he was doing he usually said he was just trying to figure something out by thinking. This same man later became one of America's foremost inventors. His "wasted time" was preparation for much more productive efforts than any which those who accusingly asked the question had ever demonstrated. What should be considered "wasted time" depends to a large extent upon what our purposes and long-time goals are.

Democracy takes longer but is more educational. Taking time to try to teach the learner how to help plan his own work is admittedly harder, and it is unquestionably more time-consuming initially to "make an assignment" through teacher-pupil cooperation than through teacher dictatorship. However, frequently the shortest road is the longest way from a long-time standpoint since the next time an assignment is to be made, the learner is still about as immature as before in assignment-making if the dictator type approach is used. Obviously, the teacher can dictate an assignment more rapidly than an assignment can be worked out by the teacher in cooperation with the pupils. But the teacher who makes the latter approach is trying to prepare the learner for the time when he, the teacher, will no longer be present to dictate what steps should be taken next.

Cooperative planning promotes motivation. Another point frequently neglected by those who argue for teacher-dominated assignments of the popular sort is that such assignments do not meet to a marked degree the real motivational and instructional needs, interests, abilities, and purposes of more than a small percentage of the group. This is particularly true if all assignments are made with the expectation that every learner in the group should do the same thing. Individual differences in needs, interests, purposes, and abilities make it virtually impossible for a teacher alone to make assignments that will even approach meeting the recognized or unrecognized needs of each learner in the group. Even if an individual tutor were economically feasible for every child in our schools, this might be undesirable psychologically if not downright educationally dangerous if it would tend to deprive the learner of the experiences necessary in preparation for independently recognizing and meeting his own problems.

Getting things done vs. *learning how to do.* Experimental evidence (8) has also shown that teacher-dominated and teacher-dictated assignments are not particularly economical in the long run even if the primary goal is the accumulation of information. Thus, there are two main reasons why it is *not* wasteful for the learner to have a share in the decisions affecting what he shall study: (1) he will learn more if he does participate; and (2) he will acquire facility in planning his own work if he is encouraged to do this under the guidance and direction of the teacher.

SHOULD THE IN-CLASS AND THE OUT-OF-CLASS WORK ON PROBLEMS BE INDIVIDUAL OR GROUP?

This is not a question to which one should attempt to give a final answer except after studying the specific situation in which the answer would apply. However, there are some general considerations which, if kept in mind, will facilitate a wise decision on this question.

Both individual and group learning needed. Typically, it is best to have a combination of individual and group work, since some problems, such as a consideration of the bases or criteria one should remember in trying to decide wisely what to study, can frequently best be attacked by the group as a whole. Other problems, such as some phases of preparing for a specific occupation into which the learner plans to enter, may best be done largely on an individual or small group basis.

Purpose is a major consideration. One of the most important factors to be considered in deciding whether the work will be individual or group is the purpose the individual has in working on a problem and the conditions under which the results of study are to be carried out. For example: If a learner is developing plans for improving his ability to help set up a community playground program, it is extremely important for him to meet and work with other individuals. These persons should represent the various points of view of those in a community who are likely to give time and thought willingly to the development of such a program.

In any specific situation there are usually factors that make one lean in the direction of having most activities group activities, and accompanying these there are generally considerations that impel one toward encouraging individual work almost exclusively. The decision about whether individual or group work is to be carried on in a particular situation should be made by those most concerned in that situation; a consideration of the questions and comments in the following paragraphs will frequently help in making a wise decision.

What type of practice is likely to be most profitable? With which of these two methods, the individual or the group, do I (or we) have greater facility in working on this type of problem? If the answer is the individual approach, then the group approach should probably be selected as the one with more educational potentialities, the method in which the learner has the most to learn. If, on the other hand, the group approach will involve *too many* new learning problems, then perhaps learning how to attack this type of problem through the group approach should be reserved till a later time, so that the situation will not be *too* upsetting and difficult in the immediate situation. Each situation should involve some difficulties for the learner so that opportunities for learning will exist; however, too many difficulties at any single time are likely to result in an excessive number of failure experiences. This should, of course, be avoided.

What help can the teacher give? With which method is the teacher or other leader in the group more skillful in giving help? Here, similar considerations to those given in the preceding paragraph would be involved. The value to the teacher and other leaders of learning that this skill will have should be weighed against the values of acquiring other important learnings if it appears that all cannot be managed at the same time.

Use of a "practice problem." Will using a "practice problem" with all the group working on it provide a valuable transition step from the type of learning to which the pupils are most accustomed to a more functional, democratic type of problem-solving learning? Pupils who have thought of getting an education as largely a matter of memorization for test purposes will frequently be lost if they do not see a group, guided largely by the leadership of the teacher, work out the approaches to, and the solving of, a problem of recognized importance to almost all in the class group. Such an approach would typically involve at least the following steps: (a) identification of a variety of problems that might be attacked; (b) selection of a problem of accepted importance; (c) statement of the problem in clear and meaningful terms; (d) breakdown of the main problem into the main sub-problems that would form the chief lines of attack; (e) getting possible solutions to each of the sub-problems; (f) getting and weighing each of the probable advantages and disadvantages of each of the proposed solutions; (g) arriving at a tentative over-all conclusion based on available evidence on the main problem itself. After this "practice problem" has been worked through by the whole group many individuals will feel better fortified to attack an individual problem.

Combination of individual and group work possible. Would a compromise between the individual attack on a problem and the group attack be feasible? For instance, the large group might be divided up into several smaller groups. Each of the smaller groups would work on a different problem from that of every other group and each individual would have more opportunity to work on a problem he recognized as important to him and still get some help from the two, three, or four others in his group who were working on similar or at least closely related problems. This might be called the sub-group approach.

Would it be well for some pupils who feel that they can manage it to strike out on their own individual problems with the guidance of the teacher while the remainder of the group makes a common attack on some common problem of recognized importance to most in the group? This approach will sometimes help to take care of individual differences in needs and in level of problem-solving ability.

Commonality of important problems. Is it possible to get a common problem of sufficient importance to all to justify everyone in the group working on it? It is doubtful whether the most important problem for study of any single pupil in a class is also the problem of paramount importance for every other member of the group to work on for long. However, some of the considerations previously mentioned may sometimes make it advisable for all to work on a common problem for a time at least. This may be true particularly on problems such as those of technique, use of resources, record-keeping, and evaluation.

Varied attacks needed. In all of this work it should be kept in mind that there is no single approach that is best for all groups. Therefore, it is important that each group try out various approaches to find the ones best suited to its needs. A picture of class consideration of this problem may be useful. The dialogue below is based on stenographic notes taken in a high-school English class (1, pp. 61-62).

"*Martha:* Why not let the class work together on the goals everybody has mentioned? Then divide the class up according to goals a few have set. Then let certain ones work on goals they alone have set.

Teacher: What would be the advantages of the plan, Martha? It would be easier for everybody to work together on the same goals.

Martha: Well, if we did that, we would waste each other's time. Some would be working on things they already know.

Ruth: I don't think the plan would work. Everybody will get all mixed up.

Roy: It will work if we plan careful enough.

Teacher: How would we plan it, Roy, so that we won't get all mixed up, as Ruth said?

Roy: Well, we could have one day in the week when everybody will be working on goals in speaking—since that was a goal everybody had.

Miriam: We could organize like a club and have a chairman and let everybody talk—say, on books or movies or radio programs.

Martha: That will give us a chance to improve in listening, too.

Roy: Then on some days we could divide into small groups and work at different tables. We could have one or two days a week for people to work on separate goals.

Teacher: I believe the plan may work. But does anyone else have a better plan? (silence) . . . Then suppose we begin with the plan Martha has suggested, and Roy and Miriam have supported. If we find that it isn't working, we can try another way. Does everyone understand the plan? (It is summarized.)"

The details for whole-group, small-group, and individual work were planned by a committee appointed by the class to work with the teacher. A week's schedule was suggested and submitted to the class for approval. The schedule included two days a week for the class to work as a whole on common goals (one of these two days the class would meet as a club); one day a week for free-reading; one day for small groups to work on special goals; one day for individuals to pursue particular aims. If an individual did not have an aim common to a small group, it was suggested that he might work on particular aims two days a week.

"In order that the whole group, small groups, and individuals might have clearer directions in their work, the students made detailed plans in writing for every separate study. Each plan included: What I (or we) expect to gain from my (or our) study; how I (or we) plan to go about gaining my (or our) purposes; ways I (or we) will use to measure my (or our) progress toward my (or our) goals. In the beginning, slow-learners needed much help in making their plans, but as they had further experience in planning, they grew in ability to plan more carefully.

"The teacher comments on one thing he learned in going through this experience with his pupils during the year, 'It was found necessary to have individuals make short-term as well as long-term plans. Less gifted pupils in particular had to have frequent stopping places along the way.' "

Two more examples of individual and group work emphasize additional points (1, pp. 66-68).

"Making Individual Contributions to Group Effort

"Children of the second grade, pupils of Mrs. David Phillips, organized into small committees to build a community: *

" 'Wouldn't it be fun to have a grocery store in our room and play groceryman every day?' a child suggested. Someone answered, 'We don't have enough room.' We decided to measure and see if we

---

* Fair Park Elementary School, Abilene, Texas.

did. A committee was appointed by the room chairman to do this during our planning period the next morning.

"The committee found a space large enough for the grocery store. The next step was planning the store. What materials were to be used? What fixtures would be needed to open a business? It was decided that apple boxes would be used for the shelves, and corrugated cardboard for the walls. The children secured the apple boxes from their groceryman. Two children brought baskets to carry the groceries in. One child's father sent mattress boxes from the place where he worked. The janitor helped with our construction when heavy nailing or special boards were needed.

"Several committees had been appointed by this time, such as a measuring committee, building committee, art committee, and reading committee. Each child was on the committee to secure the things to be placed in the store.

"After the building and arranging committees had completed their work, a price committee was selected. It was this committee's task to place the price on each item in the grocery store.

"It was while we were writing our thank-you note to the child's father who had given the boxes that a child suggested we add a post office to our grocery store. Another suggested we might have a community center with several stores. A committee began work on the post office, following the same procedure that had been followed in building the grocery store.

"The committees worked with persistence. The art committee undertook heavy responsibility in working out a pattern for the walls and painting appropriate pictures for the board behind the community center. The book committee assembled a book of stories and poems about our project. The reading committee found stories for us to read and dramatize. The health committee found charts on proper foods and checked the grocery store to see if the groceryman was 'on his toes.' The program committee presented a program each Friday afternoon, composed of something interesting we had found out during the week. The health committee encouraged us to keep our streets and homes clean. The policeman and his committee helped us in securing our wraps and getting in and out of the building.

"Civic pride was seen at its best on a day that the weather was too bad for us to play outside. I had been out of the room, and upon returning found that the art committee was adding a coat of paint to the walls. They were so intent in their work that I could not refrain from asking the reason for the new coat of paint. They answered with great pride, 'We're having visitors Thursday, and we want our community to look its very best.' I knew then that the second-grade room had truly become theirs, and not just a place where they had to spend so many hours each day.

"Sharing Responsibility for Long Periods of Time

"How sixth- and seventh-grade children organized into committees to care for rats and study nutrition is related by Marcia Ott: *

" 'Oh, rats! Boy, what fun! Let's get 'em!' Such was the reaction received when the sixth- and seventh-grade group was told they, too, might experiment with white rats. The class had read with interest a number of experiments that had been made in science laboratories in which white rats had played a leading role.

"We were told by the Kansas City Dairy Council, with whom we placed our request for two baby rats, that it would be several weeks before they would arrive. In this interval we devoured every scrap of information about scientific experimentation obtainable. We were going to be scientists! Vitamins, minerals, proteins, carbohydrates, fats, liquids, and calories meant something to us now.

"We planned for our new additions as carefully as a family does for a new baby. It seemed as if we could never answer all the questions or run out of wondering. 'Where will we get food for them?' 'What shall we feed them?' 'Who will feed them?' 'How old are they?' 'Will our rats' eyes be open?' 'Where shall we keep them?' These were samples of the many problems raised.

"The Dairy Council helped us a great deal by providing a fine technicolor movie which pictured other boys and girls conducting experiments with white rats. They also gave us a booklet entitled, 'Watch Them Grow.' They answered in detail many of our queries.

"At last the great day came. The rats arrived, the girls squirmed a bit, and the boys heroically planned to take complete charge. However, when we took the lid off the round wooden crate stamped 'Scientific Laboratories—Madison, Wisconsin' and saw two soft, bright-eyed little creatures peering over the edge, the girls and boys alike were thrilled.

* George B. Longan School, Kansas City, Missouri.

"Duties were assigned and committees established such as: feeding, cleaning, recording, obtaining food, and weighing. During the experiment each child served on at least two of the committees.

"From a long list of suggestions the names Abbott and Costello were chosen for the names of the rats. Since our experiment was to be in nutrition we had to plan carefully the diet of each rat. Abbott was fed a well-balanced diet; Costello's diet was typical of the diet of many of the children in the room, a majority of whose mothers work. Each rat weighed 64 grams upon arrival. It was going to be fun to watch what happened.

"For cages we used two wire wastebaskets and improvised lids of cardboard. We learned after cleaning up spilled milk several times that paint cans placed in the bottom of the cage would not do. One boy brought baby food cans and we naively tied them with string to the sides of the cages. Abbott beat Costello in chewing the string and knocking his can over. From then on the cans were securely wired to the cages.

"Every morning the cleaning committee disposed of the food and drink left over from the night before. They scrubbed the cans and cleaned the cages. Each rat received clean strips of crumpled paper. The feeding committee cut up the food, mixed it a bit, put fresh water, milk, or coke in the cages and our rats were ready for a new day. Each afternoon before leaving school we checked to see if our charges needed more food and fresh papers. Then we carefully covered the cages to protect them against the lower night temperatures.

"A chart picturing each rat's diet was on the wall behind the rats. Between the two charts was a graph on which we recorded the weights of each rat in grams.

"Proudly our room gave an assembly for the other upper-grade rooms telling them of the experiment, showing the movie we had seen, and displaying our charts, graph, and the rats. Carefully, too, we planned and gave talks to the smaller folk and left Abbott and Costello with each primary room for a half day. Our room soon became the most popular place in the entire building."

In considering group work we should constantly keep in mind that any group is made up of individuals, that motivation is individual. Thus, the kinds of things that an individual learner in a particular group considers important for him to work on depend upon the goals he has set or in setting for himself. The exact nature of these goals differs with each individual in a group. In this fact lies one of the major challenges faced by a teacher or other leader of groups.[1]

HOW WILL TEXTS OR COURSES OF STUDY BE COVERED IN THE PROBLEM APPROACH?

Text vs. *learner needs.* This is a pertinent and difficult question to answer adequately. One decision the teacher probably has to make for himself is this: Will I teach what the course of study tells me to teach if I feel it is far from the best thing for the pupils with whom I work? Obviously, there are arguments of weight on both sides of the question. What many teachers have tried to do is to give some attention to the regular text and then spend the rest of the time on having the pupils work on the types of things that they and the students feel to be the most important and best to study. From the writer's observation this approach, if conscientiously undertaken, usually leads to the spending of a decreasing amount of time upon the course of study material and an increasing amount of time upon those problems that the teacher and learners see as the ones they really need to study. Another related possibility is directly to raise the problem with the learners themselves and see what suggestions they have to offer. A study of this and related curricular problems can be a very valuable educational experience for the learner if he is properly guided.

Texts and courses of study should be suggestive. It should be emphasized here that frequently, and perhaps usually, courses of study and texts are intended to be suggestive. Too often teachers have assumed that because material is in a text, or because topics are in the course of study, it is mandatory that they be taught. Actually, those who planned the text, or course of study, never expected slavish or rigid adherence to the organization of materials or topics presented. Typically, texts or courses of study should only be thought of as helps, not requirements.

Changing courses of study. An approach to this problem, which many teachers have almost entirely neglected, is the possibility of working to change the local or state course of study. Too many teachers have thought of their jobs almost entirely in terms of relatively narrow and restricted classroom activity and too little in

---

[1] For additional discussion of groups the reader is referred to Chapter 11.

terms of influencing the larger local, state, and national framework within which the classroom teachers operate. The typical answer to this suggestion seems to be: "Oh, I am only one teacher or student and can't do anything." Enough of these "one teachers" or "one students" who see their work in a perspective larger than the immediate classroom can revolutionize our whole educational setup and make it more possible, and incidentally more remunerative, to do a good job of teaching and learning. A few of the specific approaches to this problem, which have been used with desirable results by certain teachers, are these: Take an *active* part in local, state, and national organizations and help make them vital functioning parts of the educational machinery. Determine the educational views and policies of regularly elected officers in the various governmental branches that have to do with the schools. Discuss these views and policies with the officers and others who have some share in their election. An indifferent attitude on the part of many teachers helps to account for many teachers' getting considerably less remuneration than a large number of unskilled laborers. Write, and encourage others to write, articles, short or long, on educational problems. These may be published in the school paper, the local newspaper, the state educational organ, or national professional publications. Many teachers and learners say: "I can't do that," but in many cases the only real reason that it is not done is that the teacher or learner has not practiced trying to do it. Many teachers and students are in a better position to write realistic material than some of those who actually are writing and publishing. Very many of the undesirable restrictions under which we labor in the educational framework could be revised or eliminated if we only tried to do so.

Modifying text setup. Instead of purchasing or requiring each and every learner to purchase the same text, many teachers are only encouraging a small number of pupils to purchase the text and the others help get other materials that are frequently of much more value to the majority in the class. For example, an English teacher who believes that not more than six of her ninth-grade class can profitably read *Macbeth*, the "required" text, will help the pupils plan to get only three or four copies of the text. The rest of the money that would normally be spent on the text is then spent on relatively easy reading materials, magazines, and perhaps a newspaper subscription could be included. These materials can be supplemented with helpful materials selected from discarded magazines and newspapers from various homes in the community and filed for the training in filing and for future use. Such a system will not only provide considerably more valuable and appropriate materials than the old one, but will also be more economical in the long run.

MOVING FROM TEACHER-DOMINATED ASSIGNMENTS TOWARD LEARNER-TEACHER SELECTED PROBLEMS

Variety of approaches needed. When the teacher really recognizes the student's need to learn how intelligently to select problems for study, he has passed the first hurdle. The second and more difficult hurdle is that of learning *how* to help the student develop this ability. Some illustrations which are suggestive in this connection for the teacher who wants to learn and improve have already been given in the material on problem identification, since the two processes are closely related. There is probably no single best way to attack the task of teaching intelligent problem selection. The *wide-awake teacher is prepared to try a variety of approaches,* choosing the one that seems most appropriate in a particular situation. The following paragraphs picture approaches and ideas that some teachers have already found usable. The illustrations are taken from particular subjects or areas but similar *methods* can be applied in all areas.

Sayward (11, pp. 272-74) studied traditional required high-school courses in mathematics and decided they have served largely as preparation for advanced work in mathematics or related fields *even though this did not seem to be what most high-school students would need most.* Sayward and her associates made a specific study of what mathematics a woman needs in actual life outside the school. From this study was developed a functional course in mathematics. This course put emphasis not only on mathematics as such but also on building up a social and economic background for the *use* of mathematics. Elements of economics, sociology, government, history, and law were taught where necessary to make the functional mathematics meaningful. The course eventually included problems related to practical logic, money and banking, thrift and investments, business law, taxation, insurance, history and mathematics, elementary statistics, and graphs.

The results of the study mentioned in the preceding paragraph produced a course that was characterized by: (1) an emphasis upon the mastery of mathematical fundamentals taught in a meaningful setting, in problems likely to arise in situations in which the student might reasonably expect sometime to find himself; (2) the production of well-motivated students who were themselves suggesting realistic problems related to mathematics that they would like to study, such as, "How do you figure out a tax on real estate with the tax rate expressed in so many different ways?"; (3) students being prepared for intelligent participation in activities involving mathematics both in business affairs and in matters of more general interest; (4) students learning to understand the contribution and relation of mathematical thinking to social development; (5) students getting some understanding of the mathematical implications in current economic problems such as the economic undertakings of the government, business cycles, inflation, and world-wide economic relationships; (6) students getting a better appreciation of the need for a balanced personal budget and for saving.

The same type of thing that Sayward has done with students taking mathematics may well be considered by teachers in many other fields.

Key approaches in vitalizing work. Certain key approaches are desirable to keep in mind as frequently profitable to utilize. Below are five that are adapted from ones that Sims (14, pp. 430-31) found useful:

1. Continually question students about the worth of their study.
2. Encourage students to prepare specific plans concerning what to do and how to do it, to choose materials, to make bibliographies, to write units, to acquire skills needed in teaching, to prepare or get instruments for use in work, etc.
3. Continually encourage students to be realistic in study, constantly questioning the practicality of proposals and plans.
4. Encourage students to focus study on problems likely to be faced, instead of spending time in preparing elaborate term papers or in studying for exams.
5. Plans set up should indicate how *they* are to be carried out in a democratic fashion rather than imposed on other teachers or pupils.

Change in teacher goals, methods, and resources. A significant indication of what may happen to a teacher's goals, methods, and resources when these are critically questioned is pictured by Rose (10) who started out to teach English as she had been taught with a theme on Monday (subject assigned by the teacher), grammar drill and spelling on Tuesday, literature on Wednesday and Thursday, and oral composition on Friday. She reports that for the first four years she never questioned any of the subject matter she taught nor the ways by which she taught it. Grammar drill was the same for everyone and consisted of what was in the text whether the individual child needed it or not. All students were required to read the same magazine (*Scribner's*), the same short stories, the same essays, the same poems, from the same book regardless of the probability that some could read as well as *average* college freshmen and others only as well as *average* fourth or fifth graders.

Breaking with tradition. Sometime after hearing "low rumblings of adapting our teaching to the needs of the child and his community" Rose began to make gradual changes in one phase of the teacher-learner relationship after another. In oral composition once a week the children were allowed some choice in the things they might talk about and a greater attempt was made to have each feel at ease on his feet. In written composition Rose still continued at first to choose topics but tried to select those that might be of real interest to a high-school child and attempted to give the individual learner some choice in deciding exactly which topics he would use. The reading program was liberalized and two class free-reading periods a month were scheduled.

Large unit teaching. The next step in her regeneration reported by Rose is experimentation in large unit teaching. A major unit on share-cropping and tenant-farming sprang from Markham's *The Man with the Hoe.* Her purposes were to teach composition, oral and written, around interesting subjects, to encourage reading to modify the attitude of the pupils, and to prepare them for their common vocations. The latter two were new for Rose. A natural and vital situation produced interest and industry.

Meeting needs of "non-academics." The next steps involved attempts at individualizing the instruction of non-college boys and girls and trying to help the pupils do better the desirable things they are likely to do anyway. To help meet the needs of non-academics two large units were worked on during the year: a unit on vocational exploration and a unit on personal equipment. More student planning and participation were encouraged in the classes.

Prospective out-of-school reading and writing played a large role in the decision about what would be studied. Imaginary employers were interviewed, talking on the telephone was practiced, skill in direction-giving and entertaining conversation was developed through practice, and functional letters were written. Reading resources were broadened and one basic text was found to be no longer practical. Variety in terms of difficulty, interest, and maturity of reading resources was provided. Better magazine and newspaper reading was emphasized. Grammar study put emphasis on use, and intensive study of such things as adverbial adjectives and retained objects was dropped.

Long-time cooperative planning. The next major step taken by Rose was to work with the students at the beginning of the school year in planning units of common interest to the whole group. These students were in a double period English-Social Studies class. The group was later divided into several groups to work on particular phases of interest pertaining to the larger topic. This step led gradually to the clearer realization that students did not all have the same interests or needs at the same time. The appreciation by both teacher and learners of this important aspect of individual differences initiated the practice of having each individual with the guidance of the teacher select problems upon which he could work by himself or with others investigating similar problems.

Discussion technique. Selberg (12, p. 127) has described a method she found helpful: "A developmental discussion technique is used to analyze the problem for study. The situation and incidents involved are presented in logical order so that the student can see some relationship between them. The students are then given the opportunity to state that relationship in the form of a unit problem. The problem must be evaluated for its correctness and comprehensiveness. Criteria are set up with the help of students to decide what standards a unit problem must satisfy." Examples of the criteria used are "Is it worthwhile? Is it comprehensive? Is it within our scope of learning? Does it emphasize only one idea?"

Alternate assignments. When the teacher is still in the stage of giving assignments, it is usually feasible to substitute for the typical one-assignment-for-all alternate assignments each time work is to be done outside of class with the explanation to each student that he may select the one which seems most appropriate to him. In other words, the learner is encouraged to *select* and do the assignment he thinks would be best for him. Learners should also be encouraged to have sound reasons for the selection of one problem rather than another. One method of providing such encouragement is to have each learner write down his reasons for his selection. If this is done with guidance over a period of time, improved bases of problem selection are likely to be developed. A class that was working on health problems was given this assignment: Pick out the one of the following problems which you think it would be best for you to work on and summarize in writing the best answers you can give to it: (a) What changes might be made in and around our school to improve sanitary conditions? (b) What are the probable causes of infection from cuts and bruises and what might we do to reduce the probability of such infections? (c) What precautions should the camper take for his own safety? As a part of the assignment or during subsequent discussions the pupils may be urged to examine critically their reasons for selecting one problem for study rather than another.

Use of criteria. When the learner has done his best in selecting a problem, it is frequently well to go over with him in conference a set of "criteria to aid in deciding what to study" and see with him the extent to which he has met these criteria. The student can carry on this practice on his own after the teacher has gone through the procedure with him several times. If the learner is encouraged to *record* his needs, goals, and plans, he has a better basis both for selecting problems and for evaluating his selective processes.

WHAT ARE SOME RESPONSES TO LEARNER SELF-EVALUATION OF PROBLEM-SELECTION ABILITY?

Already this question has been partially discussed indirectly. For example, see the discussion under "What are the criteria that should usually be considered in the actual selection of a problem or problems for study?" The criteria described there were worked out democratically through student-instructor cooperation.

Additional insight into initial learner attempts at self-evaluation in the area of problem selection may be seen in the representative answers of learners to four questions answered after twelve weeks of work with emphasis on process learnings: [2]

[2] Similar self-evaluation might be used in most high-school or college courses. The actual responses would differ depending upon the area of problems being studied and upon learner and teacher purposes in the course.

Question 1. Am I improving in the ability to pick out problems of importance for me to study? Evidence?

"I think that I am improving in the ability to pick out problems of importance for me to study because the subjects which I see as important to me now did not appeal to me at the beginning of this semester, before I had studied valid criteria for the selection of problems."

"In thinking of educational problems and connecting them with my practice teaching, I have become more conscious of the practical problems I need to study if I am to be an efficient teacher. I now have a broader vision of problems which may arise in the classroom."

"At the first of the semester I chose discipline as my problem. It was a good, very general problem. I learned a lot. But the next problem I selected with guidance was character education and personality adjustment. I was now getting down to more specific things. This problem, by the time I have finished it, will have taught me a lot about boys and girls themselves, about how to help them become better adjusted to life with sound principles of conduct. The next problem which I chose was that of reading. I can't say that good reading habits are more important than character education, but a person can certainly miss a lot of pleasure in life if he doesn't enjoy reading, let alone its great help in problem solving. Here, too, is something concrete I am learning how to help children in."

"The problems I attempted to study have been very useful and will be more so in my teaching. I realized the need and value it would be if you had a course in which problems were worked on that would be useful in the future. I never dreamed there was one and certainly not in 'History of Education in the United States.' I took the course to be a dry history course; but it was just the course I had been waiting for, in which I had the opportunity to study problems which every teacher will face, and not study the historical summary of what happened in education years ago without any tie-up with current problems which I am facing or am likely to face."

"I feel that I now know more about the problems I will have to face when I teach and can choose problems that I will have to face. An example of this: I did some research work on juvenile delinquency, a phase of which is truancy. I certainly will come across one or more truants in my teaching career."

"I believe I have become very conscious of problems that might help me as a teacher. I have visited classes and after observing them I consider the main problems that existed and how the study of such problems would prove valuable to me. I chose the problem of discipline in the beginning as it at that time seemed paramount to me but now after I have made a study of it I find it leads me to many more problems which prove just as important, such as how to care for individual differences and how to help fit the learners for community life."

Question 2. Are the results I am getting in my study ideas which are likely to be of value to me? If so, when? How?

"Now I am learning how to approach study, keep records of and use a variety of resources for the study of a problem. These are some of the things that will also help me in the future along with the actual solutions to the problems upon which I have worked. I have learned to relate the approaches, solutions, etc., of problems to other problems. I find, too, that a student can get more from his work if he is allowed to help make his own plans of study."

"For my problem I made it a point to choose something I knew would have a very definite value for me and one that I had not had much previous experience with. From my study of how to teach mentally retarded and delinquent children I have learned better how to deal with some of the pupils in my practice teaching class. There have been working situations where I may try out some of the methods I have studied. In many cases they have worked. For example, in one case of apparent mental disinterest or retardment I found that individual aid to the pupil helped a great deal. In another case of delinquency in its early stages, allowing the student to have a part in choosing what he was to study helped solve the problem. In the future, when I am teaching, my classes may represent a wider range of individual differences and mentality than they now do. If this is the case, I feel that I shall be more competent to deal with them, since I have spent a good bit of time in studying the problems connected with such range. I feel that I have been very fortunate in taking a course of this type at the same time I am teaching. There are many ways in which it helps me to know how to deal with my problems. These values, at least some of them, would be lost if the courses were not taken concurrently."

"Yes, all the problems will be of value to me in teaching and in married life. The problems will help me to carry on better conversations, and will help me to solve many more problems I will later meet. Realizing that people forget so very much of what they learn, I feel that the material I have learned from my study, 'How can the commercial teacher develop desirable personality traits in her adolescent students?' has been material that I will not use in the capacity for which I learned it. I feel that I should have made my problem something that would help me now. Such a topic as this, 'How can I develop a personality that will enable me to be a better teacher or worker?' would have helped me more in the long run because I know that a teacher cannot teach and develop desirable personalities if she, herself, does not possess such a personality."

"I see my problems now, as I did not before, as questions that I can study and probably find a usable solution for. Although I have not written up all of my study of 'Supervisor relationships' I feel that I have already put this into use. This subject fits into the subject of personality and I have found that some of the material of the other subject has been helpful in this way, even if I do not feel I shall use it for the purpose for which I studied it."

Question 3. Have I been working on something that represents a real need to me? Evidence?

"I believe that my problem does represent a real need to me, for when I begin teaching the problem of discipline will prove very important. I must understand and expect certain forms of misconduct and be able to cope with the situation. But, first of all, I should know those things which prevent misconduct and should try to use them to their best advantage (such as making the work in the class useful to the students and actually showing them how it is likely to be useful)."

"Yes, I have selected problems which are directly related to my field. I have already used some of the solutions in my teaching (the subjective examination problem, for example). I have also studied problems which involve the home life of my students. This will be a need to me in the home project visits and problems."

"My work on present-day problems of home economics teachers has centered my attention on problems that I will probably meet in my own teaching. I feel that all of the problems I have studied are of real need to me. I need to know what has been attempted by others on these problems. I need to know the problems of home economics teachers now so that I may study them, read, and search for possible solutions. This needs to be done so that I will know how to cope with problems of a similar nature that I will most likely meet."

"As I have indicated in my records, there is a great need for my studying this problem. I not only plan actually to build this cottage, but I also plan to help any of my students with similar problems that they need help with. One main objective of Industrial Arts (my major) is to prepare students to take care of themselves during unusual situations. During the last depression many high-school students finished school and went out into life facing great difficulty. There were many students that finished school who couldn't own their own homes because of a lack of finances to build. Had they known how to build their own homes and furniture they could have done this with less than half the money otherwise needed. It is such a problem as this that I want to help my students with."

"I plan to be a teacher. That statement alone is enough evidence that I need to determine my aims and objectives so that I will know why I am teaching. Further, I have never studied anything concerning the history of my field so I had taken this as fulfilling a real need."

"There has been a change in the state course of study and a type of curriculum called the core curriculum has been introduced. Many teachers are being called upon to conduct a class of this kind and they hardly know what to do about it. Since I may be called upon to teach such a class I need to prepare myself for such a situation. This represents a real need in me."

"I have never heard of a class yet in which all the students read as well as they could and should. Surely my classes will be no exception. Until last week I did not even know what 'Remedial Reading' was so what problem could I need to study more?"

"Every home economics teacher faces students who absolutely 'hate home economics.' They have the wrong opinion of what it is and believe that you can learn it as well at home. Naturally, they have an unpleasant attitude in class. More than likely they will be problem students for the teacher and they must be managed with interest and great care. A teacher is not able to do this without some training and experience. Therefore, I certainly believe I have been working on a problem that represents a real need for me."

"There is a definite need for me to learn how to teach delinquent and mentally retarded children. This, I feel, is a dire need among all teachers. The general trend seems to be to have a teacher learn to teach the normal children and 'hit or miss' on the ones who tend to fall below or above the average. While I do not expect to teach a class of pupils who are all below the normal level of mentality, I need to recognize such when I see them and be able to deal with cases if I get them."

Question 4. Do I have specific goals and am I making progress toward them? Describe.

"When I began the problem I felt that the average student in junior and senior high school thought of science as something he just had to take for no particular reason. I therefore began to see just what the aims of science were and what benefit a student who was not going to college could get out of it. With these aims and a knowledge of the benefits I can point out to the student that science is not a waste of time and I can conduct the class along channels that will bring out the basic purposes of the work. I also wanted to find out just what things would be developed most and methods of test-giving which are most appropriate for science."

"I have listed some of my goals in my folder. These are in the form of problems, for example: 'What is a functional program of home economics?', 'What is my role in making a community more livable?'. My principal goal has been to find out some definite problems that home economics teachers are facing today and to find some possible solutions to them. I have studied on a few of the problems that are met but I feel that I have climbed several rungs of the ladder in this. I have planned the immediate goals I wish to obtain before this course is completed. I want to study the core curriculum in a home economics program, and then organize and retype parts of my folder."

"The main goal in my problem in this class is: How may I bring democracy into my home economics classes? My other goal is to find what the most important things are for me to do in order to be a good home economics teacher. What methods of teaching will I use? I am studying the methods of all of my teachers and have found good points in all of them, but have decided I want to use the teacher-pupil cooperation method primarily. I want the student to feel that he can depend on me for guidance."

I. *Related to goals*

    A. Teacher dictation of assignments may seem to get quick immediate results. However, since the learner is being deprived of an opportunity to get his own learning under way, systematic learning after the teacher is no longer there is not very probable. Hence, the goal should not simply be to get an assignment made but rather to, improve the learner processes in the selection of problems. This rightly implies that learning *the process* of wise problem selection should be a fundamental goal for both teacher and learner.

    B. The importance of having the learner see the intrinsic significance *to him* of everything he studies cannot be overemphasized. This may seem to take much time but in the long run will pay rich dividends if techniques for doing it effectively are aggressively studied by teacher and students.

    C. Of paramount importance is the goal of having the learner work on problems in such a way that he will carry over his learnings into out-of-school situations. Unless this is done, the long-time values that can come from learning intelligently to select problems for study may be lost.

    D. In developing problem-selection ability an attempt should be made to keep the selection of a particular problem on a sufficiently tentative basis so that the learner will be willing to restudy selection continuously and move to the study of another problem if such a change is indicated in the light of new evidence.

II. *Related to the role of the teacher*

    A. The teacher begins to have a new role to play when he moves in the direction of democratic assignment-working on problem selection. Instead of teaching what, when, and how subject matter will be learned, the teacher's main purpose in this regard will be to help the student learn how to take the initiative in getting his own learnings started. The teacher will attempt to help each learner build a self-starter as a part of his processes for self-teaching and self-learning.

B. Effective progress in teaching problem-selection abilities frequently starts with the teacher's analyzing and improving his own selection of personal and professional problems for systematic study and may start when the teacher asks himself such a question as "How can I effectively know *my own* skill in selecting the professional or personal problems I need to study so that I may teach more happily and more effectively?"

C. Too great emphasis by the teacher on speed in teacher-learner assignment-making or the setting up of problems is likely to result in work poor in quality and quantity. The teacher's role in this area is not to hurry the pupil over problem-selection activities but rather to emphasize the importance for immediate and long-time motivation of such activities.

D. Some initial diagnosis of what is already known by each individual learner should usually precede problem selection. The more immature the pupils in problem selection, the more of this the teacher may have to do initially. Gradually, this responsibility should be assumed by the learner. It is usually a waste of time for a student to be encouraged to work on a problem with which he has already become fairly proficient. A part of the teacher's role is to get or to prepare diagnostic tools that will be of help in this process.

E. The teacher may expect challenging and even exciting returns to himself in promoting problem-selection abilities on the part of the learners. This presents a sharp contrast to the boredom sometimes noted when teacher domination of assignment-making or problem selection results in about the same teacher activity year after year.

F. As preparation for teaching the learner how to select wisely what he should study, the teacher will do well to build up a thorough understanding of methods and resources other teachers have found useful in developing problem-selection ability.

III. *Related to the role of learner*

A. To learn how wisely to select problems the learner must *have actual experience or practice in selecting problems.*

Preferably, this practice should be with the guidance of a skilled teacher who has studied and practiced intelligent problem selection himself.

B. The learner needs to develop ability to diagnose his own needs and problems and to relate these to the skills and abilities he already has. He must recognize that it is impossible for the teacher to do a thorough job of this for each pupil with whom he works. Even if the teacher had so few students that he could attempt to take all responsibility in this field, it would be educationally indefensible to build up such learner dependence upon the teacher. If a thorough diagnosis shows the learner already proficient in the wise selection of problems it is important for him to study, then little time should be devoted to this, and other areas of learner weakness should be emphasized.

C. Unless the learner has had much guided practice in problem identification, selection, and solution, he should start with relatively simple problems or assignments and build up techniques for more complex areas.

D. By all means the learner should attempt to select problems (or assignments) for study which he recognizes as important to him.

E. A record by the learner of steps taken in deciding what to study will facilitate more rapid improvement in efficient problem selection.

IV. *Related to developing democratic teacher-learner interpersonal relations*

A. The teacher and learner should together set up criteria to help in the selection of problems.

B. One test of learner and teacher effectiveness in assignment-making is the extent to which the learner himself has improved in the ability to decide wisely what he should study at a particular time.

C. To encourage each learner in a class to identify and evaluate his purposes in a course, the teacher may ask him to write down these purposes. The teacher should reciprocate by writing down for his own and the learners' benefit his purposes in teaching the course. This process will tend to bring both teacher and learners face to face with their respective goals and motivation in the course. A scale of learner motivation can be used running, perhaps, from "forced to take the course for credit" to "wanted opportunity to work with guidance on specific problems related to this course." Such a scale may help the learner objectify his status with respect to motivation.

D. In selecting possible problems for study careful attention should be given to considering what problems should be attacked individually and what ones by the group as a whole.

E. Principles that guidance experts have found effective in helping the individual assume greater responsibility for his own problems can well be considered for application in effective teaching.

F. If the teacher wishes to try to make a very gradual break from teacher-dominated assignments, he may consider listing several problems or assignments from which the learner with guidance may pick those that seem most appropriate to him. The pupil should be encouraged to give reasons for, and reasons against, selecting for study each of the possible problems or assignments.

G. Developing readiness for wise problem selection will frequently take the form of helping the learner develop his intrinsic purposes for study in the area involved. For example, before a learner is psychologically prepared really to profit greatly from the study of history or any other subject, it is of paramount importance that he see the intrinsic values to be derived from such study. When this readiness is developed, problem selection can proceed on a more intelligent basis.

H. Both learner and teacher should avoid the possible pitfalls of merely working on that which is interesting if thereby they really try, consciously or unconsciously, to escape from real issues on problems that should be faced.

V. *Related to difficulties likely to be encountered*

A. Old ideas, attitudes, and habits relating to the question of what constitutes education and schooling tend to change slowly if at all. In like fashion, ideas, attitudes, and habits relating to the question, Who should select problems for study? will be likely to take time to change. Difficulty in producing rapid change should be expected.

B. The influences on the learner of the use by other teachers of teacher-dominated assignment techniques tend to put a brake on the speed with which the learner can be taught to assume responsibility in selecting his problems for study. This makes the problem of promoting desirable change in assignment-making difficult but not insolvable. Even under optimum conditions learning efficient problem selection is a complex developmental process that may take years to develop to a high degree of efficiency.

C. A certain amount of confusion and bewilderment on the part of the teacher is to be expected if he is not already a master in developing democratic problem selection with learners. As with learners this "puzzlement" should serve as a challenge or spur to the mastery of a new process.

D. "Mistakes" on the part of the learner are to be expected as the learner develops his abilities in deciding what it is best for him to devote his time to. It is better that such mistakes be identified and ironed out of his learning processes now than after he leaves school when guidance is no longer easily available and when the mistakes are likely to be much more costly. Patience on the part of the teacher is important, for only through practice will the learner learn.

E. Some confusion and bewilderment are necessary concomitants of the effective learning process. If the learner has no trouble at all in doing his studying, it is very doubtful whether the learning is very profitable for him.

F. A high degree of democracy in guided problem selection by learners involves the use of techniques and skills on the part of the teacher and the learner that take years to develop. Continuous, persistent striving for improvement in problem-selection ability will produce results profitable to both teacher and learners.

BIBLIOGRAPHY

1. Association for Supervision and Curriculum Development. *Toward Better Teaching*. Washington D.C.: The Association, 1949.

2. Class of 1938, University High School, Ohio State University. *Were We Guinea Pigs?* New York: Henry Holt and Co., 1938.
   Pictures secondary-school setup where self-education is being developed in certain areas.

3. CROUT, VELMER E. "Mathematics in General Education." *The Southern Association Quarterly*, 3:475-81; August 1939.
   Work on meeting functional needs of boys and girls shown. Tie-up with football interests and other interests depicted.

4. GILES, H. H. *Teacher Pupil Planning.* New York: Harper and Bros., 1941.
   Steps toward democracy in classroom are pictured. Many examples used from actual classrooms. Importance of interpersonal relationships emphasized. Useful bibliography.

5. HAND, HAROLD. "The Case for the Common Learnings Course." *Science Education*, 32:5-11; February 1948.
   Gives excellent case for eliminating traditional subjects as required ones and substituting a direct attack on societal and youth problems.

6. MIEL, ALICE. *Changing the Curriculum.* New York: D. Appleton-Century Co., 1946.

7. Parker District High School Faculty and Southern Association Study Staff. *Parker High School Serves Its People.* Greenville, South Carolina: Parker District School, 1942.
   Shows how a school works toward discovering and meeting the individual and personal needs of pupils. Special attention given to analyzing work of school in developing good citizenship, health, vocational abilities, and community improvements.

8. Progressive Education Association *Informal Committee on Evaluation of Newer Practices in Education. New Methods vs. Old in American Education.* New York: Teachers College, Columbia University, 1941.
   Pictures newer experimental methods and gives objective and subjective evidence on their values. Useful bibliography.

9. RATHS, L. "Improving Classroom Discussion." *Educational Research Bulletin*, 24:6-13, 28; January 17, 1945.
   Describes study of use of discussion as elementary classroom technique. Indicates one set of criteria for deciding worthwhile problems and discusses some purposes of discussions.

10. ROSE, ELIZABETH. "Changes in My Teaching of English since 1935." *High School Journal*, 24:5-11; January 1941.
    Pictures changes in teacher's attitudes and methods in attempts to meet better the needs of each learner.

11. SAYWARD, R. K. "Mathematics Breaks with Tradition." *High School Journal,* 22:272-74; November 1939.

    Pictures mathematics "taught and studied not as an abstraction that bears no relationship to life but rather as an integral part of that knowledge which will function in the lives of all men and women."
12. SELBERG, EDITH M. "Developing Problem-solving Ability in Students." *Science Education,* 23:126-33; March 1939.

    Gives suggestions one school has found valuable in developing and teaching the scientific approach in the solution of problems. Report differs from many in that learners help select problems, help plan methods, work on skills necessary to carry out plans, and participate in evaluation.
13. SIMPSON, RAY H. Students Help Set Up Criteria To Aid in Deciding What To Study. *Journal of Educational Research,* 36:192-99; November 1942.

    Learners are given practice in an early step in effective learning. Effect on motivation considered.
14. SIMS, VERNER M. "Problems Relating to Effective Study for Workshop Participants." *The Southern Association Quarterly,* 7:418-31; November 1943.

    Excellent analysis of problems related to teaching teachers, supervisors, and administrators how to select and attack problems.
15. TUTTLE, H. S. *Dynamic Psychology and Conduct.* New York: Harper and Bros., 1949. pp. 237-41.
16. WALLACE, W. CHREITZBERG, J., AND SIMS, V. M. *The Story of Holtville,* Deatsville, Alabama: Holtville High School, 1944.

    Gives vivid picture of a developing high school in action together with some description of the origins of what is happening.
17. WATERS, E. A. *Study of the Application of an Educational Theory to Science Instruction.* New York: Bureau of Publications, Teachers College, Columbia University, 1942.

    Excellent description of how science classes were individualized. Graphic description is given of procedures actually used. Also gives educational theory on which the classes were based. This is a contribution to Education 864.

6

PROBLEM SOLUTION FOR

EFFECTIVE LEARNING

Problems to consider

How is effective problem solution related to problem identification and selection?

How may one diagnose his problem-solving ability?

What attitudes are needed to improve in problem-solving?

Should we assume that the goal in school is: (1) to learn the solutions to all problems to be faced, or (2) to learn effective processes of solving new problems?

How should the decision be made about whether to work on a problem individually or in a group?

How can intrinsic motivation to solve problems be obtained?

How may we decide whether the learner is improving in problem-solving abilities?

When and how should work on an old problem be discontinued and attacks on a new problem be started?

Introduction. As has been suggested in preceding chapters the key phases in teaching the learner to teach himself are the processes of problem identification, selection, and solution. The last of these, problem solution, will be discussed in this chapter.

Before starting a discussion of key points related to the improvement of problem-solution processes it would be well to see clearly the relationship between this and the points made in the three preceding chapters. If problem identification and problem selection are exclusively or even primarily in the hands of the teacher, the real problem the learner frequently feels he faces is "How, with the least effort, can I please the teacher or keep him from pestering me by giving additional assignments over and above that given to most students in the class?" The chief problem being recognized by the learner too frequently becomes one of avoiding unpleasantness with the teacher. In doing this the learner may give attention to secondary problems such as algebra assignments or English questions but the basic problem of the learner is to get the assignment done because the teacher made it, not because he sees any intrinsic value in it. The actual relationship of the learner to the problems will determine the extent to which he really puts his heart into getting solutions to them. Unless the learner participates in identifying and selecting the problems on which he works, his efforts in trying to solve them are too frequently made to keep the teacher quiet, to get a mark, or to get credit in a course. Sound motivation for problem solution is largely dependent upon the learner's participating in helping to identify and select the problem.

Purpose of problem-solving? One other point should be discussed in these preliminary comments. In promoting problem solution it is important to consider: What are our purposes? With some teachers the purpose is only to help the learner get the answer with the implied assumption that the primary function of the school is to help the learner get, while he is in school, all the solutions he will need when he gets out of school. The theory that the important thing in a class is to cover so much material is probably an outgrowth of this point of view. In a rapidly changing world this approach does not seem to be particularly sound, since the school graduate will constantly be running into new problems to which the solutions he memorized in school do not apply.

An alternate approach and one which is much sounder psychologically is to place most emphasis not upon memorizing solutions but upon *learning the process* of problem solution. This will involve such things as helping the learner to build up a technique of analyzing his own strengths and weaknesses, of seeing what skills are involved in problem solution that are not merely following a pattern the teacher has shown, and of learning a variety of approaches to problems. If the learner builds up sound problem-solution approaches which he has had much practice in using in trying to solve problems, he is in a good position to meet new problems in a changing world. This is particularly true if practice in problem solution is tied up with problem identification and selection practice.

Most of the following questions are based on the assumption that it is more important for the learner to improve the processes involved in effectively solving new problems than it is for him to memorize the solutions to problems which someone else has already put in a book or lecture. It should be recognized that most of the answers to these questions will be ones of degree. The questions are designed to point up areas for improvement.[1]

Organization of problems

1. Has the problem on which I have been working been organized into practical sub-parts for careful analysis?
2. Do I see how the solution of each sub-problem will contribute to the solution of the primary problem?

Possible solutions

3. Have a sufficient number of possible solutions been considered in trying to arrive at appropriate conclusions?
4. Do I have persistence in seeking possible hypotheses that may be helpful in working out solutions to my problems?
5. Have the probable advantages and disadvantages of each alternative solution been sufficiently investigated?
6. Am I sufficiently critical of possible solutions?
7. Do I usually have a great desire to understand *both* sides of a debatable question?
8. Do I have an attitude of thoroughness in searching for facts?
9. In considering possible solutions to a problem, have I usually made a deliberate search for negative instances that might throw doubt on the solutions?
10. Do I have much flexibility in my approach to problems?
11. To what extent do I have the ability to hold my mind sufficiently open to all controversial issues?

---

[1] These questions are phrased primarily for individual diagnosis by the student in teacher-training courses where teaching and learning methods are studied. It is also suggested that high-school students can and should be trained to ask themselves similar questions.

12. Do I consciously try to avoid emotional attitudes and stereotyped thinking?

Conclusions drawn

13. Are the conclusions I have drawn based on logical evidence that is a part of my study record or on snap judgments?

14. Are my conclusions based on sound reasonable thinking or on petty prejudicial beliefs?

15. Do I make a conscious effort to avoid letting prejudice influence the conclusions I reach?

Evidence of more effective problem-solving

16. What evidence, if any, do I have that I am learning more effective problem-solving?

17. In my most recent learning did I do what I planned to do? If not, were valid reasons for the changes shown? If so, did I give enough consideration to changes that might have been advisable?

WHAT ATTITUDES AND POINTS OF VIEW CONTRIBUTE TO EFFECTIVE LEARNING OF PROBLEM-SOLUTION PROCESSES?

Purposes in problem-solving. It is important for the teacher and learner to realize the attitudes and points of view that affect the learning of problem-solution abilities, since these tend to determine to a high degree the extent of learning success. If attitudes or points of view are found upon diagnosis to be unsatisfactory, they themselves provide a point of attack and certainly should be taken into account as the learning process evolves.

As has been suggested before, the learner should think of problem solution not simply or even primarily as a matter of getting solutions to the problems being studied. Rather, *the primary purpose should be to improve in the process of problem solution so that he may be better able to meet and to solve the subsequent problems he will face.*

In golf, the player should keep his eye on the ball; in learning, the student should constantly keep his eye on the problem being attacked. At frequent intervals the learner needs to emphasize in his own mind exactly what it is that he is trying to do. In effect, he asks himself the question, What are the problems to which I am trying to get answers?

PROBLEM-SOLUTION PRACTICE LADDER

Learner consciously devotes a major share of his time trying to improve his techniques for getting possible solutions to problems that are meaningful and important to him. Teacher checks sufficiently often to see that this is happening.

Learner is encouraged to get possible solutions with guidance to problems he is facing or is likely to face but is not encouraged to give conscious attention to improving the process of problem solution he himself is using.

All learners in class are encouraged to work out possible solutions to problems *they* as a group have identified and selected as a group.

All learners in class are urged to work out with a minimum of guidance solutions to problems that are posed by the teacher.

Learner is directed to study through the steps others have taken in solving problems that are meaningful to the learner.

Learner is directed to go through certain formal steps in solving problems that are largely meaningless to him.

Learner is directed to spend time memorizing information or the solutions to problems that others have solved and gets no practice in learning how to solve them himself.

READ UP ⟶

Which of the rungs above best describes the problem-solution practice I am getting in my class or classes?

What can I do to move higher on the ladder?

PROPOSED SOLUTION TRYOUT LADDER

Possible solutions to meaningful problems are tried out with appropriate guidance and the apparent merits of each proposed solution are carefully evaluated. This may be done in a group if that seems desirable to those concerned with the problem, but the individual actively participates in the process.

Possible solutions to meaningful problems are tried out by the class or group with the majority of learners taking a rather passive role.

Possible solutions to a problem whose meaning is somewhat unclear to the learner are tried out by him.

Possible solutions that are meaningful to the learner because he has helped to develop them are tried out in the learner's presence.

Possible solutions whose meanings are obscure to the learner are *actually* tried out by someone else in the learner's presence.

Possible solutions to problems of limited meaning to the learner are *verbally* tried out by someone in the learner's presence.

No solutions to problems are tried out even mentally by the learner.

READ UP ⟶

Which of the rungs in the ladder above best describes the solution tryout practice I am getting in my class or classes?

What can I do to move higher on the ladder?

Dynamic desire for post-school improvement. A second attitude that needs to be emphasized involves a continuing desire to improve beyond the period of the course being studied. This means that the learner should be shown or led to see why it is he is studying what is being studied. It means that an important part of the teacher's work is to build up a continuing desire, which is internally motivated, to improve in systematic learning. It also means that the teacher's role to some extent will be one of taking a decreasing teacher responsibility and we must, of course, have a constantly increasing sense of responsibility on the part of the learner for setting his own goals, one of which is to improve in problem-solving ability.

Experimental attitude. A third attitude that should exist, or if it does not exist, should be developed, is one of willingness to try out new methods, particularly new methods of attacking problems and getting solutions to them. It profits the learner relatively little to repeat over and over a process with which he is already fairly familiar. For example, the learner gets relatively little in terms of improving his learning processes by day after day sitting in class and copying down the outline of the talk his teacher makes. In the same fashion he gets relatively little in process improvement from continually copying down the outline upon which an author wrote a text. Improvement always involves change and change involves trying out new methods and approaches with which the learner is not at the moment very familiar.

Use of service learning processes. A fourth attitude or point of view is a consciousness of and willingness to use key service activities which support problem identification, selection, and solution. For example, the learner needs to articulate his thinking through systematic record-keeping, which will involve the organization of the ideas he gets from various sources into the framework of his own problem. An idea recorded tends to improve in clarity over the idea that floats hazily in the mind of the learner. Another service activity that the learner will do well to consider using is that of purposeful reading. The ability to read and to get answers to problems involves different skills from that of reading to memorize the details in the book for a test. Reading for problem solution involves much scanning of a variety of materials to find out whether they promise to give help in answering the specific problems with which the learner is concerned. Of course, after such materials have been located, it will be important for the learner to read for details and to get the specific suggestions the material affords. There should be the willingness to get and use a great variety of resources and to take the point of view that ordinarily there are always resources available if the learner is willing to search for them in an appropriate fashion. In other words, the learner is not stumped if in printed materials he does not find the answer to his problems. In that case, he would resort to interviews, conferences, observation of others facing similar problems, and the other types of resources that are more thoroughly discussed under the chapter "Learning How To Obtain, Select, and Use Resources Effectively."

Need for a variety of solutions. Closely tied up with the willingness to use a variety of resources is the willingness and desire to get a variety of possible solutions rather than simply to get a single answer to a particular problem. In many fields, particularly social studies, English, and perhaps science, there are a variety of possible answers to realistic problems. The function of the learner then becomes one not of getting *the* answer but rather of getting a variety of answers which he would consider using under a particular set of circumstances.

Objectivity and willingness to accept criticism. A fifth attitude whose importance cannot be overemphasized involves the desire to be objective, open-minded, and fair in an analysis of the evidence available. This means that the learner will try to get and think through the evidence on both sides and give for each solution an impartial mental trial.

Finally, the learner will welcome guidance and the constructive criticisms of others and will not be too sensitive to such criticisms, realizing that from them he can profit.

HELPING THE LEARNER RECOGNIZE THE NEED FOR SOLUTIONS TO HIS PROBLEMS

Intrinsic motivation. Above all else it is of paramount importance to help the learner appreciate the intrinsic importance to him of getting a solution or solutions to the problem being attacked. Unless the learner sees *why* it is good for him to work on a problem, any work he actually does on it is likely to be done primarily to keep the teacher from bothering him. To have strong intrinsic motivation it is usually necessary for the learner to see *why* he needs a solution and how and where such solution could actually prove useful. The problem must not only be worthy of the learner's best efforts but he *must visualize its solution as important to him.* All other problems are largely spurious, insofar as the learner is concerned. It is for this reason that we again emphasize the importance of helping the learner directly to share in identifying and selecting his problems for study.

Adequate problem solution demands that the learner really understand the problems on which he works. There is usually no better way of helping him understand them than to have him share in getting the problems lined up initially; in other words, one of the best ways of guaranteeing understanding of the problem is to enlist the cooperation of the learner in identifying and selecting problems for study.

Recording ideas. Closely related to the needs for intrinsic motivation and a clear understanding of the problem to be studied is the need for a clear-cut breakdown and *recording* of the major problem and the sub-problems upon which its solution is dependent.

Types of success in problem-solving. Coupled with the need for a clear-cut recognition of a problem and its sub-problems is the need for some realization of different types of success in working out a solution or solutions to the problem. In many mathematics problems there is a single correct answer toward which the learner is shooting. On the other hand, in many social, political, and economic problems there is no single "best" solution but rather a variety of possible solutions, any one of which might be considered "best" in a particular set of circumstances. In the first case, the learner sets for himself the job of finding and proving *the* solution. In the second area the learner may wish to become familiar with each of a variety of possible solutions, together with the probable advantages of each. A third type of goal the learner might have in attacking problem solution would be to study *the processes* involved in effective problem solution so that he would be in a better position to meet problems more effectively in the future. This latter type of problem study has unfortunately been neglected in most of our classrooms. If we are to try to improve thinking in our classrooms, it is important to study and improve *the process* of problem solution.

How can the teacher work with the learners in such a way that problem solution attempts will be most fruitful in improving the quality of future problem-solution behavior? There is no single best answer to this question but there are a variety of suggestions that will help the thoughtful teacher if considered.

Breaking down the problem. After the problem has been defined, the next major step is to go about planning the solution of the problem. A first subordinate procedure usually necessary here is that of breaking down the big problem into manageable sub-problems for attack. One method is described by Selberg (20): the unit problem is analyzed into subsidiary or minor ideas, which become the basis for the contributing problems. These latter problems must be evaluated "in a manner similar to that used in originally selecting the big problem itself," also, "each contributing or subsidiary problem should involve one important phase of the unit. These problems are next arranged in logical order by the students, or student, so that sequential learning takes place." The tentative nature of this blueprint for study should always be emphasized by the teacher. As learning proceeds, changes in the original plan or outline of the sub-problems are very likely to become necessary. These changes may involve such steps as adding sub-problems, eliminating or combining some sub-problems, or rearranging the sequence of the problems. These modifications are ordinarily a sign of developing perception regarding what the big problem being studied involves, and are necessary and desirable parts of the problem-solution learning process.

Recording plans for attacking the problem and its sub-problems. In addition to getting a blueprint of the problem and sub-problem it is usually desirable for the student to write down a tentative blueprint of his plans for attacking the problem. This would include such things as the resources he expects to use, including human resources, any suggestions he wants to keep in mind in attacking the problem, the dangers he hopes to avoid in working on the problem, and sometimes a time schedule of the work activity he expects to follow.

Formulating hypotheses. After the sub-problems have been set up, it is usually well to encourage the learner to formulate and record some alternate hypothesis that he can base on his past experience or past use of resources on problems similars to this one. His own hunches and ideas about possible solutions should be formulated and written down to clarify his own thinking and to have for consideration in evaluating his growth during the total process of working on the problem.

Getting resources, keeping records, using reading. The learner should be encouraged to use such service learnings as critical reading, keeping a record, and getting and using materials or resources. These three service activities will each be discussed in a chapter later, but at this point it might be well to emphasize a few ideas that are particularly tied up with problem solution. Most readers have been trained in the past to read simply to get the information in a certain number of pages or in a particular chapter or book and have not been taught to read to any great extent to get suggestions and ideas that would help to answer a particular problem that is pertinent to them and upon which they are working. This means that one of the key types of reading that needs to be developed is that of reading for specific information pertinent to particular problems. It also involves the ability quickly to skim over nonpertinent reading material which under other circumstances might be read quite intensively. Closely tied up with this work of reading is the ability to spot probable sources of help on particular problems. The use of such sources as the *Reader's Guide,* encyclopedias, the *Education Index,* tables of contents, book indexes, and other similar resources contributes to the type of reading that is most needed in getting help on the problems being studied.[2]

As important as the ability to pick out relevant ideas is the ability to decide what should be written down in the student's record of his learning. Such questions as this should be considered: Should I write down only what I agree with or also what I disagree with? What should I attempt to remember? Should I put down what is to be used for later comparison and conclusion-drawing or should I attempt only to put down that which suggests specific action? Certainly the record-keeping for effective problem solution should involve pulling out key ideas and placing them in the sub-problems

[2] Most of the resources mentioned in this sentence are appropriate for both high-school students and the professional educators. The *Education Index* is primarily for the latter group although some high-school students can profit from its use.

to which they appropriately belong rather than the conventional student practice of simply copying down the outline of each author in sequential fashion.

In the matter of getting and using resources it is usually important that the teacher encourage the getting and using of a wide variety of points of view particularly on controversial problems. In doing this the learner should attempt to evaluate the adequacy of various sources and should learn how to make wise judgments concerning the validity of the ideas he gets. In many learners this involves breaking down the old idea that what is printed is the gospel truth. Practically everything written on a controversial issue is biased, that is, the writer or speaker looks at the problem from his particular standpoint. There is no simple way of learning this ability to evaluate critically the worth of various resources but it can be developed if teacher and learner are conscious of the problem and attempt to develop critical abilities in trying to get solutions to the problems they are attacking. It is important that students realize the value of the human resources usually found in the community. Frequently such human resources can give the student fresh ideas and points of view that are sometimes difficult to get from printed sources. The teacher should encourage the learner to realize that someone else, in fact usually many others, have met the same or a similar problem and that part of the job of learning effective problem solution is finding who these people were and what conclusions they came to as a basis for action.

If the concept of guidance as helping the learner better to help himself is adopted, we quickly see that this is closely akin to good teaching. In good teaching the teacher no longer has a monopoly in deciding what is to be studied, when and how it is to be studied, and how much of it is to be studied. The teacher no longer has a monopoly in selecting all the resources to be used in study and in deciding when each resource will be used. The teacher no longer constructs, administers, scores, and interprets all the tests without the help of those most concerned—the learners themselves. Rather, the best teacher, the one who teaches the learner how to teach himself, is the one who recognizes that, because the learners cannot do a very good job of solving problems (one of the important steps in the learning process), he must give the learner much guided practice in this step rather than simply giving him the solution to the problem and telling him to memorize it.

Get many possible solutions. Ordinarily, the teacher should encourage the learner to get a variety of possible solutions rather than simply *a* solution to a particular problem. The reason for this is that most social, political, and economic problems actually have a variety of solutions, any one of which might be best in the particular situation where the learner may need to use it. Therefore, it is important that the learner see and be ready to use any one of a group of possible solutions.

Evaluation encouraged. Through class and individual questioning the teacher should encourage the critical examination and evaluation of all proposals, giving probable arguments for and against each. Each proposal should be considered on its merits rather than on the authority of the resource alone; although the teacher knows, we assume, the commonly accepted solution or principle, he needs to be careful not to short-circuit the learners' thinking by trotting out the answer too early. If some emergency required an immediate answer, then the teacher would take over; if learning is the primary purpose, then that needs to be done by the learner with only appropriate guidance from the teacher.

Constantly the teacher should encourage the student in self-questioning and self-evaluation of the processes he is using. Some of the questions that may be raised for consideration and evaluation of learning procedures are the following: (*a*) How is an hypothesis to be tested? (*b*) What constitutes a solution to the problem? (*c*) What constitutes evidence? (*d*) What resources may be used? (*e*) What constitutes an authority? Who are most likely to be authorities in the area in which work is being done? (*f*) What use could be made of first-hand observation of things and happenings? (*g*) Could some first-hand experimental evidence be obtained on the problem? (*h*) How can action be planned for resolving conflicting views and suppositions?

The importance of helping the learner select important ideas, form conclusions, evaluate conclusions, and apply what has been learned has been summarized by Selberg (20, pp. 128-29): "The student may be taught to summarize the main ideas from each experiment, from each reading source, or from the interview. These subsequently may be formed into more comprehensive meanings. This involves the process of generalizing and here the student is directed to note similarities and dissimilarities among the ideas presented in the assembled sentences. Before the generalization is accepted the student must decide whether it is based upon the data which he has obtained, whether it is stated in correct English form, and whether it answers the problem. He can further verify his conclusion by obtaining more information, by applying it to a concrete situation, by interviewing an authority, by experimenting or by reading another authoritative source. The latter procedures have been found to be very helpful for showing the student how necessary it is to obtain accurate, reliable, and sufficient data and how important it is to base conclusions on the evidence he has obtained. Often when the tentative conclusion has been verified in one of the above ways it becomes the final conclusion to the problem. If problem-solving procedures and conclusions are to change the behavior of the student, these must be applied in these everyday experiences."

". . . after each new technique has been used, the student is asked to review the procedure, to determine where errors and mistakes were made in its use and to ascertain the points of the method."

". . . abilities are presented gradually and progressively throughout the educational experiences of the student. With younger children one can begin with a formulation and evaluation of problems, with the critical evaluation of sources and with the simpler ways of obtaining information. With older students this process is shortened and many of them can devise ways and means of their own."

Learning to solve problems vs. *"Covering subject matter."* "Under such a program of education the teacher cannot 'cover as much subject matter' as other teachers who may be encouraging a factual method of learning. But the amount of subject matter covered will probably have to be sacrificed initially if educators believe that the ability to solve problems (and identify and select them) is an important outcome of learning."

Ordinarily, it is desirable for the teacher to decrease the "assigned" tasks, and increase the problems attacked. It is very important that the teacher try not to kill or, at best, anesthetize the normal curiosity of children by encouraging the docile acquisition of unneeded information, from the learners' standpoint, from the printed page as has been done in many schools.

Enticing sidepaths. With students unfamiliar with the problem-solution approach it is frequently desirable to help them decide when to leave a problem while studying in the library and go off on an enticing sidepath. Students will run across material that is interesting but has nothing whatever to do with the problem to be attacked, and a part of the job of the teacher is to guide them in making these side excursions only under appropriate circumstances, which frequently means cutting down the number of bypaths to be trod regardless of how enticing they may appear.

Varied approaches needed. Emphasis has already been placed upon the importance of using varied resources. A similar emphasis needs to be placed upon the desirability of using a variety of approaches in attacking the problem. An approach that is good for one problem may be relatively poor for another. In addition, in trying to get varied possible solutions to a problem, we also need to build varied attacks upon problems that are likely to be met after the particular schoolwork is over.

Leadership training. Those students with considerable experience in getting solutions to problems should be encouraged to get leadership training and practice through guiding those more inexperienced in using resources and in developing attacks for problem solutions.

AN EXAMPLE OF INDIVIDUALIZED PROBLEM-SOLUTION OPERATION

How does a class operate in which instruction is individualized? The answer to this will partially depend on teacher skills, learners' backgrounds, and community needs. One answer is given by Smyth (22, pp. 249-50) who pictures a high-school class in the third semester of its work. "Its membership consisted of twenty-eight pupils of low average ability, seven of whom claimed they were planning for college. It is doubtful whether more than three or four actually will go. During the previous two semesters, pupils had felt common needs for the studying of the following problems:

1. What can my school do for me and what can I return to it?
2. What should be my educational plans?
3. What opportunities does my home offer for educational advancement?
4. What opportunities does my community offer?
5. How has America developed her free public school system?
6. What are the essentials of the American ideal of democracy?
7. How can I develop myself so as to become a better member of society?

"As the work progressed there was a growing tendency for the pupils to discover some problem within the class problem. Therefore, by the close of the first year, pupils were largely setting for themselves the task of working out an individual problem.

"When the questions of ways of working and problems to be chosen were raised at the beginning of the third semester, pupils were very decided in their convictions that each one should be allowed to make his own choice of problems to be studied. A week was used in reviewing the past year's experiences of pupils' plans for education and careers and for re-examining ways and means of evaluating choice of problems. Also the class reviewed and criticized the ideas they had previously gained regarding pupils' obligations and responsibilities related to the task of working out their problems. Likewise, as the need arose, pupils discussed and reached conclusions regarding ways of sharing the information gained and evaluating their work. Another week was consumed in pupils' planning lists of problems which they felt they needed to study during the semester and detailed plans for their first problem. The process demanded browsing in books, magazines, and newspapers, radio broadcasts, and conferences with parents and teachers. By the third week pupils had filed with their instructors 'criteria sheets' justifying their choices and signifying estimates of the time their problems would take. Time estimates ranged from one to five weeks depending on the nature of the problem, amount of reference materials available and ability of pupil. The instructor prepared for ready reference, alphabetized roll charts containing pupils' working plans for their problems and their time estimates. Later she made charts which grouped problems having a common subject and helped pupils plan their programs for their sharing periods. At first the great diversity of subjects to be dealt with baffled the instructor who wondered how she would ever be able to bring any sort of unity into the class sharing period. The very first day of reports by pupils on their problems allayed her fears, because pupil attention and class discussion which followed were the best she had ever experienced. Pupils asked questions frequently and pointed out related angles of their own particular problem to the question of the hour. As time went on they saw and pointed out relations revealed to them from previous reports made in class as well as from their newspaper reading or radio listening that had been stimulated through their understanding of problems presented by their fellow students. The idea that perhaps pupils integrate their experiences better in such a situation of diverse problems than they do in a course devised under the most logically organized plan any teacher can conceive was becoming more apparent to the instructor. An oral test on the subject of national conscription prepared and administered to the class by two pupils revealed that pupils who had not studied, as their own individual project, problems related thereto, had gained so much information from class presentation and discussions that they were able to compete favorably in the contest. One very poor student surpassed all of her classmates on the test.

"The pupil-teacher planning for individual needs and interests necessitates anticipation of the pupil's entire social studies program for his high school career. In order to provide a well rounded plan for his work as is possible, areas of work sheets are kept up to date by him and charts showing fields that he should continue to explore are devised with him by the teacher. Effort is made to aid him in getting as full as possible a picture of the whole social studies field in the time his high school schedule will permit. In most cases four semesters of work are required; in some cases five or even six semesters are possible. In several cases, pupils who feel their future educational plans demand rigid courses in chronological history have worked out their plans for such courses and have followed their plans through very well. A case in point is that of three boys whose future educational career required, they believed, entrance units to Annapolis. Arrangements were made for the boys to be placed in the same social studies class in order that the teacher might give them time together on their common problem. Frequently they have contributed to the class well organized accounts of the historical development of mankind. They also aided pupils needing ancient historical background for their particular problems.

"Is such classroom procedure as has been described a revolution? No, rather it is evolution. Is it 'Progressive Education'? We are making no such claims but we sincerely hope pupils are progressing in the sense that they are growing and developing in their selection of problems to be studied and their understanding of their own and society's needs. Is this an experiment and are they 'Guinea

Pigs'? We do not consider such to be the case. We have no interest in conducting an educational experiment, but we are vitally interested in challenging girls and boys to become increasingly self-directive in a field that presents a life situation of personal and social problems which must be faced continuously by individuals from the cradle to the grave. Individualized teaching becomes an adventure for the teacher on a trail where pupils and teachers collaborate in the pursuit of commonly recognized goals. Learning, to be effective, must be motivated from within and must become a part of the experiences of daily living."

WHAT ARE THE SIGNS OF SUCCESS IN PROBLEM-SOLUTION ACTIVITIES?

By knowing some of the signs of success in problem-solution processes the teacher and learner will be in a better position to evaluate and to make improvements in problem-solution activities. The following signs of success are suggestive only:

More problems are recognized by the learner.

The scope and interrelationships of problems are better recognized.

An increasingly critical and evaluative attitude is taken toward the work by the learner.

The appropriateness of the method of attempting solution is considered in relation to the purpose the learner has. (An example of this is a group of administrators who were trying to get the answers to little, specific problems as opposed to another group of administrators who were learning improved methods of getting along with and working with their staffs of teachers on the job. The latter group was attacking the *process* of arriving at solutions, the former was simply attempting to get the solutions to a small number of problems.)

Is the behavior of the individual in school group, family, and community improving? This demands an analysis of what good and poor behaviors are taking place in the community.

Increased assumption of responsibility for the learning process on the part of the learner will be shown.

Additional help in the measurement of probable success of problem-solution activities can be got by making use of the questions in the first part of this chapter.

HOW LONG SHOULD A SINGLE PROBLEM BE WORKED ON?
WHO SHOULD DECIDE WHEN A CHANGE IS TO BE MADE?
ON WHAT BASIS SHOULD A DECISION BE MADE?

Since there are many factors to be taken into consideration when decisions of this sort are to be made, it is obvious that it is not something that should be decided except after some additional study of the factors that have been discussed under the following questions: What are the possible methods of helping learners determine their needs and problems? (Chapter 3.) What are the criteria to be considered in the actual selection of the problem for study? (Chapter 5.) However, the following suggestions in addition to those that have already been given should prove helpful.

Avoiding impossible goals. We should not encourage the learner to set up for himself the goal, which is impossible of achievement in most problems, of *completely* finishing the study of the problem by exhausting all possible resources. When an elementary, high-school, or college group of students are first asked, "How long do you think you should continue the study of the first problem you take up?", many of them will reply, "Until we have finished the solution of it." For instance, if an individual in a social-studies class were to study the problem "What are the ways in which we might improve democratic participation in our schools?", he is starting the study of a problem that can really never be entirely finished. What he should do, of course, is to pursue the problem to a point where he gets some suggestions of value, which he and those with whom he works will try to put into practice. All of this is not intended to imply that the learner or learners should be encouraged to jump too rapidly from one problem to another but rather to recognize that the law of diminishing returns usually begins to operate after a reasonable amount of time has been spent on a particular problem. This usually occurs long before all of the evidence on the problem has been accumulated.

Keeping conclusions tentative. Since *all* of the evidence on most problems is never accumulated the learner should be taught to try to get the best *tentative* conclusions he is able to draw in a reasonable amount of time rather than try to reach completely final conclusions.

Re-examination of relative need for studying various problems. At periodic and relatively frequent intervals the learner with the help of the teacher serving as an advisor should re-examine the probable advantages and disadvantages of studying each of various other problems upon which it might be advisable for the pupil to work and then should weigh these carefully against the probable advantages and disadvantages of continuing a study of the problem he is now investigating. For example, the high-school student mentioned before who was studying "What are the ways in which we might improve democratic participation in our school?" after one or two weeks should reconsider other problems on which he might be spending his time and, in the light of an analysis of these, determine whether it is probably best for him to continue this study of democracy or go to some other problem. Fairly regular periods of summarization and evaluation of what has been done and how it has been done will be valuable in encouraging such reconsideration. Attempt to lead the learner to ask himself often: What would be the best and most profitable problem for me to study?

Tentative summaries to be made. If the learner after a re-examination with the teacher's help of the problems upon which he might profitably study is in doubt about whether he should continue with the problem now being studied or shift to another problem, it is frequently well to suggest that he summarize what he has done on the problem upon which he has been working, list tentative conclusions, note still-unanswered questions, and then start on a new problem with the expectation of returning to the old one at a later date and in the meantime be on the lookout for additional help on the unanswered questions that have been noted.

Recording reasons for shift from one problem to another. When the learner seems to have a tendency to go too rapidly from one problem to another, constantly encourage him to *write* down before every proposed shift the probable advantages and disadvantages of changing from one problem to another.

Before leaving the study of a problem. Before the learner leaves any problem, even if the departure is only to be temporary, encourage him to get his records in order so that his time will not have been wasted. The organization of his records will also crystallize some of his thinking on the problem. (See the section on records [Chapter 9] for suggestions on ways of doing this.)

Intrinsic value vs. *pleasing teacher.* Encourage the learner to avoid basing what he studies primarily on what he thinks the teacher wants him to do rather than upon something that he thinks, after due consideration, will be of maximum value to him. His thinking should, of course, be more and more based on a careful analysis of what will really be best for him to do.

Using conclusions. When a pupil feels he has finished the study of one problem try to help him put his tentative conclusions into action as frequently as this seems wise after thoughtful consideration. Emphasize that conclusions without planned action are frequently valueless.

Teacher evaluation. Many helpful suggestions for the teacher can frequently be obtained if he will encourage the learners to answer such questions as these: In what ways do you feel the teacher helped you in this problem? Remembering the number of learners with whom the teacher is working, how would you suggest he might be of more help to you and others in your class? Sometimes it is well to have the answers to these questions anonymous.

Analyzing processes in problem-solving. At the end of the study of any problem it is usually well to ask such questions as: How could I have done the work more economically? What kinds of resources should I have used more extensively? Does it now appear that I was wise in trying to study this problem? How can I do better next time?

Who should decide when to change problems? Should the learner or the teacher decide when a change from one problem to another is to be made? Typically, this should be a cooperative decision with both the student and the instructor explaining their respective points of view. These points of view should be accompanied by reasons in each case. This may be done either through notes or through personal conference. Frequently, the former is satisfactory after a working relationship has been established and it is sometimes more convenient and less time-consuming. If motivation is to be on a high level and the learner is fairly proficient in problem identification, selection, and solution, the final decision should largely rest with the learner himself; otherwise the work is likely to degenerate into mere busywork.

Learning how *more important than the end answer.* It cannot be overemphasized that learning *how* to identify, select, and solve problems more effectively is even more important than the conclusions reached on any single problem. In education, learning the proper process of teaching oneself is much more important than any other result one may achieve.

HOW THE TEACHER CAN HELP BRING WORK TO A CLOSE ON
A PARTICULAR PROBLEM IN A PROFITABLE WAY

After a tentative decision has been made that it would be well to shift the work from one problem to another, the question arises "What should be done before the old problem is left?" or "How can the teacher help the participant to bring his work to a close so that he may get the maximum value from it?"

In this, as in most other educational problems, there is perhaps no single best answer. However, it is frequently well to raise such questions as the following with the learner:

Would it be well for you to take each sub-problem and summarize your tentative position or conclusion on the basis of the conflicting evidence that you have used from various resources?

Might it be advisable for you to reorganize your material around a main problem or group of sub-problems?

Would it be desirable to reorganize the material within certain sub-problems in which you have a lot of material that is somewhat conflicting with respect to the type of behavior it would indicate is desirable?

Would it be desirable for you to crystallize the values that you have got out of your work on this particular problem both in terms of information and ideas gleaned about the possible solution to the problem, and in terms of the method or approaches you used in working on this problem? What are the weaknesses of your problem-solution processes that have been exposed by work on this problem, and how can they be eliminated?

How can the results of your study be organized for action or behavior change? Such a consideration is extremely important if we are interested in learning which will produce changes in behavior as opposed to learning which is simply an accumulation of information or knowledge.

What suggestions can you give for the improvement of relations with those with whom you worked, including the instructor, other students, and other individuals whom you may have used in the course of your study of the problem?

Are the records of the development of your plans and processes adequate? In other words, are they in such a form that they will be useful in attacking this or similar problems at some future time?

What group work, including perhaps a summary or group criticism of the results of your work, would be of help to you in future work and also perhaps help others who are attacking similar problems?

What should happen to the record of your study after you have finished work on a particular problem? Might it be desirable to consider including this as a part of the school report to your parents, which would go along with a report card or other type of evidence of progress that would go to the home?

Is this the type of problem on which you should reach a specific solution, or is it the type which will build informational background upon which you can better reach conclusions when such are necessary for action?

Should your resources and references be put in a more usable form for future utilization?

Would it be desirable for you to keep at least parts of this problem open as you begin an intensive attack on another problem?

What suggestions growing out of your experience in attacking this problem should you nail down concerning things to do or things not to do in attacking problems?

What new problems have emerged as a result of your solution or attempted solution to this problem? In other words, what problems are you now conscious of that before the study of this problem you had not considered as important?

What type of constructive criticism or evaluation would be helpful to you if done by the instructor or other students who are working on somewhat similar problems?

Have you noted for future reference a time when it would probably be desirable either to return to the study of this problem or to use some of the material and ideas that you have gathered in attempting to get solutions to this problem?

In what specific ways has your thinking about the problem that has been attacked changed?

What ideas or procedures that were relatively new has your study of this problem given to you?

If you were starting another study of a similar problem, what different approach would you make?

What approaches for getting and using resources in the solution of the problem could you have used to save time?

What types of reading skills and abilities does it appear you need to improve as a result of your study on this problem?

Have you made sufficient use of human resources in attempting to get possible solutions to this problem? If sufficient use has not been made, why?

To what extent was your initial tentative outline adequate?

AN EXAMPLE OF STUDENTS' EVALUATION OF ONE ASPECT OF PROBLEM-SOLVING PROCESSES

Some clarification of learner reaction to individual problem solution as an aid in developing open-mindedness may be had from reading learner comments to one question of a rather comprehensive self-evaluation questionnaire largely constructed by the group of students and then answered by them individually. The question was: *Am I improving in the ability to hold my mind open sufficiently on all controversial issues?* (Each paragraph represents a different student.)

"I have tried to make myself see that there are good points on each side of a question and I try to respect the other fellow's opinion, even if I do not agree with it."

"I think I have become more open-minded since I have participated in the discussion in this class. Many of the opinions voiced made my 'blood boil' but I have tried to turn them over in my mind and see if there could be a good point there. Many times I have been able to see a different angle of the question by this procedure."

"At the first of the year I had prejudices which were foolish, I know, but which I couldn't help. Not all of these have disappeared but they have decreased and I don't get mad in a discussion as easily as I did."

"I don't believe I have improved in this respect (improved my 'open-mindedness') because I think I've always been very open-minded."

"I don't know that I am improving in this. Sometimes, I'm afraid I become a little too certain that what I am arguing for is right. However, I don't mind listening to the other person's opinion, but he has to prove he is right and give evidence that he is right before I change my mind."

"There is still plenty of room for improvement for me here. I have an open mind and am usually very willing to have my opinion changed if I can be made to see where I am wrong. However, there is still some of the old 'Man convinced against his will is of the same opinion still' in me. I feel that I have progressed to some extent though. I don't feel that I am narrow-minded but just a little hard to convince."

"I know that I have developed somewhat in my ability to see the other person's side of the question. When this class first met, I was very set in many of my viewpoints, although other persons had decidedly different ones. At first I could not see their points of argument, now I feel that I do have that ability. I feel that I now weigh conclusions more carefully than I did before. I do not always change my mind, but at least, I have the feeling of certainty when anyone again broaches the subject, and I have reasons, more or less, why I have the viewpoint I possess. Before this experience, I can say that I often had strong viewpoints, but had few reasons to back them."

"The many controversial issues which have come up in class have been very beneficial to me. I have listened—and joined in—the discussions, and have derived many worth-while conclusions from them. However, this does not mean I have closed my mind and become 'set' in my thinking about these issues."

OPERATING PRINCIPLES AND SUGGESTIONS FOR PROBLEM-SOLUTION PRACTICE

I. *Goals in solution practice*

    A. Learning the how, the process, of problem-solving is of more importance to the learner in school than memorizing solutions or conclusions already reached by a lecturer or textbook writer. Learners should be encouraged to work through problems rather than merely to memorize information.

    B. A goal in problem-solving in a school learning situation should usually be to get a variety of possible solutions rather than to get "the" solutions. In actual situations where the problem or a similar one presents itself one "solution" will probably be best in one situation and another "solution" in another situation.

    C. Learning how to set up a tentative skeleton outline of problems being attacked and to place appropriate ideas gathered in this outline is an ability that needs to be developed for effective problem-solving.

D. The teacher trying to guide learners into solving problems more intelligently should above all attempt to use the scientific method of problem solution in facing his own personal and professional problems.

II. *Methods in problem solution*

A. The need for multi-method attacks on problems should be emphasized.

B. The relation of method to purposes and goals is important. A good method for one purpose might prove to be a poor method for another purpose. Strong intrinsic purposes must be developed for effective problem solution.

C. Methods of problem solution good for one person might be relatively poor for another depending upon such factors as stage of development, initiative, and purposes.

D. One of the profitable aspects of developing the solution to a particular problem should be the improvement of problem-solving techniques in attacking other problems. In fact, in an educational situation the primary goal in solving problems will not be simply to get the best solution to the problems being studied at a particular time, but rather to learn better ways of arriving at solutions to these and *to other problems later to be encountered as well.* The learner needs aid in finding and improving methods of working out his own solutions to his problems.

E. Teacher imposition of highly formal methods of attack on problems may actually hinder the learner from starting at the stage of problem-solving where he now is and thus keep him from really developing a sound personal technique in solving problems.

F. Learning by copying down a lecture or memorizing for a test is likely to discourage the development of a problem-solving attitude by leading the learner to believe that education is copy and memorization. Only what is practiced is learned. Thus, to develop problem-solving ability one must practice the solution of problems. This may be obvious but frequently it is disregarded.

G. For attack, break down the main problems that have been selected into sub-problems. List the breakdown of sub-problems so that additional problems can be added without recopying.

H. While attacking the problem the learner should constantly keep a clear formulation of it and its sub-problems in mind. He should continually ask himself: For exactly what purposes am I trying to get these answers?

I. The desirability of organizing ideas as acquired into the learner's tentative framework or pattern of problems cannot be overemphasized.

J. The greater the amount of actual learner tryout of proposed solutions the more likely it is that problem-solution techniques will soundly develop.

K. A key test of the amount of actual problem-solving learning is suggested by the question: Are the methods of problem solution practiced in the learning situation actually remembered and *used* subsequently in similar problem situations?

III. *Attitude of the learner*

A. The learner should keep an open mind until much evidence is in or until a decision has to be made regarding which solution to a problem is probably best under particular circumstances.

B. The learner should constantly have an attitude of studying the efficiency of the methods he is using.

C. *How can this method be used in solving other similar problems should be a continual learner attitude in problem-solving.*

D. A key part of learning to solve problems is developing the ability to detect that which is in error or illogical. Each idea and suggestion acquired that gives promise of helping to solve the problem should be looked at critically and evaluated in terms of ideas and evidence already held by the learner. Such analysis should be done while the context in which the idea was presented is clearly in mind.

E. Possible solutions to problems should be given severe "mental tryouts." Critical comments giving possible strengths and weaknesses of suggestions recorded will indicate that the learner has forseen some of the probable advantages and disadvantages of the ideas studied.

IV. *Use of resources in problem solution*

    A. Digestion of ideas obtained from various resources and their organized assimilation into the ideas already held on the problems being studied are primary requisites for effective and economical learning.

    B. The mistakes made by a child are not corrected in a profitable sense by giving him "right" solutions. Rather, what the child needs is guidance in diagnosing his technique in problem solution and in building up stronger and more meaningful techniques.

    C. In a class where learners are acquiring abilities connected with problem solution, it is much more important for the teacher to suggest possible approaches and possible techniques than to try to give a pat answer ("the right answer," "the gospel") to every controversial issue that develops.

BIBLIOGRAPHY

1. Association for Supervision and Curriculum Development. *Toward Better Teaching.* Washington, D.C.: The Association, 1949.

2. BLITCH, L. W. "Achieving Certain Educational Objectives through Work with Eighth-Grade Pupils." *High School Journal,* 26:123-37; May 1943.
   Pictures a teacher's attempt to help learners develop initiative, indepedence, dependability, poise, cooperativeness, social sensitivity, and problem-solving ability.

3. BROGAN, PEGGY DUNN. "Building Self-Respect in Children." *Childhood Education,* 19:5-8; September 1942.
   Three excellent illustrations of democratic problem-solving with young children. Effect of method on personality well analyzed.

4. BROGAN, PEGGY DUNN. "Scientists in Kindergarten." *The Nation's Schools,* 34:20-22; December 1944.
   Shows how even five-year-olds can use the scientific method and profit from it.

5. COVELLO, LEONARD. "A Community-centered School and the Problem of Housing." *The Educational Forum,* 7:133-43; January 1943.
   Shows how a pressing local problem can be a vehicle for education.

6. CROW, L. D., AND CROW, A. *Educational Psychology.* New York: American Book Co., 1948. pp. 16, 74, 75, 234-35, 311-20, 334-36.
7. DIEDERICH, PAUL B. "How To Run Away from an Educational Problem." *Progressive Education,* 19:167-68; March 1942.
   How to act if we really do not want to meet educational problems. Facetious, but very stimulating.
8. ERICKSON, EDITH F. "The Study of a Problem." *The Clearing House,* 26:82-86; October 1951.
   Problem-oriented classroom activity is described. An attempt is made to adapt methods to purposes.
9. FAUNCE, R. C., AND BOSSING, N. L. *Developing the Core Curriculum.* New York: Prentice-Hall, 1951.
   The core curriculum is defined and its educational basis is discussed. Detailed help is given to teachers and administrators who wish to try out this approach.
10. HILGARD, E. R. *Theories of Learning.* New York: Appleton-Century-Crofts, 1948, pp. 16, 195-98, 300-20, 343.
11. MATHESON, E. "A Study of Problem-solving Behavior in Pre-School Children." *Child Development,* 2:242-62; May 1931.
    This early experiment with children shows that at a very early age children can solve problems in situations where an opportunity for looking over the total situation is given.
12. MAXWELL, P. A. "Solving Problems of Action." *Journal of Experimental Education,* 6:101-5; September 1937.
    Gives a somewhat hypothetical procedure for the solution of practical problems.
13. MILLER, HELEN RAND. "Unified Studies: An Escape from Edutional Feudalism." *The Clearing House,* 26:20-24; September 1951.
    Describes some changes in teachers and learners when attempts are made to move from autocratic to democratic teaching-learning situations.
14. National Society for the Study of Education. *The Psychology of Learning.* 41st Yearbook, Part II. Bloomington, Illinois: Public School Publishing Co., 1942, pp. 415-43.
    A psychologist analyzes the problem-solving process, ways of teaching problem-solving, and practical suggestions for developing ability in problem-solving.
15. NOAR, GERTRUDE. *Freedom To Live and Learn.* Philadelphia: Franklin Press, 1947.
    Describes day-to-day care activities of a junior-high group.

16. PARKER, S. C. *Types of Elementary Teaching and Learning.* Boston: Ginn and Co., 1923. pp. 263-332.
Suggests activities to improve problem-solving ability.

17. ROMINE, STEPHEN. "What One Teacher Can Do." *The Clearing House,* 26:111-13; October 1951.
Suggests some approaches a teacher can use even without a faculty renaissance.

18. ROSE, ELIZABETH. "An Experiment with Non-academic Boys and Girls in Senior English." *High School Journal,* 24:319-29; November 1941.
Gives areas of emphasis, problems attacked, and methods of work.

19. RYAN, W. CARSON, AND HOLTON, S. M. "'Here and Now' in Secondary Education." *High School Journal,* 35:16-21; October 1951.
Emphasizes the need for relating the educational program to the present.

20. SELBERG, EDITH M. "Developing Problem-solving Ability in Students." *Science Education,* 23:126-33; March 1939.
Gives suggestions one school has found valuable in developing and teaching the scientific approach in the solution of problems. Report differs from many in that learners help select problems, help plan methods, work on skills necessary to carry out plans, and participate in evaluation.

21. SKINNER, C. E., editor. *Educational Psychology.* Revised edition. New York: Prentice-Hall, Inc., 1945. pp. 213-31.

22. SMYTH, TEXIE. "Making the Social Studies an Adventure in Individualized Teaching." *The Social Studies,* 32:247-50; October 1941.
Pictures evolution from formalized, subject-matter social studies to a plan designed to help meet the needs of individual learners.

23. SNYGG, D., AND COMBS, A. W. *Individual Behavior.* New York: Harper and Bros., 1949.
A psychology book that emphasizes the learner's point of view.

24. Southern Association of Secondary Schools and Colleges (Staff Report by FRANK C. JENKINS, *et al.*) *Co-operative Study for the Improvement of Education.* Durham, N. C.: Duke University Press, 1946.
Largely a reprint of the February and August, 1946, issues of *The Southern Association Quarterly.* Gives excellent pic-

tures of the purposes, methodology, outcomes, and implications of the Southern Study.

25. UNZICKER, S. P. "What Kind of Activities in Science?" *Science Education*, 25:42-48; January 1941.
    Emphasizes need for teachers to be quite clear about goals. Gives excellent help in suggesting: (1) techniques connected with raising problems, and (2) techniques connected with solving problems.

26. WEBER, JULIA. *My Country School Diary*. New York: Harper and Bros., 1946.
    Gives detailed description of steps taken in improving a rural school program.

27. WILES, KIMBALL. "Are We Developing Skill in Purposeful Fact Collecting?" *Journal of Educational Research*, 38:617-23; April 1945.
    Presents data relative to problem-solving habits of certain students.

28. WOOD, G. C. "Techniques for Developing Problem-solving Abilities through Science Teaching." *Science Education*, 23:78-83; February 1939.
    Although teacher selects problems and apparently all learners work on the same ones, this article does suggest specific techniques found of value in developing some phases of problem-solving.

Part Three

DEVELOPING SERVICE ACTIVITIES WHICH
CONTRIBUTE TO EFFECTIVE TEACHING-
LEARNING ATTACK

7

BASIC CONSIDERATIONS RELATED TO

DEVELOPING EVALUATIVE ABILITIES

Some problems to consider

What is evaluation? How may we evaluate the adequacy of evaluation?

What is the relation between evaluation and self-evaluation?

How does evaluation differ from each of the following: diagnosis, testing, marking, and critical thinking?

What are the arguments for attempted teacher monopoly of evaluative processes?

What are the arguments for learner participation in systematic evaluation?

What difficulties may we expect to encounter if cooperative teacher-learner evaluation is attempted?

How old must learners be to start self-evaluation?

What is the teacher's role when learners participate in evaluation?

Introduction. The evaluative questions given in the initial part of Chapters 3, 5, and 6, and those appearing in the first of four subsequent chapters (Resources, Record-keeping, Intra-Group Relations, Reading) are primarily related in each instance to the evaluation of that phase or step of the learning process being discussed in the chapter in which the set of questions appears. The evaluative questions that follow are essentially for the purpose of directing attention to evaluating evaluation and to broader aspects of problem attack. These questions tend to be more inclusive of several learning steps or processes than are those in other chapters. Obviously, no student or teacher can give a favorable answer on *all* of these questions; they are to be used to discover weaknesses in our present practices.

Questions relating to diagnosis and improvement

1. Am I continually asking myself what it is best for me to do?
2. Do I do sufficient planning for future work?
3. Do I sufficiently often review my methods of work in a systematic fashion with objective and subjective tools? (Such tools as check lists, tests, questions such as those in this list, and inventories may be used.)
4. Can I pick out many of the specific mistakes or weaknesses and strengths that characterized my working on problems recently and so make a conscious effort to improve my abilities in problem identification, selection, and solution?
5. Can I identify the values I have got from selecting and working with problems recently so that I may capitalize on these assets in working with other problems?

Questions relating to attitudes, interest, and self-responsibility

6. Is my attitude toward my work such as to produce the most desirable results?
7. Is there evidence that my interest in my self-development is improving?
8. Am I getting definite satisfaction out of the methods of learning I am using because they are both challenging and pleasant to use?
9. Do I take a sufficiently critical attitude toward my own efficiency?
10. To what degree do I accept the responsibility for my own progress in learning and go ahead without being told almost every step to take?
11. Is my school participation primarily on a draft basis or because I see the importance to myself of actively participating in group and individual learning procedures?

Questions relating to time being given to work

12. Is the quality and quantity of my work consistent with the importance or urgency of the problems I face or am likely to face?
13. Is the time being spent on my work commensurate with the values being received?

14. Have my effort and time spent been sufficient to produce desirable results?

Questions relating to results of work

15. Through activity on the problem on which I am now working, am I gaining a much fuller appreciation of the significance of other problems?

16. Do the quality of my work and the values I am getting from my study measure up favorably with that which I am capable of doing?

17. Were some phases of my problem identification, selection, or solving overemphasized at the expense of equally important or more important parts?

Questions relating to systematic self-evaluative practice

18. Am I getting sufficient practice in evaluating my own activities?

19. Am I progressing in the ability to evaluate the end products of my work?

20. Do I constantly seek to improve my ability in self-evaluation?

EVALUATION AND SELF-EVALUATION

In order to understand the place and function of self-evaluation in effective learning, it is desirable, as basic background, to have a picture of various concepts of evaluation. In the following paragraphs an attempt is made to give this essential background and to summarize some key features of evaluation.

WHAT ARE SOME CONCEPTS OF EVALUATION?

There are several differing concepts of evaluation currently believed, knowingly or unknowingly, by different educators. Four points of view ranging from the simple and inaccurate to the psychologically sound are presented below.

Evaluation and marking. First, there is the erroneous point of view that "evaluation" and "marking" are practically synonymous. This concept is represented by the mimeographed instructions recently presented to students by a professor of education in one of our large American universities. We quote the gist of these instructions as they pertain to evaluation. "Evaluation in the course will be based upon three things. First and principally (about one-

EVALUATION LADDER

Learner assumes major responsibility for self-evaluation of his learning processes and seeks help and guidance from others as needed. Teachers periodically check to see that learner is seeking needed help.

Teacher and learner attempt to set up and use evaluation suitable to the individual learner's needs and purposes.

Teacher and learners attempt to evaluate amount of information memorized.

Teacher attempts to do all evaluating but is interested in checking on areas of learning, such as attitudes and processes, in addition to amount of information memorized. *Or* learner has minor share in determining method of evaluation although he does not actually evaluate himself.

Teacher attempts to do all evaluating and restricts himself almost entirely to measuring amount of information memorized.

Work is carried on without any systematic evaluation by anyone.

READ UP ⟶

Various levels of evaluation are shown on the ladder above. In the classes in which I work, on what level of the evaluation ladder do we operate? What can I do to move higher on the ladder?

half), the student's mark will be determined by the quality and inclusiveness of his reasoning as manifested in an analytical essay. Secondly, the student's mark in part (about one-fourth) will be based upon his performance on the short check-up tests or required reading. Thirdly, the remainder of the student's mark will be based upon his written reports of his visits to schools." Note the implication that not only are marking and evaluation practically synonymous but that all of the evaluation will be done by the professor. Neither position is defensible.

Evaluation as a look backward. A second point of view is one expressed by Cureton (3, p. 308) who believes both evaluation and guidance involve judgment with this distinction, "Evaluation looks backward and judges the past, while guidance looks forward and judges the future. Since the future, fundamentally, is always more important than the past, it follows that guidance is intrinsically a more important type of activity than evaluation." This latter position is certainly questionable, even if we accept Cureton's definitions, in view of the dependence of any intelligent guidance upon a consideration of past behavior and achievement.

Evaluation related to objectives. A third concept of evaluation that is similar to, but more specific than, the preceding one is expressed by Smallenburg (18, p. 550). "Evaluation may be defined as the process of collecting, analyzing and interpreting evidence indicating the extent to which the major objectives of an educational program are being achieved." This definition, while more adequate than preceding ones, places definite limitations upon the nature and possible purposes of evaluation.

Evaluation as a basis for action. A fourth type of definition of evaluation, which is more descriptive and adequate, is represented by the paragraphs below.

Troyer (20, p. 530) indicates, "Evaluation may be defined as the process of making those value judgments by which one determines his courses of action. Evaluation in teacher education is the process of making value judgments in the acceptance, rejection, and clarification of identified professional goals, working assumptions, appropriate experiences through which the goals may be realized, and in assessing and appraising of evidences of progress toward the goals. Self-evaluation is the same process with the student serving the dual role of evaluatee and evaluator."

Mead (11, p. 46) emphasizes one phase of Troyer's definition in these words, "The writer's point of view is that while evaluation may involve measurement it is not measurement. It is not data. *Rather, it is a search for values.* It is not a static process. The more useful the data, the more accurate and truthful the data, the more worthwhile may the evaluations be."

Orata (13, p. 650) well distinguishes between measurement and evaluation in this way, "The term measurement implies refined, exact, quantitative, and standardized assessments of things or states of being in an impersonal and objective manner. On the other hand, the terms 'appraisal' and 'evaluation' are usually associated with *values,* with *processes of growth and development* toward a goal that does not remain fixed. Measurement places emphasis upon accuracy and reliability; evaluation on validity and social utility. Measurement deals primarily with subject matter, attainment and information; evaluation, with experience and motivation. Theoretically, evaluation has the upper hand, but in practice its friends and critics praise and condemn it on the same grounds . . . evaluation has made its most lasting and significant contribution, first, in its insisting upon evidence for what are generally regarded as intangibles in education; second, in its theory that testing is an integral part of the educative process; third, in its exploration of new sources of evidence; and finally, in its suggesting a plan for comprehensive evaluation."

Conclusion on nature of evaluation. To summarize some points concerning the nature of evaluation in education we conclude:

Evaluation and marking are *not* synonymous. In fact, the basic purposes of evaluation are likely to be neglected if evaluation is used primarily for marking purposes.

In considering evaluation related to teaching and learning, we should be concerned with:

Specific identification of the goals toward which the evaluation is oriented. It should be recognized that these goals will be constantly shifting.

Both subjective and objective measurement of past and present status with respect to goals being considered. The description and measurement of methods and procedures that helped to promote or retard movement toward goals is of major significance.

The utilization of appropriate objective and subjective data by the evaluator in determining possible courses of action.

The planning of future activities in terms of best available evidence.

Evaluation is a continuous process which is constantly being carried on by both the learner and the teacher, whether either or both realize specifically what is happening.

In addition to considering what evaluation consists of and when it takes place, the student of evaluation is interested in the problem, "Who should evaluate in a teaching-learning situation?"

Evaluation in education is the process of making judgments concerning past and present situations, learnings, materials, or processes, so that one may more wisely direct his future activities.

WHAT IS THE RELATION OF EVALUATION TO DIAGNOSIS? TO TESTING? TO CRITICAL THINKING? TO MARKING?

Diagnosis and evaluation. A key part of the evaluating process in most situations can be labeled diagnosis. In diagnosis, the self-evaluator attempts to determine answers to such questions as: Where am I? What is my status in certain respects? How did I get into this position or status? What are my major strengths and weaknesses? What are the ways I can capitalize on my strengths and eliminate my weaknesses? To get the evaluating process under way, it is usually necessary or desirable for the learner to make a diagnosis of himself and the situation of which he is a part.

Testing and evaluation. Ordinarily, such diagnosis will involve some testing. The testing may be formal or informal, subjective or objective. Tests are essentially tools to aid in a diagnosis of such things as abilities, processes, and learnings. This is done so that the evaluator may have more accurate and perhaps more objective data upon which to reach the conclusions at which he arrives in evaluation.

Critical thinking and evaluation. The quality of thinking, particularly critical thinking, is largely dependent upon the accuracy of the evaluative judgments the individual makes. Indeed, in some respects, good evaluation and critical thinking are almost synonymous. It is for this reason that training in effective self-evaluation is one of the best ways of promoting critical thinking.

Marking and evaluation. Evaluation, testing, and critical thinking can, of course, go on without any *marking* at all. Marking certainly should be relatively unimportant as compared with evaluation. However, it should be pointed out that when marks are given they presumably are based on some kind of evaluation. It is unfortunate that the nature of the evaluation which sometimes results in marks is so unclearly understood by many teachers. Marking may be thought of as an appendage to evaluation that should assume decreasing importance as more valid motivators for learning are developed.[1]

WHAT ARE SOME OF THE POSSIBLE PURPOSES INVOLVED IN SELF-TESTING AND SELF-EVALUATION?

Need for purpose in evaluation. No type of measurement or evaluation is likely to be useful until the tester, whether he be learner or instructor, has one or more sound purposes in mind for doing the testing or evaluating. Unless the purposes involved in giving each and every test are carefully considered, the time, effort, and materials used are likely to be wasted; evaluation without clear-cut purposes is also likely to be relatively ineffective.

Some years ago when it was the vogue to give school-wide standard tests, a particular principal was very derisive of any school that did not give school-wide achievement tests. On investigation it was found that this principal did the following: (1) bought enough tests for all the pupils, (2) gave the tests to all the pupils, (3) had the tests scored by several clerical workers, and then (4) *took the tests home and filed them carefully away in the top of his garage.*

The next year the same process was repeated like a ritual. When this principal was asked why he did this he responded: "Why naturally every good school gives standard tests. I would feel that my school was not modern or up to date unless I gave these tests." Obviously, this principal's testing program was a wasteful process primarily because his purpose, to try to be modern just for the sake of being modern, was a poor one. This clearly indicated a lack of thoughtful planning.

The aim of the writer in giving the list below is to suggest for consideration some of the possible purposes of self-evaluation.

---

[1] For a more detailed discussion of marking the reader is referred to the section of Chapter 14 titled "Marking Uses and Dangers."

To improve interpersonal relations between teacher and students. If the learner feels that he is participating in the class evaluative processes, he is more likely to feel that it is his class and learning is largely his responsibility than he will if the teacher monopolizes evaluation.

For motivation purposes. If the learner has made an analysis of his strengths and weaknesses, he is more likely to do work with intrinsic motivation than if such a diagnosis has been made by the teacher alone.

To help the learner do a better job of evaluation when he leaves school. The learner is going to evaluate whether he is properly trained to do it or not, and if the teacher can help him improve in the process, the time taken to do this will certainly be well spent.

To help take care of individual differences. Unless the teacher helps the learners develop the process of self-evaluation, it will be impossible for him adequately to take care of individual differences since he will not have sufficient time to diagnose and evaluate each individual situation, ability, and purpose. If the learner is trained to do this himself, it will tend to help make it possible for the teacher to individualize work and still give more actual guidance to the learner himself.

To help uncover the real purposes and motivation the learner has. As long as the teacher tries to do all the evaluating, it is doubtful if he can get very far underneath the surface; however, with the learner cut in on the process, evaluation can become individual and uncover real motivation.

To serve as a basis for identifying important problems and selecting the most desirable of these for study. When this is a conscious purpose of self-evaluation, it can serve as a basis or guide for valuable future work.

To help provide the teacher with information necessary for the effective guidance of individual students.

To help clarify goals and to aid the learner and the teacher in seeing more concretely the directions in which such goals are moving.

To aid in identifying strengths so that they may be held to and improved.

To help identify weaknesses so that they may be eliminated or mitigated.

To help the individual to determine more wisely his present needs and probable future needs.

To promote the ability to decide wisely what resources to select for study.

To help the learner develop more functional and purposeful reading skills.

To help the learner improve in his record-keeping.

To help get a mark. As long as teachers are expected to give marks to students, one of the ways of getting these so that they will be accepted by the learner is to have the learner help in setting up the goals and aid in deciding the extent to which he has reached such goals.

To help the learner appreciate the importance of evaluation in problem identification, selection, and solution.

WHAT ARE THE ADVANTAGES AND DISADVANTAGES OF ATTEMPTED TEACHER MONOPOLY OF EVALUATION?

Most of the discussions of evaluation in professional educational literature are based on the assumption *that all evaluating in the classroom should or will be done by the teacher.* We wish to have the reader question that assumption by weighing some of the advantages and disadvantages of attempted teacher monopoly of evaluation.

Possible advantages of teacher monopoly of evaluation. One of the major advantages of attempted teacher monopoly of evaluation is that it appears to make evaluating a simpler process. As soon as the learner begins to participate in the evaluation processes, we have more factors involved and the role of the teacher is not as clear-cut.

Another major advantage of teacher monopoly of evaluation, from the standpoint of some teachers, is that it is less trouble for the teacher. As it has usually worked out, it means that the teacher needs to pay little or no attention to individual differences and gives the same test to all, regardless of individual purposes, goals, or abilities.

Combined with the advantages of simplicity and lack of trouble for the teacher we have teacher monopoly of evaluation in line with the philosophy that a learner should not do something till he can do it well. The argument is made that the teacher can evaluate better, therefore the teacher should do the evaluating.

This is a questionable assumption, for even if the teacher could evaluate better than the learner could for himself, improvement in learner evaluation could hardly be gained through the teacher's practicing evaluation. Thus, the question becomes, "Is our purpose to get the best evaluation possible or is our purpose to teach evaluation?"

Teacher monopoly of evaluation is also what many high-school and college students and teachers have been led to expect, and thus they are somewhat upset if a part of the responsibility for evaluation and some practice in self-evaluation devolves upon the learner. This expectation on the part of high-school, college, and even graduate students sometimes makes it more difficult to develop self-evaluation in older students than it is to develop self-evaluation in younger students regardless of the greater maturity of the former.

Disadvantages of teacher monopoly of evaluation. Perhaps the major disadvantage of attempted teacher monopoly of evaluation is that the learner is eliminated from practicing an important phase of the learning process, namely, evaluation, and when it *is* carried on by him it is likely to be without the guidance and direction of the teacher.

A second major disadvantage of teacher monopoly of evaluation, which tends to result from the first, is that we have shown in out-of-school situations a relatively poor quality of evaluation actually done by the products of our schools. This is largely because learners have been given little or no guided practice in self-evaluation while in school. If we anticipated that the learner would have a teacher at his elbow for the rest of his life, this particular disadvantage might not be so important. Obviously, this is impossible, and consequently we need to consider whether the learner will be able to evaluate properly after he leaves school.

Another disadvantage of teacher monopoly of evaluation is that it tends to put major emphasis upon the memorization of end products or solutions rather than upon the improvement of learning processes and techniques. It also tends to make the learning process, in the mind of the learner, a responsibility of the teacher rather than of himself. If a learner does not participate in a key part of the learning process, in this case self-evaluation, the process itself is likely to be considered the responsibility of someone else who is "running the show."

One of the most serious disadvantages of teacher monopoly of evaluation is that it makes the evaluation in terms of developing individual goals and purposes a virtually impossible task. It tends to result in relatively static goals which have been set up by someone besides the learner and frequently are not clearly understood by him.

There is a strong tendency for teacher monopoly of evaluation to place primary emphasis upon extrinsic motivation such as grades, rather than on diagnosis, in an attempt to see where and how the learner himself can make progress. When goals are thought of in terms of values, it is especially difficult, if not actually impossible, for the teacher to set them.

Who should evaluate. Woody (21), in criticizing the evaluative techniques of the Evaluation Committee of the Eight-Year Study, makes this significant comment (21, pp. 490-91): They "are applying the same techniques employed by those who developed the standardized achievement test. The only difference in the two groups of workers is in the type of values being measured. Instead of measuring mechanical processes of arithmetic or reading, as done by the pioneers of the testing movement, the test workers of the Progressive Education Association are attempting to measure cooperation, planning, social sensitivity, or interest. They are using the same statistical techniques, same formula for standardization and interpretation. *In most cases they are attempting to develop instruments of measurement in the abstract divorced from purpose or from the activities of group living.* [Italics mine.] They stress end points of achievement rather than the process of achieving. They emphasize isolated elements of behavior rather than an element in relation to the behavior of the organism as a whole." Woody implies that the learner should have some share in the evaluative processes that concern him and his learning.

This point is emphasized by Sims (17, p. 76): "To evaluate an educational endeavor is to pass judgment on its worthwhileness—the goodness or badness of the endeavor. This judgment is made, of necessity, by each person who examines the endeavor, and is made in terms of the values held to by the particular examiner. What one labels 'good' or 'bad' on an educational enterprise depends not alone on what is observed or counted but upon such factors as the observer's ideas of the nature of learning and of the purposes of education. Thus, two persons examining the same educational experiment may come to entirely different conclusions concerning its worthwhileness. *It is a misconception of the nature of the evaluative process to think that one person can evaluate for another. All that one can do for another is to present data from which evaluation may be done.*" [Italics mine.]

WHAT ARE THE POTENTIAL VALUES AND DIFFICULTIES IN ATTEMPTING TO HAVE BOTH THE TEACHER AND THE LEARNER PARTICIPATE IN EVALUATION?

If a learner is to acquire the ability to evaluate better than he now does, he must have guided practice in the process. Orata in a significant paper, "Evaluating Evaluation" (13, p. 649), supports the thesis that the development of learners' self-evaluation is desirable: "The pupils, themselves, can aid materially in making appraisal of their own progress if they are made to realize the significance of evaluation for them, and are encouraged to make appraisals, and if properly managed and motivated an evaluation program of the kind suggested can be organized without putting an undue burden upon the teachers or the pupils."

In a concluding paragraph, Orata (pp. 652-53) makes the following statement: "If evaluation is to be really progressive it should be, in fact, an integral part of the total educative process. A pencil-paper type of test made in advance by someone on the outside for someone else to use or to copy is inappropriate for a kind of program for which the newer schools stand. Evaluation, to be an integral part of the educative process, should grow out of or emerge from that process. No one, not even an expert, should evaluate the work of someone else, if the philosophy of progressive education is accepted as a point of orientation. In fact, *the teacher should not evaluate the work of the pupils; they should do the evaluating themselves. If not, why emphasize the objective of self-direction, which obviously includes the process of evaluation of one's performance in the light of the goal that has been self-determined? The evaluation function of the teacher is to provide situations whereby the pupils are led to evaluate their own procedures in the light of the criteria that they, themselves, had formulated.* [Italics mine.] In like manner, the function of an expert in evaluation, if there be one, is not to make tests for teachers to use or to copy, but to guide them in integrating their evaluation function with their teaching procedures."

Some more specific advantages of dealing the pupil in on evaluation are the following:

The work is likely to become more purposeful.

More opportunities are likely to present themselves for developing individual initiative and responsibility.

Only through practicing self-evaluation can self-evaluation be learned. We learn only what we practice.

The teacher is likely to be able to individualize instruction if such processes as self-evaluation are continually improved. The learner is then able to do a major part of his own diagnosis with a minimum of guidance, and so free the teacher for guiding learners in identifying, in selecting, and in solving their individual problems.

Troyer (20, p. 535) appropriately raises the following questions regarding possible hazards of self-evaluation:

"Does self-evaluation provide an undue temptation toward apple-polishing, cheating, and otherwise beating the game? . . ."

"Is there a grave danger that through self-evaluation the student may become too introspective? . . ."

"Will it be too much to hope that he will continue this process of self-evaluation after he has found a job, especially if he has guidance?"

To these questions may be added this: Will the learner be apt to be too upset by being partially put on his own in the matter of evaluation?

HOW OLD MUST LEARNERS BE TO START SELF-EVALUATION?

Reasoning starts early. Can high-school students learn to have a major share in evaluation? How about the elementary-school child? Is he too immature to be encouraged to develop self-evaluative abilities? McConnell, outstanding educational psychologist, says (6, p. 448):

"In fact, if allowances are made for differences in knowledge, experience, and language development, it appears that children and adults reason in essentially the same fashion. The errors which young subjects make are not different in kind from those which adults exhibit when they meet very unfamiliar situations."

"The evidence, however, suggests that children—even pre-school children—can reason. Investigations have shown that children as young as three years can discover a principle and apply it to new situations."

Self-evaluation is done by very young children. Since self-evaluation may be considered a key part of reasoning ability, there seems to be evidence that most preschool children are capable of certain types of self-evaluation. The point can be illustrated from actual occurrences. The first example comes from the N.E.A.'s Eleventh Yearbook of the Department of Supervisors and Directors of Instruction (4, p. 194). It describes a first-grade group discussion in their first day of school.

FIRST GRADE GROUP. FIRST DAY OF SCHOOL

TEACHER: "How do you like our pretty room?

CHILDREN: "This is a good room." "It is as pretty as the kindergarten was."

TEACHER: "Do you see anything in it in which you are especially interested?"

CHILDREN: "We like the clay table." "I like the hammers and saws." "Oh! I like to paint pictures."

TEACHER: "We have many interesting things in our room now, and we will probably have more later. Do you think we should make plans for caring for the different things so that we can always find them when we want them?"

CYNTHIA: "We can all take care of them."

JIMMY: "I can take care of this room, Mrs. Houston. I can take care of it all by myself."

TEACHER: "Shall we ask Jimmy to do all the work of caring for this room?"

NORMA: "We could take turns; he could do it one day and someone else could do it the next."

TEACHER: "Maybe we could think of a way so that each of us could do something to help, every day. Does that seem like a good plan?"

BERYL: "I think that is a very good plan. I could sweep the floor. Sometimes I sweep the floor with my little broom at home."

TEACHER: "Let us think of everything that will need care in the room. I will write them on the blackboard as you tell me."

The following list was developed with the help of the children and with pertinent suggestions to guide their thinking injected by the teacher:

The clay table
The work bench
The supplies, scissors, paste, etc.
The easel and paints (four children)
The library
The flowers
The science table
The sewing table
The game table

The weather news
The milk money
The dusting
The lockers
The floor
The chalk
The erasers
The cloakroom
The pan and sponge
The windows

The preparation of the milk luncheon:

Shaking and opening the bottles (two children)
Setting the places (two children)
Distributing the straws (two children)
Serving the crackers (two children)
Removing the crumbs and bottles (two children)

TEACHER: "Now we know what needs to be done. How shall we decide who will take care of all these things?"

RICHARD: "You could choose us."

TEACHER: "All right. I shall choose one person and then that person can choose another until we have each received a room duty. Who would like to care for the clay table? (Many voices say "I.") I will choose Mary Kay, and I shall write her name by the clay table so we can remember. Now, Mary Kay, you choose someone to care for the work bench."

MARY KAY: "I choose Bernard."

In this way each child in the class was chosen for a position of importance in the group. No point was made of the relative suitability or the efficiency of the child chosen. Some who at this stage gave little promise of ability proved to be very faithful and rose to the role expected of them by the group. The teacher also assumed a task, that of washing the slate blackboard, for she felt that she, too, should be a member of the cooperating group. Having arrived at the "division of labor" necessary for practical cooperation, the teacher then led the children to plan for a time in the day when they could work together, each doing his part in the routine care of the room.

Six-year-olds evaluate rest period. A second illustration of learner participation in evaluation in a democratically operated classroom is described by Brogan (2, pp. 5-6).

"A teacher and her thirty six-year-olds were discussing their plans for the day. Several suggestions were written on the board and the job seemed about complete when a small hand waved frantically in the air. 'Miss Brown, you know, I been thinking about something. It's not very good to always have rest time because that old floor is so hard it doesn't feel like resting.' A new thought. Something even Miss Brown hadn't thought of. All the schools she had ever visited had children rest on rugs on the floor, but she herself had never tried to see if it were restful or not.

"Other children began expressing their thoughts on the subject. Maybe they shouldn't have rest time at all. They never felt tired. But that would never do because doctors who have studied about boys and girls knew that they needed to rest and Miss Brown would be a bad teacher if she let them make plans like that. Maybe they ought to just sit on chairs to rest—or take turns using the eight cots in the rest room—or put three chairs together to make a bed for everyone.

"Miss Brown thought they might try two or three different ways and see which one worked best. Sitting on chairs proved to be very unsatisfactory, and most children were back on the floor before the rest period was over. Taking turns on the cots didn't work either, because all children needed the rest and it took too long to use them in shifts. There were not enough chairs to put three together to make temporary beds, and anyway they were as hard as the floor. Finally, it was Janet who suggested, 'Maybe we could all do different things at rest time just so we are quiet and really rest,' and Bobby added, 'Yes, my favorite way to rest at home is to look at a book.' So a list of legitimate rest time activities was made, and a satisfactory solution to the problem was reached. There was a half-hour rest time declared each morning when children were free to lie on rugs and sleep or to look at books, to listen to music, or to use the rest room cots."

Miss Brogan's analysis of the incident just described is also significant: "... the very fact that the children and teacher were sitting down together to discuss daily plans is significant. In order to maintain their self-respect, children must have the feeling that the daily living of the group depends upon worthwhile contributions from all members of the group.

"Secondly, and even more important is the fact that the teacher herself had an unanswered question about group procedure. She admitted frankly to herself and to the children that there are situations where children's opinions and help are really needed. Many teachers feel that it is an admission of inadequacy ever to be in a situation where they do not know the *one right* way to do the things, and in many schools it would be very unwise for a teacher to make such an admission. But obviously this teacher works under conditions which help her maintain self-respect. She feels free to call upon administrators for help and to make suggestions for change. Therefore, she sees the need for children to have this same feeling, and is able to deal with this kind of situation—in fact, even to arrange events so that such situations are certain to occur.

"Probably the most significant of all was the way in which the entire group responded to the situation. The little girl had been *thinking about* their group procedure and the rest of the group, including the teacher, sat down to help think about the problem. Children who are allowed to maintain their self-respect—to know the feeling of being important to someone or some group—are thinking children because there is some reason for them to think. They do not follow directions blindly because of fear of punishment nor do they accept any pattern of procedure suggested merely to win a false kind of approval. They know that the happiness of the group depends largely upon their thinking and resulting action. Suggestions are not made in a selfish or defiant way, because they did not have the feeling that they were fighting against some plan the teacher was trying to make them adopt. It was an important job to these children, and individual wants were amended and woven together to arrive at the one procedure which was considered best for the group."

Improvement in thinking can be taught to children. From a psychological standpoint, the significance cannot be overemphasized of actually helping the children think and then with them using the results of their thinking. Children may not be able to verbalize it, but they quickly sense whether they are being given a real chance to participate in the planning of classroom activities or whether the teacher is just working them around to do something that was cut and dried to begin with.

Self-evaluation of many types can be developed at a very early age. It is unfortunate that many of our schools actually put a damper on self-evaluation by conditioning children to expect only teacher evaluation in school.

WILL LEARNER SELF-EVALUATION ELIMINATE THE NEED FOR TEACHER EVALUATION?

Developing learner self-evaluation should not decrease the amount of evaluating done by the teacher. Rather, the kind and purpose of evaluation done by the teacher will change.

Instead of the teacher's being almost exclusively concerned with attempts to do all the evaluating for the learners, the teacher's evaluative efforts will be partially directed toward analyzing and improving his own activities. In other words, the teacher will do more and more evaluating of his own behavior and spend relatively less time trying to evaluate for others.

One picture of the teacher's role in situations where self-evaluation is being developed is given by Smyth (19, pp. 248-49):

The teacher must develop new planning techniques "built up from recognized needs of not only the skills, habits and understandings of each pupil, but much more than heretofore the teacher must know a great deal about each member of the class."

Needed knowledge of the learner "demands acquaintance with all available records, possibly questionnaires and many personal contacts with the individual and anyone who may be able to contribute desired information concerning him." This requires "a new type of recording to indicate pupil progress as well as useful information about him."

"Pupil analysis and pupil guidance become almost consuming activities of a teacher's class time and preparation time."

"New techniques for class planning must necessarily include long-range and daily planning. The former will contain briefs of the group's background of experiences in the social studies: charts of problems studied; lists of possible problems, charts of pupils' choices, time estimates, and progress made; goals to be attained in skills, habits and responsibility; devices for improving pupil reporting and for unifying the work of the class. Daily planning involves a multiplicity of details such as providing needed help for individuals, materials, library passes, and in interpreting materials, conferences for checking progress, advice regarding organization, devices for encouraging or admonishing pupils as the need arises. Time must be provided for planning with pupils various types of classroom activities involving individuals, small groups or the class as a whole. Schedules for work periods, reporting periods and periods for discussions of classroom problems must be anticipated and provided for in daily plans."

"New methods for evaluating the whole program, its execution, and pupil reaction must be studied."

Teachers evaluate themselves. In a program that is meeting individual needs, the teacher emphasizes self-evaluation and helps the learners develop abilities concerned with evaluating their activities. One illustration of what happened when a group of teachers and administrators decided to investigate their own reading abilities and their own use of these abilities in identifying and solving professional problems has been described by Simpson (16). For a consideration of the results of the study the reader is referred to the chapter on reading improvement. Other aspects of learner and teacher self-evaluation are discussed in the following chapter.

Evaluative principles. The operating principles suggested in this chapter are combined with those derived from the discussion in the next chapter and will be found at the end of the next chapter.[2]

BIBLIOGRAPHY

1. ARSENIAN, SETH. "Own Estimate and Objective Measurement." *Journal of Educational Psychology,* 33:291-302; April 1942.
   Pictures need for training in self-evaluations and suggests changed emphasis in guidance and teaching.
2. BROGAN, PEGGY DUNN. "Building Self-respect in Children." *Childhood Education,* 19:5-8; September 1942.
   Three excellent illustrations of democratic problem-solving with young children. Effect of method on personality well analyzed.
3. CURETON, E. E. "Evaluation or Guidance." *Journal of Experimental Education,* 8:308-40; March 1940.
4. Department of Supervisors and Directors of Instruction. *Cooperation Principles and Practices.* Washington, D.C.: The Department, National Education Association, 1939.
5. ENGEL, F. E. "Democracy Enters the Music Class." *High School Journal,* 22:290-92; November 1939.

[2] The writer has intentionally avoided including the material typically included in books on tests and measurements. For such material the reader is referred to: H. H. Remmers and N. L. Gage, *Educational Measurement and Evaluation* (New York: Harper and Bros., 1943); H. A. Greene and others, *Measurement and Evaluation in the Secondary School* (New York: Longmans, Green, 1943); W. J. Micheels and M. Ray Karnes, *Measuring Educational Achievement* (New York: McGraw-Hill Book Co., 1950).

Describes guidance techniques and evaluative methods in trying to meet pupil needs.

6. GATES, A. I., *et al. Educational Psychology.* New York: Macmillan Co., 1948.

7. GREENE, MARY. "Attempts To Meet the English Needs of College Preparatory Seniors in Waynesboro High School." *The Southern Association Quarterly,* 7:453-60; November 1943.
   Emphasizes determining needs, using resources, and evaluation.

8. JENKINS, FRANK C. "The Southern Association Study." *The North Central Association Quarterly,* 16:389-95; April 1942.
   Briefly depicts changes in instructional procedures; evaluation procedures; administrative procedures; relationships among pupils, teachers, and parents; and shows contributions to betterment of committees as a result of the study.

9. JENKINS, FRANK C., AND STAFF. *The Southern Association Study: A Report of the Work with the Thirty-three Co-operating Secondary Schools.* 1938-1941. Nashville, Tennessee: University of Tennessee, Commission on Curriculum Problems and Research, 1941.
   Discusses origin, nature, and work of the Study. Describes significant aspects of work with schools consciously trying to better the education of youth. Very useful for those who wish to improve their ways of working with teachers.

10. JONES, CARLESS. "Does This Apply to You?" *The Clearing House,* 13:299-302; January 1939.
    Emphasizes need for self-evaluation on the part of the learner and teacher.

11. MEAD, A. R. "An Oversight in Current Education Practices." *Journal of Educational Research,* 35:43-46; September 1941.

12. MULHOLLAND, V. M. "Growth and Progress in Greenville High School, North Carolina." *The Southern Association Quarterly,* 3:540-47; November 1939.
    Shows students, teachers, and administrators working together, and attempts evaluation of activities.

13. ORATA, PEDRO T. "Evaluating Evaluation." *Journal of Educational Research,* 33:641-61; May 1940.
    Discusses with critical comment the shift in emphasis from measurement to evaluation. Gives comprehensive bibliography.

14. ORR, M. L. "How Do the Graduates of the Montevallo High School Experimental Program Fare in Their Academic Work at

Alabama College?" *The Southern Association Quarterly*, 9:110-18; February 1945.

Brief picture of experimental work with some evaluation of results.

15. Progressive Education Association (Informal Committee on Evaluation of Newer Practices in Education). *New Methods vs. Old in American Education*. New York: Teachers College, Columbia University, 1941.

Pictures newer experimental methods and gives objective and subjective evidence on their values. Useful bibliography.

16. SIMPSON, RAY H. "Reading Disabilities among Teachers and Administrators." *The Clearing House*, 17:11-13; September 1942. Reprinted in *A Secondary Anthology of the Clearing House*, 19:85-88; October 1944.

Shows present reading skills and use of reading to help solve professional problems. Also suggests needed changes.

17. SIMS, V. M. "Evaluation in the Southern Association Study." *School and Society*, 57:76-79; January 16, 1943.

Analyzes purposes of study and staff concept of evaluation, gives criticism of most testing evaluation to date, and emphasizes the developmental nature of the study which implies evaluation would not be "blueprinted" from the beginning.

18. SMALLENBERG, H. "Developing a Program for Evaluation of Pupil Growth in the Burbank Schools." *Journal of Educational Administration and Supervision*, 28:550-53; October 1942.

19. SMYTH, TEXIE. "Making the Social Studies an Adventure in Individualized Teaching." *The Social Studies*, 32:247-50; October 1941.

Pictures evolution from formalized, subject-matter social studies to a plan designed to help meet the needs of individual learners.

20. TROYER, MAURICE E. "Self-Evaluation in Teacher Education." *Journal of Educational Research*, 35:528-43; March 1942.

Excellent analysis of possibilities in developing self-evaluation in teacher education. Has significant implications for all learning.

21. WOODY, C. "Nature of Evaluation." *Journal of Educational Research*, 35:481-91; March 1942.

22. WRIGHTSTONE, J. W. *Appraisal of Experimental High-School Practices*. New York: Bureau of Publications, Teachers College, Columbia University. 1936.

Summarizes some progress in construction and application of new measures to the curriculum experiments in several progressive high schools. Results of testing matched experimental and conventional secondary schools are shown.

23. WRIGHTSTONE, J. W. *Appraisal of Newer Practices in Selected Public Schools.* New York: Bureau of Publications, Teachers College, Columbia University, 1935.

Attempts to give some objective and subjective appraisal based on experimental evidence of results obtained in "newer type schools."

8

DEVELOPING SELF-EVALUATION

Some problems to consider

How may the teacher go about encouraging self-evaluation by the learner?

What diagnostic tools may be used in developing self-evaluation?

Can or should learners construct and use their own self-evaluative resources?

What principles may we use to help us in developing functional, democratic evaluation?

WHAT SUGGESTIONS MAY BE MADE FOR ENCOURAGING SELF-EVALUATION BY THE LEARNER? [1]

The primary purpose of the suggestions given in the paragraphs under this heading is to present some picture of possible ways of developing an interest and facility in self-evaluation. Training in self-evaluation will take much time and should involve much guidance. Significant overnight results should not be expected. Some of the suggestions below are more applicable for older learners and others for those who are younger. For convenience, the suggestions have been grouped under nine main headings.

I. *Suggestions involving the use of tests made by others*

Encourage the learner to send for and to study test catalogues. [2]

---

[1] The student is encouraged to re-examine the self-evaluative questions near the beginning of Chapter 7.

[2] This is the type of suggestion that may be of most use to students who are teachers or prospective teachers. However, some of the more mature high-school students may also profit from use of this type of suggestion.

Study different types of printed tests and determine their possible uses.

Help the learner develop criteria for the selection of particular tools for his special purposes.

Study tests and evaluative aids which other learners have made and used.

Sometimes it may prove desirable to write to other schools and interview learners from or in other classes.

Have the learner help select, take, score, and analyze the available tests which relate to his purposes. The learner should analyze the results in terms of his own needs, interests, and abilities. Status and progress in skills can also be determined in this fashion.

Under some circumstances it may be desirable to have students compare their individual scores and group norms with published norms of standardized tests.

Use most tests early rather than late in the year so that the results can be utilized for goal-setting and planning. If tests are given at the end of the year, they frequently have little or no effect on the actual educational progress of the learners concerned.

II. *Suggestions involving the use of the learners' own records*

Have the learner use the diary type of daily evaluation of what has been done each day. This may be extended gradually into long-range planning for future activities.

Keep and use comprehensive records for evaluation of own and others' work.

Have the learner list what he has done during the week and then help him evaluate the probable worth of each part of it.

Ask each learner periodically to take his personal educational record (see Chapter 9 on Record-keeping), and list his major strengths and weaknesses in learning, as he sees them. He should be encouraged to follow this list up by writing, under each of the weaknesses, the steps he thinks he can take to eliminate it. After the learner has done this, it may be used as a basis for discussion of his plans with the teacher. The list of strengths and weaknesses and the steps to be taken for improvement themselves become a part of his personal educational record.

Ask each group of learners to do for the group procedures the same type of thing that was suggested for the individual in the preceding paragraph.

Have each learner regularly turn in for study and suggestions by the teacher his record of work accomplished and in progress, together with his plans for future work. In examining these the teacher notes desirable and questionable features and writes some comment designed to help the learner improve his procedure. It is recommended that these and other interpersonal communications be made a part of the record for future use.

Systematically encourage the learner to write down and follow up suggestions he and others have made for his own improvement. Diagnosis, a phase of evaluation, is not likely to be very valuable unless the ideas gleaned from it are put to use and result in the improvement of learning.

III. *Suggestions involving the use of assignments*

Evaluate which of two or more assignments would probably be better for him (the learner) giving the advantages and disadvantages of each.

Seek the active cooperation of students in the study of many problems growing out of working together. Such cooperation, which will tend to encourage learner evaluation, may be done through planning committees, grading committees, meetings of representatives to plan improvements, meetings on types of assignments, and meetings on the use of records. Questions should frequently be raised concerning the methods of teaching and learning being used. Also encourage the learner to consider whether what he is doing could better be done at some other time or place. There should be many opportunities for the learner to weigh the values of various types of activities.

Consider using the following type of examination (adapted from Rose).

1. Meet in the library.
2. Give each child a separate problem.

3. Tell each child to make a bibliography of all material pertaining to his subject in the library; at least the card catalogue, *The Readers' Guide,* and the vertical file, should be used.
4. Have each learner outline one article, properly noting its source.
5. Have the pupil, without the original article, summarize its content from his own outline.
6. Ask the pupil to list the ways he might obtain information outside the library. De-emphasize memory assignments.

Have each learner rank 1, 2, 3, 4, the paper record or project of four of his classmates. Ranking should be done on the basis of criteria set up by the group. His own paper, record, or project may also be included in the ranking.

IV. *Suggestions involving the use of letter-writing and/or direct contact*

Write to other schools requesting samples of types of tests, and/or inventories, and/or report cards that are somewhat unusual.

Study approaches other people have used in gaining an understanding of measurement and evaluation.

Study measurement and evaluative techniques used by storekeepers, farmers, bus companies, advertising agencies, etc.

V. *Suggestions involving the use of reports to parents*

Write evaluations of the worth of what has been done to take home to parents. This should, of course, be preceded by a *description* of what has been done.

Keep a record of parents' comments, complaints, or criticisms, of the school or its work and study these as a basis for improvement.

VI. *Suggestions involving promotion*

Have the learner help the teacher and others decide whether he should stay with the same teacher or subject another year or go on with the group he is in. This might be approached by listing with him the possible advantages and possible disadvantages of change.

Suggest that each student draw up a statement of the bases that would be adequate for grading himself. The teacher could add or subtract from the initial lists drawn up by the learners.

VII. *Suggestions involving problem children*

Have each behavior problem child write down on paper his difficulties, problems, sources of dissatisfaction, etc., and evaluate these as to their effect on him. Aid him in writing plans for improvement.

Encourage the learner through conference or interview to give the parts of his situation that he feels are causing him difficulty and attempt to get him to offer possible suggestions for improving or changing these causes.

VIII. *Suggestions involving the next group or class*

At the end of the year have the learners check back over their work of the year and evaluate it in terms of the standards set up; then have them make recommendations for similar classes in the future. The same thing might be done at midyear.

Have each pupil at the end of the year write a letter to a next-year pupil suggesting possible approaches to the work so that he will get the most out of it. These suggestions may be in the form of letters or notes. Sometimes it is best to have them entirely anonymous.

IX. *Questions relating to school policy on evaluation*

Some schools have found it desirable to hold a series of conferences on the objectives, program of studies, and evaluation policies of those schools. In these conferences, teachers, parents, and students participate. At a conference in Shaker Heights, Ohio, reported in *Learning the Ways of Democracy* (5, p. 414), we find the following questions were discussed:

"1. To what an extent should students be given an opportunity to evaluate their own progress? What use should be made of such evaluation?

2. In what ways can the school use more effectively the evaluation of students by parents?
3. Should the evaluation program include published tests which are widely used by the school?
4. Should a curriculum which has been planned to meet student needs in Shaker Heights be modified to enable students to make better scores on tests published for nation-wide use?
5. What use should be made of test results? Should they be given to parents? To students?

   a) Intelligence tests.
   b) Tests dealing with habits of thinking, study skills, interests, appreciations and attitudes.
   c) Tests of academic achievement."

Encourage each learner and each teacher to gain a clear understanding of the purposes and reasons for self-evaluation.

TOOLS FOR DEVELOPING SELF-EVALUATION

There is an almost unlimited number of tests, check lists, and questionnaires which can be developed and used in encouraging self-evaluation. Some of these are given with illustrative answers later in this chapter. Here we will call attention to three different types, two for students and one for the teacher as a learner.

Individual class discussion analysis. Self-appraisal by individual students is more common than group appraisal. In the Hamtramck, Michigan, public schools a questionnaire was used for the purpose of guiding both students' self-analysis and teaching. It dealt with classroom discussions and is typical of a number of other direct approaches to the evaluation and development of classroom procedures. The questionnaire [3] used is as follows:

"This questionnaire has been made for the purpose of finding out why more students do not take part in class discussion. If we are able to find out the reasons, we may be better able to help students develop the ability to express themselves in the presence of others. The survey will be useless IF YOU DO NOT ANSWER TRUTH-FULLY.

[3] Educational Policies Commission of N. E. A., *Learning the Ways of Democracy* (Washington, D. C.: National Education Association, 1940), p. 415.

I. Check one word only.

How often do you take part in class discussion?

a. Always ....   c. Seldom ....
b. Frequently ....   d. Never ....

II. If you seldom or never take part in class discussion, check the reason or reasons for not doing so.

1. I am not sufficiently prepared.
2. I am afraid to talk in front of any large group of people.
3. I am afraid the teacher will criticize me.
4. I am afraid the class will criticize or laugh at me.
5. I am not interested enough in the class to bother taking part.
6. I think it is foolish to take part in discussion when I can pass the course without doing so.
7. I am too lazy.
8. The class is so disorderly and noisy that it is useless to try to take part in a discussion.

Add any other reasons that are not listed above.

III. If you take part in discussion frequently, check the following reasons for doing so.

1. I take part in discussion so that I will get a better mark.
2. I take part in discussion because I like to express my ideas.
3. I take part in discussion because I believe it helps others to hear my ideas.
4. I take part in discussion because I believe that everyone has something worth while to contribute and that if I do my share others will do theirs.

Add any other reasons.

IV. Do you feel that small group discussions help you to understand the problems? Yes...... No......
Whom would you rather have conduct the discussion?
Teacher...... Chairman......"

Need for teacher self-evaluation. For effective teaching of evaluation and particularly self-evaluation it is important that the teacher practice self-evaluation himself. Such practice not only helps the teacher to improve himself but also sets an excellent example for students. Experience with such self-evaluation will also give the teacher a keener appreciation of the problems the learner faces in acquiring self-evaluative abilities.

Although spring is the traditional time for a final evaluation of the learners' work, summer or early fall is usually a good time for the alert teacher to look back over his work of the previous year and see in retrospect where materials, attitudes, and procedures have been inadequate, so that planning for the new year's work can go on intelligently and effectively.

Simpson (17, pp. 47-48) in an article titled, "Teachers, Here Is Your Final," has given one set of questions which are illustrative of a quiz each teacher may administer to himself. Excerpts from that article are given below.

"Provide for individual differences in academic ability. During the last school year did you:

1. Systematically diagnose and record for each child his chief strengths and weaknesses? Yes...... No......
2. Have your pupils help plan their assignments? Yes...... No......
3. Have the pupils help in the construction, administration and scoring of at least some of their tests? Yes...... No......
4. Have as much concern about the very rapid learner as about the very slow learner? Yes...... No......
5. Enlist the aid of the learners in the selection of appropriate materials for their needs? Yes...... No......
6. Attempt any systematic check on the success of your teaching in previous years as reflected in the activities of those whom you have taught? Yes...... No......
7. Help provide reading materials for daily use which had a spread in difficulty of at least five grades? Yes...... No......
8. Have different standards of promotion for each youngster? Yes...... No......
9. Objectively compare the achievement of each youngster with what he should be achieving? Yes...... No......
10. Give youngsters a major share in planning their work and deciding when it should be done? Yes...... No......
11. Try out some major change in your teaching materials or methods? Yes...... No......

"Professional development. During the last school year did you:

12. Read at least four professional magazines in the average month? Yes...... No......
13. Study at least four professional books? Yes...... No......
14. Become familiar with at least one new standard test? Yes...... No......
15. Attend at least one professional convention? Yes...... No......
16. Participate actively in your teachers' meetings? Yes...... No......
17. Write at least one professional article? Yes...... No......

"Aid youngsters in developing socially. During the last year did you:

18. Help youngsters make plans for out-of-school activities? Yes...... No......
19. Have a sufficient number of small clubs at your school? Yes...... No......
20. Have a committee or group of pupils help select, provide and care for materials in your room? Yes...... No......
21. Have youngsters help make at least 80% of their assignments? Yes...... No......
22. Encourage the youngsters to make rules for activity and conduct in the classroom? Yes...... No......
23. Have a group of youngsters responsible for halls, cloakrooms, toilets? Yes...... No......
24. Encourage pupils to study and work out many of their problems together? Yes...... No......
25. Permit pupils to have partial charge of the main library (if any) or the classroom library? Yes...... No......
26. Have pupils help decide when the classwork should be done? Yes...... No......
27. Consciously mark a pupil on the amount of social progress he made during the year? Yes...... No......
28. Discuss more than once with pupils the problem of how to work most effectively with others in a committee? Yes...... No......
29. Encourage pupils to bring magazines, newspapers, or other materials to school for the use of other pupils? Yes...... No......

30. Give any test designed to measure social development? Yes...... No......
31. Aid children in intelligently carrying on a conversation in the subject which you teach? Yes......No......
32. Leave the classroom for fifteen minutes or longer and find the pupils capable of carrying on profitably without you? Yes...... No......
33. *Jointly* decide, with the pupils and the school administrators, upon what materials (textbooks, pamphlets) available money shall be spent? Yes...... No......"

The intelligent teacher diagnoses his weaknesses and then systematically sets about to eliminate them. The questions given above should suggest some ways in which a teacher can improve his work during the school year. *Continuous* diagnosis and systematic attempts at improvement are, of course, necessary for best results.

Administrators need to evaluate themselves. Administrators may make a check on their own activities by using the set of questions given under the title, "Are Your Teachers Learning?" (14, pp. 16-19).

SUGGESTIONS INVOLVING CONSTRUCTION AND USE OF OWN SELF-EVALUATIVE RESOURCES

The purpose of the following list is to suggest possible approaches to the teacher and learners who are interested in encouraging self-evaluation through guided learner construction and use of evaluative tools. The suggestions have been grouped under four headings: I. Soundness of goals, problem identification, objectives, and problem selection; II. Planning; III. Methods of work after planning; and IV. Use of resources, including printed materials.

I. *Soundness of goals, objectives, problem identification, and problem selection*

Study possible goals and objectives and then set up specific ones for self. Tests should be built around individual purposes and problems of importance.

With guidance make up own tests after goals and objectives have been set up. Tests should be for learning purposes rather than for marking purposes.

Have each learner help make out a list of qualities and abilities upon which he thinks he should be marked. Have the class then together do the same thing for the group as a whole. Since marks in many schools set the stage for what is to be emphasized by the learner, this may focus attention on worthwhile objectives.

Have some or all pupils share in the formulation of a tentative report card after careful consideration of what it should include and why.

Help the learners make specific tests which they feel will measure such specific and important phases of functional learning as: ability to get appropriate materials to solve a problem, using resources wisely, organization of ideas, method by which conclusions are reached, etc.

Encourage the learners to set up a list of questions they will ask the school's graduates regarding what they did do in school and what they now feel they should have done.

Help the pupils to get evaluations from prospective employers on the needs and characteristics of employees.

Help the pupils analyze the possible purposes and uses of tests. What things of importance can be measured? The great variety of things that can be measured should be emphasized. For example, high-school girls can make out individual appearance and personality rating charts, indicate present status and goals for the year, and make a second rating at the end of the year. Self-rating can be checked against rating by others.

Have the learner describe a short story or recreational book with the purpose of interesting other pupils in it. Help him measure success in terms of the number who heard the report who actually read the book or story as a result of being stimulated by selling talk, blackboard description, poster, or cartoon.

Have the learners set up standards for evaluation of oral reports given in class.

In the fall have the learners study the carry-over value of the preceding winter's experiences in terms of what was actually done during the summer—i.e., What was read? What kinds of activities and thinking carried on in the preceding winter were continued and actually used? How were activities tied up to schoolwork?

Raise this question with the students: "Should we try to cover the course of study or do what seems to be best to us if the two conflict?"

Help the pupils set up questions we should raise in selecting a problem for study.

Have each pupil evaluate himself in terms of the level of motivation upon which he operates.

Study the approaches other learners have used in determining soundness of goals, objectives, and problems selected.

Study the probable situations each pupil is likely to be in on some future occasion.

II. *Planning*

Have a short time each day to check on and evaluate progress. Have a day every two weeks or oftener for intensive evaluations. How could work have been bettered and how shall we better it in the future?

Plan the next day's or the next week's work *with* the learners.

Where there is conflict or disagreement on what procedure should be followed, encourage the learners to list the advantages and disadvantages of each method or plan.

III. *Methods of work after planning*

Study the methods of work that others have used with profit.

Encourage the learner to measure, evaluate, and feel free to criticize constructively each and every contribution to discussion made by the instructor, or the pupils. Analyze and evaluate the worth of each argument presented.

IV. *Use of resources, including printed materials*

Have the learners help set up standards for quality of comics, short stories, books, newspapers, advertisements, records, etc.

Have the pupils evaluate the arrangement of the room and the school in terms of functional learning and encourage them to suggest changes in terms of the ways things could be improved. For example, if there is no room for small group activities, arrange seats on skis so that they can be shifted around easily.

Let the pupils aid in evaluating the things they will need to provide for a livable room situation and the arrangements suited for doing a particular task.

Variety of approaches needed for learning self-evaluation. It should be pointed out that no single suggestion will work with every group or every individual in a group. It is a part of the function of the instructor to encourage the learners to try out as many suggestions as are necessary to obtain the desired results. If the learner and the instructor are persistent enough, self-evaluation will gradually become an integral part of the learner's activities.

**AN EXAMPLE OF A SELF-EVALUATIVE TEST
WITH ILLUSTRATIVE ANSWERS**

The nature of learner self-evaluation will perhaps be clearer if an illustration of a teacher-learner constructed test is given together with illustrative answers. Such a test, which was constructed by the writer and some of his students, together with illustrative answers, is given below. The test is preceded by some orientation material.[4]

Traditional purposes of history tests. Many, perhaps most, history tests are simply checks designed to test the amount of information the pupils or students have "learned" (frequently merely memorized) during a particular period of time. The primary purpose in the minds of most teachers in giving tests has been to determine the relative status of the pupils so that a mark based on competitive standing may be given. In the mind of the learner the primary purposes have simply been (1) to pass the course, and (2) to wangle as good a mark as can be obtained without too much effort. So true is this, that many teachers and their students sometimes have difficulty in conceiving of tests where the purposes of teacher and learner are different from those already indicated. This discussion represents an attempt to give a picture of other purposes in history testing that are based on psychologically sound principles of learning.

Methods of teaching and learning employed in class. Before the writer gives the test with illustrative answers made to various questions, a very brief description will be given of the methods of teaching and learning emphasized in a history class in which the test was employed.

Purpose of study. The study of history was approached by each student as *the getting and using of some of those written records which gave promise of helping him to recognize, meet, and solve more effectively the present and prospective problems that he as an individual was now facing or would be likely to face.* This, of

---

[4] First appeared in *The Social Studies,* 33 (December, 1944), 363-70.

course, meant that an attempt was made to individualize the instruction and study of the learners in the group. For instance, one student who expected to become a teacher attempted, with the help of the instructor and other resources, to set up the types of problems he would be likely to face. Then he worked to get reasonable solutions to these problems, recognizing that one solution might work best in one place and another might be more desirable in a different situation. Another student planning to be a social or welfare worker did the same type of thing for his field. In other words, each student worked on problems he expected later to meet. Methods of selecting problems wisely have been described elsewhere.[5]

Resources used. Each student was guided in learning how *to select more wisely and use more effectively materials that promised to give help on the problems he had set up.* No text as such was used in the course. Any and every type of printed resource (as well as many other resources such as interviews, observations, and correspondence) was considered suitable grist for his attentions if it promised to give help on the problems he recognized or was led to recognize as important. These materials included magazine articles, newspaper editorials, and news items, books, pamphlets, report cards, etc., all of which were considered functional history materials if they gave the desired help.

Reading history merely for the sake of getting historical information was avoided. Rather, the purposeful study of problems gave the student direction in the selection of materials and in the guidance needed in deciding the type of ideas he would try to get from them.

Teaching the learner to teach himself. In all of the work an endeavor was made to teach the learner to be better able to meet his own problems and to learn how to teach himself. Teacher dictatorship in assignment-making, in the selection of materials, in the use of materials, in the purchase of materials, in testing and evaluation, was guarded against, for it was recognized that this would never lead to independence of thinking and study on the part of the learner.

Keeping own records a phase of history study. The records the student kept of his own educational activities and the skills he developed in keeping them were looked upon as an important phase

---

[5] Ray H. Simpson, "Students Help Set Up Criteria To Aid in Deciding What To Study," *Journal of Educational Research*, XXXVI (November, 1942), 192-99.

of his history study. Stress was placed on the fact that the student was actually gaining a better insight into the meaning and uses of history through writing some of it, i.e., his own educational history. *Students evaluate some phases of their work.* As has already been pointed out, the individualized type of instruction makes it necessary and desirable to build up within the learner the ability to evaluate continuously his own work. It was emphasized that evaluating and testing should be primarily a checkup on past thinking and activities so that we might redirect our future activities into more profitable channels. With this in mind a test whose origin has already been described elsewhere [6] was answered outside of class by each of the students over a period of three weeks starting about the middle of the semester. The test questions and illustrative answers are given primarily to show how testing and test questions may be developed to focus attention upon learning and learning improvement and thus wean the learner (and the teacher) away from the idea that tests should be used almost exclusively to determine marks and credits.

I. *Questions relating to goals toward which to work and problems upon which to work.* [7]

1. *Am I improving in the ability to pick out problems of importance for me to study? Evidence?*

"When I first began work on my problem, which deals with the teaching of delinquent and mentally retarded children, I had no clear concept of what to look for in the library or what phases of my problem to attack. I was inclined to look at random and write down almost anything I found. However, after a week or so I found that I was not getting anywhere and that I had only a hazy conception of the goal I was seeking. My material seemed lifeless to me and somehow it had no organization. From suggestions received in class and from some careful thinking on what I wanted to do with my problem I gradually 'caught on' and began organizing my paper and my work in terms of problems. I had to go back over the work

---

[6] Ray H. Simpson, "Students Attempt Self-Evaluation of Work in Educational Psychology," *Journal of Educational Psychology*, XXXIII (March, 1942), 225-31.

[7] These questions are particularly appropriate for teachers and prospective teachers in methods courses and educational psychology courses. The same basic ideas can be used by students in secondary schools.

I had done and I found that by placing my information under specific problems, my work took on a new aspect for me. I began to visualize myself in an actual teaching situation and I asked myself what problems would confront me. By this use of imagination I saw and felt new problems all the time. I have started working on these problems which are real to me and from them have discovered the goal I would like to work for and through their solution I am reaching it."

"I think that my last problem I picked out to study was the most important problem that I could have chosen. It was made up of one large problem which can be broken down into small ones. This enables me to get the practice of solving the many smaller problems. The best evidence of the importance of the problem to me is that it meets all of the criteria that we set up as a basis for selecting a problem. I have already taken advantage of some of my study by selecting and buying a lot in accordance with the results of my study. This problem study will also help my industrial arts needs for a general knowledge of carpentry and buildings."

2. *Are the results I am getting in my study likely to be of value to me? If so, when? How?*

"I have tentatively decided upon my aims and objectives in teaching. This will certainly be of value to me since it will help to decide how I teach. It will also help determine what I teach my pupils. For one thing, for instance, I have decided that I am not going to teach to cram factual knowledge down my pupils, but rather to teach them to think for themselves and to help them acquire abilities necessary for facing life's problems."

"I have learned something of the history of my profession. This is valuable to me since I really should know a little of the background of what I am teaching. I can also use my information in trying to make various phases of physical education interesting to my pupils."

"I have made a complete study of the relationship of physical education and the core curriculum. This is of value to me because I now realize what I as a teacher of physical education can contribute to such a curriculum should this ever become necessary."

"The main reason why my results are of value to me is that I probably will not have another opportunity to study things I really need with the help of the teacher. My other subjects from now on will be outlined for me and I will have no choice as to what I will study."

"I am planning to keep my folder for reference when I do my practice teaching and when I begin my actual teaching. In some parts of my work I have found tests that teachers may give to themselves to evaluate their own teaching procedures. I think they are excellent and want to have them on hand to test myself to see if I really am doing the best I could do."

"I want to use some of the ideas that have been used in other communities for improvement of the communities in which I teach. This work has proved of immediate value to me also. I am interested in knowing what is being done in other communities. I am interested in what other people in my field of work are doing as well as the improvements in the whole field of education."

3. *Have I been working on something that represents a real need to me? Evidence?*

"I think so. I want to know the characteristics of a democratic school and how to get cooperation among the pupils. I want to know how to develop them in every way possible so as to make them have a feeling of freedom and belonging. I want my classroom to be so democratic as to instill in the pupils a feeling of love for cooperative recognition of the rights of others, and a desire to exercise their own abilities. I want to make democracy foremost in their minds and actions and by study of the problem of democracy in the school I am preparing myself for this."

"This topic and any other that I am working on has a twofold meaning, first, for a solution of the problem itself; second, for a good system of keeping records. I have developed from this work a set of notes that will be of great assistance when I start teaching. It will also give me a chance to pass on to other learners a system by which they, too, can tackle a problem which is troubling them or others."

4. *Do I have specific goals and am I making progress toward them? Describe.*

"My major goal has been to try to learn the many different methods one can use in the teaching of mentally retarded and/or delinquent children. Also, I have placed as a goal the desire to learn to organize my work and materials better, to see problems more clearly, and to devise better methods for handling general problems which might come up in the school room. I feel that I have made definite progress toward these goals for in my study I am gathering much material on methods and am learning the use of it. My work seems to be better organized than it formerly was and has a more connected central idea. From class discussions I have learned a great deal about general problems of all types and have gotten many specific suggestions which have helped me in my study."

"My ultimate goal is to make myself a better teacher. I have had lesser goals but they all led up to my final purpose. I have studied problems that I believe have aided me in my purpose. I have learned other things through class discussions such as: how to keep good records, factors in grading, taking care of individual differences, how to select a problem, desirable characteristics of a teacher, approaches to solving the problem of cheating. I have also improved in using the library and other resources."

II. *Work with others*

5. *Am I progressing in the matter of my contributions to class discussions? Evidence?*

"I have found that I seem to want to discuss my side of problems in class more than I did earlier in the course. Often I like to give some actual classroom experiences that I have had for the benefit of those who are not doing teaching now."

"When I first came into this class I felt that I knew so little of the problems of education as I had had only one course in education previously. I felt that my idea about the subject would probably be so 'far-fetched' that it would be disregarded. Then, I began gradually to volunteer information and found that my opinion was respected just as much as anyone's opinion. I feel that I have asked some questions that stimulated thought in the group which seems a desirable thing."

6. *Do I indirectly help myself by helping others? If so, indicate in what ways I have helped others.*

"I have referred other students to references and materials which they have found helpful, and might otherwise have missed."

"I believe anyone can gain by helping others for in doing so he makes obstacles clear in his own mind. If a person can explain something that is useful and helpful to others, it points out to him the important points of his topic. I have discussed controversial issues with others and thus seen opposing sides more clearly. Also, by criticizing other pupils' folders and giving them suggestions for improving their work and records, I have helped myself."

7. *Have I been sufficiently willing to accept suggestions for improving my work? If so, give some specific instances.*

"I have been willing to accept suggestions and try them out and then see for myself whether they are desirable for my work. For instance, it was suggested in class that we organize our work under specific problems. I went back over my material and did this and found it to be the most helpful suggestion I have had. I also followed a good many of the useful suggestions for keeping personal records and have improved in this ability."

"I feel that I have been very willing to accept suggestions for improving my work. Evidence of this is that I have found a very satisfactory method of arranging my research work, only after I had tried my own way, together with other methods suggested by the instructor and by other members of the class. Looking over my progress reports, I see that I have changed my method of writing several times. The first way that I made these reports was that of giving in my own words the viewpoints and material of several different authors. I made no criticisms of their works and did not give any of my own thought on the subject.

"The next step forward that I took was the instructor's suggestion that I give more of my own ideas to guard against my work becoming 'busywork.' I saw where the instructor was right, and in my next week's work, I inserted my own ideas and gave instances when I thought the author was not altogether right, or where his plans would not fit in with my present program of schoolwork. I think this was a good suggestion because it made me begin to really ask myself, 'What is the answer to my question?'

"Then I began asking myself different questions that would lead finally to the answer to my first main question. These I wrote at the heading of the report and then I attempted to see what answers authors give for these simpler questions.

"Next, I made a general outline for each week's work so that anyone could pick up my folder (record) and see exactly what I

had done, and what I planned to do. The next conscious improvement that I made was that I summarized what I had discovered
and made plans for what I would do in the future.

"I think this sequence gives some indication that I progressed in
my method of work through accepting freely the suggestions of
others who, I thought, should be in a position to give good ones."

III. *Records and organization of work*

8. *Am I progressing in my ability to keep records that
include the type of materials I am likely to need later on?
Evidence?*

"Especially on the problem on which I am working at present I am
keeping records of material that I will definitely use later on. I
have records of sources of material to be used later on. I have taken
every problem and listed reasonable possibilities and then stated
my conclusion or decision. Although I have not made a complete
list of material to be used, I do intend to make this list as soon as
I have made all of my decisions."

"In my problem I have organized the materials in such a way as
to help me later on. In placing them under specific problems I
shall have a sort of file of problems and later on when the need
arises I can go directly to the specific problem and get some suggestions for possible answers to it. This ability has a carry-over
value for other subjects as well. I have found this same method
useful in my other subjects."

9. *Am I improving in the ability to organize my work?
Evidence?*

"Previously I sat down and wrote out an outline, and then filled
in. Now I make a temporary outline and set my specific topics or
problems written on separate sheets. After this, I take each sheet
that has a heading and expand on them from the material collected
from books and articles. Then I write my personal view on the subject. Now I can look at some material and tell if it is of any value
to me, because I have my general outline in mind."

"For this question I would like to contrast the organization of the
study of my first problem, the aims and objectives of physical education, with the study of my last problem, the core curriculum and
physical education. For my first problem I just made a list of my

objectives after studying the parents', teachers', and pupils' viewpoints. But for my last problem I had a definite outline which was as follows:

"(1) What is the core curriculum? (2) Relation of core to physical education? (3) Ways physical education is connected with core curriculum? (4) What are the implications of the core curriculum? (5) What is the task of the physical education teacher in this new curriculum? (6) What methods should be used? (7) How should guidance be carried on? (8) What are ways to organize a class? (9) What are special problems I am likely to face in trying to use the core curriculum in my teaching? What are possible solutions to each problem?"

IV. *Initiative*

10. *Am I learning to plan my work more effectively? Evidence?*

"When I go to the library for work on my problem I now have a clear idea in mind as to what I am going to spend my time doing. I have found that by putting down ideas before beginning work saves endless time that was formerly wasted. I feel that I have progressed by doing this. There is still plenty of room for improvement, however. I still find it hard to study at regular times."

"I have not only learned to plan my own work more effectively in this course but in every course I am taking and in the spending of my time out-of-class. The discussions we have had on record-keeping have been most beneficial to me for my personal improvement. I now keep a daily record on my calendar of everything I am supposed to do for a day and how long I should spend doing this. I have saved much time that would otherwise be wasted."

11. *Am I improving in the ability to go ahead with my study without being told almost every step? Evidence?*

"Now I see that every part of my study leads directly or indirectly to another part of it. I think that this is some evidence that I am improving in my ability to proceed without being told at every point what to do next. Other evidence of this is that my study is seeming more useful to me than it seemed at the beginning of the semester."

"At the beginning of my work on my problem, I was at a loss

as to where to get material and how to organize it, and just what kind of material I should get. Then I had to ask for help and guidance, but now I find much less trouble along these lines."

V. Interest in work

12. Is my interest in the work growing? Evidence?

"I think that one sign of my progress is that I am becoming more interested in the general topic and wish to go into the subject more thoroughly than I had originally planned. Since I wrote my first study into an article form, I have been studying personality tests. I think that this is an interesting study, and I have a very intense interest in it from an objective as well as a personal viewpoint."

"At the beginning of the semester I thought that the study of a problem was a waste of time. I worked because I had to. After I really understood the significance and benefit to be obtained, I began to take interest. Now I enjoy working on my problem and on the class discussions."

VI. Open-mindedness and objectivity

13. Am I improving in the ability to hold my mind open sufficiently on all controversial issues?

"At the first of the year I had prejudices which were foolish, I know, but which I couldn't help. Not all of these have disappeared but they have decreased and I don't get mad in a discussion as easily as I did."

14. Are the conclusions I have drawn based on evidence? If so, illustrate.

"I now feel that my answers and conclusions are based on reasoning and evidence. For instance, when I entered this class, I had many of the same ideas and factors in mind that I now have, but the difference is that now I can give at least one reason why I hold a conclusion. One specific idea I had upon which I changed my mind was the one that teachers and associates could discover the desirable traits and the undesirable ones after they had known the person a short while, because I felt that such traits always were the first thing you noticed about a person when you met him. Now I see that personality tests have a great value to persons interested in changing or developing personality in others. My reasons for changing my mind are listed in my progress report (record)."

"No, on personal opinion I am afraid."

VII. *Use of available resources*

15. *Am I learning how to use the library and other resources better in study? Evidence?*

"I have learned the wealth of usable material to help solve current problems which is contained in current periodicals. Heretofore I have used books for study almost exclusively. Another main source I have used a lot is talking with people who can help me. I have learned that it is a good idea to check ideas of experienced people with ideas that are read from books."

"I think that I have improved tremendously in the use of the library. In the first place, I did not even know of the existence of the *Education Index* until this semester. I did not realize the importance of magazines and pamphlets nor the wealth of information they contained. This was a new aspect of the library which I for some reason took to be primarily for amusement and pastime. Why or where I got this idea, I do not know."

16. *Am I learning how and where to get some materials which are not immediately available? If so, give examples of what has been learned.*

"I find I can get much more help from the librarian than I ever thought possible before. I once thought the librarian just checked out books. I also find that many of the other teachers are able and willing to give me valuable help on some of the problems upon which I have worked. This is the first semester in which I have used sources of this type."

"I have found that educational publishing concerns are frequently a good source of help on some problems. Also, the federal and some state governments have much free and/or inexpensive material which is quite helpful on some problems."

17. *In my study am I placing too much dependence on books and not enough on other resources available? If so, what resources should I probably use more?*

"Yes, I think I am inclined to do this. Some of the resources which I should use more are the juvenile court, to learn at first hand what methods are used for delinquent children, and interviews with teachers who know specifically about teaching mentally deficient children."

"There are other resources which I should probably use more. It seems that there is such a wealth of knowledge in the field of personality in the library that I have studied it very little outside of these books. I have used some of my ideas that were gotten from observing friends and members of my family. Other sources that I could get information from are the radio, movies, teachers, and discussions with some members of the class."

VIII. *General method*

18. *Am I giving sufficient consideration to the methods of study and teaching used in class and out of class so that I might sometime try them myself? If so, show this by indicating:*

(a) *What the outstanding characteristics of our methods are.*

"The method used which was most outstanding to me was that of the self-check or the records which we keep. The student has a sense of responsibility, definite work and assignments, work which will be of definite interest and help to the individual."

"The thing that I am most interested in is the fact that, in the class, interest is never at a standstill. It isn't dull and lifeless like so many courses in rote learning. The strength of it lies in the fact that the students have a considerable share in choosing what they will study and for this reason are more willing to work. The democratic method used in handling the class and planning the work has impressed me."

(b) *Possible weaknesses and possible strengths of the methods* (Note: Two answers concerning weaknesses and two concerning strengths are given).

"We don't learn facts about the history of general education in the general, conventional sense. For example, someone might ask us who wrote the first textbooks for children, and we might not know. But to me that is not very important and I think the history we studied was much more important."

"This type of approach to learning is so different from what many students are accustomed to that it is difficult for some to appreciate and take adequate advantage of it."

"One of the greatest strengths about this course is that we use our own judgment in almost all things. Few courses I have had before help us develop our judgment. I feel that writing the important facts gleaned from a variety of sources together with the expressing of my own thoughts in relation to them has been a very good way of learning, and also of thinking. The method of study which we use in this class requires the development of initiative."

"The student learns the means and habit of testing himself continually so that he can progress more rapidly in his learning."

19. *In my work in other classes am I using some of the ideas about study methods gained in this class? If so, illustrate.*

"I have used the ideas and methods in my practice teaching, particularly in the matter of keeping records. In my future teaching I plan to let the students have more freedom in the choice of special problems to study."

"Yes. One of the most valuable (ideas) is directly related to and results from the study of my problem. I have begun to consider the material taken up in other classes, not only for that which seems important for passing exams, but also for the things I will probably need when I begin teaching science and related subjects. I have been using the method of record-keeping we developed in all of my courses. As a result of this, I find when I get ready to review that I am able to tell much better what material I have, when it was obtained, and from where it came; I have followed one suggestion of using separate notebooks for each course and have found this most useful. I received the suggestions for using the *Education Index* in this course and have used them in four other courses. . . ."

"The suggestion of using other sources than textbooks and magazines has been of much help to me in studying and compiling material in other projects. I have used this method in three other courses. One thing I have learned in this class has been of paramount importance to me and will help me in the remainder of my life. I have learned to analyze a problem, think it through, and then try possible approaches to a solution."

20. *Give one or more suggestions for improving classwork so that it will be more profitable to me.*

"I believe *my* classwork may be improved by taking a more active part in the discussions. The classwork on the whole seemed

very interesting although I think it would be more profitable to me
if we finished a topic completely [?] rather than skim the top and
then skip to another one. For a while I thought there were altogether too many loose ends dangling around but I do not feel this
way at the conclusion of the course."

"I suppose more teacher dominance would have been more profitable in my case since I have been used to it ever since I started to
school. However, I approve of this method of teaching and intend
to use it myself when I teach."

IX. *Evaluation and self-evaluation*

21. *Am I learning how to check up on what I have done so
that I may improve my future work? Evidence?*

"I recently have begun to evaluate my work with certain specific
goals in mind. I find that with the goal in mind my work is more
inclined to direct itself to this goal in a straight line, rather than get
waylaid at different paths toward this goal."

"When the students looked at the folders and wrote criticisms, I
think that was one of the best helps there could have been. This
evaluation of other students sort of made me check to see whether
my work came up to my standards. Also, I took their suggestions
and tried to do something about them."

22. *Am I sufficiently conscious of my present weaknesses? If
so, indicate what I think they are and indicate what steps I
think I should take in trying to eliminate them.*

"This type of examination helps me to see my weak points. I wish
I could have read one of these about two months ago. One great
weakness of mine is to have a 'set' opinion on some few matters
that have been brought up in class. I have tried to be open-minded
but some few opinions voiced are so entirely different from anything I have been associated with in the past I have a hard time
trying to see the other person's point of view. I am trying hard to
see why the other person should feel as he does and am trying
to see the good in his opinion."

"I feel that I am more conscious of the weaknesses in my work
that I have improved upon than the weaknesses that I still possess.
Some of my original weaknesses have been modified, and some
completely done away with so far as I can judge. One weakness

that I am very conscious of is my lack of thoroughness. I have heard it said of one girl: 'She stops at nothing short of perfection.' I wish that I could overcome my habit of working fast and carelessly. I realize the importance of such habits as care and thoroughness and hope that I am acquiring them at the present. I feel that the best way to do this is to do my work on time."

23. *Add one additional question that I think would be appropriate in this self-examination.* (NOTE: This was somewhat difficult since the original questions were set up by the class under the leadership of the instructor.)

"What have been the chief factors which have motivated me to work in this course? How does this list compare with a similar one from another course I took at the same time?"

"Do I see some importance in doing everything that I do? (Note added by student: This question should be taken into consideration very thoroughly. I think that the teacher should impress upon the students' thoughts the importance of their work. I feel that the attitude which the student takes in this matter is largely a reflection of the teacher's attitude. One teacher whom I have at the present time says such things as these very often: 'I know this textbook isn't any too good, but seems like we have to have something to keep you all busy.' 'There's nothing important in this chapter, but you'd better read it because you know we're going to have a departmental exam.' 'If I give you all a cut today, will you be ready for a quiz next time?' 'You all can sleep in my class, just so you don't snore, and wake up your neighbor.' The students usually laugh at such remarks, so the teacher thinks that he is going over big, but the students don't, and they don't like it. There are also sincere professors who can't get up interest in their work, because they haven't set up specific goals toward which to advance.)"

24. *Contrast this method of examination with the ones I am more familiar with by giving outstanding characteristics of each.*

"This method of examination is the most fair examination of this type. It gives you a chance to think through the question and time to form your conclusions and write them down more logically. You are calm and do not have to do it until you get in the mood. The tenseness that is present during an examination is absent. The other method of examination just tests what facts pop into your mind and the conclusions you draw without sufficient thought. If you had had a chance to think over the question, you would probably have answered it entirely differently."

"With this type of exam there is little desire or need to cheat. Facts stated are things that the student already knows or can obtain in some legitimate manner. I think that by the use of this type of examination the teacher can evaluate his success in teaching as well as the students' success in improving."

25. (a) *Give what I think are the possible weaknesses of this method of self-examination.*

"This type of test is relatively new and perhaps confusing to some students. Most students are used to cramming for exams and they might not treat this test seriously enough."

"A person can easily give the right answer to some of the questions. Sometimes students are prone to put down what they think the teacher wants them to put down."

(b) *Give what I think are the major values to be derived from a test of this sort.*

"This type of test is a sort of review. It helps one to evaluate his work and see just where he stands. It encourages planning in the fields in which you have weaknesses. It makes one conscious of the practical side of the course. It is really a learning procedure in that one learns to write his ideas in such a way that another person is able to study his work methods. One learns to think by approaching the questions as problems to be solved."

"Instead of simply requiring facts this test emphasizes thoughtful opinions based on facts."

**OPERATING PRINCIPLES
FOR EFFECTIVE DEMOCRATIC EVALUATIONS
IN LEARNING SITUATIONS**

I. *Principles related to purposes*

    A. A primary purpose of evaluation should be to help the learner see where and how he can become more efficient in learning.

    B. The learner should have many guided evaluating experiences so that he can evaluate with greater efficiency in school, and, even more important, be able to carry on wise evaluation after he gets out of school.

C. With appropriate guided evaluative experiences, the courses of action taken by the learner should tend to be gradually improved.

D. Evaluative experience is a search for sounder values.

E. Learning to evaluate better may be one purpose of evaluating in a particular situation.

F. Goals and purposes in evaluation should be re-examined frequently and appropriate modifications should be made.

G. All concerned with evaluation should remember that the school is primarily a place for learning rather than merely a place for demonstrating perfect performances. Learning self-evaluation will involve making some mistakes.

H. Mental health is a primary goal of self-evaluation. No individual or group is likely to remain mentally healthy long unless self-evaluation is developed.

I. Teacher self-evaluation can constitute an important basis for teacher and learner improvement.

J. Evaluation of learning activities *in progress* (such as term papers) is frequently more helpful in improving learning than evaluation of the end products of learning, since the former is the real basis for the latter.

K. Evaluation of group goals, procedures, and resources is frequently a worth-while procedure.

L. Learning effective self-evaluation is a problem that takes much time and effort, and cannot be achieved overnight or even in a month, semester, or year.

M. Neither testing nor evaluation should be thought of as primarily for marks or grade-getting purposes.

N. The fundamental purpose of evaluation is to make living better and happier.

O. The proper evaluation of a process used in making a conclusion is frequently more important than the conclusion itself. The process of learning and its improvement is more important than the end product of learning.

P. Effective evaluation should never be divorced from basic goals.

Q. The learner should be encouraged to develop a critical attitude toward his own efficiency. The development of the ability of the learner to evalute aspects of his own efficiency so that he may intelligently go about improving his work is at least as important as the development of the ability to memorize an assignment given by the teacher!

R. One of the primary goals in self-evaluation is to improve the quality of motivation in the learner. Intrinsic motivation is likely to be stimulated if the learner is taught how to diagnose his needs and set up plans in line with those needs.

S. Evaluation should help the student discover strengths, weaknesses, and methods of eliminating the weaknesses and capitalizing on the strengths.

T. The development of self-evaluation will tend to improve character through eliminating some of the motivation for cheating that is common in many traditional classrooms. When the learner begins to see that he studies, really, to help himself, rather than primarily to get good grades, he will begin to see that when he cheats he cheats himself in the long run.

II. *Who should evaluate in learning situations?*

A. Each teacher and each learner should attempt with appropriate help to set up his own guiding principles for effective evaluation, since it usually is, or should be, *his* responsibility.

B. All concerned should have a share in deciding the purposes and procedures of the evaluation to be done. The learner's share should increase as he gains additional facility. Autocratic evaluation not only presents an impossible job for the teacher because of the number of pupils, but also remains low in quality because of the magnitude of the job, and because none but the learner himself is in the best position to evaluate his own work. Individualization of education demands democratic evaluation.

III. *When should evaluation take place?*

A. Evaluation should be thought of largely as a beginning rather than an end process.

B. Evaluation should begin as soon as work is started; thereafter, frequent opportunity should be provided for the student to judge the worth of his work. The teacher's evaluation should begin with his preplanning.

C. All policies relating to both goals and procedures should be given frequent re-examination by those setting up the policies.

D. Evaluation should be thought of as a continuous process which always goes on concomitantly with other phases of learning in which the student is engaged. It is a continuous appraisal for continuous reorientation.

E. Procedures for evaluation should be developed by all those using them.

IV. *How can self-evaluation be developed?*

A. Frequent re-examination of procedures used in evaluation should be encouraged.

B. Doing and thinking should be tied up. The quality of evaluation will be reflected in basic improvements in the lives of those involved. Emerson said, "Your actions speak so loudly that I cannot hear what you say."

C. Identification and writing-down of specific goals constitutes one of the first important steps in evaluating procedures.

D. Effective diagnosis of where one is with respect to specific goals constitutes an important phase of evaluation. Diagnosing where one came from and how he got where he is, is also frequently helpful. Thus, learning self-diagnosis is a significant part of learning self-evaluation. Strengths to exploit and weaknesses to eliminate should become clear with diagnosis.

E. The probable value of any testing instrument in a particular situation should be weighed against the probable value of other alternative instruments or procedures. Evaluation by the learner should be oriented around the goals and purposes he recognizes as important to him.

F. A well-kept personal educational record constitutes a good basis for certain types of evaluation desirable for effective learning.

G. A record should be kept of evaluative activity.

H. An important part of evaluation is to set up specific behavior changes that will be put into effect to improve self-efficiency. Unless evaluation results in present and future improvement, it is of doubtful value.

I. Self-evaluation for learning purposes should *not* be thought of in terms of allowing students without guidance to do whatever they want to do.

J. Learners may evaluate the work of each other for practice in evaluation and to give reciprocal help.

K. An important procedure in developing self-evaluation is helping the learner to build up appropriate criteria to guide him in wisely making various types of decisions.

L. Learners may be encouraged to write brief criticisms about their own work or papers.

M. Procedures for weaning teachers from monopolistic practices in evaluation need to be studied, particularly by the teacher himself.

N. Reviewing, and studying the method of problem-solving used by others in reaching conclusions is frequently helpful in improving one's own problem-solving techniques. Studying the records of other students is one application of this principle.

O. Frequent opportunity should be provided for the student to judge the worth of his work.

P. Work should be evaluated primarily on an individual basis.

Q. The learner should develop the ability to decide wisely when he needs guidance and should learn how to go about getting it from a likely source.

R. Since goals should change in effective learning, evaluative processes should also be in a constant state of flux.

S. Evaluation should be made up of frequent and systematic looks backward on past work, and should be tied up with systematic plans for changes in future work in the light of what has been seen. This should result in improvement.

BIBLIOGRAPHY

1. Association for Supervision and Curriculum Development. *Toward Better Teaching.* Washington, D.C.: The Association, 1949.

   Chapter Eight is particularly useful in giving a variety of illustrations in which pupils and teachers cooperatively evaluate shared activities.

2. ALILUNAS, LEO. "Experiment in Self-Evaluation." *Nation's Schools*, 30:25; July 1942.
   Self-marking experiment with applications in social studies and English.

3. BOWMAN, LILLIE LEWIN. "Self-Evaluation at Tenth-Grade Level." *California Journal of Educational Research*, I:15-19; January 1950.
   Describes a program of self-evaluation in secondary schools which is "a cooperative project involving administrators, counselors, teachers, and students ... the ultimate goal of which is to lead students in making sequences of desirable choices which foster security and satisfaction."

4. EARLY, L. J. "A Pupil-made Test in Social Science." *Elementary School Journal*, 43:29-32; September 1942.
   Describes procedure used in learner test construction and utilization.

5. Educational Policies Commission of N.E.A. *Learning the Ways of Democracy*. Washington, D.C.: National Education Association, 1940.
   "A Case Book of Civic Education" much of which relates to self-education. An analysis of democracy in education is made and many illustrations are given.

6. FLAUM, LARRY. "Tests as a Co-operative Activity." *School Activities*, 13:347-48; May 1942.
   Students' testing committees work with teacher in deciding tests to be used.

7. JENKINS, FRANK C., et al. "Cooperative Study for the Improvement of Education. *The Southern Association Quarterly*, 10:3-132, 369-488; February and August, 1946.
   Also published in one volume, *The Southern Study*, by "The Commission on Curriculum Problems and Research of the Southern Association." Describes in detail a somewhat unique approach or method of seeking school improvement. Contains "a case history of the efforts of a group of school people to learn a method of work which to them appeared worth mastering. Attention is devoted to identifying this method, to describing how it was put into operation, and to describing the kinds of educational outcomes which emerged."

8. JENSEN, H. T. "Three Thousand Students Evaluate an Education Course." *Educational Forum*, 7:127-32; January 1943.
   Shows teachers can obtain appraisal of worth of course from students. Implies need of students to know purposes of course and problems involved in course.

9. McALLASTER, ELVA. "A I a Good School Citizen?" *The Grade Teacher*, 59:48; May 1942. ·
   Gives self test questions through which the learner may check himself on neatness, work habits, sportsmanship, and courtesy.
10. McMILLIN, MARTHA. "Self Checks for Eighth-Graders." *The Instructor*, 53:28; June 1944.
    Describes a questionnaire designed to help students evaluate themselves in social living and citizenship.
11. RATHS, LOUIS E. "Evaluation in the Secondary Schools." *High School Journal*, 34:100-3; April 1951.
    Offers four suggestions for developing an evaluation program for the high school that is based on the shared thinking of the students, faculty, and community representatives.
12. ROCKOWITZ, MURRAY. "Know Thyself: Techniques in Pupil Self-Evaluation." *High Points*, 33:50-56; October 1951.
    Suggests procedures with which teacher and learners may wish to experiment.
13. ROGERS, SARAH. "A Description of a Teacher's Work with Tenth-Grade Pupils in English-Social Science." *The Southern Association Quarterly*, 7:347-65; August 1943.
    Good illustrations of materials selection, procedures, record-keeping, and evaluation.
14. SIMPSON, RAY H. "Are Your Teachers Learning?" *The School Executive*, 61:16-19; December 1941. Abstract in the *Loyola Educational Digest*, 379.15-3617; March 1942.
    Gives diagnostic questions for administrators to ask themselves and discusses possible significance of answers.
15. SIMPSON, RAY H. "Students Attempt Self-Evaluation of Work in Educational Psychology." *Journal of Educational Psychology*, 33:225-30; March 1942.
16. SIMPSON, RAY H. "Use of a Self-evaluative Test in Individualized History Study." *The Social Studies*, 35:363-70; December 1944.
    Describes an evaluative instrument used in an unconventional history class where realistic problems were identified and studied by individual students.
17. SIMPSON, RAY H. "Teachers, Here Is Your Final." *The Clearing House*, 16:47-48; September 1941.
18. WRIGHTSTONE, J. W. "Can Pupils Help Evaluate Their Growth?" *The School Executive*, 62:22; August 1943.
    Pictures how learners help define objectives, set up tests, and evaluate achievement.

9

DEVELOPING ABILITY TO KEEP

PERSONAL EDUCATIONAL RECORDS

FOR EFFECTIVE LEARNING

Some problems to consider

How is individual learner record-keeping related to effective learning?

What is the relationship of clear thinking and learning to an individually organized record of problems and possible solutions to them?

What are the possible purposes a learner may have in keeping personal educational records?

What are some suggestions for improving record-keeping?

How may the instructor and other students help the learner improve through periodic study of his record?

How may the student eliminate some of his learning weaknesses through systematic evaluations of his learning record?

What are the principles to remember about record-keeping for effective learning?

Introduction. Writing down what one thinks helps to clarify one's thinking. Recording the suggestions of others aids us in relating our own ideas to those of others. Critical, written comments by the learner help him understand, interpret, and organize his own ideas and utilize those he gets from other sources.

Traditionally, record-keeping by the student has been largely a matter of copying what has been said by an instructor or written in a book. Such record-keeping has tended to stifle creativity and thought. Its purpose has usually been to pass tests, and other purposes have largely been neglected.

In this chapter an attempt is made to picture record-keeping as an integral, stimulating, and necessary part of the learning process. The evaluative questions listed below are designed to point up problems related to record-keeping for effective learning.

EVALUATIVE QUESTIONS RELATED TO EFFECTIVE RECORD-KEEPING [1]

Goals and purposes

1. Does my record of study contain clear and specific statements of the goals and purposes that form the framework of my activities?

2. Is there evidence that the record has been made for intrinsic purposes rather than to have something that will look nice for the teacher to see?

3. To what extent would my record reflect my goals to another student or to my teacher by giving a clear picture of my tentative plans for future activities, immediate and distant, so that he could be in a better position to help me?

Organization of record with appropriate sections

4. In my record of study, do I have a well-organized tentative outline or table of contents (with tentative paging, preferably) that reflects the main questions and sub-questions about which I am concerned?

5. Do I continually revise my working outline in terms of new evidence and a better appreciation, or a growing appreciation, of the problems being attacked in relation to my needs?

6. Is my record set up in a sufficiently elastic fashion so that new ideas concerning my particular question or problems can be added without recopying ideas already listed?

7. Does my record contain a section where I list new problems as their significance is appreciated by me in my study of present problems?

8. Have I tried to make sufficient use of my record in noting

---

[1] These questions are phrased primarily for individual diagnosis by the student in teacher-training courses where teaching and learning methods are studied. It is also suggested that high-school students can and should be trained to ask themselves similar questions.

points to be asked in conferences or interviews and by keeping in my record the suggestions that grew out of the discussion?

9. To what extent have I given my own reactions and criticisms of ideas gleaned from various sources *as the ideas were recorded?*

10. Do I have a section organized for use by myself and others which includes appropriate information about resources already utilized, including such items as people interviewed, tests examined, observations made, and letters written?

Comprehensiveness and economy of record

11. To what extent would my record present to another student or my teacher a clear picture of what I have done and thought, with emphasis on what has been thought and done most recently?

12. Does my record indicate that I may be somewhat "pen or pencil lazy," neglecting the values that accrue from writing down what I am thinking?

13. Are ideas placed in *my* outline as they are acquired? Or is the uneconomical method of copying other people's outlines used first? In other words, am I improving in the ability to organize without recopying the material obtained from various sources?

Personal educational record and conventional history

14. Have I seen the relationship between personal educational records (history) and history in the more conventional sense?

Plagiarism

15. Have I consciously avoided plagiarism in my record?

Evaluation and the record

16. Is there evidence in the record that it is really furthering my thinking and learning? (Revised outlines, indications of changes in thinking, thoughtful analyses might be indicators of this.)

17. Is there evidence in my record that a critical and thoughtful attitude has characterized the use of all resources? (This is opposed to a mere parroting of ideas.)

18. To what extent have I used my record in measuring what I have done and in planning next steps?

19. Do I have a section in my record listing difficulties I have encountered in (*a*) getting and using ideas, (*b*) deciding what to study, and (*c*) keeping an effective record?

RECORD-KEEPING LADDER

Learner with a minimum of teacher guidance keeps a comprehensive record of his needs, identified problems, reasons for study of particular problems, and self-evaluations and uses these extensively in setting up goals and in planning steps for meeting these goals.

Each learner keeps reasonably extensive records of his needs, problems, problem solutions, and activities and uses these somewhat in planning future work.

Each learner keeps a very sketchy record of his *needs,* problems, and attempted solutions.

Same as rung below except that learner adds some comments on his own initiative.

Learner keeps a teacher-dictated record of group problems, needs, and attempted solutions.

Teacher keeps some record of class needs, problems, and attempted solutions to problems.

Neither teacher nor learner keeps a record of learner needs, problems, or attempted solutions to problems.

READ UP ⟶

In the teaching-learning situation of which I am a part, how high on the Record-keeping Ladder would I come?

What can I do to move higher on the ladder?

20. Does my record show that I have examined my own strengths and weaknesses in record-keeping?

21. Does my record indicate too great a dependence upon printed materials for ideas and not sufficient use of other types of resources?

22. Am I progressing in my ability to keep records that include the type of materials I am likely to need later on?

WHAT IS THE BACKGROUND OF THE PROPOSAL FOR THE DEVELOPMENT AND USE OF PERSONAL EDUCATIONAL RECORDS?

Adequate records, a part of all efficient learning. Since it is here proposed that the keeping of efficient educational records (personal educational histories) become an integral part of all the learner's activity, a brief picture of the background of this proposal will be given. Although history classes are used for illustrative purposes, it should be emphasized that the teaching of efficient record-keeping is a part of the work of all teachers in all classes. This is true since adequate records are necessary for efficient learning regardless of the area in which the learner is working.[2]

Value from history studied. "What uses or values have you derived from your study of history during your school career?" This question was put to two classes of university juniors and seniors who were just beginning a study of the History of Education in the United States. Each of the students had studied history for at least ten semesters and in some cases the number ran as high as twenty-two semesters. The answers strongly indicated something that the writer, who has taught history classes on the elementary, secondary, and university levels, has long suspected, i.e., that students see relatively little value derived from the hundreds of hours spent on history as it is now usually taught. Such answers as the following were frequent: "I have a vague and hazy background of European and United States history. I usually made good grades in these courses, but this was a direct result of memorizing my work. I do not feel that I have gained very much from these courses as we usually had so much to cover in one semester's work I did not

[2] It is increasingly recognized that not only the speech and English teachers but all teachers should be concerned with oral and written expression if transfer of training to out-of-school situations is to be achieved. Keeping a record (history) of personal learning activities in science, social studies, and mathematics classes, for example, not only improves the quality of learning in these subjects but also improves the learner's efficiency in written expression in these subjects.

see the relation between one country's history and another or between one century and another."

Purposes in social studies. Another conclusion, rather arresting and challenging to history teachers, that was gleaned from the answers was that most students seem to have the idea that the primary purpose in studying history is to memorize facts and more facts and fix these in mind so that time will not dislodge them, at least not till after the final examination. The use of these facts seems to have little, if any, connection in many students' minds with the purposes of studying history. Answers like the folllowing seem significant: "I have learned how to study history—to cover every detail in studying and never forget the main facts." "I have gained from the history courses the foundation of the world and America." While a few students mentioned using historical facts in understanding conversations and literature, no reference at all was made to using history to improve specific or even general political, economic, or social situations in the communities in which these students live or have lived. No attention was given to the possibility of improving personal records or "personal histories" as a significant value that might accrue from the study of history. In general, some students could perceive no value in their history as it had been taught and studied; even those who could see value saw it almost exclusively in terms of the amount of information memorized rather than in terms of the ways the study could improve their own lives and those of others.

The following incident contains an illustration of the thesis that our history students and more broadly our social studies students have been almost exclusively concerned with the memorization of information and that they have gained little if any facility in actually dealing with or even in recognizing relatively simple social problems that confront them from day to day. In a particular high school a class had been studying the topic of social security for some time. While the students had docilely memorized such things as some of the California social security laws, old-age pension provisions in Texas, and federal laws relating to unemployment, the work did not seem to have much real meaning or interest for the pupils. One day as the teacher, who was rather discouraged about the results or lack of results from his efforts, was about to enter the schoolhouse he happened to note the condition of a large tree near the entrance of the building. At the bottom the tree was supported only by a shell since most of the trunk near the ground had rotted away. At that moment the teacher had what psychologists call insight. Here was a real and immediate problem of social security! If that tree were to fall, as it would be likely to do in a high wind, it would no doubt at least damage a part of the school building and perhaps wreck several cars. At the worst its fall might even cause death or injuries to pupils, teachers, or townspeople. The teacher thought perhaps we can make "social security" a functional problem rather than merely the routine memorization it is now. When the problem was raised before the social studies group, the pupils were immediately enthusiastic. Never having had much, if any, experience in actually meeting and doing something about a real social studies problem, the pupils made some suggestions of questionable merit and others that indicated more thought. The first reaction of many was, "Let's get a saw or an ax or whatever one uses to cut a tree down and do it right away." Others raised objections to this, pointing out that they might do as much harm as the wind in bringing it down unless proper steps were taken. Finally, discussions were held and committees were formed to work on such problems as the following: To whom does the tree belong? To what administrative officer—principal, superintendent, or school-board member—should we go to get permission to have the tree cut down? What steps should be taken to safeguard property in bringing the tree down? What uses might be made of the wood? Could suffering from cold by the poor nearby be alleviated by proper distribution of the wood? Enthusiasm was rampant!

Some, with uplifted nose, may say that this is not studying history or social studies, but the teacher and pupils were confident that here were problems of law, of getting along with people, of getting things done, which were more significant and vital than memorizing such facts as the provisions of the latest wage-hour law. Parenthetically it may be pointed out that more facts and certainly more usable facts were learned in the study of these problems than were learned with the "fact memorization approach." *Records* of individual and group questions, problems, plans, and results were kept as the work progressed.

In attacking and solving such problems as the relatively simple one given above, as well as problems in many other areas, the writer and the learners with whom he has worked have found well-kept records to be an indispensable part of efficient learning. Training in effective record-keeping should be given in all classes, but the fact remains that it has not been given to any great extent, largely because the following *psychological principles of efficient learning and teaching have been frequently violated in student and instructor approaches to record-keeping study in most fields, including history.*

I. *Principles related to motivation, purpose, and the selection of appropriate subjects for study*

In social studies as well as in other fields the distinction between study for solving problems and activity for recreational values should be clearly recognized. The recreational values of history and social studies should be seen and developed, but they should not be used to the exclusion of work-type study designed to improve living in the home, school, community, and in other areas. In this connection it should be noted that mere learning can be dangerous. Too many teachers are happy if only the child is busy. Many times mere "busyness" involves an escape from the real problems that should be faced by the individual. A specific illustration of this is a fifth-grade group of pupils who spent some four months studying a unit on the South Sea Islands. This unit involved a study of the housing, sanitation, communication, government, occupational activities, and other aspects of the community. Within two blocks of the school in which the fifth grade spent the four months studying about living in the South Sea Islands there were terrible slum conditions that represented the type of situation in which at least 90 per cent of the children in the fifth grade involved were living. In this situation the students were extremely interested and enjoyed studying about the South Sea Islands but it was done at the expense of attempting to improve actual living conditions in the community that the school presumably served. It might be argued that study of the South Sea Islands would eventually produce changes in living conditions in the immediate community. This argument does not seem to have too much strength when we consider the fact that transfer of training is likely to be very small unless the learner and teacher see some direct relation and make direct applications to the immediate situation. The learner only learns what he practices.

If we accept the desirability of continued learning after students leave school, then we must recognize that a major goal of teachers should be to help learners learn how to educate themselves. If this purpose is not emphasized, it is very probable that learning in a systematic way will practically disappear after the student leaves school.

As an orientation for effective learning the student should be guided into a clear recognition of his present and probable future problems. In building up this effective basis for future study, written records can be of great value.

Closely related to the principle suggested in the preceding paragraph is the fact that the learner himself should participate in the selection of specific problems for study. This does mean that for purposes of motivation and in order that the learner may be able to continue such activity after he leaves school, he must participate in the early steps of the learning process. In order to learn how to select specific problems for study in an intelligent fashion it is important that the student be given considerable guidance in setting up sound criteria to aid in the selection of problems.

A few comments may be made at this point concerning the type of problems upon which learners should be encouraged to work. All problems studied should be related to the felt needs of the student, starting with close immediate ones and gradually reaching farther and farther out as broadening and deepening ability on the part of the learner makes this feasible. The learner should start, ordinarily, with relatively simple problems and as he develops skill in analyzing and actually doing something about these, he should advance to problems that become progressively more difficult.

Generally speaking, problems studied should be such that the student actually can do something about them after study. Closely related to this principle is the conclusion that the use the learner sees he is likely to be able to make of facts to be learned should be directly tied up with the learning of these facts and this, indeed, involves a fundamental part of functional learning. When facts or principles are memorized without the learner's seeing the context in which they will be used, it is rather probable that the facts and principles will be forgotten before it is time to use them, or, if they are remembered, it is doubtful that when the time for use arrives the particular facts can be pulled out for functional use unless at the time they were learned they were tied up with the problem situation in which use was expected.

II. *Principles related to general methods of carrying on group activities*

Democratic procedures that involve cooperative planning and study on the part of learners and teachers facilitate desirable learning. This means that students should participate in the making of practically all the assignments, not only for motivational purposes, but also to develop skill in this area so that pupils may be more likely to continue to learn after they leave the teacher. Such cooperative planning will also give many opportunities for the development of leadership of small and large groups in the class. This not only makes it more possible for the teacher to take care of individual differences, but it also provides a valuable type of learning experience for the student and aids his social development.

Rather than a one-way broadcasting system, the teacher doing the broadcasting, the class should usually be a multi-way stimulation between teacher and learners and learners and other learners for the exchange of ideas. Learner initiative in selecting and developing reasonable solutions to problems should be encouraged and developed rather than penalized. This means that much of the time of the learner, in fact most of the time of the learner, will be spent on constructive and creative thinking and not on memorization of facts or ideas that the teacher and/or textbook has presented to him.

Closely related to the points in the preceding paragraph is the fact that the learner should have experience and guidance in organizing points, ideas, and materials himself. Memorizing of teacher and/or textbook organizations, which may themselves be excellent, is likely to result in a *disorganized* clutter of information in the mind of the learner, for he has not shared in making the organization. In other words, it is possible and very frequently happens that the learner can regurgitate an organization he has memorized from a lecture or from a textbook but still in his own mind have a completely unorganized or disorganized understanding of the basic issues involved because he has spent his time memorizing the organization of someone else rather than attempting to develop, with teacher guidance, an organization that basically is meaningful to him. The learner should have frequent experience in reaching his own tentative conclusions and the teacher should specifically guard against the uncritical acceptance of teacher "directions" and textbook "gospels."

Learning how to improve methods of studying regardless of the field is certainly as important a goal as the sheer amount of information gleaned from such study. The digestion and application of knowledge are as important, if not more important, that its mere acquisition.

III. *Principles related to the selection and use of materials*

The learner should have a share in the acquisition and selection of most of the resources that he uses in study. Unless he gets practice in these abilities he is not likely to be able to continue to carry them on after he is no longer with the teacher. A critical and thoughtful attitude should be developed in the learner and teacher in the selection of all materials or resources used. This, of course, implies the setting up of sound criteria for the selection of resources.

All materials utilized should give some answers to problems recognized by the students as important ones he needs to face. (In this discussion we are omitting resources that are used strictly for recreational purposes.) In many situations, magazines, pamphlets, and newspapers form an excellent source of materials for present use and for filing for future use.

IV. *Principles related to the evaluation of activities in the study of history*

Evaluation should be primarily (*a*) to check on past activities for the purpose of finding major strengths and weaknesses in study, and (*b*) to aid in capitalizing more and more on strengths and eliminating weaknesses. Evaluation should be directed by the goals and purposes set up and recognized by the students with the help and guidance of the teacher.

Evaluation should be thought of as a continuous or at least a very frequent process rather than merely as a weekly, a monthly, or a semester happening. In all phases of evaluation the learner should be trained to participate both for the motivational value behind such evaluation and because the learner needs to know how to do such evaluation after he gets out of school.

It may be re-emphasized here that record-keeping for effective learning is closely tied up with the application of sound educational procedures of other sorts. This is particularly true of procedures tied up with motivation, methods in group activities, resources, and evaluation.

The individualized personal educational history (a form of record-keeping) proposed here represents an attempt to encourage the application of the basic principles described above to the study of problems *in all classes*, not merely in history classes alone.

WHAT ARE THE POSSIBLE PURPOSES A LEARNER MAY HAVE IN KEEPING PERSONAL EDUCATIONAL RECORDS?

The writer has been concerned for some years in trying to find more vital approaches to the study of history. During a discussion of the possible purposes of studying history with students who were beginning a study of the History of Education in the United States, the point was developed that one of the sound purposes might well be the development of the efficient use of personal educational records. History has been defined as "the written record of man's achievements." Now with the written record of what "man" would the student be most likely to be concerned? The answer almost immediately strikes one: with the written record of his own achievements, of course. Thus, this section is concerned with the question of the possible purposes a learner may have in keeping personal educational records.

It is interesting and significant to note that the implications of the problems that are being raised concerning the effective study of history are closely tied up with similar problems in certain other areas. For instance, is music best taught without the learner ever having some experience in the making of music himself? Is the appreciation of the short story likely to be deep if the learner only reads and analyzes the short stories of others and makes no attempt at short-story-writing himself? Psychologically, it appears that it is possible to appreciate history, music, or short stories without creative activity in the area, but this appreciation and use of the medium or subject is likely to be greatly enhanced if the learner also has a variety of experiences in which he actually tries to create history, music, or short stories, as the case may be.

The following list is suggestive of the possible purposes a learner may have in keeping personal educational records. It was developed by the writer in cooperation with several of his classes.[3]

[3] These possible purposes as stated are directly applicable to the teacher or prospective teacher who is a student in a methods course or an educational psychology course. Similar purposes may be considered by the high-school student.

I. *Purposes primarily concerned with learning the skill of efficient record-keeping*

To improve in the ability to keep useful records of one's activities. A concomitant purpose is to improve composition skills.

To study and compare the values of different kinds of records so that one may teach others how to use them effectively.

II. *Purposes primarily concerned with getting the study of a problem under way*

To list needs one has and problems one faces.

To list sources of help on a problem and encourage selective and critical choice of materials useful in analyzing a particular problem.

To aid in systematizing or organizing ideas already held before the present study.

To aid in the sketching of plans for further work.

III. *Purposes primarily concerned with facilitating work in progress*

To aid in the pursuit of learning on a basis largely independent of the teacher.

To encourage the selective and critical choice of materials useful in analyzing a particular problem.

To aid in the functional use of the library through recording useful sources, useful bibliographies, useful tests, etc.

To motivate the student to work harder and more regularly through being able to see tangible objective results to which he attributes some value.

To keep conferences, classes, and appointments straight and to facilitate the use of out-of-school resources. Closely related to this is the use of records in preparing for a conference to make sure the questions one wants to get considered are discussed.

To aid in keeping, for later use, the key points of an interview, a conference, or other resource situation such as observations and field trips.

To serve as a guide for assignments, learner-made or teacher-learner-made.

To help one get a clear picture of the advantages and disadvantages of each proposed solution to a problem so that one may have the basis for sound conclusions based on a reasonable amount of available evidence and a fair consideration of differing points of view.

To aid in tying new ideas into the pattern of those already held on a particular subject. Making a record of ideas forces one to objectify and clarify them sufficiently to write them down.

IV. *Purposes primarily concerned with credit-getting, the acquisition of high marks, and other realistic but "non-intrinsic" motives*

To help get an acceptable mark.

To help the teacher have more of a basis for giving marks.

To get social recognition through having the record of one's work posted, exhibited, or shown to others.

V. *Purposes primarily concerned with improving future work*

To prepare for later evaluation of attitudes, interests, and needs.

To help the student improve his work by providing the material for checking over what he has done and how he has done it. This is a directly functional use of personal history and will provide the learner with a clearer understanding of what history is through writing some himself.

To aid in reviewing what has been studied by showing the step-by-step procedures toward the goals of the individual or a group in which he is participating. Facts pertinent to problems attacked are also likely to be more clearly understood and remembered if they are written down, preferably in problem context.

To aid the teacher and other students where reciprocal learner help is encouraged in guiding the student more effectively by revealing his progress in what has been done and the difficulties he encountered in its accomplishment.

VI. *Purposes primarily concerned with activities more distant in time*

To help one get a job. The record should provide some objective evidence of past learning and thinking.

For later recreational use (diaries, for example).

To have ideas organized for ready reference when a particular problem comes up that is closely related to one already studied.

For help in a prospective occupation. If training for teaching is properly handled for example, the new teacher will have a whole battery of possible solutions to many of the problems he will face.

To provide a basis for similar courses that may be taken in the future.

To keep a list of places from which one may obtain material or which one may use as resources.

Obviously, there is some overlapping between some of the purposes. On the other hand, it has been found that *the pursuit of one purpose may militate against the achieving of other purposes.* For instance, a student who has been trained to study and to keep records only with the idea of memorizing information to pass tests frequently has a very difficult time developing study and record-keeping for some of the other specific purposes indicated above.

WHAT ARE USEFUL SUGGESTIONS FOR EFFICIENT RECORD-KEEPING?

As with other types of learning, it is important that those trying to teach and learn efficient record-keeping have some guides for the acquisition of the varied abilities involved. After a considerable amount of experience with the teaching of functional record-keeping the writer, with the help of numerous students, has evolved the following suggestions for consideration. For convenience the suggestions have been grouped under five headings: I. Purposes and possible uses of records; II. Sources of help and bibliography; III. Organization of records; IV. Improvement of approaches to record-keeping; V. Plans for future work.

I. *Suggestions related to the purposes and possible uses of records*

A clear statement of goals, purposes, and specific problems tied up with the study of a major problem should constitute an important part of the record. Such statement or statements should be put down initially when the problem is started. When goals, purposes, or problems change, the record should clearly indicate these changes with reasons for them. This suggestion is based on the assumption that goals, purposes, and problems should be dynamic and change as the thinking and procedures of the learner improve. The learner should keep in mind that a good record for one purpose may be a poor record for another purpose. This means that the students should carefully think through the purposes for studying and the relation of such purposes to the making of records. The type and completeness of one's record should be closely related to the purposes he has.

The student should usually give his own reactions to ideas gleaned from various sources—if his purpose is to do more than merely parrot the ideas of others. Initially, it is frequently wise to require that learners put their own reactions to all groups of ideas listed in the record at the time the ideas themselves are gathered. This requirement can be lifted as soon as learners see quite clearly the need for thinking through ideas got from outside sources and incorporating them or the valuable parts of them in the thinking and record of the learner.

In starting to study, it is usually well to state the main question to which the learner wants to find the answers, and then subdivide this main question into minor questions which will facilitate an analysis in the study of the problem. The main question and these sub-questions should clearly reflect the learner's purposes and aims in studying the problem or problems.

In group activity the advisability of keeping group records similar to individual records should be carefully considered. These, if kept, would give particular attention to *how the group works* as well as to major decisions the group may have reached. The latter is ordinarily emphasized but the former aspect of group records has frequently been neglected.

II. *Suggestions related to sources of help and bibliography*

In the record all sources of help utilized should usually constitute a part of it. These resources will include such ones as people interviewed, tests examined, articles read. References should be included in such a way that one can return to them quickly if necessary. For instance, listing the *Education Digest* is too general a reference to be of quick help. Difficulties encountered in getting ideas and using resources should also be listed for help in the record.

Closely related to the suggestions in the preceding paragraph is the idea that it is well to keep a list of resources, animate and inanimate, that the learner thinks should constantly be kept in view as possible sources of help. Particular attention should be given to the listing of out-of-school resources. Sometimes it is well for the learner to examine "a good record" in progress. This will give him additional ideas about how to set up such lists of resources for best and most functional use.

Plagiarism should, of course, be avoided. Direct quotation marks should accompany direct quotations. Acknowledgment of all sources of help by at least a bibliographic reference is a desirable goal, although sometimes, of course, we cannot identify the original source of a particular idea we want to include.

A critical and thoughtful attitude should accompany the use of all resources. Particularly to be avoided is blind acceptance, as the whole truth, of an idea either because it is printed or because an "authority" has spoken it. In recording ideas derived from a particular source it is sometimes well to indicate whether the origin of the idea is theoretical, based on the experience of the writer, or based on controlled experimentation. Frequently, it is well to clarify one's own ideas by writing them down even before any outside resources are used.

A few points on the relation of records to conferences and interviews are probably appropriate. It is usually desirable to bring all pertinent records to a conference in which the learner wishes to get direct help from others. In addition, it is frequently wise to prepare for a conference or interview with an instructor, another student, an employer, or someone else, by listing the points about which the learner wishes to inquire or which he wishes to discuss. During the conference or interview it is frequently desirable to make a written record for future reference of any suggestions made, so that such points will be available for use when needed. Unless this is done, over 50 per cent of the points made in a twenty-minute conference are likely to be rather quickly forgotten. Obviously, such points will be of little or no value unless the learner is in a position to consider them at the appropriate time. Ordinarily, enough data should be given in the record so that someone else, such as the instructor or another student who is attempting to give help, will have a sound picture or background of what has been done and what is projected for future study. Some students may object that this will involve too much writing. However, an idea not clearly enough stated to be meaningful to someone else frequently is actually somewhat unclear to the student himself. Ordinarily, such things as copies of letters written to distant individuals or organizations and answers to the same should be included as a part of the record. The student should also usually consider the advisability of making an annotated bibliography.

III. Suggestions relating to the organization of the record

Ordinarily, notes should be organized as taken under the *framework of the learner's problems* and not just in the author's organization of *his* ideas, as is frequently done. If the student continually attempts to organize new ideas into *his own* framework of problems and in answer to the questions he has raised, with the help of the instructor, in his own mind, he is not only becoming basically acquainted with the new ideas and principles, but he is also seeing, or attempting to see, their relationship to his own thinking. In addition, he is gaining practice in creative organization of his own.

Frequently, the simplest records are the least effective and most time-consuming. For example, records with no bibliography, no organization on the part of the learner except that of the authors quoted, no change from type of record-keeping used for years, or records made just to pass a test or get a mark may be simple, but they are likely to be ineffective for functional learning. To copy is simple; to think and write down the organization of one's thinking is much more difficult but vastly more effective. In this matter of organization the learner should consider periodically whether he should take time out to regroup or reorganize the ideas he has made a record of.

A word of caution related to the purpose of the records is probably appropriate here. The learner should definitely avoid spending time getting his notes looking nice just for the teacher. Of course, notes should be legible and should be taken with a definite purpose, but the learner should not feel that everything should be in final form every time the teacher or another student sees it. Records for learning purposes should be developing, which means that there will always be room for additional progress. To put down what he wants and what he feels is most likely to help him, rather than just what the teacher wants, is likely to be a most profitable procedure for the learner. Sometimes a section on miscellaneous ideas or information to give the teacher an overview of what is being done is valuable. In this, the student should include in brief form a list of his activities, interests, problems, and progress toward objectives. It is usually wise for him to head his papers and sections of his records so that he and others can tell at a glance the contents of a page or section of his record. A table of contents and some sort of tentative paging are usually necessary to facilitate improvement and the economical use of records.

It is of basic importance that we keep in mind the fact that the digestion of ideas is as important, if not more important, than the mere acquisition of them. One test of the quality of the digestion of ideas is the extent to which a student is able, in his own words, to tie up new ideas in an organized fashion with related ideas already held.

IV. *Suggestions on improvement of approaches to record-keeping, including some on evaluation*

The student should constantly examine his own strengths and weaknesses in record-keeping. Such study should be accompanied by attempts at greater utilization of recognized strengths, and the rapid elimination of weaknesses. A report on progress in this direction should constitute a part of the record. Such a report might include an indication of difficulties encountered in deciding what to study, when to study, and how best to record ideas gleaned from various resources. This may be put in a specific part of the record. If mistakes are listed as they are recognized, the learner is more likely to eliminate them in future activities.

It is frequently well for the student to study the records of other students periodically in order to gain ideas for the improvement of his own record. Such ideas should be listed in his record as well as a list of suggestions made by others for improving the record. Discussions held periodically with others on how to improve records provide one basis for such ideas.

The teacher may provide space in a filing cabinet in which the learner is encouraged to place information that he feels might create a better understanding between himself and the instructor. The folder might contain information concerning the students' activities, interests, problems, and progress toward his objectives. The instructor's comments may be added. Such a system can avoid embarrassment and keep the teacher and learner team working harmoniously together.

As the record is made, consideration should be given for use of similar record-keeping procedures in other situations. The learner, for example, may consider how his record-keeping in other classes may be improved and actually set about improving it. He can list what has been done in this respect and evaluate it. The student may also want to consider how he can later help others with whom he may be working to improve their records of learning. This point is particularly important for teachers and prospective teachers to consider.

Frequently, the learner should consider whether he is writing down too much or too little for most efficient record-keeping in view of his purposes. In particular, the learner should avoid writing records just for the sake of writing records. He should also avoid being "pencil lazy or pen lazy." Writing out ideas and plans that have been thought through is an excellent method of discovering for ourselves what, if anything, we are actually thinking. It is valuable at frequent intervals to go through the record, analyze the progress made, and then write critical comments concerning the work.

V. *Suggestions relating to plans for future work*

It is always well to keep in the record tentative but somewhat detailed plans for future work. Planless work is frequently a waste of time. For the practical and economical utilization of ideas acquired, plans should usually be made for such utilization at the time of the acquisition of the ideas or principles. Otherwise, the ideas or principles are likely to become "cold" and unusable within a relatively short period of time. A dynamic phase of the plan for future work would be a section containing additional questions or problems that are suggested by continuing problem attack that would seem to form a useful part of later planning and study.

Usually the records should contain "pupil-teacher assignments," teacher assignments, and/or self-made assignments. One sheet or one section of the record should probably be reserved for this purpose.

❉ ❉ ❉

The suggestions given above, which have grown out of actual use of records in solving actual problems, should not be accepted uncritically by the reader. Rather, each suggestion should be examined carefully by the reader and then rejected or used as his best thinking dictates. The suggestions are designed to promote active thought by students and instructors on ways in which they may develop more adequate and more effective record-keeping.

HOW MAY THE INSTRUCTOR HELP THE STUDENT EVALUATE HIS WORK THROUGH PERIODIC EXAMINATION OR EVALUATION OF THE LEARNER'S RECORD?

In promoting the study of individual problems, it has been the practice of the writer to hold as many planned, informal conferences with each individual student as are feasible. What is feasible will depend on teacher-learner ratio and on other job commitments of the teacher. Since time limitations often make it impossible to have such conferences frequently enough for the instructor to keep in close touch with the work of each student, a system of periodic (usually weekly) inspections of the progress reports or records of each student has sometimes been instituted by the writer after discussion of the problem with the students. Thus, each student hands in his complete progress report, *including all work to date,* about once a week, the instructor looks it over, makes some comments or suggestions, and hands it back during the next class period. Students are encouraged to seek help through this type of teacher-learner correspondence. Below are some of the representative suggestions the writer finds, on checking over progress reports, he has made to students. Although some of these students were rather mature, similar types of suggestions would be appropriate for younger students. Usually not more than three or four suggestions were made to any one student at a single time. The suggestions are given with the hope that they may prove helpful to other teachers or prospective teachers who are attempting to develop individualized study approaches, but find time limitations a serious handicap. The items also suggest a method of encouraging learner thought and independence.[4] (Notes to a student were usually headed by the student's name.)

I. *Suggestions to students relating to materials and other resources*

Would it not be well for you to consult the *Education Index* and the *Readers Guide* for the names and sources of articles that might

---

[4] These suggestions were made to teacher-training students. Similar ideas with modified language can be used with high-school students.

prove helpful on your problem? (The use of appropriate pamphlets, tests, courses of study, questionnaires, and inventories was also suggested through this type of question.)

I think you would find it profitable to discuss this problem with Mr. A_____ and Mrs. B_____. Mr. A_____ has had special experience in the area in which you are working and Mrs. B_____ has already studied much on this problem.

Might it not be advisable for you to write to_____(naming an individual, company, or institution) for additional information on this problem?

Let me urge you to request a conference with Professor_____, to discuss this problem. He is particularly interested in it and I think he could give you some valuable help.

If you can arrange it, I believe an interview with Mr._____ (a local employer) would give you a different point of view from the one you are getting. If you do this, let me suggest that you prepare a series of questions to have in mind during the interview to ask of him if you get a chance.

Have you seen and used_____(naming a particular resource)? If so, how did you react to it? If not, I suggest you try it.

Are your references complete enough and specific enough for you to find later or order if you should want to do so? How would you quickly locate an article whose source you have simply designated as being in the "Journal of Educational Psychology"?

Would it not be advisable to visit_____where the type of thing you are discussing is being carried on?

Might a systematic survey of materials or opinions help you reach a better conclusion on this problem?

Are you familiar with the current magazines in your field? Would it be well to include the names of these together with the address and cost of each?

Would it be a good idea to list the resources you plan to use in the study of this new problem? This list would be tentative, of course.

Are there resources you would like to have but find they are not now available?

Are you handing your record in for inspection sufficiently often?

Are you not depending too much on books and not enough on other sources for new ideas?

Please list specific difficulties you have and upon which you should get help. It might be well to have a special sheet for these. Please leave the suggestions of other students and myself in your record.

II. *Suggestions to students regarding emphasis in working on problems*

Are you giving too much attention to mere accumulation of materials and not enough to how you can actually *use* this information?

Might it be well to make a test or check list to outline points of emphasis and/or check on understanding and utilization of what is being done?

Are you writing down enough so that you will have a sufficient basis for checking back on your plans and approaches when you later want to use them? Are your records complete enough?

Do you feel that you are keeping your conclusions tentative enough in view of the fact that you have sampled only a few points of view or lines of evidence? Are you justified in making such a statement as, "The cause of World War II was_____"?

Are you handling this work too much as an assignment, instead of trying to prepare yourself better to meet situations you are likely to face in the future?

Are you giving sufficient place in your record to your own ideas and thinking regarding the information you are collecting?

Are you utilizing the suggestions about records and problems that were made in class? I suggest that you review your notes on these points.

Are you being sufficiently critical in the selection and acceptance of ideas you are getting?

Are you giving sufficient attention to an analysis of your own strengths and weaknesses of study? Not to know how to do this, or not to do it, is in itself a major weakness.

Are you making a sufficient effort to transfer to your own field class suggestions made regarding some other field?

Have you given adequate attention to the suggestions you and I worked out together at our last conference?

Remember there is no easy road to learning. Consistent effort is necessary for consistent results.

III. *Suggestions to students regarding organization of record*

Are you copying too much the organization of someone else and not organizing the material to meet *your* probable needs and sound purposes?

Are you organizing your materials so that you can foresee the probable uses for it.

Do you need to take time out to pull the loose ends together and get a new over-all view of your problem and the progress you have made in attempting to solve it?

Could you not organize your materials into a more consistent framework? I shall be glad to talk this over with you.

Would it be well to crystallize your tentative organization into a table of contents?

Are you putting a heading over each section of material so that you can find it when you want to do so?

IV. *Suggestions to students regarding plans for future work*

What difficulties would you be likely to encounter in giving the tests you mention in your record? (Other questions of a similar sort will sometimes encourage the learner to think through probable future difficulties.)

The main problem you are attacking is: How may we eliminate malaria in our community? Might it not be well to work initially on such sub-problems as these: What is the cause of malaria? How is malaria carried? How may malaria be prevented?

Have you considered whether this is the best time and place for you to study this problem? Might it be better to study some other problem such as_____(suggest one or more) and study this problem next summer or later in the year?

Might it be well for you to enlist the cooperation of another student and jointly work with him on this problem?

Are you considering how you may help others, whom you may be working with at a later date, to use this problem approach to study?

Should you now carefully consider whether it is advisable to start working on a new problem? It might be well to let your ideas on this problem "ferment" for a time.

Are you giving sufficient attention to tentative plans for future work?

Do you think you are getting a sufficient amount out of your study to justify the time you are spending on it?

I suggest that together we talk over your plans for future work.

Might it be well for you to visit work in progress of the type that you are studying?

Have you projected in your own mind the types of situations you are likely to face and then set up your plans to prepare yourself to meet these situations more effectively?

Would it be well to organize an annotated bibliography for future use?

What suggestions could you make for improving your own work? Remember that continuous diagnosis and evaluation should be planned for as an integral part of your work.

I suggest that you talk over your problems more with others. See how they react to the plans you have set up.

Might you be able to tie up this work with the work you are doing in_____(naming another course)? Such an arrangement would give you plenty of time to make an intensive study of these problems.

Have you discussed your plans with_____and_____(naming two other individuals)?

Additional comments lauding work well done were also frequently included. It should be noted that the response to this instructor-student relationship was gratifying and more than paid the instructor in satisfaction for the additional time and effort he put out.

HOW MAY THE LEARNER HELP HIMSELF THROUGH A SYSTEMATIC SELF-EVALUATION OF HIS OWN EDUCATIONAL RECORD-KEEPING?

As has been previously indicated, one of the main purposes of keeping educational records is to improve our skills related to this activity. Means by which the instructor and fellow students can help in this regard are listed under other questions. In order to get record-keeping improvement maximized, it is vital that the learner himself continuously examine and re-examine his own efficiency in keeping records that are most useful to him. In record evaluation, as in all other evaluation, it is strongly recommended that the type be increasingly emphasized which will (a) help the learner make changes in his future work by having him see some specific weaknesses in his study approaches, and (b) develop in the learner the ability to carry on his own evaluative activities with a decreasing amount of dependence upon the instructor. No one is able to remember, without written aids, all the details he needs to consider when the solution of a major problem is attempted. Students and instructor should consciously attempt to de-emphasize two phases of evaluation that tend to produce an ineffective use of all types of study: (a) evaluation that is used almost exclusively to get a mark, and (b) evaluation that is almost entirely the responsibility of the instructor.

One group with whom the writer worked decided with the instructor's aid that the two following questions would be useful for them to consider individually: (1) Am I progressing in my ability to keep records that include the type of materials I am likely to need later on? Evidence? (2) Am I improving in the ability to organize my work? Evidence? To suggest the types of self-evaluation the questions produced and to indicate the factors that students consider important in record-keeping ability, the following illustrative answers to each of the questions are given.[5]

Question 1. Am I progressing in my ability to keep records that include the type of materials I am likely to need later on? Evidence?

"Evidently, I am progressing very well in my ability to keep records of the type of material that I will need to teach my home economics classes. I am collecting pamphlets and getting addresses from which I may obtain information. I am also making illustrations for clothing classes and ordering posters."

"Yes. In my field I feel that the majority of teachers do not know what generalizations the student should acquire. I question whether the mastery of the laws of chemistry or physics is not as important as the learning of the general principles that should be acquired, such as scientific thinking. In working on my problems I have kept a record of everything that would be useful along this line. I have also kept a record with comments of some good examinations."

"Especially on the problem on which I am working at present, I am keeping records of material that I will *definitely* use later on. I have records of sources of material to be used later on. I have taken every problem and listed reasonable possibilities and then stated

---

[5] High-school students can be encouraged to consider similar questions.

my conclusion or decision. Although I have not made a complete list of material to be used, I do intend to make this list as soon as I have made all of my decisions."

"In my problem I have organized the materials in such a way as to help me later on. In placing them under specific problems I shall have a file of problems and later on when the need arises I can go directly to the specific problem and get some suggestions for possible answers to it. This ability has a carry-over value for other subjects as well, for I have found this same method useful in many other subjects."

"Yes, before I started this course I had never kept a record except for the 'money budget' in freshmen problems. Since taking this course I have been keeping a record in all of my classes. I am sure they will help me later on."

"I feel that I am progressing in my ability to choose the factors, for my record, that are important now and have been useful to modern teachers and psychologists. Evidence of this is the part of my record where I have shown the work of other teachers and have tried to point out where their practices might be used effectively by me.

Question 2. Am I improving in the ability to organize my work? Evidence?

"Previously, I sat down and wrote out an outline, then filled it in. Now I make a temporary outline and set down my specific topics or problems, which are written on separate sheets. After this, I take each sheet that has a heading and expand on it from the material collected from books and articles. Then I write my personal view on the subject. Now I can look at some material and tell if it is of any value to me, because I have my general outline in mind."

"In the beginning of the course I could never seem to find the correct topic under which to place material. Several suggestions from the instructor have helped me to devote more thought to this. I am able to tell at a glance now what problems I have, and I am able, to some extent, to give possible answers to any of the questions. The possible approaches have been worked out by some present-day teachers."

"At the first of the semester, I thought I couldn't do all of my work, but I learned by better organization that I would have more time. Also, by looking at the folders of others, I learned the organizations of others and gained some help."

"Formerly, I was inclined to study for fact memorization and my learning had no positive carry-over value for me. Since I have learned to organize my work in my mind, as well as on paper, I find that it helps me immeasurably in study, as well as for future use."

"On my first problems I was more or less studying, but I was not quite sure how to organize them or just where I was going next. On my latter problem I took the smaller problems and took them step by step as I would see them. I studied the different solutions to each, then decided on the best solution for each problem in the light of the evidence I could get."

"For this question I would like to contrast the organization of the study of my first problem, namely, the aims and the objectives of physical education, with the study of my last problem, the core curriculum and physical education. For my first problem, I merely made a list of my objectives after studying the parents', teachers', and pupils' viewpoints. But for my last problem I had a definite outline, which was as follows:

- a) What is the core curriculum?
- b) What is the relation of the core curriculum to physical education?
- c) What are the ways physical education is connected with the core curriculum?
- d) What are the implications for education of the core curriculum?
- e) What is the task of the physical education teacher in this new curriculum?
- f) What methods should be used?
- g) How should guidance be carried on?
- h) What are the ways to organize a class?
- i) What are special problems I am likely to face in trying to use the core curriculum idea in my teaching?

When we first started all this writing and keeping of records in the curriculum laboratory work, I thought it was sort of foolish. Since then I have changed my mind. I find that it clarifies my ideas and helps me organize them if I write them down."

Questions that may be used in the evaluation of one's own record and record-keeping abilities, in addition to the two given here with illustrative answers, may be found at the beginning of this chapter and in the section that follows this one.

HOW MAY LEARNERS HELP ONE ANOTHER THROUGH A RECIPROCAL STUDY AND EVALUATION OF EACH OTHER'S RECORDS?

Individual records of personal educational progress provide one of the best avenues through which learners may help themselves through helping others. As is the case with most worth-while educational activity, in the early stages it is very important that the teacher give considerable advance thought to the projected activities. In attempting this type of activity, the instructor with the aid of the learners should consider their needs and purposes in connection with record-keeping evaluation and then cooperatively develop a systematic approach or series of approaches so that goals may be reached to as large a degree as possible. It should be emphasized that merely telling learners "Now you help one another through studying each other's personal education histories" may do more harm than good. There is no effective substitute for careful pre-planning on the part of the instructor and students.

For example, in one group's approach to reciprocal record study these four questions were developed and answered by each learner for two or more records of others:

1. What are the strong points of this record?
2. What are the possible weaknesses of this personal educational record?
3. What are suggestions for improving this record?
4. What ideas have I gleaned from studying this record that are likely to be of value to me?

The answers relating to a particular record, together with the name of the student contributing them, were kept in the record to aid the writer of the record in improving his work, particularly his record-keeping. Illustrative answers to these questions by a group with no previous experience of this type are the following:

Question 1. What are the strong points of this record?

"Mr. S. seems to have started work on his problem after feeling a real need for work in that field. He evidently uses his material effectively, because his notes are concise and to the point. He does not include irrelevant material."

"He has given the opinions of several authors as well as his own views on the subjects he has studied."

"Miss B. has used a great variety of resources and her conclusions reflect a well-rounded point of view."

"She has given careful attention to listing tentative plans for specific activities to be carried on in the future."

"Mr. S. is working on a problem in which he has strong motivation because he is definitely facing it right at the present time."

"She has made a careful division of the main problem into specific sub-problems and she is making considerable progress in solving these sub-problems."

"Changes in the record reflect considerable improvement in the selection and organization of material since the semester started."

"Miss K. gives a variety of specific examples of materials she could use in actual teaching."

"The record shows clearly the types of things that Miss V. believes the teacher, the learner, and the community may do in working out solutions to the problems."

"Specific sources and references for each problem have been carefully listed."

"Miss P.'s goals and purposes in studying these problems have been specifically set up and listed."

"Miss S. is collecting a variety of materials that will help her later."

"She has picked a subject that specifically runs parallel with her life work."

"She has improved very much. Her first work sounded very 'bookish,' but the latest work seems to be in her own words and shows she is doing more thinking herself."

Question 2. What are the possible weaknesses of this personal educational record?

"She has no table of contents or index and it is hard to find various parts of the material quickly."

"He has not used a sufficient variety of references and resources to get the proper perspective on the problems."

"It seems that Miss T. has been just going through books without first setting up her own organization. The result is that her material is a compilation of the organizations of the authors she has examined and there is much overlapping of ideas."

"She has not divided her work into sub-problems that would make it much easier to handle."

"The work is presented in too much of a discussion form, which makes the record so long that it is hard to see the picture as a whole."

"She should be more critical of what is read and heard, attempting to pick out the strong and weak points of all the materials examined."

"No dates are used in the work, which makes it difficult to see clearly trends in thinking and study."

"There are not sufficient headings to show just what sub-problems each part of the material is giving a partial answer to."

"None of Miss B.'s own comments are included in the record; there seems to be much mere parroting of the work and ideas of others."

"References probably should be given separately for each topic."

"Too much dependence has apparently been placed on books and not enough on other resources, such as professional magazines and other educators."

"He should show quotations through the use of quotation marks. He should give credit for an idea where credit is due."

"The record does not contain a bibliography, an item that I have found to be a great time-saver. Also, there is no general outline of the study."

Question 3. What are some suggestions for improving the records?

"Make a bibliography and a problem outline to study by."

"Write notes in clearer outline form under appropriate sub-problems."

"Make the bibliography more complete and accurate."

"Consult a greater variety of sources before drawing conclusions."

"Reorganize your folder in terms of the specific problems and sub-problems upon which you are working. Tentatively discard material that is not pertinent."

"Write some of your own conclusions and ideas that have resulted from your study. Do not merely copy the ideas of others."

"Use a greater number of examples in your work."

"In using references only select and record ideas that seem to have a bearing on the problems and sub-problems you are studying. Do not record everything just because it is written down."

"If you would give more time to your problem you would be more satisfied with the results."

"Outline short-time plans specifically and long-time plans in general so that you will have a tentative schedule for your study."

"Instead of organizing your material after you have accumulated a lot of it, I suggest that you organize it as you get it. I have found this saves much time."

"Make a table of contents so that you can turn quickly to various sub-problems."

"Use 8½ by 11 paper rather than the little sheets you are now using. It will make it easier for you to use your record."

Question 4. What ideas have I gleaned from studying this record that are likely to be of value to me?

"This record suggests a method by which I can summarize my problem material into a usable final form."

"The idea of specifically presenting a problem and including possible methods for solving it."

"I think that, instead of first collecting my material and then organizing it, I should first set up a tentative organization and place related ideas together as I get them. In this way I will have materials relating to a specific sub-problem together and it will take less time to reorganize them later."

"Her record gave me an idea of a problem I should work on which I had not thought about before: How can I promote democracy in a physical education program?"

"Her references suggested some new sources of material that I plan to use."

"I see I should use the *Education Index* more and generally expand the number of resources I use."

"I got the idea of how a good outline is developed. I also now see the importance of giving suffici nt detail in my record so that what I am presenting is clear."

"The record suggests some practical ways in which my problem and the material I am getting on it can be applied."

"I think the idea of getting samples of the different types of tests from publishers is one that will help me later on."

"It so happens that I intend to teach the same subject as Mr. J.

His ideas should prove very valuable to me. For example, he gave the advantages and faults of certain methods that I had intended to use in teaching. With the ideas I derived from his records I can better pick out the more valuable methods and be conscious of their strengths and weaknesses."

"Mr. S. has included some notes that are directly to the point in my problems."

Additional proposals for reciprocal evaluation. Five additional methods of reciprocal evaluation that have been used with profit are the following:[6]

Method I

_____record analyzed by_____

1. List favorable features of the record.
2. List features about which you think a question should be raised.
3. Give specific suggestions for improving the record using the following lists, which we have cooperatively worked out in class:

   a) Purposes of records
   b) Suggestions for keeping good records

Method II

(Sometimes appropriate if given about one week before the end of the semester.)

1. What five individual educational records in the class do you feel have been particularly well worked out? (All records will have been made available to each student for a specified period of time.)
2. Give the outstandingly desirable features of each of the five records you have selected.

NOTE: In doing this it may be well to identify the records by number only, rather than by name, and thus largely eliminate

[6] These suggestions are phrased for use with students in teacher-training methods or educational psychology courses. Similar proposals can be phrased by, with, and for high-school students in any course where attention is given to improving personal educational record-keeping.

the personal factor. Also, a very rough rating of each of the better records can be made by totaling the number of times each record is mentioned. A rough rating of each rater can be obtained by finding how many of the top five records, as evaluated by the whole class, he mentioned in his individual ratings.

Method III

For Reciprocal Evaluation of Folders or Records

With respect to each of the following questions, and using the record being examined as a basis for your answers, indicate (*a*) status, and (*b*) indications of needed improvement.

1. Organization of ideas:
   a) Did the student attempt to see and specifically identify the main problems of his study?
   b) Did the learner systematically divide the main problems into sub-problems for effective attack?
   c) Are there indications that the learner gave careful consideration to a sufficient number of possible problems before actually selecting the first main problem he worked on?

2. Does the record show that the student is making progress in solving sub-problems? Evidence?
3. Does the record have a guide or table of contents so that parts of it may be quickly found?
4. Does the record contain an adequate bibliography? Are the individual references sufficiently complete?
5. Does the record show an increasing use of a variety of resources?
6. Does the record show that the user has in mind specific purposes for keeping it? If so, what do you think they are?
7. Does the record show the learner is constantly or periodically making plans for future work? Evidence?
8. Are there indications that the record-maker sees and is eliminating weaknesses in his record?
9. Are there indications that the learner sees purposes and methods of record-keeping that he may later use with his own students?

10. Are there indications that the learner keeps his records with him during study and uses them at appropriate times?

NOTE: The questions given above may be revised and used with (a) purposes of records, and (b) suggestions for improving them.

Reciprocal evaluation of records not only gives suggestions for improvement to the learner whose record is being studied, but it also suggests changes the evaluator should consider making in his own record.

Method IV

Suggested Reciprocal Evaluation of Record-keeping for Effective Learning

_____'s record rated by_____

Before each letter indicate status of record being examined by using a 5-point scale. If record is very high on the point being rated give it a 5; if extremely low give it a 1. Use ratings in between for other indications of merit. The higher the number, the better the rating.

I. *Objective evaluation questions on records*

( )   A. Adequate table of contents with paging to show what is in record and where it is, and does this tie up with rest of record?

( )   B. Bibliography in conventional form in some order with one copying?

( )   C. List of possible problems set up so it can be added to? Indications that list of possible problems is being added to as study proceeds?

( )   D. Breakdown of at least two problems?

( )   E. *Use* of problem breakdown in placing ideas obtained?

( )   F. Ideas set up under sub-problems in such a way that additional ideas can be readily placed without recopying?

( )   G. Have *professional goals* been clearly indicated?

( )   H. Have specific purposes for working on group of problems being studied been indicated?

( )   I. Have tentative plans for rest of semester been indicated clearly?

( ) J. Have own reactions and criticisms of ideas gleaned from various sources been given as ideas were *first* recorded?

( ) K. Has plagiarism been avoided?

( ) L. Are questions to be asked in conferences or interviews indicated?

( ) M. Are records of conferences or interviews given?

( ) N. Is each page in record headed so that one can tell at a glance what is in it?

( ) O. Is record set up in sufficiently elastic fashion so that ideas concerning any particular question or problem can be added without recopying ideas already listed?

II. *Subjective evaluative questions*

( ) A. Are there indications that the *Education Index* (the teacher's bible) is being much used?

( ) B. Is there evidence that note-taking has been selective in nature (as opposed to putting down ideas not related to problems being studied)?

( ) C. Does it appear that the learner is able to put down ideas obtained without a lot of recopying?

( ) D. Is there objective evidence that a critical and thoughtful attitude has characterized the use of resources (as opposed to mere parroting of ideas)?

( ) E. Is there evidence that the record has largely been made for intrinsic purposes rather than to have something for the teacher to see?

( ) F. Does the record indicate that ideas are put down in sufficient detail to be useful a year from now? (Or is the learner pen or pencil lazy?)

( ) G. Does the record indicate sufficient use of other types of resources (conferences, interviews, observations, letter-writing, friends, classmates, teachers, etc.) besides printed materials?

( ) H. Is there evidence that about the right amount is being written in the record rather than too much or too little?

( ) I. Are there specific indications that improvement in all steps of the learning process (see mimeographed sheet on "Purposes of class as seen by instructor") is being sought?

( ) J. Does it appear that the material would actually be useful to the individual on the job or in getting a job?

( ) K. Can another person get a *clear* picture of the learner's purposes, and of what has been done?

( ) L. Does it appear that sufficient effort has been put forth?

( ) M. Have sources and resources used been quite varied?

( ) N. Are there indications of considerable creativity in the organization of problems?

( ) O. Are there indications that the learner is writing down many of his own ideas in addition to those received from reading?

( ) P. Are there evidences that the individual is getting *and using* suggestions on study procedure and resources from others?

( ) Q. Does the learner seem to be conscious of the specific weaknesses he has?

( ) R. Does it appear that the record is being used as a vehicle for efficient learning?

( ) S. Are there indications that the record-keeper did a good bit of thinking himself, both in organization of problems and in listing possible solutions to problems?

( ) T. Does it appear that the learner really understands what he puts down?

( ) U. Has the learner used a good balance of "theory" resources and "applied" resources?

( ) V. Does it appear that the recorder is thinking about using methods learned in other courses and other situations?

Method V

For Reciprocal Evaluation

_____'s record rated by_____

To what extent:

a) does it appear that the learner is really concerned about his present and prospective problems?

b) is it clear what the learner was trying to do?

c) was the learner thinking rather than simply copying?

d) does it appear that the record might be useful when the person got on the job?

e) does it seem that an appropriate variety of resources was
used?

f) does it seem that the learner's ideas have changed during
the semester?

Comments: _____

_____

_____

WHAT KIND OF LEARNER RECORDS CAN CONSTITUTE ONE PART OF THE REPORTS FOR PARENTS?

Learner records as a part of the "report card" that goes home to
parents have several possible advantages. They provide the student
with a realistic type of functional composition; they give the parents
a picture of what their child is doing in school *from the standpoint
of the child himself.* Such reports also make it possible for the
school to keep its channels of communication to the homes of the
community more open. Such reports keep parents better informed
about what the school is doing and, when it comes to paying larger
salaries to teachers or otherwise financing better schools, parents
are more likely to support such moves.

Wallace (12, pp. 77-79) gives a record written by a senior high-
school student. The record is reproduced below.[7]

"MY SIX WEEKS' REPORT, SECOND SEMESTER

Jane Ernestine—Sr. II

"I feel that I have accomplished a great deal in the past six weeks.
I have worked very hard to get as much done as possible during
these remaining weeks, as I wanted to work even beyond my goals
set at the beginning of school.

"I have done more cooperative work during these weeks than
ever before, and I feel that it has been a great help to me. One of
these six weeks was spent in registering people in the community
for war ration books, and during that time I carried on all my regular work at home, because I wanted to keep up with my planned

[7] By permission of the publisher.

work. I feel, however, that this experience was a valuable one, in which I learned the importance of being accurate, dependable, and cooperative.

"In my English work, I have done a good bit of study from the textbook concerning office work, social manners, and fundamental English, such as the parts of speech and their uses. I have also spent much time in studying a copy of the Cooperative English Test and have looked up the sources of the questions. I have worked very hard to improve my vocabulary and spelling and I feel that I have made progress. During home-room discussions, I have learned to enter into the activities more than before. I have also written several reports, one of which is on the war effort of the school. I have read the following books during the past six weeks: *Flight Surgeon, The Merchant of Venice, American Bred, Landfall, The Tragedy of Macbeth, Travels with a Donkey, Ethan Frome, A Lantern in Her Hand,* and *Sky Service.* I feel that I have used my time to good advantage in working toward my goals.

"I have carried on my work in bookkeeping, and I feel that I have been successful in reaching my goals. I have studied five chapters from my textbook and worked problems from these in my workbook. I have made an extended study of these subjects: the work at the end of the fiscal period, merchandise inventories, daily inventories, work sheets, balance sheets, profit and loss statements, classification of accounts, adjusting entries, closing entries, promissory notes, personal and collateral surety, interest-bearing notes, interest expense, bank loans, accrued interest, and methods used in paying notes. I have also done some work for the home economics department in which I completed the canning records for the year of 1942. I typed these reports and used the adding machine to make final calculations. I feel that work of this type is of great value to me.

"My work in Latin-American history has been most interesting. I have read interesting facts concerning dollar diplomacy; Latin America and World War I; the Good Neighbor Policy; the Pan-American movements; the conferences at Mexico City, Rio de Janeiro, Buenos Aires, Santiago, Havana, Montevideo, and Lima; the results of these conferences; the developments of economic relations; and the effects of the present war and problems brought about by it. I have also written several reports on matters of interest and presented them in class. I feel that I have learned a great deal, which helps me understand and appreciate the relationships of the Americas.

"I have studied very hard on literature. I have read and studied the history of American literature and have begun that of English literature. I have studied the periods of American literature and the best and most beloved authors of each period. I have also read some of their best works. In my study of English literature I have studied the section on the beginning of English literature, which contains examples of epic poetry, narratives, and travel stories. In the next section I studied ballads and something of Geoffrey Chaucer's life and works. In the section on the Elizabethan period, I have studied drama and lyric poetry. In order to find more to help me pass the Cooperative Literature Test, which is one of my goals, I began this week to look up each subject mentioned on an old test. Thus far, I have about seventeen pages of notes to help me. I feel that I have learned much on a subject of utmost importance.

"During these weeks I have completed my third book of shorthand and feel that I have made good progress. This book was a review of my first two books and introduced quicker and better methods of phrasing. I intend to spend the remaining weeks in review of these books and also put into practice what I've learned. I shall work to increase my speed in dictation, which is now 80 words per minute. My goal for the year was 60, but now I should like to reach 100.

"I have typed a great deal recently—putting into practice what I have learned previously. I can now type 55 words a minute, which is better than the goal I set in September. I have on several occasions typed postal cards, letters, and newspaper articles. I also typed a complete play for a junior high-school group, which was excellent practice for me. I feel that by doing things of this kind, I am really accomplishing something in my work. I have continued my study of letter forms and also my practice work on things such as stories and reports. I have done another new type of work in making out forms and filling in data. I intend to continue doing jobs of this kind so that I may really be equipped for future work.

"Last week I passed a standard government clerical test, which I took in Montgomery. On this examination I was tested on English grammar, vocabulary and spelling, penmanship, arithmetic, and general intelligence. The test is that given all those applying for clerical jobs in this division.

"I feel that I have made progress in all of my subjects, and I intend to work even harder during the remaining weeks in order that I may reach my goals."

The type of report described above gives a clearer picture of student activity in school than is usually got through exclusive use of teacher reporting. The latter should supplement learner reporting as it does in the situation reported by Wallace.

There are many possible ways of writing reports for home use (letters, stories, compositions, cartoons, poems, etc.), but perhaps the primary value that can come from them is the encouragement they give to thinking about the purposes of school activity, why particular things are being done rather than other things, and a consideration of what is being got out of school.

OPERATING PRINCIPLES FOR THE DEVELOPMENT OF EFFECTIVE LEARNER RECORD-KEEPING

I. *Purposes of record-keeping*

A. The keeping of records is an indispensable help in making an evaluation of progress.

B. Records tend to stimulate perseverence and keep the learner working toward definite goals.

C. In learning record-keeping the student will make many mistakes in the beginning, but he will profit by them later as he will find out how to approach his problems and keep an efficient report of what has been done and what he purposes to do.

D. Good records tend to permit the learner to know his own weaknesses and oftentimes inspire him to do better despite these weaknesses.

E. The teacher, as a learner, should keep an adequate record of his plans and problems, so that he can improve his own learning and teaching skills.

F. Getting practice in keeping the type of records the learner will need outside of school should be given major consideration.

G. One use that can be made of the record in school situations is to help the parents see what is being done at school, why it is being done, and how it is being done.

H. An attempt should be made to keep the record in such a manner that it will be useful for future reference.

I. One of the most important principles to be kept in mind, in evaluating a record, is raised by the question, "Is the record usable?"

II. *Content of the record*

A. Materials included must be those that are most meaningful and helpful to the learner in his work on his assignment or problem. The contents of the record should seem important to the learner himself.

B. One of the most important parts of record-keeping is a clear statement of the goals, purposes, and specific problems being studied.

C. It is important that the record be not merely a compilation of ideas derived from various resources. It should also contain the student's own reactions to the ideas and his criticisms of them, in terms of situations that he feels he is likely to face or situations that he has actually faced.

D. Records should be in sufficient detail and clear enough so that they can be reread after two weeks or two years and still offer meaningful suggestions to the learner.

E. The record should emphasize the practical aspects and implications of what has been learned and not merely be a compilation of theory.

F. Frequently it is desirable to record weaknesses in method or solution as well as successes.

G. In most cases records should contain several possible solutions to a particular problem, rather than "the solution." The reason for this is that in many types of problems one type of solution will work best in one situation and another type of solution will work best in another situation.

III. *Organization of the record*

A. Records should be individual and original. No two learners should keep exactly the same kind of records if teaching is to be what it proposes to be, a democratic movement to develop individual differences.

    B. Different parts of a record should be set up in a flexible fashion so that they can be added to as the occasion arises without recopying.

    C. It is frequently advisable to make an index or a table of contents so that material can be easily found. Pagination should be flexible so that new pages may be added without recopying.

    D. Ideas put into the record should be put in the learner's outline rather than copying the outline of the person who wrote the book or article from which the ideas may have come.

    E. Frequently, study should be made of ways of keeping a record economically; that is, putting down the information in organized form as it is acquired rather than getting a lot of unorganized ideas and then trying to organize them after the information and background of the ideas are cold.

    F. The bibliography should be set up in such a way that additional references may be added without additional recopying.

IV. *Help from others in keeping records*

    A. In order to keep effective records the learner should be guided regarding proper form and content of his record.

    B. It is advisable for the teacher to examine student records from time to time and offer suggestions about the ways the learner may improve his work.

    C. Frequently, it is advisable for the student to have his record checked by other students and give reciprocal ideas on improvement.

    D. It is frequently desirable for the student to experiment with different types of records. Showing the student some "good" records may be advisable at times.

BIBLIOGRAPHY

1. Association for Supervision and Curriculum Development. *Toward Better Teaching*. Washington, D.C.: The Association, 1949.

    Pages 244-50 are particularly useful in giving actual examples of learner record-keeping.

2. Class of 1938, University High School, Ohio State University. *Were We Guinea Pigs?* New York: Henry Holt and Co., 1938. pp. 274-94.
   Describes some learner record-keeping procedures that can be adapted to other situations.
3. COOK, NELLIE E. "Real Problems for Youngsters." *Educational Leadership*, 4:169-74; December 1946.
   Article is made up largely of children's diary accounts of how they planned and carried through a project.
4. FREE, RAYMOND J. "We Measure Growth Together." *Educational Leadership*, 4:464-68; April 1947.
   Emphasizes that learner evaluation is a significant part of the learning process.
5. GILES, H. H. *Teacher-Pupil Planning.* New York: Harper and Bros., 1941. pp. 110, 122, 236-51, 376-79.
6. GRIM, PAUL R. "Youngsters Take a Hand." *Educational Leadership*, 4:438-41; April 1947.
   Emphasizes the role of the child in appraisal and record-keeping.
7. IRISH, BETTY. "What Is a Good Report Card?" *Educational Leadership*, 4:433-34; April 1947.
   This is a "timely allegory" on report cards and teacher-parent relationships.
8. LINDSEY, MARGARET. *Children's Records of Their Use of Time in School as a Means of Evaluating the Program of the Elementary School.* Ed. D. Report. New York: Teachers College, Columbia University, 1946.
   Report is based largely on study of diaries of their activities made by fifth- and sixth-grade children in two schools chiefly distinguished by the rigidity of their time and activities programs. Children kept records for five days of what they did from the time they entered school until they left in the afternoon.
9. LINDSEY, MARGARET. "School Time—Quantity and Quality." *Educational Leadership*, 4:151-56; December 1946.
   Here is an excellent, brief description of the use of learner diaries (records) of school activities in two contrasted elementary schools, one "developed under rigid requirements of distribution of time and activities and the other developed in a framework of freedom for teachers and children to plan cooperatively their use of time in school. . . ."
10. MULHOLLAND, V. M. "Greenville Improves Pupil Progress Reports." *High School Journal*, 23:17-20; January 1940.

Pictures modifications in report cards with reasons back of changes.

11. ROGERS, SARAH. "A Description of a Teacher's Work with Tenth-Grade Pupils in English-Social Science." *The Southern Association Quarterly*, 7:347-65; August 1943.
    Describes some record-keeping procedures.

12. WALLACE, W., CHREITZBERG, J., AND SIMS, V. M. *The Story of Holtville*. Deatsville, Alabama: Holtville High School, 1944.
    64-65 and 74-83 are particularly helpful.

13. WILLS, OLIN J. "New Reports for Old." *Educational Leadership*, 4:435-38; April 1947.
    Describes how parents, teachers, and children worked to improve reports in one situation.

14. WRINKLE, W. L. *Improving Marking and Reporting Practices in Elementary and Secondary Schools*. New York: Rinehart and Co., 1947.
    Analyzes some record-keeping practices related to marking and reporting to parents.

10

LEARNING HOW TO OBTAIN, SELECT,

AND USE RESOURCES EFFECTIVELY

Some problems to consider

What are the common weaknesses, related to resources, that are frequently shown by learners?

What are the possible purposes a learner may have in using resources?

What measuring instruments are of aid in diagnosing weaknesses in getting, selecting, or using resources?

How should texts or courses of study be used if functional problems are to form the primary basis for study?

What are the ways of helping students learn how to acquire appropriate resources?

How may students be helped to select the best resources from those available?

What steps may be taken to help learners use resources more effectively?

How can an antiquated textbook system be modified to take care of individual differences?

What principles do we need to keep in mind in helping learners acquire abilities related to resources?

Introduction. Resources should be thought of as a means to an end and not the end itself. Memorizing ideas acquired from resources is likely to be a wasteful process from an educational standpoint, largely because the learner frequently does not see any really valid reason for the memorization. In the utilization of resources, the learner ordinarily should have clear-cut purposes in mind for their use. Such purposes may be quite varied in nature, ranging from such a one as learning how to use resources effectively to using the resources for sheer enjoyment alone. Purposeful use of resources by the learner while in school will tend to promote continued purposeful use of resources after the learner leaves school

Each of the following self-evaluative questions is phrased as it might be asked by a student who is a prospective teacher or a teacher. After writing answers to the questions the learner-prospective teacher or learner-teacher should consider writing down the implications of his answers for future plans for improvement and continued learning in the field of getting, selecting, and using resources.

**EVALUATIVE QUESTIONS RELATED TO ACQUIRING,
SELECTING, AND USING RESOURCES EFFECTIVELY** [1]

Getting resources

1. Have I thought of learning how to get appropriate resources, particularly those not locally or readily available, as an important phase of my improvement in learning efficiency?

2. Is the money that is being spent in connection with the resources for my learning being economically used? Are we getting too many materials of one kind and not a sufficiently wide variety of materials? If the answer to the latter question is yes, what changes would I suggest for a similar class or grade next semester or year?

3. Do others and I bring materials to class frequently that might be of value to other students in the group?

Using resources

4. Have I thought of learning how to use appropriate resources more effectively as a significant goal for me?

5. After initial orientation in a field, do I use resources in a directly purposeful fashion to try to get answers to specific problems, or do I just use, in a rather aimless way, anything on the general subject being studied?

---

[1] These questions are phrased primarily for individual diagnosis by the student in teacher-training courses where teaching and learning methods are studied. It is also suggested that high-school students can and should be trained to ask themselves similar questions.

6. Do I make sufficient use of such parts of a book as the preface, table of contents, chapter summaries, index, reference sections, charts, diagrams, and pictures?

7. In my study am I learning how to use the library, including the classroom library, if any, and other resources better?

8. Have I become sufficiently familiar with, and have I learned how to use, a sufficient variety of resources besides books, including magazines, interviews, actual experiences, tests, questionnaires, inventories, observations, conferences, and correspondence? Have I made sufficient attempts to observe the practical solutions made by other people who are now facing and solving, with varying degrees of success, resource problems on which I am now working?

9. Does it appear that most of the ideas that I am getting from resources are really being incorporated in my thinking?

10. To what extent am I able to ferret out and apply, in my own field, *methods* and *materials* reported as being helpful in subjects or areas other than that which I am studying?

Evaluation

11. Have I developed the ability to distinguish between objective evidence, logical evidence, and opinion? To what extent do I check on the adequacy of source materials? Are printed resources considered promoters of thinking or as always giving "the gospel truth"?

12. Am I reviewing my use of resources sufficiently often and constantly trying to evaluate the worth of specific resources?

13. Do I keep a list of difficulties encountered in getting, selecting, and using resources?

Resources for the future

14. Am I building up a good file of resources for future personal and/or occupational use?

OBJECTIVE EVALUATIVE TOOLS FOR MEASURING ABILITIES RELATED TO ACQUIRING, SELECTING, AND USING PRINTED RESOURCES

Frequently, a good self-diagnostic approach to needs relating to the getting, selecting, and using of printed resources is to encourage the learner to take and self-score one or more of the available tests, questionnaires, or inventories. Five of these will be briefly discussed.

FINDING-RESOURCES LADDER

Individual learner assumes major share of responsibility, with needed guidance, in learning ways of getting appropriate resources. He practices methods in getting resources that will help him solve problems identified as important to him.

Learners, as a group, study ways of getting appropriate resources and actually practice getting needed resources.

Learner is frequently encouraged to get additional resources suitable to his needs and goals.

Learner is occasionally encouraged to try to get additional resources himself.

Learner is frequently shown how others get resources to be used in systematic learning, but he does not get practice himself.

Learner is occasionally shown how others get resources to be used in systematic learning, but he does not get practice himself.

Learner gets no practice in finding resources appropriate to his needs.

READ UP ⟶

In classroom situations of which I am a part, how high do we come on the finding-resources ladder shown above?

What can I do to move higher on the ladder?

SELECTING-RESOURCES LADDER

The individual learner assumes the major responsibility for intelligently selecting the resources that are likely to be of most value to him in meeting his problems. He, with appropriate guidance, studies ways of improving his process in this regard.

The teacher helps the individual learner improve in selecting appropriate resources and aids him in studying the problems he has identified as important to him.

Teacher and learners, as a group, cooperatively select resources for use in studying problems.

Materials are largely teacher-selected, but occasionally learners are given some option on which of several teacher-selected materials they will use.

Teacher selects, but explains reasons occasionally.

The few resources that are available are selected for use by the teacher.

Few resources for study are available and these have been selected by neither the teacher nor the learners.

READ UP ⟶

In classroom situations of which I am a part, how high would we be on the selecting-resources ladder shown above?

What can I do to move higher on the ladder?

Test on the Use of the Library for Elementary Schools by L. R. Reed is published by the Chicago Planograph Co., 517 S. Jefferson, Chicago. This is a thirty-five minute test designed to discover how well the elementary-school child can use a library independently instead of waiting for the librarian's help. There are two equivalent forms of the test and each has three main divisions. The first division is titled "Does the Library Contain the Book You Want?" Illustrative directions in this section are: "Below you will find the descriptions or the titles of books, together with several words under which you might look for them in a dictionary card catalog. For each write the number of the best answer in the blank space at the right." "Each of the following statements lists a topic on which you might wish to find a book, together with possible words under which to look for it in the dictionary card catalog. For each write the number of the best answer in the blank space at the right." "Three cards from a dictionary card catalog are shown. Below them are five questions that can be answered from the cards. Study the cards and write the answers to each question in the blank space at the right."

The second section of the test is headed, "Can You Find Material in Books?" Illustrative directions in this section are: "Below is a list of seven parts of a book and also a list of statements that are to be completed by writing the number of the part of the book in which you could *best* find the information. The same number may be used more than once." "In column A you will find the names of ten people. In column B there are five kinds of reference books. If you know which people have produced each kind of reference book you can more easily find the reference book you want." "In the blank space at the right of each type of reference book put the number of the person who has produced a book of that kind. Put *one* number *only* in each blank and *do not* write the same number *more than once.*"

The third main section is headed "Can you find material in magazines by using the magazine indexes?" The directions in this section read: "The following entries appeared in the *Readers' Guide* for 1932-1935. By means of them you could find articles in magazines. Numbers have been placed in circles above portions of the information contained in the entries. Below are questions about the entries. Answer them by writing the number of the correct item from the *Readers' Guide* in the blank space at the right. For each use *one* number *only* and *do not* use the same number twice."

Junior High School Tests. "Library Tests for Junior High Schools" was prepared by the Committee on Tests of the School Library Association of California, under the direction of Jeannette Vander Ploeg, and was published by the California Test Bureau, 5916 Hollywood Boulevard, Hollywood, California. This test was designed "as a diagnostic test to secure as accurate an indication as possible of each pupil's familiarity with that particular library usage. . . . As far as it was possible the questions are more general than specific in regard to certain library policies and book collections in order that they might be applicable to many situations." This test has two equivalent forms and each of them contains the five following sections: (1) the book, (2) the arrangement of books, (3) card catalog, (4) dictionary and encyclopedia, and (5) miscellaneous books.

The Peabody Library Information Test, by Louis Shores and J. E. Moore, and published by the Educational Test Bureau, Minneapolis, Minnesota, covers three levels: elementary, high school, and college. These tests attempt to measure knowledge of shelf arrangement, the Dewey decimal classification system, the use of the information on catalog cards, in dictionaries, in encyclopedias, knowledge of the common reference tools, the alphabetization of books, and the simple bibliographical forms.

The Use of Library and Study Materials, A Test for High School and College, by Mary Kirkpatrick, L. R. Thompson, and H. Tomlinson, is published by the Steck Company, Austin, Texas. It is divided into two main parts. The first is designed to measure a student's ability to locate information, and the second to measure certain aspects of his ability to understand the material once it has been found.

Tyler-Kimber Study Skills Tests, by H. T. Tyler and George C. Kimber, is published by Stanford University Press, Stanford University, California. This test attempts to measure the "skills and fundamental understandings of study techniques useful in practically all fields of academic work, together with a single highly accurate measure of study-skill mastery. The eight separate measures are:

    I. Finding What You Want in the Book
   II. Using an Index
  III. Using General Reference Books
  IV. Recognizing Common Abbreviations

V. Using the Library Card Catalog
VI. Interpreting Maps
VII. Knowing Current Periodical Literature
VIII. Interpreting Graphs

After tests have been given and self-scored by the learner, he, with needed guidance from the teacher, should make a list identifying his major strengths and a list indicating his most serious weaknesses, as shown by the tests results. This analysis should be followed by a *written* plan for working to eliminate his weaknesses. Frequent checkups should be made by the learner and the teacher to determine the progress that is being made in improving abilities in getting, selecting, and using printed resources.

SOME EXAMPLES OF LEARNER RESPONSES TO EVALUATIVE QUESTIONS RELATED TO RESOURCES

Some learners have had little or no systematic training in getting, selecting, or using resources in an economical and profitable fashion. This, unfortunately, is too true even of many college students. Some excerpts from students' evaluative statements may be helpful in giving a picture of student reactions to guided learning, related to resources.

Question 1. Am I learning how and where to get some materials that are not immediately available?

". . . I have written to several different people about articles and booklets listed in magazines. Some of the replies have been quite helpful. . . ."

". . . I have found that the federal and some state governments have much free and/or inexpensive material that is quite helpful on some problems. . . ."

". . . I find that many of the other teachers are able and willing to give me valuable help on some of the problems upon which I have worked. This is the first semester in which I have used sources of this type. . . ."

". . . I find that students who have gone to schools that are out of the ordinary in some respect frequently have some worth-while ideas. . . ."

"...The Library of Congress has been found to be a useful source of help on some problems...."

"...I have discovered the great value of interviews with people who have worked on the same problem if I go with some specific things written down that I plan to ask them in the interview...."

Question 2. Am I learning how to use the library and other re-sources better in study?

"...I have learned the wealth of usable material to help solve current problems that is contained in current periodicals. Heretofore, I have used books for study almost exclusively...."

"...I am beginning to see the value of people as sources. Before, I had only thought of using printed sources...."

"...I think that I have improved tremendously in the use of the library. In the first place, I did not even know of the existence of the *Education Index* until this semester. I did not realize the importance of magazines and pamphlets nor the wealth of information they contained. This was a new aspect of the library, which I for some reason took to be primarily for amusement and pastime. Why or where I got this idea, I do not know...."

"...One main source I have used to a large extent is talking with people who can help me. I have learned that it is a good idea to check the ideas of experienced people with the ideas that are gleaned from books...."

"...Yes, I am certainly learning how to use the library. I learned only this week, through your help, about the tests in the file. I have no excuse for not having known about these, except that I had never had them pointed out to me...."

"...I rather confess that I have been accustomed to, many times, copying any material in my notes that made any direct or indirect mention of my particular study. This material was very quickly relegated to the realms of the wastebasket upon completion of the study. Since the inception of this study I have attempted to record only data that might bear directly on my problem or that might be of value to me in a closely related study. Consequently, I have data organized in such a way that what I have should be valuable to me. Because it has been weeded it will not be necessary to do away with it after next week. I will not have to search through reams of material to find what is wanted. I have learned that busy-work for its sake alone is worse than no work at all. . . ."

". . . Being of a very practical nature I have smothered in the past under the necessity for the collection of a lot of pious data for formal term papers, which could have no value to anyone under any conceivable circumstance. Naturally, I was delighted to learn that voluminous material and data were not expected in this course and that what we collected should bear directly on our problems. Therefore, I have collected and selected material that is valuable to me. Being able to do this I have had my problem constantly in mind and have recorded information and deductions with a purpose of using them. Everything being vital, I have in mind the use that shall be made of what I have in the study of this problem. No record is made of anything that is absolutely worthless or that might be useful in some other study. I find that when you have a problem in mind and work toward its solution as you gather material, you will record it in such a form as will be immediately of value as the need may arise. . . ."

Question 3. In my study am I placing too much dependence upon books and not enough on other resources available?

". . . I believe if I would use more up-to-date magazines it would be better. I don't believe I have done enough searching along that line. . . ."

". . . I think I am depending too much on books—I should interview and observe more than I do. . . ."

". . . Maybe I have been doing too much book reading and not enough question asking. . . ."

". . . Yes, I think I am inclined to do this. Some of the resources which I should use more are the juvenile court, to learn firsthand what methods are used for delinquent children, and interviews with teachers who know specifically about teaching mentally deficient children. . . ."

". . . There are other resources that I should probably use more. It seems that there is such a wealth of knowledge on the field of personality in the library that I have studied it very little, outside of these books. I have used some of my ideas that were gotten from observing friends and members of my family. Other sources that I could get information from are the radio, movies, teachers, and discussions with some members of the class. . . ."

INDIVIDUAL DIFFERENCES AND AN ANTIQUATED
TEXTBOOK SYSTEM *

PHYSICAL EDUCATION EQUIPMENT
REQUIREMENTS IN SCHOOLVILLE

Each child is expected to buy or rent by the end of the first week of school tennis shoes as indicated below:

Grade	Size Shoes
1	2
2	3
3	4
4	5
5	6
6	7
7	8
8	9

Shoes may be gotten at the Podunk Shoe Store.

Physical differences known and given attention; mental differences known.[2] If such a notice as that above were sent home to parents by a school system, both parents and children would be rightfully indignant, because obviously the shoes that will fit one third grader may be much too large or too small for another third grader. We

* Adapted from an article by the author, "Of Shoes and Textbooks," *Illinois Education,* 37 (January, 1949), 157-58, 177-79. Also in *The Education Digest,* 14 (May, 1949), 7-9.

2 This section is written with the assumption that the teacher and prospective teacher of secondary-school students needs to have an understanding of the problems faced by elementary teachers. Many of the complaints of secondary teachers about the students they get are due to lack of understanding of the individual differences of children as they come to school and the normal spread of these differences as the students progress through school.

It is recognized, of course, that individual differences should influence other phases of teaching in addition to the selection of textbooks.

have as great individual differences in mental ability as in size of feet within a particular grade level, yet in thousands of our school systems we expect all of the same age to use books of the same difficulty level.

Modern American schools have inherited a textbook acquisition system that was set up before the nature of individual differences in mental abilities had been objectively established. *Unfortunately, this inherited system is still permitted to remain in effect in many of our schools by the school boards, school administrators, and teachers, the system being that of expecting or requiring all learners to buy, rent, or accept the same text or group of texts simply because all the learners happen to be on a particular grade level or in the same course.* Why is it that we expect or require all children in a particular grade level to use the same book? The reason probably is that the differences in mental ability are not so obvious as the tangible differences in physical size.

Although we have very clear-cut objective evidence that there is approximately as great a spread in mental ability as there is in the size of feet, we still have in many schools an antiquated textbook acquisition system which requires each learner in a particular grade level or a particular class to get exactly the same materials. The effects on the individual and his adjustment are probably even worse than would be the effect of having the same size shoes for all learners in a particular grade level. We say worse because we are affecting the attitudes, habits, and abilities of those who are forced to use the materials, and the mental effects of uniform materials are frequently worse than the physical effects that too small or too large shoes would produce.

Objective evidence on individual differences. What is the objective evidence relating to the differences in mental ability that should be expected among school children at a particular grade level? A summary of that is given in capsule form in Table I.

What are the key facts and implications represented by Table I? One is that the good first-grade teacher is prepared to teach youngsters on at least five different average grade levels of ability. A second is that only about 50 per cent of six-year-olds are ready to begin to read, since experimentation shows that a child should ordinarily have a mental age of at least six or six and one-half before he should be encouraged to read. This means, of course, that a major share of the work of the first-grade teacher is to promote reading readiness. This is also true of the good second-grade teacher. A third implication is that it is foolish for the second-grade teacher to expect all the learners coming to her to be able to read an average second-grade reader. Learners are made differently and should not be expected to achieve at the same level. Finally, coming to the area of primary emphasis here, *it is extremely unsound to have all learners at any particular grade level required to buy, rent, or use the same materials.*

TABLE I

EXPECTED MENTAL CAPACITY OF 25 SIX-YEAR-OLD FIRST-GRADE CHILDREN ENTERING AVERAGE SCHOOL (approximate)

Number of Pupils	Mental Age	Average Mental Grade Level
2	8	3rd
6	7	2nd
9	6	1st
6	5	High Kindergarten
2	4	Low Kindergarten

Effect of increasing age on spread of mental ability. What happens to the spread of mental ability as this group of 25 learners moves up through the elementary school? Let us take a look at them when they reach the sixth grade (assuming progress of one grade per year).

In the sixth grade we would expect a *range of mental age of about nine years.* We would expect about 5 of the 25 children to have an average mental age of 11 years, 4 an average mental age of 10 years, 3 an average mental age of 9 years, 2 an average mental age of 8 years, 1 an average mental age of 7 years. Going up from the average in the other direction we would expect 4 with the mental age of 12, 3 with the mental age of 13, 2 with the mental age of 14, and 1 with the mental age of 15.

Translating the same picture into average mental grade level expected, which would probably correspond closely to average reading grade level, we find a range again of nine average grade levels running from average second- to average tenth-grade level with about 5 of the learners with average sixth-grade ability. This information is summarized in Table II. The small number of cases makes the distribution a rough approximation.

TABLE II

**EXPECTED MENTAL CAPACITY OF 25 ELEVEN-YEAR-OLD
SIXTH-GRADE CHILDREN IN AVERAGE SCHOOLS**
(assuming progress of one grade per year)

Number of Pupils	Mental Age	Average Mental Grade Level
1	15	10th
2	14	9th
3	13	8th
4	12	7th
5	11	6th
4	10	5th
3	9	4th
2	8	3rd
1	7	2nd

Significance of spread of ability shown. Does it make sense to expect a learner with average second-grade ability and another learner with average tenth-grade ability to buy the same book, which is most likely to be of average sixth-grade difficulty? The chances are the book would be entirely too difficult to the first youngster and too easy to be challenging for the second youngster. Expecting all learners in a particular grade level to get the same text simply does not make sense. The fact that individual differences in ability tend to increase the older children get is illustrated by comparing Table III with Tables I and II.

In Table III we note a spread of reading ability in the tenth grade of twelve average grade levels in one school system and thirteen average grade levels in the other school system. Incidentally, the youngsters in each of these school systems were required to purchase and use the same English books!

Lack of learner practice in evaluating and acquiring books. Another major difficulty with the present archaic textbook acquisition system in many schools is that it virtually deprives the learner of practice in evaluating and selecting and acquiring books for use. We do not propose to discuss this problem here, but the effect of this weakness tends to be that when the learner leaves school he does not know how intelligently to select or acquire books and other resources to meet his needs, and consequently many learners, particularly the lowest 50 to 60 or 70 per cent who do not acquire this training at home or somewhere else, actually make relatively little use of books.

Arguments against having texts meeting individual needs. At this point it would probably be well to take a look at the arguments against having youngsters get or use a variety of textbooks. The first argument that is sometimes given is that the child will be embarrassed if he is not using the same book as other children in the grade or course. The question arises: Will he be more embarrassed trying to use a book that is too difficult for him or using a book from which he can get some success and achievement? Psychologically, the latter is much better.

TABLE III

ACTUAL READING ABILITY STATUS OF 565 TENTH GRADERS
IN A LARGE MIDWESTERN CITY AND OF 380
WHITE TENTH GRADERS IN A
SOUTHEASTERN CITY

					Midwestern City	Southeastern City
Average	16th	Reading	Grade	Level	2%	3%
"	15th	"	"	"	3	1
"	14th	"	"	"	5	2
"	13th	"	"	"	8	12
"	12th	"	"	"	7	11
"	11th	"	"	"	10	8
"	10th	"	"	"	14	12
"	9th	"	"	"	13	14
"	8th	"	"	"	14	19
"	7th	"	"	"	13	10
"	6th	"	"	"	5	7
"	5th	"	"	"	5	1
"	4th	"	"	"	1	

A second objection is that the administrator, the school board, or other administrative officials decide these problems and that the teacher can or should only be concerned with using what is given to him. This argument assumes a dictatorial state of affairs where neither the teacher nor the learner has a share in decisions that vitally affect their welfare.

Another argument sometimes given by the teacher is that it is too much trouble to buck the administration. A teacher may get "in Dutch" if she attempts to recommend or promote a change in the textbook system.

Some insist that one teacher cannot do anything. Obviously, in the long run one teacher can do much if she works tactfully and intelligently with her colleagues.

Sometimes it is argued that standards must be maintained and the only way to maintain standards is to use the same books. Objective evidence indicates that higher standards will be maintained—although it will not be a single standard for all—if appropriate resources are used in particular situations.

Another situation sometimes has a subtle influence: when a bookstore has a practical monopoly on the selling of books, it is much less trouble for the bookstore simply to hand out the same set of books and get a nice profit than it is to have a variety of texts for the same grade, or to have the school use the resource acquisition problems as a learning vehicle to help children acquire the ability and practice the habit of getting and using appropriate resources.

A final objection, sometimes raised, is that it is too much trouble for the teacher to help learners use a variety of materials. The writer will grant that many teachers who have been accustomed to assigning so many pages for the next day will need to change their methods, but this is necessary for good teaching, anyhow. The alert teacher is willing to change.

SUGGESTED CHANGES IN THE RESOURCE ACQUISITION SETUP

What resource acquisition setup would we envisage as being in line with what is objectively demonstrated about individual differences? A picture of the changes in four school systems will help to give some answers to this question.

School A starts a book fund, saves the learners money, and begins to meet individual needs. Let us look at School A. Here the school children originally bought their books each year and resold what they could at the end of the year. A careful study was made and it was found the average buying price for elementary books was $10.50. About $5.00 of this could sometimes be got for resale of the books at the end of the year, leaving a net cost for books of $5.50 a year. After advising parents of the study and its results, the school asked each child to pay $5.00 into a book fund at the beginning of the year (in lieu of the $10.50 spent before) with the understanding that the money would be spent for books that would stay in the classroom.

How was the money used? Each teacher and her pupils were allowed to spend as much as her pupils' book fund permitted. Instead of spending the money to get thirty identical copies of the same book, each teacher began to build up a well-stocked functional library, each part of which would help meet the resource or reading needs of some children. Some of the money went for books labeled for the grade that purchased them but no more than eight books of any one type were purchased. A newspaper and several magazine subscriptions were bought in the upper grades. Reading readiness materials of various sorts were purchased in the first, second, and third grades.

Books high in maturity level and low in difficulty level were purchased in most grades to help take care of those with a reading level below average. This group, of course, usually amounts to about 50 per cent of the typical class. To locate these books much use was made of lists set up for this purpose which give, for example, the information that Barley's *When Grandfather Was a Boy* (Ginn) has a vocabulary level (one measure of difficulty level) of average third grade and interest level of average fifth grade and costs $.72.

How did the plan develop? First of all, the teachers found it stimulated *them* to study and learn a lot. They became acquainted with book lists they had not known about before. They were challenged to find different ways of grouping and developing leaders in their classes. They found the *Education Index* a ready source of help in time of trouble. They found faculty meetings and other ways of getting suggestions and help from others a definite must. They learned to make assignments and help learners make their own assignments in such a way as to take care of individual differences. Teaching became a thrilling, challenging experience.

After the second year of the book-fund system, each classroom began to have a wealth of resources and at less expense to the children than ever before, since books were being selected to meet needs and were staying in use rather than gathering dust at home or being thrown away. After three years the school was able to cut the book-fund fee to $3.00 (3/5 of what the cost had been before) and also spend some of it on music and art materials, which originally had been extra expense and could only be afforded by parents with above-average means.

School B starts a resources fund and learners get practice in evaluating resources. In School B they originally had a book rental system with primary-grade children paying an average rental of $5.00 a year and intermediate children paying $6.50 a year. In this school the setup was changed so that each child paid $4.50 a year into a resource fund; this was allocated to each teacher according to the number of children he had in his class (or classes) with the understanding that it be spent on needed resources.

In this school the teachers were concerned about the fact that most learners did not know how to get or evaluate resources themselves, and incidentally, when they graduated from school did little of this. They decided that not only did the youngsters need to know how to use materials but they also needed to know how to select and get them. Thus, in School B the learners in each class were dealt in on the process of evaluating, selecting, and ordering the resources that would be acquired during the year. Intermediate learners helped primary groups in functional letter-writing and other processes for which it was thought the younger children were too inexperienced. Also, in the spring of each year, recommendations were made to the next year's class regarding resources it would probably be best to consider getting.

So, in School B, democracy was not only read about and talked about but was actually put into practice in the selection and acquisition of needed resources. Those who were concerned helped to make the decisions that affected them.

School C. Teachers use evaluations of past students and set up book packs. In School C, the children in a particular grade or class rent different packs of books, which are returned to the school after a particular group has used them.

Each pack is different, but all sell for the same amount. They are tied and ready for rent when school opens. What is to go into each pack is worked out by the teachers using their own judgment on the probable needs of incoming groups. The suggestions of similar groups the year before regarding additional resources needed were carefully noted down and taken into account in ordering for the ensuing year.

This program does require planning by the teachers but can be done *on school time* if the administration will help teachers set aside as much time as is needed in the spring to make plans for the fall.

In School C, this plan was first used in the English classes. It worked so successfully that it was adopted in the school as a whole.

School D gives students varied resource practice. School D was a conventional high school where decisions regarding the selection and use of textbooks had been a monopoly of the administrators and teachers. The staff decided to give the students some freedom in the exploration of materials through the use of several books instead of one textbook.

Instead of the students all buying the same set of textbooks, a book-fee system was instituted and the money was used to buy several kinds of books. It should be emphasized that this, which can give appropriate materials of greater variety, actually costs the learner or his parents less than the system where each student in a particular class is forced to get and to use the same textbooks.

In School D students helped select the books, helped make and keep the classroom library cards for them, and, best of all, did much reading of a better sort than they ever did under the old system. When new books arrived, students were so anxious to use them that at least one group volunteered to help get them ready. Many learnings of a desirable sort were by-products of such activities. Among other activities these included such things as fixing book cards and pockets, entering trade items, checking invoices, looking up author numbers, and checking the *Standard Catalog* for class numbers and subject headings. Magazines, pamphlets, bulletins, and other materials that the learners felt would be helpful in their study were also selected, ordered, and used by the students with the guidance of the teachers and the librarian. Not only did all of this self-direction on the part of the learners help them do a better job of learning what they are conventionally expected to know, but it also resulted in their learning how better to get and use resources for effective learning.

Important also were the improved attitude and motivation shown when the selection, acquisition, and use of materials changed from an autocratic to a democratic procedure.

Antiquated text system can be made modern without additional cost. In summary, evidence has been presented that the uniform text acquisition setup as constituted in many schools appears outmoded when seen in the light of objectively demonstrated differences in mental ability and other psychologically important characteristics of learners. Wide-awake school systems that are making use of what is known about individual differences are using resources money in such a way that it helps rather than hinders the development of individual abilities. Antiquated methods of acquiring resources that pay little or no attention to individual differences can be revised and vastly improved without extra expense to the teacher, the learner, or the taxpayer.

SUGGESTIONS REGARDING THE ACQUIRING OF RESOURCES

A key part of the development of abilities related to resources is tied up with learning how to get appropriate resources. The suggestions given in the following paragraphs may be divided into four main groups: (1) those related to purpose and resources, (2) those related to evaluation of ability to get appropriate resources, (3) those related to encouraging learners to develop abilities in obtaining resources, and (4) those related to practice in getting resources.

Purpose and resources. It is extremely important that the learner clearly understand his purpose in studying and using resources if he is to make the getting of resources meaningful. This, of course, means that ordinarily it is undesirable to consider resources except in the context of problem identification, problem selection, or problem solution.

The emphasis in learning the process of getting resources should be upon acquiring *new* ways of getting resources. There is little profit to the learner, from an educationl standpoint, in going over and over again the same practice in getting resources that he has used in former years or in other courses. Thus, it is a part of the job of the teacher to be quite familiar with a variety of ways of getting resources and to study possible ways of leading learners to see the desirability of trying out these approaches.

In addition to encouraging the learner to acquire new ways of getting resources, it is important that each learner see the need and desirability of developing materials to meet his own needs and problems, which are somewhat different from those of every other learner. It is also of paramount importance that the learner see the necessity of improving ways of working so that his getting of resources will not only be more adequate but also more economical. This leads us to a final point concerning purpose, which is that the learner should be led to recognize that learning how to get appropriate materials is as important, if not more important, for useful education as is memorizing information. In our traditional schools this ability has been practiced so little and given so little attention that many learners do not even realize that it is a key part of the learning process that will have to be carried on after the learner leaves school, by the learner himself, if systematic improvement is to result.

Diagnosing ability to get resources. The problem of diagnosis of ability to get appropriate resources in an economical fashion has already been discussed to some extent under the heading of "Objective Evaluative Tools for Measuring Abilities Related to Acquiring, Selecting, and Using Printed Resources." Wiles (17) has pointed out in reporting a thought-provoking study he made of college students' abilities in fact-collecting that teaching learners how to locate information to solve their problems is one of the most important functions a teacher performs.

After studying the fact-collecting habits, indicated in a library test, of a group composed of teachers and prospective teachers, Wiles concluded the evidence was clear that one-half of those in a college class were not sufficiently skilled in the use of elementary tools in their chosen field. At least one-third of the group had a glaring deficiency in purposeful fact-collecting skill. After completing his exploratory study, Wiles saw the following implications (17, p. 623):

"a. It is not safe for an instructor at the upper undergraduate or graduate levels to assume that his students possess techniques of locating information for effective learning...

b. Reading out of reference texts does not guarantee that students will learn to collect information...

c. All graduate work is not successful in producing efficient collectors of information...

d. More examinations that test skills and techniques should be given. However, the test should be given at the beginning of the class work, not as a final examination. Each teacher should make sure that the students possess the skills that will enable them to be successful in the class work. Skills must not be estimated or assumed but must be determined by actual evaluation. Not all students will need assistance with study skills, but specialized training should be provided for those with deficiencies."

Wiles (17, p. 622) also listed certain errors or weaknesses that seemed to prevent students from making an efficient use of the library:

"1. Seeking magazine articles on topics by scanning current magazines without use of index.
2. Securing one reference at a time.
3. Thumbing through books looking for specific information without using index of book.
4. Shifting from one source to another without adequate reason—students exchanging material when they were not working on same topic.
5. Reading titles of books on reference shelf to discover one dealing with topic.
6. Not compiling a list of references sufficient to keep busy the full period.
7. Unable to find appropriate headings in the *Education Index*.
8. Checking on available material by going to shelves instead of using library file cards.
9. Not being sure of problem before starting work.
10. Unable to locate references in card catalog."

Resources to which to give more attention. The reader is referred to the section in this chapter titled, "Individual Differences and an Antiquated Textbook System," for a discussion of getting resources largely from the standpoint of text and initial materials that will be purchased by the learners. At this point it might be well just briefly to indicate a variety of resources that both learner and teacher should constantly keep in mind as possible helps in attacking problems: letters, radio, films, interviewing authorities in the field of the problem being studied, personal experience and observation, experimenting, pictures, bulletins, conducting surveys, bulletin boards, cartoons, panel discussions and oral reports, listening to the radio, obtaining data from field trips, slides, television, observation in the community, and observation of demonstrations of various sorts.

It would seem to be particularly important to encourage learners to make much greater use of non-printed materials in discovering their present and prospective problems and in getting ideas about how to solve such problems. More use should be made of such resources as planned interviews, where men and women of various occupations and activities are asked such questions as: What do you now wish that you had gained out of school that you might have gained out of English? Out of social studies? In most communities there is a wealth of usable reading materials such as old magazines, pamphlets, and newspapers. It is desirable that learners be helped to collect these and then follow this up with a systematic organization of usable material in them.

Resources should be collected during school experience with an eye to future use out of school. "What materials might I need in the future?" might well be a question to be frequently considered. This might include such things as getting the address of a useful source, the name of a publisher, or where to get certain types of resources.

Much more material should be used that is problem-centered rather than merely information-centered. For example, most historical information and most histories are written from a chronological standpoint rather than from a problem-centered standpoint. Increasingly, there are more and more materials that are set up as definite aids in helping to answer problems and using such material should be encouraged.

Suggestions related to practice on getting resources. Learners are most likely to practice appropriate resource-getting activities out of school if such resource activities are carried on in school. Therefore, it is of paramount importance that the teacher be familiar with a variety of possible activities that learners may be encouraged to carry on while in school which will train them in various processes connected with the acquisition of resources. Following is a list of some suggested activities:

The learner should continuously participate in the getting of resources used by him. Spoon-feeding must be eliminated since a study of getting resources is not something that can be done by the teacher for the student.

Give students practice in ordering books from publishers and get the learners' names put on a list for new publications in various fields. Encourage learners to write to publishers for names of books on specific school and community problems. Sometimes committees of pupils may write to publishers for catalogs of books of various types. Wilson's *Children's Catalog* is an illustration of one source that the children might learn to check. A similar type of thing may be done in getting tests and other resources for self-evaluation.

Teachers and other learners should, through actual experience, learn how better to use correspondence as a method of finding out about and getting an evaluation of materials helpful in identifying, selecting, and solving problems. Such materials would include, among other resources, tests, books, magazines, newspapers, and pamphlets. This type of practice can also provide much practical and functional composition work.

Training in the use of the library is of key importance. This may involve setting up a library in the classroom for illustrative purposes or so that the learners may actually gather together materials and organize them for learning purposes. Class trips to the library will be advisable. The teacher may want to encourage learners to spend a certain amount of class time each week in practicing using the library in various ways.

Encourage each pupil to keep a list of the problems he faces for which there seems to be little help or few resources available and then be on the lookout for such materials. Such lists may also be gathered together and the whole class can offer suggestions that will be of help to individual members of the class. Consider setting up material bureaus partially operated by the learners in each school. Such bureaus will assemble and keep in order basic bibliographies, addresses, and descriptions of services available.

Help learners develop for use by brothers, sisters, and themselves as well as teachers and parents, lists of books suitable for presents on Christmas or birthdays. Give such a list to the local newspaper or bookstore and distribute it in the homes.

Encourage youngsters, parents, and teachers to contribute books to the classroom and school libraries, as well as magazines that are no longer being used in the home. Sometimes special days may be observed for the addition of such materials.

Encourage various clubs, classes, etc., to promote a collection of particular materials that will be of help on special problems or projects.

Practice using the state library or state agency that is responsible for promoting better use of resources in the state.

Request permission from the public librarian or the school librarian to bring, periodically, a group of books to the classroom where they will be left in use for a certain specified amount of time. These books preferably should be partially selected by the learners and should be tied up with the problems upon which the learners are working. Teachers as learners should have a system set up so that a continuous supply of new professional stimulation comes to each teacher each week.

In many schools it is found desirable to allocate so much money each year for professional materials. These are then circulated and used by the teachers in the system. Instead of each teacher in the school system subscribing to the same professional periodical each subscribes to a different one and these are then circulated systematically among the teachers.

Making acquisition of resources functional with learner participation. Making a course functional with active learner participation usually is one of the main goals of the teacher who wants his work to be of value to his students. There are many ways of attacking this problem, but the approaches made by Greene (4) in a college preparatory English course are suggestive not only for English teachers but for teachers of other subjects as well.

After discussing various types of colleges, the class decided it would be well (1) to get the exact requirements in English for college entrance and (2) to ascertain the nature of freshmen college English. To do this the class members composed letters and sent them to fifteen colleges. Not only was this good communication experience, using functional composition, but the pupils felt that if they could get a clear picture of what they would need to know and to have accomplished they would do more purposeful work in English.

The answers obtained from the letters were very helpful in indicating to the students the skills stressed by the various colleges and universities. Many specific weaknesses or deficiencies that colleges had found prevalent in high-school graduates were also noted in the answers. The points made in the letters were grouped and tabulated and they provided the basis for setting up individual goals.

Another resource for familiarizing students with college requirements used by Greene's class was that of getting student opinion. The high-school seniors found that freshmen college students visiting in the town or high school were very glad to discuss problems and requirements they had experienced in college. Some even came to school and led discussions of freshmen college work. Letter-writing to college freshmen could also be used as a source of information and motivation.

Greene's class also decided it would be well to determine students' needs. One approach was to use tests that included writing a theme, participating in oral work, and measuring reading, vocabulary, and general English (including pronunciation, punctuation, capitalization, grammar usage). Note that the tests were not given *at the end* of the semester or year for the purpose of getting a grade, but early enough in the school year so that the student would have a chance to work on his weaknesses. It is significant also that the learners understood the purpose for taking the tests and apparently felt the tests could help them identify individual needs.

After the pupil had identified his specific weaknesses, he set up with the teacher a tentative work program to try to capitalize on his strengths and eliminate his weaknesses. It should be emphasized that the diagnosis that had been carried on using the approaches and resources indicated above showed that each learner needed to be handled as an individual.

Results also showed the need for a *great variety* of resources on various maturity and difficulty levels.

In Greene's class not only was great use made of a variety of printed books and magazines, but movies, radio programs, student-constructed tests, and self-evaluative questions were also utilized as resources in functionalizing the work of the class.

DEVELOPING ABILITY TO SELECT RESOURCES

Students learn only what they practice. Since students learn only what they practice, learners should be participating continuously in the selection of the resources they use. Democracy of choice should govern, being both psychologically sound and also in line with professed American traditions and ideals. Time spent in learning how to select materials intelligently may be considered wasted by the uncritical teacher or student. Actually, gaining practice in this important skill is likely to be much more valuable to the learner than having a teacher turn over to him a lot of ideas to be memorized.

Student attitude toward a resource important. As one aspect of the cooperative teaching-learning process, the teacher should respect the student's point of view on what resources he thinks are most helpful to him. It is relatively undesirable for the teacher to try simply to use absolute standards of goodness in selecting resources without sufficient concern for the purposes, abilities, and points of view of those who will actually use the resources. The teacher will do well to encourage the students to recommend appropriate resources to each other. A resource recommended by another student will sometimes be used with more zest than the same resource recommended by the teacher. As one phase of this practice in selecting resources, it is sometimes desirable to encourage each student to submit a list of his five favorite books, authorities, magazines, etc., in order to encourage him to consider the factors in selection, and to follow this up by having the student give reasons for his choices.

Developing criteria for selecting resources. A key phase of helping learners develop intelligent resource-selection abilities is helping them set up sound criteria to aid them in selecting such appropriate resources. These criteria may be set up by a group or may be formulated individually. Some of the possible ones that the teachers and learners may consider using are suggested in the following paragraphs.

Differences in purpose in using resources. In the first place, it is important that the teacher attempt to help the learners see the difference between using resources for pleasure and using resources for help in solving problems. In the first case the criterion should be largely one of whether it will help in problem identification or problem solution. The most important criterion should be, "Will this resource help me in more clearly identifying problems or getting possible solutions to them?" Also, we might illustrate this by suggesting that the teacher attempt to lead the learner to see the difference in purpose between recreational reading for enjoyment of the process and other functional work-type reading where the purpose should be to get help in identifying or solving recognized problems.

It is desirable to encourage the selection of resources largely in terms of recognized needs and problems identified as important to study. Also, selection of resources with a variety of points of view should be promoted.

Avoid sticking to resources labeled with the name of the course. Frequently, it is well for the learner to select materials or other resources that are not stamped with a label of the particular class in which he is studying. Too frequently the learner uses only those resources that are labeled history, geography, arithmetic, or whatever the subject is that he may be studying at a particular time. This tends to close his mind to the possibility of using other potentially helpful resources.

Another criterion to be considered by the learner is the question of whether the ideas in the resources are based largely on opinion, on experimental research, or on sheer logic. Use may be made of each of the three types. It is important that the learner recognize the type of resource he is using and make appropriate allowances for bias or error.

Re-evaluation of resources after use. After the student has selected materials and used them to help identify or solve problems or for recreational purposes, it is desirable to encourage him to go back over his basis for the selection of the materials and analyze additional bases that he should have considered or given greater weight to in deciding what to use. If this is done over a period of time, the learner will be able to select appropriate resources more intelligently. Obviously, inconsistency in available evidence and bias toward some particular evidence should be carefully considered by the learner.

In this connection it may be pointed out that many textbooks, for example, show palaces, temples, and ordinary houses of old, but omit serious discussion of pressing problems such as the housing of today and its related problems of real-estate lobbies, obsolete city building codes, too-rigid trade-union restrictions in certain areas, rental leases set up almost entirely to protect the landlord, and other problems the learner may need to know how to attack.

Skyscrapers, state capitol buildings, statues, and museums are pictured and discussed, and no attention is given to the wretched conditions under which millions of our people live, or to specific techniques we, as citizens, might use to improve the situation. There is a fundamental need for textbooks that are reoriented to help the learner identify and solve problems, so that he may get the type of help he most needs to prepare for a happier and more effective life.

Giving guided practice in the selection of resources. How the teacher can encourage guided practice in the selection of appropriate resources will be discussed in the next few paragraphs.

Very frequently it is desirable to present the learner with such a choice as: Here are three sets of materials you might use in facing the problem you're working on. Which do you think you should start with? Why? Which of these that you have used before have given the most help? What kind of help did each give?

Often it is desirable to emphasize the use of different neglected parts of a book. We refer particularly to such parts as the index, table of contents, preface, tables and charts, and other parts of the book that learners frequently disregard. Frequently, the learner may need help in diagnosing his apparent problems and needs in order to get some sound orientation for the selection of material. This orientation should be in terms of the purposes of the learner himself, rather than in terms of the purposes of the teacher alone, wise though these may be.

Until the teacher is acquainted with the student, he should lean in the direction of recommending too easy materials rather than those that may prove too difficult. If the learner has no difficulty with the complexity of the resource, he is more likely to learn to like it and use it than if he constantly has the feeling that he can "hardly catch" what the resource is talking about.

As is more extensivey discussed in the chapter on record-keeping, the learner will do well to keep some record of resources used, how they were evaluated after use, and then utilize such material as a basis for a comparison of the different resources used.

Key questions for consideration are: What resources commonly unused in conventional education should be used much more in functional democratic education? Why have such useful resources been neglected in the past? What specific materials should be considered basic for students to help develop their ability to teach themselves? What are my weaknesses in the ability to select resources appropriately?

Occasionally, it may be desirable to have each person who uses a book or magazine write several sentences giving his reaction to it. These reactions may be recorded and other learners may use them as one basis for selection of materials. Again, the teacher may want to put a sheet of paper at the end of the book or magazine for this purpose so that such comments may be kept for future use. These may be filed in a particular place in the classroom that is accessible to students who are looking for certain types of resources. Some learners, if such comments are filed, may find it interesting to write their own notes before they see those made by other students.

Obviously, there are several ways in which such types of evaluation of resources can be used in the intelligent selection of resources.

Recreational vs. *problem use of resources.* In attempting to develop intelligent use of resources, it is very important to emphasize to learners the difference between materials that are used primarily for recreational purposes and those that are used largely to get help in identifying or solving problems. In the first case, the situation is similar to that of a family going for a drive on Sunday afternoon. The purpose here is not primarily to get any place in particular, but rather simply to enjoy the scenery during the period while they are out. In the problem type of reading and other types of resource use, the learner is primarily concerned with getting help either in identifying problems, or in getting possible solutions. In our analogy this would be similar to using a truck to get material from one place to another.

Resources for problem identification. Using materials to help identify the problems the student needs to consider is an important skill that has been largely neglected. The learner should always attempt to get and use materials on an intrinsically motivated basis. Otherwise, the use of the materials is likely to do more harm than good. The learner must also see the different purposes for reading and using resources.

Free use of resources. It is sometimes wise to have free periods in which the learners are studied as they engage in activities involving the free use of various types of resources. In this setup, the schoolroom should have a variety of materials from which the learner may choose. A study of behavior, or a record of behavior in such a situation, will frequently aid the teacher materially in evaluating the probable carry-over value of the getting, selecting, and using of resources when the learner leaves school. Habits of using resources should definitely be geared to the type of habits we would like to encourage outside the school. For example, if we want students to use resources like the Consumers' Research or Consumers Union bulletins to aid in intelligent and economical buying after they leave school, they should practice using that type of resource while in school, where guidance in improving approaches and techniques can be had.

Making more use of key parts of books. This and the next few paragraphs will be primarily concerned with suggestions about improving the use of printed resources. The first suggestion is primarily concerned with books, since books form one of the key resources in our culture. The writer has found in a recent study that a large proportion of college students make relatively little use of certain important parts of the book, parts that are important particularly if the book is read in a purposeful and meaningful fashion. Included in these parts are the following: preface, table of contents, chapter heads, chapter conclusions, index, title page, illustrations, pictures, charts, diagrams, and frontispieces. Obviously, there is a good reason for having each of these parts in the book, if included, and it would seem rather important that learners be taught their use through practice in using them.

Changing use of texts. In the school, where reading was intrinsically motivated, texts would be used primarily as references, rather than for reading sequentially from cover to cover. By this we mean that the learners would have certain problems and certain types of things they would be looking for in the texts, and would not go simply to the text for purposes of memorization to take care of the inevitable test. In other words, the emphasis would be on getting ideas for help in solving problems, rather than for helping in passing a test. Tests would be used more for learning purposes than for marking purposes. Thus, instead of students thinking of a test as being used to get a mark, they would think of it more in terms of the help its results can give in self-analysis of weaknesses and strengths, and thus aid in improving the types of work being done.

Types of resources needing more attention. Two types of books that would seem to need to be given much more attention are dictionaries and indexes of various sorts. In other words, students should be given much guided practice in the use of the dictionary and in the use of such indexes as the *Readers' Guide.*

Other types of resources in the use of which learners need additional guided practice are pictures, cartoons, and charts. Again, if the learner is to use and understand these best after he leaves school, it is of vital importance that he get practice in using them while he is in school.

Need for learner organization of ideas. There would seem to be a need in most of our schools to provide more time in the reading program for the child actually to assimilate the material into *his own organization* of ideas. Having a chance to develop meaningful connections between what he reads and what he already knows is very important for the learner. This also will be facilitated if, before reading, the learner attempts to set up his purposes in reading and attempts to see clearly what it is that he is trying to get out of his reading.

Using human resources more effectively. Moving from the use of printed resources to the use of non-printed resources, we raise the following suggestions: to get learners acquainted with available facilities, it is frequently wise to request assistance of those already intimately familiar with them. Librarians and more experienced learners are examples of such individuals. Also, the teacher may frequently direct learners to other learners whom he thinks might be of help in offering suggestions about the use of resources.

Most of our learners need additional training in getting the most out of conferences or interviews. For current problems and current topics, often an interview with someone who has experience in the field or with the problem being studied will be able to give more current and more up-to-date information than written resources. However, in order to get the most out of a conference or interview, it is important that the student be given guided practice in preparing for such an experience. One way of doing this is to practice such conferences or interviews in mock sessions in class. It goes without saying that the interviewer should know exactly what it is he is trying to get answers to in the interview. His questions do not necessarily have to be written down or be in view of the person being interviewed, but for purposeful learning the student must know specifically what information he is trying to get. Also, he should remember that it is important for him to let the person who is being interviewed talk most of the time, and his, the interviewer's, function is to raise questions and get reactions, not argue or attempt to persuade the authority about the problem being discussed.

As has been suggested, learners should be encouraged to think in class. This is the time for getting additional ideas of a sort different from those that the student can get from books or from other resources. If this principle were applied, we would have fewer lectures and more exchange of ideas in classrooms, since the same type of thing that can be obtained from lectures ordinarily can also be had from printed or mimeographed materials in a more economical fashion.

Eliminate uniform assignments. The mass assignment of a certain number of pages is a thoroughly outmoded procedure, and it would largely be eliminated if what is known objectively of individual differences were actually taken into account.

Early in the learning process, with a particular group, it is desirable to discuss the resources that might be used, or that the learner would consider using in identifying and solving particular problems. It is desirable also to encourage the direct use of appropriate facilities through incidental mention in discussion of problems that are taken up in class. Sometimes it is well to go with the learners the first time to resources that are new or unfamiliar to them. Some class periods can appropriately be taken up with the teacher asking the learners questions concerning the use of specific resources, and giving various learners an opportunity to help each other in using them.

Put the filing system on a problem basis. In order to facilitate the use of materials, it is desirable that a continuously operating and continuously improving filing system be set up in the classroom. Materials in the file should be arranged largely on a problem basis. After the learners have been taught to select the usable parts of magazines, newspapers, and pamphlets, the teacher should help them learn how to file these for present and prospective use. In other words, the learner should be encouraged to help set up a functional folder and filing system for pamphlets, articles, and useful material, from magazines and newspapers. The teacher and learners might consider setting up a classroom "Education Index" for folder materials. This "Education Index" could give directions to the learners on where in the filing system it would be possible to find certain kinds of materials.

As an aid in placing materials in the classroom, it is frequently wise to consider enlisting the help of the manual arts department in setting up shelves and other necessary equipment for the filing of resources. This not only is helpful to the classroom teacher, but also provides a functional interclass activity that will tend to promote desirable school relationships.

Individual filing of resources. In addition to the learner's helping to set up group or class files that will remain in the classroom, it is recommended that he also be encouraged to organize and keep materials on an individual basis, with an eye to out-of-school use and out-of-school needs. In other words, the prospective housewife would be trained to set up a workable filing system and actually gather in it various types of resources that would be helpful in carrying on household tasks more successfully. The prospective farmer would be encouraged to start operating a personal filing system, which would include suggestions on methods of feeding livestock, procedures for diagnosing and treating the needs of the soil to get best production, and other related problems. This not only tends to make the classroom activities more vital and functional, but also provides a springboard for intelligent and systematic learning after the learner leaves school.

Making records help in planning the use of resources. Closely related to the arrangement of resources for functional use is the utilization of records. Before a student starts to work on a particular problem or project, the teacher might suggest that he make a list of the possible resources he might consider using in attacking it. After this has been done, the instructor and fellow students may be asked to add to the list. This helps the learner see other avenues of attack, which he perhaps had not previously considered, and thus improves his technique for using available materials.

Ordinarily, when a particular source or resource is used, it is worthwhile for the learner to keep some systematic record of where it was obtained and its values, so that he can return to it, or refer someone else to it, if an occasion should arise when this would be desirable.

Keeping a list of difficulties related to resources. As the learner attacks the identification and solution of problems, he should be encouraged to keep a list of the difficulties he encounters in trying to get, select, and use various types of materials. This can form the basis for helpful conferences or discussions with the instructor, other students in the class, or others who might be able to help the student on his particular problem. Not only is this likely to help the learner in his attack on the particular problem being studied, but it will also train him to get help from other individuals in a systematic fashion.

Additional ways of evaluating work that has been done on problems. These are optional approaches whose use teachers may encourage in reviewing work that has been done on problems. (The suggestions are made as the learner might approach the step himself.)

It is recommended that the reader review the suggestions in the preceding chapter on improving record-keeping for additional ideas on the appropriate use of resources.

a) List sources and situations (including human sources) that I have found most helpful in solving my problems. Put these in the order of their estimated value to me with the most valuable coming first.

b) List the people I talked to for help on problems during the semester. Give their names in order of the value of their suggestions to me.

c) List books used in working on my problems. Give these in order of value.

d) In order of value, list magazines used in working out my problems.

e) In order of value, list observations of activities made in the study of my problems.

f) In order of the value of the replies, list the names of individuals to whom I wrote.

g) In order of the value of their contributions to my learning, list tests, inventories, and questionnaires that were used.

OPERATING PRINCIPLES OR SUGGESTIONS FOR GETTING, SELECTING, AND USING RESOURCES

Importance of purpose. Resources for learning should be found and used as much as possible in a purposeful fashion, purposeful, that is, from the standpoint of the learner. The learner should not only understand the purposes for his using them, but should also participate in setting up those purposes. A specific purpose for the gathering of ideas from resources should displace mere absorption of ideas. The primary question about any resource should be: Is this resource likely to give me help on the problems I should study?

I. *Goals in learning processes related to resources*

    A. Learning how to select and get appropriate resources for helping solve problems should be considered an important goal in improving learning processes. Learning how to use resources more effectively is also of key importance, if the learner is to continue systematic learning after he leaves school.

B. Active participation by the learner in selecting, getting, and using materials is a prerequisite for rapid improvement in these processes.

C. Resources for learning should be found and used as much as possible in purposeful fashion. Unless the resources are found, selected, and used with purposeful behavior in mind, it is very unlikely that such resources will be found, selected, or used after the learner leaves school.

D. It is to be remembered that unless and until a person learns how to find and use materials efficiently to solve his own problems, he is not in a strategic position to teach others how to do this.

II. *Types of resources to be used*

A. The *Readers' Guide* and the card catalogue are invaluable aids in identifying and attacking significant problems. For the professional educator's problems the *Education Index* is most helpful.

B. Human resources are too frequently neglected in selecting and solving problems. Colleagues or classmates, for example, frequently can provide a wealth of help if we only make the attempt to get it.

C. Tests, inventories, and questionnaires for self-diagnosis and self-instruction have great potentialities.

D. A particularly important resource of the active learner is a record largely in his own words of what he has learned and the processes he has gone through in learning it. A list of resources used in the learning and a notation of the problems encountered should also be included.

E. Letter-writing to educational authorities, governmental agencies, educational publishers, and others who have met problems similar to those being studied frequently will produce helpful results.

III. *Procedures in getting, selecting, and using resources*

A. Improving the use of the book as a resource will usually involve getting greater value from the frequently "neglected" parts of the book: table of contents, preface, first and last paragraphs of chapters (for initial orientation), index, front thesis (if any), title page, reference sections, pictures, charts, and diagrams.

B. The professional learner should be systematically building up a personal file of resources he can use to improve his teaching or other professional activity. These should, of course, be organized for easy use.

C. Observation of others meeting the same type of resource problems is often suggestive of possible solutions.

D. Developing the ability to select critically parts of a source or resource for use is an important learning to be achieved. Also, consideration should be given to whether evidence is largely objective or largely opinion.

E. A variety of resources should be used in getting possible solutions to problems. This is very desirable to get different points of view all of which will contribute to balanced suggested solutions to problems.

F. Learners should not confine themselves to the use of particular materials merely because only those materials are labeled with the name of the course they are taking. For example, many resources not labeled "History" are very helpful in solving problems arising in the study of history.

G. Questions raised in class discussions by the active learner can help him and others better to get and to use appropriate resources.

H. Reciprocal help by learners in getting and using resources for problem identification, selection, and solution is to be encouraged.

I. As the learner attempts to improve his skill in getting and using resources more effectively, he should be constantly asking himself this question: What am I learning about the processes of effectively getting and using resources that I can teach others with whom I later work to acquire?

IV. *Goals related to evaluation, including self-diagnosis*

A. Resources should be used not only to help the learner get possible answers to problems but also to help him get his bearings, identify the problems on which he should work, and evaluate his activity.

B. Constant guided practice in the evaluation of resources which one has used or contemplates using is fundamental to improvement in getting, selecting, and using resources.

C. Resources very appropriate for one learner in a class may be most inappropriate for another learner in the same class. Some contributing factors to this situation are individual differences in needs, attitudes, skills, and basic abilities and in a feeling of just what is a problem to the particular learner concerned.

BIBLIOGRAPHY

1. COVELLO, LEONARD. "A Community-centered School and the Problem of Housing." *The Educational Forum,* 7:133-43; January 1943.
   Shows how a pressing local problem can be a vehicle for education.
2. GILES, H. H. *Teacher Pupil Planning.* New York: Harper and Bros., 1941.
   Steps toward democracy in the classroom are pictured. Many examples used from actual classrooms. Importance of interpersonal relationships emphasized. Useful bibliography.
3. GILES, H. H., *et al. Exploring the Curriculum.* New York: Harper and Bros., 1942.
   Three educators tell of their experiences in helping schools meet problems of administration, curriculum revision, and methods of teaching. Stimulating discussions of purposes of education classroom practices, growth of teachers and administrators.
4. GREENE, MARY. "Attempts To Meet the English Needs of College Preparatory Seniors in Waynesboro High School." *The Southern Association Quarterly,* 7:453-60, November 1943.
   Emphasizes determining needs, using resources, and evaluation.
5. JENKINS, F. C., *et al.* "Cooperative Study for the Improvement of Education." *The Southern Association Quarterly,* 10:3-132, 369-488, February and August, 1946.
6. KAYLOR, ALLIEGORDON. "The Contribution of the Library to the Work of Benham High School." *The Southern Association Quarterly,* 7:447-52; November 1943.
   Development of a functional library and its use by teachers and learners is discussed. Evaluations attempted.

7. KINNEY, LUCIEN, AND DRESDEN, KATHARINE W. *Better Learning through Current Materials.* Stanford, California: Stanford University Press, 1949.
   Gives details of how teachers and learners used newspapers, magazines, and other current materials in the classroom.
8. MIZELL, PHOEBE, *et al.* "Work Conference Experiences." *The Southern Association Quarterly,* 7:403-17; November 1943.
   Gives picture of improving training for in-service work through work conference experiences.
9. PETERS, C. C. *Teaching High-School History and Social Studies for Citizenship Training.* Coral Gables, Florida: The University of Miami, 1948.
   A field experiment in "Democratic, Action-centered Education (DAC)," which suggests approaches teachers have used for moving from traditional subject-matter social studies classes toward more functional citizenship training in a democratic state.
10. ROGERS, SARAH. "A Description of a Teacher's Work with Tenth-Grade Pupils in English-Social Science." *The Southern Association Quarterly,* 7:347-65; August 1943.
    Good illustrations of materials selection, procedures, record-keeping, and evaluation.
11. SHULAR, HELEN. "Procedures Employed in Developing Certain Social Concepts through the Use of High-School English Materials." *The Southern Association Quarterly,* 7:478-85; November 1943.
    Describes dual purpose: English Activities Related to Social Studies.
12. SIMPSON, RAY H. "Of Shoes and Textbooks." *Illinois Education,* 37:157-58, 177-79; January 1949. Also condensed in *The Education Digest,* 14:7-9; May 1949.
13. SIMPSON, RAY H. "Reading Problems of Teachers and Administrators and Books Found Most Valuable in Meeting These Problems." *Educational Administration and Supervision,* 28:520-28; October 1942.
    Shows actual use of auto-education in teacher-training classes.
14. Southern Association of Colleges and Secondary Schools. (Commission on Curricular Problems and Research.) "Some Evidences of Student Achievement." *The Southern Association Quarterly,* 7:253-303; May 1943.
    Gives comprehensive data and evaluations related to: (1) how pupils in secondary schools of Southern Study compare with pupils of other schools in achievement tests, and (2)

information concerning the personal, social, and intellectual development of pupils in the Study. Also gives good picture of purposes of the Study. Also purposes of teachers and learners participating in the Study are well indicated. Resources, planning, and cooperative attack on problems are given attention.

15. WALLACE W., CHREITZBERG, J., AND SIMS, V. M. *The Story of Holtville*, Deatsville, Alabama: Holtville High School 1944.

Gives vivid picture of a developing high school in action together with some description of the origins of what is happening.

16. WATERS, E. A. *Study of the Application of an Educational Theory to Science Instruction.* New York: Bureau of Publications, Teachers College, Columbia University, 1942.

Excellent description of how science classes were individualized. Graphic description is given of procedures actually used. Also gives educational theory on which the classes were based.

17. WILES, KIMBALL. "Are We Developing Skill in Purposeful Fact Collecting?" *Journal of Educational Research*, 38:617-23; April 1945.

Presents data relative to problem-solving habits of certain students.

11

DEVELOPING DESIRABLE

GROUP ROLES

Some problems to consider

Why is learning effective group behavior important?

How may the student or teacher evaluate his effectiveness in group situations?

What are some possible purposes and goals in group discussions?

What are the teacher's roles in launching and developing groups?

What are the student's roles in grouping and in groups?

How may the classroom group be nurtured?

What are the common obstacles to improvement in group roles?

How may one evaluate discussions and intragroup relations?

What are the operating principles related to improving group activities?

THE SIGNIFICANCE OF INTERPERSONAL RELATIONS

A most important need in child and adult life today is effective interpersonal relations. This is true not only on the local level but also on the national and international levels. Today we know how to produce goods in great abundance; we have not yet learned, however, how to get along with each other in mutually satisfactory relationships. Since most of our school setups involve group functioning, a study of such functioning (and malfunctioning) is of paramount importance to the teacher or the learner who wants to improve his efficiency.

Getting along with people is a key weakness in many out-of-school activities today. This reflects a major weakness of our schools in not teaching learners how to work cooperatively for mutual benefit. Many individuals, when they get into a group, actually try to meet their individual needs at the expense of the group rather than through cooperation with it. Such malfunctioning in a group is illustrated by those who become aggressors, blockers, recognition-seekers, self-confessors, playboys, dominators, or those who assume other unhealthy group roles.

Many students in our schools today, having been brought up on a fare of strictly individual learning, are not aware that behavior in getting along in a group is actually a learned activity. Group or social activity is simply one way of helping individuals achieve their purposes. A group is not a mystical something. It is an agent for helping its members identify and achieve some types of desirable goals.

Human relations have sometimes been called the fourth "R" and certainly they are as significant to human welfare as any of the other "R's."

Real democracy is practiced in everyday life. This means that if we really believe in democracy we will teach learners through our example to practice democratic procedures in their interpersonal relations. "Talking democracy" means little, if anything. Practicing democracy, on the other hand, means much, in fact, practicing democracy is the only way to learn democratic behavior.

Effective interpersonal relations is the keynote of democracy, and their development is essential to its nurture. The teacher must try not to revert to the archaic. It may frequently seem easier, in the immediate present, to get things done through dictatorial procedures, but in the long run democratic action has been demonstrated to be more effective. If we are to expect pupils to use democratic behaviors after they leave school, it is extremely important that democratic ways of behaving in interpersonal situations should be established in school. What we need is more "do democracy" and less "say democracy" both in and out of school.

One of the first objectives of the teacher and the learners should be to develop a good "social climate" in the classroom and school situation. Some of the class and individual goals should be concerned with improving interpersonal relations. Specific objectives should be set up in this as in other learning fields; frequent checks should be made to determine the extent to which these goals are being achieved.

For example, it should be remembered that good discussion technique is just as much a matter of learned behavior patterns as is good spelling or good speech. This applies not only to the leadership qualities needed in good discussions, but also to the qualities of other participants besides the leader in discussion groups. The student should learn how to criticize constructively the suggestions and decisions made by the group in which he works. He should be an active participant not only in what is being discussed but also *in considering the processes used in the discussion*. Since so much of our school activity is done in large or small groups, it is important that these large and small groups function effectively and independently rather than under the single, dictatorial guidance of a teacher who makes practically all of the decisions and merely manipulates the learners as she might a band of puppets.

Increased efficiency in learning will definitely result if the teacher and learners carefully make a study of interpersonal relations and the ways of improving them. The amount of guidance a learner needs is not related to too high a degree to his age or grade level in school. Some seventh-grade children are much more adept at carrying on appropriate interpersonal relations than many college students. For this reason we cannot simply relegate the job of promoting effective interpersonal relations to the elementary school or to the high school or to the college, but we must attempt to improve them whenever they appear to need improvement. In this as in other situations we have the responsibility for taking the learner where he is and attempting to help him develop appropriately from that point.

Since interpersonal relations in learning situations are essentially dynamic rather than static, it is important at all times that in the learning process attention be given to possible ways of improving these relations. This means that each learner, *including the teacher as a learner*, should attempt constantly to improve the interpersonal relations in the school which are likely to affect the quality of learning that takes place there. It is important that teachers and learners refuse to give up in difficult situations because of apparent limitations of resources, administration, and tradition, and that they endeavor to modify older methods as much as possible within the outside limits set by the situation. Changing such outside limits themselves may represent a key goal. The variety of methods and materials that can be used is frequently unrecognized.

So-called limits are frequently alibis for inaction. Since the student learns what he lives, it is extremely important that teachers and administrators be living examples of "do democracy." If dictatorship is practiced and democracy is preached, the latter will inevitably lose out.

EVALUATIVE QUESTIONS ON INTERPERSONAL RELATIONS IN GROUP DISCUSSIONS [1]

Goals

1. Am I sufficiently conscious of the great variety of goals group activity may help achieve, such as: efficient group functioning, awareness of broader social goals, fuller member utilization, and promotion of the growth of group members?

Attitudes and feelings in the group

2. In group discussions am I more interested in learning the truth than in proving to others in the group my preconceived ideas? If not, what should I consider doing about this?

3. In group discussion do I have a healthy respect for the opinions of others?

4. In group discussions to what degree do I accept individuals on a basis of personal worth, rather than by color, creed, class or other similar factors? In what areas am I somewhat biased?

5. When working in groups do I usually have a feeling of belonging to the group? If so, how do I show this? If not, what are the possible steps I might take to improve the situation?

Expression in the group

6. Am I able to express myself clearly and tersely in a group?

Group roles

7. Am I thoroughly familiar with the functions and techniques of group observers?

8. In group work am I willing to assume the leadership at appropriate times?

[1] These questions are phrased primarily for individual diagnosis by the student in teacher-training courses where teaching and learning methods are studied. It is also suggested that high-school students can and should be trained to ask themselves similar questions.

9. In what types of group situations, if any, do I sometimes play aggressor, blocker, recognition-seeker, self-confessor, or playboy roles? What should I consider doing to improve this situation since all of these tend to be unhealthy roles for effective learning for myself and others?

Study of group procedures

10. In the last six months have I consciously studied the development and use of democratic approaches and procedures in group operation?

11. Have I ever seriously set about to learn desirable discussion methods?

Evaluation

12. Do I know the possible ways of evaluating the carry-over or application effects of discussions or other types of group work?

13. In group work do I constantly try to appraise *my* activities so that, over a period of time, I will grow in efficiency of effort, and in contribution to the group, and thus achieve my goals through the improved productivity of the group?

PURPOSES AND GOALS IN GROUP DISCUSSIONS

Numbers make grouping imperative. The number of students who are in our schools today make it absolutely necessary to make considerable use of group activities in our educational setup. Education in group activities to be effective makes it necessary that both teachers and learners know how to work effectively together, particularly in groups. Mutually profitable exchange of ideas and guidance are necessary for effective education. Since, therefore, so much of our education is in groups, it is extremely important that those involved in these groups make a study of the interacting forces that will result in improved identification and the ultimate solution of learning problems.

Discussion groups are important out of school. Not only is group activity an essential part of in-school procedures, but it also is a successful part of a large number of out-of-school activities. In our democracy many decisions are made by, through, and after discussions. Farm groups, labor unions, religious groups, families, and clubs are illustrative of the widespread use of group activity in our

DEMOCRATIC GROUP DISCUSSION LADDER

Group is assuming major responsibility for selection of problems for discussion and the carrying on of the discussion, with the teacher assuming only an advisory role.

Problems are cooperatively identified by teacher and learners, and teacher seldom assumes a dominating role.

Problems, cooperatively identified by teacher and learners, are discussed by the group, with the teacher frequently assuming a dominating role.

There is free and frank discussion of various points of view on subjects teacher and learners have cooperatively selected but exchange is only between teacher and learner, never between two learners.

Teacher encourages questions and even permits differences of point of view but considers main role that of answering questions rather than one of encouraging critical thinking by all students in the class through the rephrasing or clarifying of questions.

Teacher permits questions but discourages any real difference of point of view or opinion.

Teacher does practically all the talking and learners' role is to copy down and memorize what teacher has said.

READ UP ⟶

Which of the rungs above best describes the class and small-group discussion practice I am getting in my class or classes? What can I do to move higher on the ladder?

culture. For this reason learning effective group operation is not only desirable in immediate learning setups while the student is in school, but is also of considerable importance to the learner after he gets out of school.

Since the success of so many of our activities depends upon effective group operation, it is important to study groups to ascertain the purposes for which they may be formed. Discussion groups in our democracy are contributers to the recognition of common needs as well as to the procedures for meeting these needs. Discussion groups have well been called the cement for building democracy.

Groups as motivators. Another purpose that those who are interested in teaching or social development may have in studying group discussion is that groups are powerful motivators to action and lead, if properly guided, to definitely improved behavior and changed attitudes on the part of those who are involved in the groups. Thus, educational and social improvement can be speeded up through the effective use of groups and group activity.

Success of the group depends on a diagnosis of the group. All groups in their operation are partially successful and partially unsuccessful. The degree of success in a particular group usually depends upon the abilities in group operation that the members bring to the group or develop after it is started. Many groups do not operate as they should, with results satisfying to the participants, and one of the basic reasons is that most discussants have not been trained to diagnose a group's difficulties. If our car or other complex mechanism that we use does not operate properly, we either try to make adjustments ourselves or get the help of an expert. If a group, which involves an extremely complex type of interaction of group members, does not seem to be moving along well, the all-too-common reaction is something like "Oh, committee work is a waste of time anyhow" or "So and so doesn't know what he is talking about." With training we would be more likely to try to find out the basis of the difficulties in group operation. This is essentially one phase of functional evaluation of groups, which can only be learned through systematic practice, preferably with guidance. We must study groups and their operation to develop instruments and skills for effectively diagnosing such groups.

How to use diagnostic results for improvement is important. Closely related to the diagnostic phase of working with the group is the improvement phase, in which ways of eliminating weaknesses shown by diagnosis are planned. Most ineffective group operations can be diagnosed and basically improved if teacher and learners make a systematic study of the difficulties and then take appropriate steps for making changes.

Such diagnosis and improvement also involves understanding and using appropriate types of group leadership and other effective roles of a good group participant.

Improvement can be made through study. In considering the study of group dynamics it should be kept in mind that sound operation procedures in a group are not primarily dependent upon inherited leadership or membership abilities. Rather, one is trained or trains himself, consciously or unconsciously, to operate effectively in a group. This is a learned ability and can be learned most effectively by elementary, high-school, and college students who operate in groups under the guidance of teachers who have made a study of such processes as are involved. All can learn effective group operation if appropriate guidance is given. It is extremely important that teachers and prospective teachers, as well as supervisors and administrators in education, become sensitive to the complexities and needs of good group operation.

Perception of possible discussion purposes has been too limited. It is unfortunate that many students and teachers only think of one or two possible purposes of group discussion when attempting to evaluate a group situation in which they have found themselves. For example, a discussion participant leaving a discussion was heard to say, "Well, we didn't get any place today, why, look, we only discussed and discussed and reached no decision for action. It looks to me like it was a waste of time."

Actually, there is a great variety of possible purposes that a discussion may serve quite helpfully and quite legitimately. For example, there is the recreational or therapeutic aspect. In this section we are primarily concerned with "work discussions" and, therefore, will not go into possible recreational purposes in any detail. However, it might be well to point out that "bull sessions" sometimes serve a very healthy function by giving the participants a chance for a verbal catharsis, which may relieve tensions that have been built up. Such "bull sessions" also frequently have a recreational value in setting up a situation for a type of intellectual struggle that can be enjoyable to many people. In evaluating any discussion it is extremely important to consider the possible purposes which that discussion may be serving.

Interpersonal relations improvement may be a goal. Sometimes the primary purpose of a particular discussion in a high-school or college group may simply be to improve interpersonal relations among members. This is frequently true when members of the discussion group are relatively unknown to each other and need to develop a common understanding in order to work effectively in later group activities. In this type of situation the discussion might be evaluated in terms of the extent to which a mutual understanding is increased among the members of the discussion group. The occasion for this use of discussion is probably most frequent in school when a new class first meets.

Growing a group. Closely related to the possible purpose mentioned in the preceding paragraph is the goal of "growing a group." This involves not only the mutual understanding previously mentioned, but also the development of operational procedures and assumptions under which the class or small group can investigate problems and propose possible solutions. It involves the development of a healthy respect for other members of the group and a consideration of, and respect for, the contributions that other members can make. An orientation discussion of common needs and problems will frequently help give the basis for the development of an effective group. A discussion of the possible organizational setups that might be used to start out the work of the group is sometimes a legitimate part of growing the group. Also, the setting up of a group organization and the selection of a leader, observer, or other type of functionary in a group may be desirable in the growing process.

Group purposes tend to parallel individual purposes. As we continue our analysis of the possible purposes of discussion, we see that a class group simply helps individuals within that group identify and meet significant problems in a more satisfactory fashion. Thus, the jobs in discussion tend to parallel in many respects the jobs that the individual learner needs to face if his development is to be satisfactory.

Clarification of needs and goals as a group purpose. An important purpose that many high-school and college groups meet initially is that of helping to clarify the needs and goals of a large number of individual members. In meeting this possible purpose a census of common needs and common problems frequently should be developed and a listing of these on the blackboard is in many cases desirable. As each proposed need or goal is stated, it is often desirable for the individual suggesting the need or goal to give his reasons for feeling that it is important. Ordinarily, this type of purpose involves no immediate action on the part of the group but gives a sound basis for later and more specific identification of problems and the selection of some of them for attack.

Identifying problems. Closely related to identifying needs and goals is the group purpose of identifying possible problems in a more specific fashion for later individual or group attack. Needs and goals tend to be rather generalized in many cases, and stating these needs and goals in the form of problems, preferably questions, points up the actual type of thing to be attacked by the individual or group. For possible ways by which not only individuals but also groups may identify problems the reader is referred to Chapters 3 and 4, which go into detail on matters related to problem identification.

Selecting problems for attack. After a large number of possible problems have been identified by the group, a common next step is to select the best among them for attack by the class or small group. Generally speaking, those selected should be considered important to almost all in a group and in addition should appear susceptible of some degree of solution by the group. For other criteria on problem selection the reader is referred to Chapter 5, which takes up in more detail some of the various aspects of effective problem selection.

Problem solution. After the group has decided which problem or problems it will attack initially, a next step is, of course, to have possible solutions suggested. These possible solutions will, in the group, get a trial run by being mentally tested out not only by the person who proposed the solution for consideration but also by other members in the group. Through such cooperative analysis and thinking the chances of a workable solution's being actually adopted are better than if a solution were considered only by an individual member of a group.

Tryout of possible solutions. After one or more possible solutions have been mentally screened for strengths and weaknesses and tentatively accepted, another possible purpose of the group is to set up ways by which such proposed solutions may actually be tried out. In other words, the group may plan ways and means of testing the "best bets" in terms of proposed solutions.

Re-evaluation. After such a tryout of proposed solutions it is frequently desirable for the group to re-evaluate a problem and its possible solutions in terms of the tryout of one or more of these proposed solutions. If the proposed solution has worked out reasonably well, the group may decide that the matter is settled. On the other hand, if the proposed solution has not been satisfactory it is quite possible that the group will want to re-examine one or more of the other proposed solutions and consider trying them out.

Group may examine how it is operating. At any particular point in all of the activity that has been suggested above the group may propose to evaluate the effectiveness of its own activities. Such an evaluation may be facilitated by the work of an *observer* whose possible functions will be discussed later, or at any particular time a member of the group may suggest that the group examine what it is doing, and why, in an attempt to improve group activities. Also, if the group is interested in improving its techniques in group participation it may desire to give frequent attention to the group processes and group roles that are shown and decide what effect such are having upon the health of the group.

Purposes of the group are important in evaluating its work. It should be pointed out that unless teachers and learners are aware of the great variety of the possible purposes of groups a group discussion may be wrongly evaluated by those participating and many of the values that may have accrued from group discussion may be underestimated. Until the possible purposes of group discussions are more clearly understood, it is not probable that groups will get as much value as desirable from their discussions. Only after a careful consideration of the possible purposes of a group can its successes and failures be fairly evaluated.

TEACHER ROLES IN LAUNCHING AND DEVELOPING GROUPS

Effective discussion groups must be grown. To be effective a group of individuals must work together for a time and, in effect, grow a discussion group. The mere bunching together of students does not and cannot constitute a well-functioning class group in a psychological sense. In fact, many classes meet physically together for a semester or a year or even longer and never really constitute a psychological group. Sometimes group growth is slow, sometimes rapid. In any case, it is important for both the teachers and the learners to recognize that, for a group to function effectively, it must be grown, and to grow in a healthy fashion it must be nurtured by both the teacher and the learners.

Discussing with learners the advantages and disadvantages of group work. It is possible for the teacher to help the group see that discussion in and of itself is not necessarily good or bad. The high-school and college teacher can help the students see the possible advantages and dangers of group work. The teacher can help the learners see the great variety of purposes for which a discussion may be held. To give the advantages of group operation free play, it is important that problems be freely raised by group members. All must feel free to talk and ask questions. Timidity and embarrassment must be quickly eliminated in a group if it is to function for the best interests of all concerned. The teacher can help the learners see that informality will frequently avoid emotional upsets that tend to keep a group from getting started off well.

Setting up appropriate groups. The teacher should be familiar with the great variety of groups that may be set up. Before groups actually start work the teacher may profitably take up with the learners the problems connected with various types of groups. Generally speaking, groups should be based on common problems and common interests. Short-time and long-time group goals and the specific purposes of individuals in a group should be studied. The student should also recognize with the help of the teacher that one of the advantages of group work is that different members may get the points of view and contributions of other group members whose experiences have been quite different from those of the particular individual member involved.

Group purpose. The teacher should help a particular group to see clearly the types of jobs that the group might do. The teacher may discuss with small groups together or with separate groups (depending on the number of common aspects of group problems) the specific jobs the group might consider doing first. A problem census may frequently be the best first step. Also, it may be desirable to encourage the group to try to attack a relatively easy problem at first, since success in this project may help the group to grow in a more adequate fashion. In effect, this means that the teacher may suggest that the group give initial consideration to a job the group can do rather quickly. The purpose of this job will be partially to get the values that come from having the task done and partially to unify the group and give it a feeling of progress. Early in its operations, the group should be encouraged to set up workable procedures and to get started quickly. Under some circumstances, where the time and place of meeting and the length of meetings has not been settled in advance, the reaching of decisions on these points may promote group cohesion.

If several groups will be operating in a classroom, it is frequently desirable that the teacher appoint a temporary leader with some experience for each group, particularly if the learners do not know each other. If the learners are familiar with each other's abilities, the teacher may suggest that they elect a leader right away. It should be remembered that sometimes relatively poor students in an academic sense may make quite successful group leaders in certain types of situations.

Finally, in getting the group launched, the teacher may want to encourage individual groups to set deadlines for particular parts of their work. This gives them something to shoot at and sometimes will help keep discussions on the beam.

Approaching groups set up for learning purposes. Common, but questionable, teacher practice in this regard includes going to a class with a relatively rigid idea in a specific sense of what will be done, when it will be done, and how it will be done. Such an approach assumes that the teacher can preplan, down to details, the exact trend of group thinking; in effect, it is likely to result in the teacher's imposing a precut plan on the group of learners. This approach further assumes that *telling how* to plan or to do is of more significance than actually planning, thinking, and doing. In this approach, the teacher tends to think of himself as an information dispenser. Such an approach tends to develop learner dependence on the teacher, lack of learner responsibility for group work, and a rather passive listening attitude on the part of the learner.

Improved practices would seem to demand that the teacher go to the group with elastic ideas about the problems the group should consider and the direction the group should take. With this approach the teacher encourages learner practice in planning discussions for best learning. The teacher stimulates the group itself to help set up long-time and short-time goals and to decide the procedures with which the group will try to reach such goals.

This suggested change in approach also is based on the assumption that learners learn what they do rather than what they are told. This approach further assumes that the teacher should encourage the students to help make decisions both on *what* is to be considered, and also on the procedures themselves, the *how* of discussion. With this approach to a class the instructor is likely to encourage genuine group cooperation rather than pseudo cooperation in which the teacher becomes the salesman and works the group around to want to do what the teacher had specifically preplanned in advance.

Number of roles the teacher practices. Common, but questionable, teacher practice in this connection has been for the teacher almost always to assume the same or a very similar role. This role usually has been one of giving directions and giving information. When the teacher assumes this role, the learners are almost forced to practice and repractice the same roles and learning processes *ad infinitum, ad nauseam.*

Under the traditional setup, the over-all role that the teacher plays is that of the dominator. This same role tends to be played day after day, week after week to the bitter end of the course with the teacher always being the keystone of the learning activities. Obviously, when the keystone is removed, the whole systematic learning process is likely to drop with a rather sickening thud.

In more desirable learning situations the over-all role of the teacher is one of guidance. However, the teacher is consciously trying to assume different roles and thus encourage the students, also, to learn the varied roles that are important for effective group interpersonal relations.

The teacher studies how and when to assume various roles. He considers carefully which roles it is probably best to assume at particular times and under certain circumstances. Obviously, such decisions are to a high degree a matter of judgment. There is no set formula or rule for such decisions. However, conscious study of the various types of healthy roles that a teacher may take will definitely improve practice in this regard. For example, at one time the teacher may support a minority position in order to see that it gets a fair hearing in a group. At another time, it may be the teacher's role to attempt to relieve tensions that seem to be growing up between members of the learning group. Still another role that the teacher frequently needs to adopt is that of "ball tosser." In this role, the teacher tries to keep the learners from always talking at him or through him, the instructor. The goal here is to get the students to carry on discussions without the teacher's assuming the leading position with every other statement.

One important difference between this and common conventional practice is the decrease in the playing of the front-center-stage part by the teacher. Actually, teacher guidance is directed toward helping the learners assume an increasing responsibility for carrying on the group operations. In one sense, the significance of the teacher's role gradually decreases as learner ability increases. In this setup we have a conscious attempt on the part of the teacher to shift the leadership to other members of the group and to give them practice in assuming such leadership. In effect, the teacher is attempting to wean the group away from the need for him, the teacher. At the present time it may appear that some teachers' egos may not stand such weaning, but if we are to consider as paramount the interests of the students, such weaning is extremely important in developing learner responsibility and initiative.

Dictatorial, laissez-faire, or democratic role? Common, but questionable, teacher practice at the present time tends to move either in the direction of dictatorial control or in the opposite direction of letting the learners do as they please, a laissez-faire role. In fact, when many teachers discuss the possibility of decreasing instruction domination in a discussion group, they immediately think of letting the learners run the show entirely on their own. Such a laissez-faire role is not seriously encouraged by any reputable educators. It is recognized that individuals left alone will not necessarily form into a desirably functioning group. A laissez-faire situation may simply substitute the domination of a student or students for former teacher domination. Neither practice is acceptable for desirable learning purposes.

More desirable teacher practice gives guidance to learners in their attempts to identify and solve problems and to get practice in running groups. Such guidance makes the running of class groups a *cooperative, democratic* venture and tends to develop a democratic group. The teacher is careful to try to steer a democratic course between the Scylla of teacher domination and the Charybdis of unguided learner domination. In a modern approach to group operation there is genuine teacher-learner cooperation in achieving better identification and solution of problems.

Purposes of the teacher as a group leader. Common, but questionable, teacher purposes in the past have been (1) to assign some work to be done, (2) to use group time to clarify points for individual learners, and (3) to check up to see that such work as has been assigned has been done.

Such practice implies that the purposes of each and every member of the class are or should be about the same. It implies that the teacher's role is one of assigning work, dispensing additional information about the content that has been assigned, and giving tests to check up on the extent to which the assigned material has been memorized by the students.

Improved practice demands that the teacher *help* the learning group set up its goals. If in the course of its work the group departs from consideration of progress toward these goals, the decision should be a conscious one on the part of the group. The teacher may sometimes assume the role of calling the group's attention to deviations from accepted goals which are taking place in the discussion.

It should be clearly recognized, however, that goals should be elastic, and that it is not the function of the teacher to keep learners from changing their goals but rather to help them make changes consciously and wisely. Another role the teacher may assume in connection with purpose is that of recognizing and helping the group to take care of the fact that different members of a group may have very different purposes and perhaps needs in a particular group operation or discussion.

Other teacher roles related to purpose might include the following:

• Helping the group and individuals in the group to re-examine their purposes periodically.

• Helping the group decide which problems are probably most crucial for consideration at any particular time. This will probably involve calling the attention of the group to some factors that may have been overlooked in deciding what would be considered for discussion at a particular time.

• Aiding the group in changing the framework of its operation in an intelligent fashion.

• Helping the group decide whether particular problems are susceptible of solution, and consequently whether it is probably desirable to take up these particular problems at this time.

- Showing interest and concern with the problems of the learners in a group. Listing the learners' concerns on the board will frequently at least give them the feeling that their points of view have been or are being considered. When problems seem overwhelming in number, the teacher as leader may consider encouraging the group to combine types of problems that seem to go together. This may help the group to have a better basis for deciding what problems should be attacked first.

Varying processes of discussion as well as varying content. Common, but questionable, past practices include the teacher's almost exclusive concern about varying what is discussed to avoid repetition of content coupled with little or no concern about varying *how* ideas are being considered or discussed. With this conventional setup the instructor tends to fall into a pattern of either always giving a lecture with a little discussion at the end or of always asking questions on text material that has been assigned. In any case, the pattern the teacher tends to follow is one of always being *the* only leader in the classroom.

Improved practice will have the teacher as much concerned about varying the processes practiced (roles practiced) as he is with varying what is discussed or considered in the group. The teacher has an understanding of the forces operating in learning in a social situation. His role is likely to reflect the fact that behavior is determined more by what is done by the learner than by what is said in the learner's hearing.

In this role of the teacher, where concern is shown for the learning processes being practiced, consideration will be given to developing the skills and understandings necessary for good group activity. The teacher with the members of the group will consciously attempt to use different discussion procedures, to invest the student leaders with different functions, to use such procedures as psychodrama to emphasize certain roles, and to have panels and committee meetings with guidance to give learners practice in these important processes.

The teacher will keep the challenge of *How* shall we operate? as constantly before the group as the more common question of *What* shall we discuss?

Teacher roles related to evaluation, including diagnosis. Common, but questionable, teacher practice in this connection has been reflected in almost exclusive concern with marks. The teacher has been little concerned with improving group operations, diagnosing individual needs, or considering ways of attempting to improve the quality of group operation.

Improved practice has the teacher assuming a role of increasing concern with helping the group evaluate itself, including diagnosis of strengths and weaknesses both of group operations and of individuals in the group. Such a diagnosis would also include an analysis of the way the group is growing. In this new, evaluative role, the teacher is concerned with the social and emotional development of the members in the group and attempts to help the learners get better acquainted with each other, and operate in the group without undesirable social or emotional strain. The teacher also assumes the role of one who is trying to help the group diagnose its needs and difficulties at any particular time in the course of group operations. With improved evaluative approaches the teacher's concern becomes primarily one of *helping individuals* improve in group activity rather than one of checking for marking or grading purposes only.

Closely related to the points just mentioned is the teacher's role of suggesting possible barriers to the achievement of group goals through procedures and/or solutions that have been proposed. The teacher may encourage the group to consider whether difficulties seem to arise out of lack of facts or technical or specialized information that the group can get from another source, or whether they arise primarily out of difficulties in interpersonal relations among members of the group during a discussion. Do the difficulties arise because members of the group do not feel free to bring forward problems or difficulties about which they might be somewhat sensitive? Is there antagonism and personal dueling between individual members which puts the group in a state of fighting itself? In general, the teacher in this role will encourage a permissive air, a relatively informal rather than a stiff and formal atmosphere. The teacher is concerned not only with judging the emotional tone of the group and its members, but with helping individual group members see how they can improve in vitally important social and emotional techniques.

Do the learners get needed practice or does the teacher monopolize practice activities? Common, but questionable, teacher roles give the teacher considerable practice in selecting problems, selecting resources, working out possible solutions, criticizing solutions, analyzing solutions, and other needed learning process activities. In other words, the teacher is front and center stage almost all the time in terms of learning practice.

Unfortunately, under current roles assumed by the teacher the learner himself gets relatively little practice—except in listening. It is not uncommon in many of our classes for the teacher to spend over 90 per cent of the time giving information. It is true, of course, that information is frequently needed, but the question may appropriately be raised, Do the learners need practice in listening 90 per cent of the time that they are in class, particularly when this one-way transmission of information is similar to the type of thing that a book can furnish?

In more approved practice the teacher attempts to assume roles that will give *learners* a chance to *get needed practice* in the interpersonal relations skills that are vitally important for good group activity. One role the teacher adopts with increasing frequency is that of becoming a good listener. In this connection, it is well to reiterate again that learners learn what they do and frequently do not learn what they are told. This means that if we want them to learn effective discussion procedures we must give them opportunities to assume leadership roles and active discussion roles rather than being largely passive observers of front-center-stage behavior on the part of the instructor.

Sensitivity to different steps of problem attack. Common, but questionable, practice on the part of teachers has been to give directions and give information to learners. When only these roles are assumed, the teacher tends to pay little or no attention to the different steps of problem-process attack in which the group may be operating.

Improved practice leads the teacher continually to recognize different steps in problem attack in any one of which the group may find itself at a particular time. Illustrations of these stages are: problem inventory, getting problems out on the table, organizing committee work, getting possible solutions, clarifying issues, coordinating activities, and other key aspects of problem attack.

In assuming roles suggested in the preceding paragraph, the teacher encourages the learners to help make decisions on procedure and on the problems to be considered. If there are general differences of opinion about procedure, the matter of procedure itself may be a problem that should have high priority for consideration.

In general, the out-of-class roles (activities) of the teacher in relation to group members may be considered a matter of considerable importance, such as individual talks with learners, particularly those who did not contribute greatly (orally) to group discussions or those who oppose or question the operation the group itself has decided on. The teacher may talk to the learner individually about problems the latter sees as of major importance but to which others in the group do not seem to attach much significance.

Sometimes a resource person coming into the group may need to be helped to see the type of role the group would like him to play. Otherwise, the resource person may become a dispenser of information and may even try to give a lecture to the group.

Generally speaking, the teacher's roles are essentially those needed for building up in the learners a major share of responsibility for the successful operation of the groups in which they find themselves.

Closely related to improving teacher roles in class situations is the problem of helping learners modify their roles in the classroom. This will be our concern in the next section.

STUDENT ROLES IN GROUPING AND IN GROUPS

Who should participate in grouping for learning purposes? To what extent should grouping be done by others and be imposed on the learners (making learners pawns in this phase of the learning process), rather than train the learner to participate in the actual grouping process itself? The latter can be done through helping the learners diagnose their needs and then guiding them in helping the teacher plan the grouping setup that will be most appropriate for meeting their needs. Such an approach gives a better basis for the continual revision and replanning of the learning setup in terms of changing individual and group needs, since the learners themselves are considering their needs and the ways in which the group or groups may contribute to meeting them.

A point made by Allport (1, p. 123) is significant here:

"... A person ceases to be reactive and contrary in respect to a desirable course of conduct only when he himself has had a hand in declaring that course of conduct to be desirable.

"Such findings add up to the simple proposition that people must have a hand in saving themselves; they cannot and will not be saved from the outside."

It is unfortunate from the standpoint of the writer that most of the professional literature on grouping has assumed that groups will be imposed upon the learners rather than that the learners can help with the grouping problem. In a recent discussion by Corey, Havighurst, and Prescott [2] only three levels of decision about grouping are suggested (p. 368): (1) the school board or superintendent, (2) the principal, (3) the teacher. Forgotten is the learner level on which all these decisions impinge and where presumably the learning in grouping should be taking place. Sound participation in all phases of the learning process will make it essential that the learner also participate in the grouping judgments or decisions which effect him. Not only is this desirable from a motivation standpoint while the learner is in school but it also will be of considerable value to him in setting up and working with groups after he gets out of school when the teacher is no longer there to direct him.

Working on the assumption that it is important for the learner to participate in the grouping process, we propose to suggest some of the possible approaches teachers may use in encouraging learners to participate actively in grouping problems.

Approaches to grouping. One of the approaches is to take up with the learners the problems related to grouping. Such questions as the following may be raised: What types of grouping might we consider for this work we have planned together? What seem to be the advantages and disadvantages of each type of grouping that has been suggested? Learners will usually exhibit good sense if given a chance on this type of problem with an appropriate amount of guidance. Planning an evaluative session on grouping would seem to be a desirable phase of the learning process after the learners have begun to give more consideration to matters of grouping.

After the learners have become somewhat accustomed to each other in a class or group, it is sometimes desirable for them to elect two or three leaders or as many as seem to be needed for the groups they have set up. The leaders may then "choose up sides" with each leader selecting those students whom he would like to work with on his group. This is one way of putting social pressure on those who in the past have not cooperated to any great extent with others in attacking problems in groups. Such a procedure usually gives a good

2 S. M. Corey, R. J. Havighurst, and D. A. Prescott, "Grouping Children: A Discussion," *Educational Leadership*, 4 (March, 1947), 365-73.

cross-section of the learners in each group and keeps in each group a number of leaders who can help others who may have less ability. A possible disadvantage of this approach is that the learner may not get into the group that is studying the types of problems he feels it would be best for him to work on.

After the teacher and the learners have worked together for some time and each has confidence in the other, a sociogram may be developed out of the learners' responses to such questions as these: With what other students in the group would you prefer to work on a problem? What student's judgment do you value most highly in this class? After the results of such questions have been ascertained, the teacher with the help of the learners may develop sociograms that will reveal isolates and other individuals who probably need special help in developing appropriate friendships within the learning situation.

Another approach is to let individual learners propose a problem around which a group might work. The procedure can be to have a learner who wishes to propose a problem group put the name of the problem on the board with his own name under the problem. As these problem names are put on the board other learners will each either propose problems for grouping purposes themselves or put their names under problem groups that have already been suggested. Too small groups or "non-filled groups" can "enlist" in other groups. For example, one student might suggest a group on, How Can We Improve Citizenship Activities in Our School? Another student might propose the group problem, How Can We Plan Our Social Activities More Effectively? Another group might consider working on, What Are the Experiences Other Schools Have Had in Improving Reporting to Parents That Might Be of Value in Our School? If a sufficient number sign their names under each of these three groups, these would constitute working groups for an appropriate period of time. Dependent upon the nature of the class will be the type of problem and the range of problems that would be appropriate.

Although the teacher has set up tentative plans for the semester, including the group work of the class, it frequently is desirable to have a "student advisory committee" elected or selected which works with the teacher in making specific and detailed plans for future activities of the class. Such a committee can meet periodically with the teacher and some aspects of student points of view can be incorporated into the planning for the class.

Another approach is to encourage each learner to help diagnose his own strengths and weaknesses and then to try to select a group on the basis of its relation to his apparent needs. For example, if the learner seems to be particularly weak in getting resources or using resources, he might elect to join a resources committee. If a particular learner seems to be weak in written expression, he might decide it would be best for him to become a part of the school newspaper staff or class newspaper committee as the case might be. Such an arrangement gives the learner some share in planning his own activities and sets up functional groups made up of learners who are in particular groups for particular purposes.

If tentative teacher grouping of the class is made initially, the learner should be encouraged to consider frequently or periodically the desirability of group placement and, if necessary, request a shift to a group where it seems his learning would be improved. With each such request, of course, the learner should be asked to submit his reasons for wanting to shift and give the teacher some better basis for helping him decide whether the shift would be desirable. In practically all class grouping situations the setup of groups should be sufficiently elastic to meet changing needs and newly recognized needs.

In general, it is desirable to encourage learners to break up into sub-groups within a small group as new needs arise. In such a situation it may be well to have an observer in the group who keeps this type of question in mind and raises it periodically. Would we do well to break up into smaller groups for more effective learning purposes?

If students are to learn how to formulate groups, they must have guided practice in setting them up for various purposes. In addition to the desirable practice learners get from helping to set up the groups in which they will function, we usually find motivation to work well and purposefully in the groups after they are set up is likely to be much healthier if the learners have helped to group themselves.

Out of school we hope school graduates will know how wisely to set up groups for functional purposes. They will, if they have had sufficient practice in doing it, with guidance, while in school.

Learner facilitation and coordination of group work. Much has been written on the training and developing of teachers and leaders of group activity; relatively little of a practical sort has been presented to help the teacher or prospective teacher to visualize the roles in which class learners should be given practice if they are to be effective learning participants in classes and smaller groups. The discussion on the next few pages has been written to help the student of teaching-learning situations visualize the roles to be encouraged.

In considering facilitation and coordination roles, we are concerned with the help the learner can give in a group when it is identifying, selecting, and defining common problems, and also, with the help the learner can give the group in getting possible solutions to the problems that are studied. The trying out of some of the solutions the group has proposed is an additional function with which we are concerned.

It is obvious that in any particular discussion the learner as a group member may enact more than one role. It is also true that during a series of class or smaller group activities, the learner should get considerable practice in as many of these roles as possible. The reason for such practice is primarily twofold: first, the learner needs to know how to carry on these roles in group situations; second, the operations of the learning group of which the student is a part are likely to be more healthy, to be characterized by stronger motivation on the part of the members, and to produce better results if most of the learners in a group are able to assume most or all of these roles with considerable facility. In other words, the learner is acquiring the skills needed for later group activity and is also at the same time helping to facilitate the work of the particular group in which he is operating. Descriptions of twelve facilitator and coordinator roles follow.

Initiator-contributor.[3] In assuming this role, the learner is encouraged to suggest new ideas or changed ways of regarding group problems or goals. He is encouraged to suggest possible solutions to problems arising in the group. He attempts to get practice in the handling of different group difficulties. He may suggest new pro-

[3] The names of the roles are those used by Kenneth Benne and Paul Sheats, "Functional roles of group members," *The Journal of Social Issues*, 4 (Spring, 1948), 41-49.

cedures or new organization for the group. This is essentially a creative role.

Information-seeker. In enacting this role, the group member seeks clarification of suggestions that have been made in the class or small groups in terms of such things as their factual adequacy and/or authoritative information. He may also attempt to get at pertinent facts after a brief explanation of why he thinks particular facts are needed.

Opinion-seeker. Here the learner is practicing the role of seeking clarification of the values pertinent to problems the group is considering or values involved in suggestions made. The opinion-seeker differs from the information-seeker in that the former is consciously attempting to get at personal points of view and personal values rather than at factual information.

Information-giver. The information-giver volunteers facts or generalizations that are "authoritative" or relates his own experience pertinently to group problems.

Opinion-giver. In this role, the learner states his belief or opinion regarding suggestions that have been made, or compares alternate suggestions that have been proposed. Generally speaking, the purpose in doing this is to try to influence the group's use of pertinent values and thus suggest what should be done.

Elaborator. The learner practicing this role gives examples or developed meanings, offers reasoning back of suggestions that someone else has made before, and tries to project his thinking into a consideration of how the idea proposed might work out. The elaborator may also, of course, attempt to show that certain suggestions do not appear to be good ones because of faulty rationale or because it does not appear that they would work out successfully.

Coordinator. The group member assuming this role attempts to clarify relationships among ideas and suggestions, he tries to pull ideas and suggestions together, or in other words, he attempts to coordinate the thinking and activities of members or sub-groups.

Orienter. The orienter attempts to define the apparent position of the class or sub-groups of the class on the goals the class or sub-groups are trying to achieve. He sometimes will attempt to summarize what has been done in order that the group may have a better orientation for proceeding with problem identification, selection, or solution. He may attempt to point out departures in the group discussion or group operations from the agreed directions or goals. Sometimes he may question the value of the direction the discussion is taking.

Evaluator. Periodically, the evaluator attempts to subject the accomplishment of the group to "standards" of group functioning. He may evaluate directly or may question "the practicality," "logic," "facts," or "procedure" of a suggestion or of some unit of the group discussion. His role is essentially to lead the class or groups into a re-evaluation of goals, standards, and accomplishments.

Energizer. The function of the energizer is to prod the group to some action or decision. He attempts to stimulate the group to both "greater" or "higher-quality" activity. He can sometimes be of greatest value when the group is delaying needed action or decision.

Procedural technician. In a sense this is a fancy name for a routine but extremely important job, which includes distributing materials or manipulating objects for the class, such as putting up maps, changing movable blackboards, or rearranging chairs or tables.

Recorder. The recorder has sometimes been called the "group memory." He writes down suggestions, group decisions, or products of discussion so that he can report back to the group what has been said about problems that have been discussed. In addition to emphasizing the gist of *what* has been said, it is helpful if he indicates the issues which students seem divided and those on which they seem to agree.

Learner roles related to building group-centered attitudes and orientation. As has been indicated before, the group is essentially an organism and it is important that the members of the organism operate as a part of the group rather than merely as a collection of individuals. The next seven roles [4] to be discussed are related to the way learners in a class or small group can help maintain and develop group-centered activity on the part of other members of the group as well as on the part of the individual himself. Here again, a particular group member may practice for learning purposes several roles in the course of a particular discussion. It should also be pointed out that most of these roles as well as those in the preceding section are also enacted by the teacher as leader. In fact, the clear-cut line of demarcation between teacher and learner tends to disappear as the group grows in a healthy fashion.

[4] Names of the roles are those used by Kenneth Benne and Paul Sheats, *op. cit.*

Encourager. In this role the learner praises, agrees with others, and, when he accepts others' ideas, he says so. He also shows a warmth and solidarity in his attitude toward other students in the group. Obviously, such an attitude must be sincere if the role of encourager is to be well played.

Harmonizer. In this role, the student attempts to mediate intra-group scraps. He tries to relieve tensions that may have arisen in the group and attempts to keep others from becoming emotionally upset and personally antagonized one with another.

Compromiser. When a learner's idea about what solution is best or what should be done by the group is in conflict with that of another learner or group of learners, when he yields status, admits an error, disciplines himself, or "comes halfway," the learner may be said to be enacting the role of the compromiser. In the interest of effective group operation, he is willing to try to reach a middle ground rather than doggedly sticking to the individual position he originally had.

Gate-keeper and expediter. The role of this person is to encourage and facilitate the participation of other learners. For example, one student may say, "Let's hear what Jim has to say about this. He has had considerable experience along this line," or he may suggest when some in the group are monopolizing the time, "Why not limit the length and number of contributions so that all in the group may have a chance to react to this problem which is of importance and significance to all of us?"

Standard-setter or ego-ideal. In this role, the learner attempts to express standards for the group to attempt to achieve in its functioning. The learner may also try to apply standards that the group has been explicitly or implicitly using in evaluating or attempting to evaluate the quality of group processes.

Group-observer and commentator. He keeps records of group processes and contributes these data, with or without proposed interpretations, to the group's evaluation of its own procedures. To handle this role tactfully the learner needs to get considerable practice. Otherwise, he is likely to antagonize certain other learners who are sensitive to criticism that might be interpreted as directed at them individually.

Follower. The reason that a follower is placed in a healthy role in a group is that he provides a friendly audience for others. His overt indications of interest or boredom may to some extent provide a sounding board for other students who are speaking more in the group than he is. Obviously, too many learners have assumed the follower role almost exclusively. In many classes, most students only play the role of follower with any facility.

Anti-group learners' roles to be avoided. In addition to the nineteen healthy group roles that have just been briefly described, we discuss below eight roles [5] that are likely to militate *against* successful group operations. The primary similarity of these unhealthy class or small-group roles is that in each of them *the learner is trying to meet his felt individual needs at the expense of group health rather than through cooperation with others in the group.*

It should be emphasized that in assuming both healthy and unhealthy roles the learner is trying to help himself, and that this is normal. In healthy roles he helps himself in a constructive way; in unhealthy roles he tries to help himself through behavior that may give some immediate satisfaction ("I really slapped him down") but tends to give a frustrated feeling over a period of time.

The conscious avoidance of the practicing of unhealthy group roles is as important for individual adjustment and group productivity as the development of healthy group roles.

Aggressor. Here the effort is to deflate the status of other learners. It may be done through expressions of disapproval of the values, acts, or feelings of others. The student in this role attacks the group itself, or the problems the group is taking up. He may joke aggressively, or show envy by trying to take credit for the ideas of other learners.

Blocker. In this role, the student tends to be negativistic. He is stubbornly and unreasoningly resistant to suggestions proposed by others. He tries to bring back an issue that the group has intentionally rejected or by-passed as being unusable in the particular circumstances involved.

Recognition-seeker. This learner tries to call attention to himself and may try to do so in a variety of ways, for example, he may boast, report on personal achievements unrelated to the work of the group, and in unusual ways struggle to prevent being placed in an "inferior" position.

Self-confessor. In this role, the learner uses the group to express personal, non-group-oriented "feeling," "insight," "ideology."

[5] Role names are those used by Kenneth Benne and Paul Sheats, *op. cit.*

Playboy. The playboy displays a lack of personal involvement in the group's work. He tends to stay at the fringes of group activity and his actions may take the form of cynicism, nonchalance, horse-play, or other more or less studied "out-of-field behavior."

Dominator. While this role is frequently taken by the teacher, some learners may also try to exert some authority in manipulating a group or in persuading some individuals in the group to do what the dominator wants done in an undesirable sense. He may use flattery, assertion of superior status or right to attention, give directions authoritatively, or continually interrupt the contributions of others.

Help-seeker. This individual tries to get "sympathy" responses from others through expressions of insecurity, personal upset, or deprecation of himself beyond "reason."

Special-interest pleader. This learner may always be arguing for the little man, the hard-worked student, the athlete, or the occupation in which his father happens to be engaged. He tends always to react to suggestions in terms of a relatively narrow frame of reference. In many cases he is actually cloaking his own prejudices and biases in stereotypes that best fit his individual needs as far as he can see the situation. A narrowness of point of view is frequently reflected in the special-interest pleader in the classroom situation.

In concluding our discussion of learner roles, it should again be emphasized that not only the learner but also the teacher tries to practice healthy roles and to avoid those roles that give satisfaction at the expense of the group.

Teacher roles and learner roles have been discussed. In our next section we discuss some ways in which instructors can nurture healthy groups.

NURTURING A CLASSROOM GROUP

As has been suggested before, a group grows like an individual organism. If unhealthy relationships exist between parts, they must be rooted out. Functional democratic working conditions must be nurtured at all times.

Teacher example of self-learning important. Generally speaking, it is vitally important for growing a healthy group that the teacher regard himself as a learner *with* the group. The teacher must consciously practice improvement and growth himself if he is to be a healthy influence on the growth of the group. Students may not be able to verbalize it but they are quick to sense preaching-learning as opposed to practicing-learning, professional stagnation vs. professional growth.

Goals, rules, and grouping need periodic reconsideration. There are several types of things the teacher should probably encourage the group or groups to do periodically. One is to reconsider their goals, particularly if little progress seems to be made by the group. Changes in rules may be encouraged to meet the changing purposes of the group. Periodically, the group may be encouraged to consider the desirability of sub-groups. These may arise out of different interests or needs or out of a desire to facilitate the work of the group. More work on group problems out of a group setting may also be desirable. The best time and place for meetings may be a point that the teacher should raise with the group. Even such a radical step as suggesting a reshuffling or reconsidering of group membership may be a service that the teacher can perform for the group.

Permissive atmosphere to be encouraged. Also, the teacher should encourage each member of a group to consider whether he feels really free in presenting any problem, and the teacher can note any difficulty that individual group members may be having in working with the group. For example, does there appear to be a lurking fear of embarrassment or ridicule? If so, whence does it stem? Is there a desirable atmosphere of permissiveness in the group? Sometimes an anonymous evaluation may be desirable in determining what the situation is in this regard. The teacher may also encourage each individual to solicit evaluation of his work by others in the group. This may be done through anonymous check sheets or other types of communication that are not likely to upset the friendly interpersonal relations that should exist in a group. In general, in this connection, it is important for the teacher to help each learner play his roles better and to practice playing new roles in which he does not have too much facility.

Keep teacher-learner channels open. All teacher-learner communication channels should be continuously open so that the teacher can help the students make adjustments. The teacher as leader may encourage each learner to talk to him about the troubles he is having with his group. "Everybody laughs at what I say." "Nobody likes the ideas I propose. But when someone else proposes the same ideas, the group likes them." Such comments as these should be considered objectively and with a sympathic attitude by the teacher. Frequently, the teacher by observation is able to see the types of things the learner does that lead other students either to laugh at him or to be antagonistic to the things he proposes in all seriousness. Sometimes the difficulty may be a matter of talking too much or even of voice inflection. Here the teacher can suggest ways of improving.

Variety of resource use to be encouraged. A large variety of resources for use by the group should be encouraged by the teacher. A sign of growth sometimes is the ability of a group to inform itself and to think straight and to correct deficiencies. Use of varied human resources should also be encouraged, sometimes for information and sometimes to help the group diagnose its difficulties or correct these difficulties if a diagnosis has already been made.

Rotation of roles. The group may be encouraged to consider whether the leader, recorder, and observer roles should be rotated. This will sometimes discourage undesirable overdependence on a leader or teacher. The group may desire to study the functions of each of these people periodically and consider how their performances can be improved.

Group disappointments and successes. The teacher may emphasize that the groups as individuals have both disappointments and successes and that one of the aspects of a group's growing emotionally is the ability to take both successes and disappointments in its stride.

In general, the teacher should develop group growth by raising questions rather than by telling the group what it should do or how it should perform at any particular time. In this way the teacher is encouraging the group to develop independence and judgment and to operate in such a way that the group can improve even if the teacher is not immediately present.

There is no arbitrary formula for group growth. All involved must study its strengths and weaknesses and attempt to have the group help individual members and meet their common purposes through the effective vehicle of group operation. It is vitally important that a large share of the responsibility for the success of the group be assumed by each student. If the meeting did not go well, he should be helped to see that he is probably partly responsible. One key sign that the teacher has been successful in promoting group growth is the assumption of responsibility for group success by all the learners in the group.

Have appropriate seating arrangements. The conventional class setup with seats row behind row and column beside column is conducive to autocratic group operation. The physical setup where the learners see the backs of the necks and heads of their fellow students usually rather effectively discourages learner-learner exchange of ideas. Regardless of how esthetically attractive the necks and heads may be, a face-to-face relationship is extremely desirable, if not absolutely necessary, for effective group learning. Sometimes a first major step a teacher can take in developing democratic group operation is to modify the essentially authoritarian setup which is all too common in classrooms.

In general, a circular arrangement of tables and chairs seems to be helpful in growing a democratic class or group. Where there are too many students in the class or where the size or shape of the room makes a single circle impractical, a double or even triple circle may be the best answer that can be suggested under the circumstances. In any case, movable class or group furniture makes it possible for the group to try out different arrangements for the same or different purposes.

The physical setting for the group discussion should be such that there are maximum possibilities for each in the group to hear easily and see the faces of all others in the group. Such a physical arrangement encourages a multidirectional exchange of ideas rather than the conventional unidirectional or at most bidirectional interchange of ideas.

Absence of outside noises, appropriate heat and light, and freedom from interruptions by outsiders, all contribute to effective group operation. *While having optimum physical conditions certainly does not guarantee effective group growth, undesirable physical conditions do make healthy group growth more difficult.* The teacher can and should try to help the learners arrange physical conditions so that desirable group growth can be rapid.

Record ideas. Usually a blackboard placed so that all can see is a helpful tool for keeping before all in the group the points different learners have made.

In addition, it is sometimes desirable to use large sheets of newsprint placed on the wall or easel on which points developed by the group can be recorded for all to see. The advantage of the sheets over the blackboard is that they can be rolled up and retained as a record of a group operation that was developed in plain view of all. The newsprint record also provides a basis for some types of future evaluation of the classwork.

In our next section we shall consider some of the difficulties frequently encountered in improving class and small-group work.

COMMON OBSTACLES TO IMPROVEMENT IN GROUP ROLES

Attitudes toward group efficiency. Perhaps the main difficulty we face in attempting to improve the quality of school group work is the general feeling on the part of many teachers and administrators, and sometimes on the part of students, that appropriate group behavior is something a person either has or does not have, something that cannot or need not be learned. This, of course, is contrary to the evidence that good group behavior is largely learned behavior, and therefore can be taught. A first major problem, then, is the clear-cut recognition that desirable activity on the part of an individual in a group can be learned and is of considerable importance.

Lack of experience in democratic groups. Closely related to this attitude is the lack of experience that many instructors and learners have had with good democratic interpersonal relations in group discussions and elsewhere. Where connections with group work have been unfortunate, the individual is likely to reject a change in the matter of interpersonal relations, because anything he has seen in a group did not appear to work out very well. It appears that many group discussions that seem to be profitless are that way because of lack of training for such discussions on the part of those involved rather than because of any inherent weakness in the discussion approach or group approach itself. Common weaknesses of teachers and learners in group activity usually go back to a lack of sufficient participation in democratically functioning groups.

Lack of training in evaluation. Most learners and teachers have lacked training in evaluating their own individual activity in a group and in checking up on the methods and means used in a group itself. This involves, of course, a consideration of the outcome sought through the discussion. Closely related to this lack of ability in individual appraisal or self-appraisal of group work is a lack of recognition of the need for an evaluation of the processes of a group. If a mechanism such as a machine breaks down in operation we tend to consider what the possible causes are and what might be done to eliminate these causes of the difficulty. In group discussion a similar attack on the problem would be in order but most learners and even teachers have not been trained to take such a step.

A rather direct result of the lack of past consideration of ways of diagnosing group behavior in operation is the common lack of attention, by both teachers and learners, to growing a group that will have some common attitudes and purposes, and that will attempt to reach individual goals through appropriate group action. Growing a group is somewhat similar to growing a plant. A strong and healthy group does not arise in full bloom. It must be nurtured and given appropriate care if it is to become something of worth. One phase of growing a group involves attention on the part of the participants to various types of roles that each may play with profit in producing a healthy group. There must also be a consideration of the types of roles that are unhealthy and that tend to harm rather than help the group. Study of this type on the part of teachers and learners has been sadly neglected in many cases.

Undesirable group training has been given. Unfortunately, with most teachers and learners we not only face the problem of lack of favorable training for effective group operations, but we also face a situation where teachers and learners have had what might be called negative training or poor group activity. In classrooms, for example, this frequently has resulted in the expectation on the part of teachers and learners that the teacher will lead practically all the discussions and the responsibility will be his for the health of the group work. Such a type of unfortunate experience gives the learner a feeling that his role in a class is a relatively passive one that involves doing what the teacher has indicated but does not include taking much, if any, responsibility in actively leading in the learning process. Such assumption of the continuously dominating role on the part of the teacher in classroom activity has also kept learners from much needed practice or active participation in taking leading roles in small group discussions. A difficulty closely related to that mentioned in the preceding paragraph is the common practice in classes of "discussions" being limited to giving answers to questions related to materials presented in the text or in the lecture. Here the teacher usually permits questions that he himself has indirectly asked on the text.

The vast experience that most learners have had with teacher-dominated groups tends to give learners the idea that this is the desirable situation, in fact, almost the only possible situation, in a reputable classroom. There has been too high a premium placed on leaders who simply give information and get the group to do what they want it to do, rather than on leaders who help the group to think through its problems and arrive at mutually profitable and desirable conclusions or decisions. Pushing the whole responsibility for the success of the group upon the teacher or other leader with the other members sitting back and taking an essentially passive role is a concept that must be overcome if we are to develop effective group interpersonal relations.

In the teacher-dominated setup, too often the teacher comes to the group with rigid ideas about what direction it will or should take, what it will do, and what conclusions it will reach. This, of course, violates the principle of effective democratic group action for learning purposes and makes the group merely a puppet in the hands of the teacher or leader.

Systematic study of group processes needed. Although great advances have been made in the last few years in studying group processes, we still lack sufficient systematic study or experimentation on techniques and methods for developing and using group procedures. Lack of sufficient experimental data constitutes a major handicap in our activities. However, enough is now known with considerable definiteness so that great strides forward may be taken by the teacher and learners who are sincerely interested in developing effective democratic group operations.

One significant way of working for improvement in group work is to study and try out some of the ways of evaluating discussions and intragroup relations. Suggestions along this line will be given in the next section.

EVALUATING DISCUSSIONS AND INTRAGROUP RELATIONS

Discussions may be profitable or unprofitable. Intragroup relationships may be healthy or unhealthy. The primary purpose in evaluating discussions on intragroup or intraclass relationships is to determine the past and present quality of key processes and relationships so that future processes and relationships may be more satisfying and productive.

Since the class is a group, the following considerations refer not only to small groups but to the class group also.

Before one is in a position to evaluate most aspects of the work of a group, or even the relationships within a group, it is vitally important that he know the "group" purposes. The "goodness" of a group depends largely on the extent to which the group activity is contributing to the group's goals. Our consideration in a preceding section of some of the possible purposes of discussion when related to this point gives us a picture of the immense complexity of evaluative problems within groups. Goals, for example, may be process ones, such as motivation of the group for later group activities. On the other hand, the group may be after production goals. Here the purpose might be, for example, to identify clearly problems of importance or to reach sound decisions. If the significance of class and small-group goals is clearly recognized, more attention will be given to them than is commonly the case.

In considering evaluation of discussions or group success it is important to recognize clearly that an analysis should include not only *what* is being discussed but *how* it is being discussed. Too little attention to the *how* of discussions sometimes results in antagonistic, bored, or apathetic behavior on the part of the members of the group. Unless a class or group gives special attention to ways of utilizing the abilities of *each* member, a relatively large amount of group potential is likely to be lost. Productive furnaces are likely to be banked unless the *how* of getting all in the group to work productively together is given group consideration.

Since group members are usually better acquainted with group purposes than outsiders, from some standpoints, they are in the better position to carry on class or group evaluation. Also, if evaluation is to be really functional, it must be a continuous process and an integral part of the total pattern of successful group operation. Periodically, the group should take time out to ask: How are we doing? Most profitable evaluation must be carried on by the group; outside experts or observers may at times supplement the group evaluation.

For evaluative purposes as well as for other uses to which they may be put, *records* of *what* a group did, *how* it did it, and *why* it was done are invaluable. Good group operation frequently demands that comprehensive records be kept.

Some issues to consider in trying to evaluate a learning group. The complexity of factors involved in evaluating a group's discussions or its intragroup relationships has already been suggested.

There is no single best way of attacking this difficult but vitally important learning problem. In an attempt to help clarify some of the angles of attack, specific evaluative questions for teacher and learner consideration have been formulated. These questions are given below and are grouped under eight headings. Categories include questions related to (1) group goals, (2) leader behavior, (3) member behavior, (4) general group methods, (5) group atmosphere, (6) plans for improvement, (7) group production, and (8) past group reactions.

A. *Questions revolving around the group goals*

1. Did the group have clearly defined purposes and goals in its discussion?

2. Did it appear that members of the group have consciously considered such questions as these: *Why* are we having this discussion? What are we trying to do and why?

3. To what extent was the group fitting its immediate goals into long-time social goals in a culture that is striving toward greater democracy?

4. Was transferring group learning to other areas of school and community group life a conscious goal of the group members?

5. In discussions where decisions were to be reached was the goal "group *consensus*" rather than merely majority vote?

6. Were group goals realistically difficult in terms of the present abilities of group members?

7. Were the group activities directed toward a goal or goals that had been consciously set up?

8. To what extent did group members seem to be motivated by a common purpose?

9. Were group goals reconsidered sufficiently often?

B. *Questions revolving around the leader*

1. What effect did leader behavior seem to have on the group?

2. Did the leader seem rather insecure and so promote a repression of ideas?

3. Did the leader assume too much responsibility for group operation and thus tend to promote irresponsibility on the part of other members of the group?

4. Did the leader seem to talk too much in the group?

5. Did the leader seem to have a preconceived detailed plan

about what should happen in the group and try to force the group into that plan?

6. Did the group leader show skill in delimiting and emphasizing areas of greatest argument?

C. *Questions revolving around member behavior*

1. What kinds of healthy member behavior operated in the group?

2. What kinds of unhealthy member behavior operated in the group?

3. Did any non-leader members in the group seem to talk too much?

4. Did all in the group seem to take a real interest in the group proceedings? If not, why not?

5. In the group did there seem to be some members who were largely rejected by the group?

6. Was there widespread participation reflecting intense member involvement in the discussion or did a few persons dominate the group's work?

7. To what degree did all the group members apparently accept responsibility for helping the group to move ahead rather than relying unduly on a leader or leaders?

8. To what extent did it seem that the individual members of the group were able to subordinate individual immediate interest to the common goals?

9. Were most contributions made in the group on the point being discussed rather than "off the beam" or "off the course"?

10. Did the contributions of members indicate that those who made them had been listening to what others in the group had been saying?

11. Did it appear that those in the group were able to rise above their preconceived notions and emotions and change positions somewhat in view of the evidence adduced?

12. Did the group operate in such a way that members were becoming better contributors in terms of the quality of their contributions and in terms of the variety of healthy group roles that they were learning how to assume?

13. Were group members talking willingly and naturally?

14. Was each group member accepted on a basis of his personal worth rather than on the basis of his family status, color, etc?

15. When a minority disagreed with the majority after discussion, did the members of the group attempt to protect the rights of the minority?

16. When a poor or unclear question was asked by a group member, did another group member attempt to restate it in better or clearer form?

17. Did attendance records in the group reflect strong continuing interest in group activities?

D. *Questions revolving around general group methods*

1. What forces seemed to be helping the group solve its problems?

2. What factors seemed to be hindering the group from reaching its goals?

3. What were the specific weaknesses in the group processes as shown by group discussion?

4. What were the strengths in the group processes as shown by discussion?

5. Did the group give sufficient attention to its own group processes in operation?

6. At what points in the discussion did the group seem to get off the track? What derailed the group? Why did we, the group, sometimes find it hard to stick to the point?

7. Is the group making any improvement in its ability to work together more effectively?

8. Was the group operating democratically?

9. Was every group member encouraged and helped to participate in group decisions that affect his and the group's welfare?

10. Did the group sufficiently often delegate authority and tasks to sub-groups or individuals?

11. Were summaries of discussions given at appropriate times?

12. Did the group at appropriate times recognize its need for information and go about getting such information?

13. If a needed decision was one of the goals of the group, did the discussion move readily toward such a decision?

E. *Questions pertaining to group atmosphere*

1. Was the group climate, atmosphere, or "personal weather" such that each person in the group seemed to feel really free to express his actual opinions and feelings?

2. Was there a warm, friendly, personalized give-and-take atmosphere in the group during the discussions?

3. At times when members of the group disagreed with each other was there an atmosphere of friendly cooperation?

4. Did there seem to be increasing tolerance of opposing opinions and willingness to listen sympathetically to positions of other group members?

5. Did some in the group seem to find it necessary to wear a "mask" to protect their ego?

6. Was the group characterized by teacher (leader) rule and learner (follower) obedience?

7. Was there an apathetic, indifferent atmosphere?

8. Was there active negativism or even open hostility in the group?

9. Did the group atmosphere seem cooperative or competitive?

F. *Questions relating to plans for improvement*

1. What steps could be taken to help the group improve in its ability to work more effectively in this type of discussion?

2. What possible improvements might be suggested to this group?

G. *Questions relating to group production*

1. To what degree did the group progress toward some production of process goals it had set for itself?

2. At what rate did it appear that the group was moving toward goals it had set for itself?

3. Since the group situation was presumably an educational one, what specific changes in member behavior seemed to be resulting?

NOTE: Answers to many of the questions already given in other categories are, of course, closely tied up with evaluation of group production.

H. *Questions relating to post-class or small-group reactions*

1. How successful did you feel the class or small-group meeting you just attended was? (*a*) Poor, (*b*) Fair, (*c*) Good, (*d*) Very good, (*e*) Excellent?

2. How do you feel you could have changed *your* behavior to have made it more successful?

3. To what degree did individual group members seem to see some of their out-of-group behavior as a phase of the tasks started in the group?

4. Did post-meeting conversations reflect interest and healthy concern about *what* was being accomplished in the group as well as *how* it was being achieved?

5. If the discussion was expected to produce a certain kind of behavior, what actually happened in terms of member behavior after the meeting was over?

Additional approaches to measuring discussions. Auer and Ewbank in their practical publication, *Handbook for Discussion Leaders,* suggest the following methods of measuring discussions (4, pp. 100-105):

1. Use of a simple, anonymous ballot to determine how individuals feel about a subject before and after discussion.
2. Use of a shift-of-opinion ballot.

Question: What should be my attitude toward consumer cooperatives?

Before discussion
(*check one*)

_____ I am in favor of consumer cooperatives

_____ I am undecided

_____ I am opposed to them

After discussion
(*check one*)

_____ I am more strongly in favor of consumer cooperatives

_____ I am in favor of them

_____ I am undecided

_____ I am more strongly opposed to them

This type of ballot does provide some basis for evaluating the effect of total discussion in shifting individual opinions. *Check before* and *after* discussion. Do not sign name.

3. The rating scale.—Participants can rank proposed solutions in order of preference.

Question: What about the "right to strike"?

Below are 5 possible solutions to this problem. Place a "5" before the solution you believe best, a "4" before the second best, etc.

_____ The right to strike is the union's only effective weapon.

_____ The right to strike should be limited only by making unions legally liable for losses to employers through unauthorized strikes.

_____ The right to strike should continue as at present.

_____ There is no right to strike when the public would be harmed thereby.

_____ Strikes should be forbidden by law.

4. Specialized techniques. — Attitude test or linear scale.
5. Evaluation questionnaire. — To get reactions and suggestions from those who attended. Use only occasionally to supplement reactions gathered informally. Anonymous. Example: (Can be adapted to situation.)

Your answers to the following questions will be helpful to those in charge of planning these discussion meetings. Please be frank. Check the answer to each question which most nearly fits your reaction.

1. Was the subject for discussion of interest to you?
   _____ Very interesting _____ Mildly interesting _____ Not at all interesting

2. Did you learn something new about the subject?
   _____ A great deal _____ A little _____ Nothing at all

3. Do you now have a better understanding of the subject?
   _____ Much better _____ Somewhat better _____ No better

4. Was the meeting as a whole an interesting experience?
   _____ Very interesting _____ Moderately interesting
   _____ Not at all interesting

5. Did the leader (or formal speaker) talk
   _____ Too long? _____ Just long enough? _____ Not long enough?

6. Did you take part in the discussion (or forum period)?

_____ More than once _____ Only once _____ Not at all

7. Will you come again?

_____ Yes _____ Perhaps _____ No

8. What suggestions would you make for improving these meetings?

9. What subjects would you suggest for future meetings?

Miel (26, p. 51) in a stimulating article, "It's Our World Again," analyzes some phases of social competence and contrasts some relatively low-level with some relatively high-level social learnings for which the school should share responsibility.

Level 1	*Level 2*
a. Maintaining self-control	Bearing a friendly feeling
b. Being kind to others	Having a concern for all mankind
c. Exhibiting tolerance of difference	Valuing difference
d. Getting along with others	Being a contributing member of a group
e. Conceiving of freedom as extending until it interferes with the freedom of another	Seeing the necessity of a cooperative search for conditions guaranteeing maximum freedom for all
f. Taking responsibility for doing one's own job	Taking responsibility for a share of the labor involved in a common enterprise
g. Being satisfied with majority rule	Working for "unanimous consent"
h. Showing obedience to authority	Evaluating and cooperating with authority
i. Understanding and accepting the status quo	Refining constantly one's conception of the "good society"
j. Acquiring the mechanical skills of reading, writing and figuring	Making full use of communication skills.

Consideration of the differences between Level 1 and Level 2 on the list above not only suggests some possible goals of group discussion but also indicates some factors in the evaluation of behavior in groups.

Post-discussion behavior evaluation. Another attempt at evaluating the worth of one type of discussion is based on comparing the post-discussion behavior of the participants with the behavior of other group participants where other group procedures, such as the lecture, were used. This type of evaluation was used by Lewin [6] and Bavelas.[7]

In the discussion approach during World War II groups of women from low, medium, and high economic levels discussed the use of glandular meats with a nutritionist and the group came to regard the problem being discussed as important to it. Group decisions based on individual decisions regarding the increased use of these meats were reached by the end of the discussions.

The results from this discussion approach were compared with those from the lecture method using three similar groups: one each from high, middle, and low income levels.

The test of the relative effectiveness of the two methods was made by interviewing each of the women in the groups to determine her use of the glandular meats. Forty-four per cent of the women in the discussion groups served one of the glandular meats while only 3 per cent of those in the lecture groups served such meats.

This type of control group approach seems to have significance in that actual behavior is being investigated.

OPERATING PRINCIPLES RELATED TO IMPROVING GROUP ACTIVITIES

I. *Principles related to goals and purposes*

    A. The goals and purposes of groups should reflect or develop common member goals and purposes. Thus, the primary purpose of the discussion group is to help members identify, select, and solve common problems.

    B. One major goal in class and small-group discussions probably should be to practice democratic living. In-school and out-of-school discussion groups are the cement for democracy, and, therefore, merit great attention in our culture.

[6] K. Lewin, "The relative effectiveness of a lecture method and a method of group decision for changing food habits" (Washington, D.C.: Committee on Food Habits, National Research Council, June, 1942). (Mimeographed.)

[7] A. Bavelas, "Group decision." Paper read before a meeting of the S.P.S.S.I., 1943.

C. Effective group behavior can be learned. It, therefore, constitutes a legitimate goal in the learning program.

D. Perhaps the outstanding weakness of our society today is shown by the striking inability of many of its members to work cooperatively with each other in meeting mutual problems. This weakness should challenge schools to revise, perhaps radically, the conventional pattern of teacher-dominated group discussions.

E. Discussion groups can be powerful motivators for more effective individual behavior.

F. The possible goals or purposes of discussions are extremely great in number and varied in type. Care should be taken so that we will not unfairly evaluate a discussion on one criterion when it may have been extremely successful in terms of achievement on one or more other criteria.

II. *Operating principles related to setting up a group*

A. The individual learner should share in decisions affecting the class and the sub-groups he is in.

B. The approaches to grouping practice are many. Opportunities for practice in a variety of these should be given the learner.

C. The purposes for which a class or group is set up should be major factors in determining who should belong to a particular class or group.

D. Whether it is better to have work done on a problem at a particular time or by a particular individual or group should depend largely on the purpose of the work and on the educational values to be derived. This in turn depends to a major degree upon the needs of the learners involved.

III. *Operating principles related to physical condition*

A. Psychologically, the seating arrangements in a class help to determine class atmosphere and the direction of communications within the class.

B. A circular arrangement in which each learner can see the faces of all, or as many as possible, of the other class members is desirable for promoting a democratic interchange of ideas.

IV. *Operating principles related to teacher activity*

    A. The teacher as the major class leader is in a key position for gearing group activities with democratic values and procedures.

    B. The teacher should be able to distinguish between autocratic and democratic leadership.

    C. A democratic teacher is able to take upon himself a great variety of group roles. In any particular situation he attempts to assume that role which will be of most value to the learners. This will sometimes be a good listening role.

    D. Studying how to get learning groups launched successfully and growing in a healthy fashion is a major task of the teacher.

    E. To promote a situation where the learners can practice different healthy roles the teacher must depart from the one or two roles played traditionally and assume many different roles at different times.

V. *Operating principles related to member activity*

    A. Democratic group operation must carry with it implicit or explicit agreements that set some limit on the freedom of the individual to do as he pleases. In the interests of the group organism's operation, different parts (leader, members) of that organism must delegate some authority and some partial control.

    B. Group members should practice ways of having each member in the group both achieve and also obtain some satisfactions from his achievements in the group.

    C. Class members should be helped to see that the large and small group discussions provide opportunities in which they may practice group skills in situations where failure is not tragic as it might be on the job or out of the school.

    D. A change must take place in the too-current idea that the teacher is almost solely responsible for class or small-group success. Added learner responsibility is essential for significant improvement in large or small group learnings.

    E. The teacher and learners need continuously to (*a*) evaluate and (*b*) plan improvement in *group goals and operations.*

F. Both the teacher and the learner need to give consideration to ways of (*a*) evaluating their *individual behaviors* in group situations, and (*b*) planning improvement in such behaviors.

G. Students should be constantly aware of the great variety of roles that the most effective group members practice.

H. Unhealthy group roles need to be identified and guarded against.

BIBLIOGRAPHY

1. ALLPORT, GORDON. "The Psychology of Participation." *Psychological Review*, 52:117-32; May 1945.
   Discusses psychological aspects of group operation.

2. Association for Supervision and Curriculum Development. *Toward Better Teaching*. Washington, D.C.: The Association, 1949.
   Gives accounts of functional discussions.

3. Association for Supervision and Curriculum Development. *Group Processes in Supervision*. Washington, D.C.: The Association, 1948.
   Written to show how democratic group processes can be used by supervisors in their work with others. The ideas given are also useful for the teachers, principals, or superintendents who are interested in improving education through working with other educators.

4. AUER, J. J., AND EWBANK, H. L. *Handbook for Discussion Leaders*. New York: Harper, and Bros., 1947.
   Gives helpful consideration of (*a*) getting discussions under way, (*b*) the leader's job, and (*c*) measuring group work.

5. BACK, KURT. "Interpersonal Relations in a Discussion Group." *The Journal of Social Issues*, 4:61-65; Spring 1948.
   Analyzes the contrasting patterns of relationships in two discussion groups. Recorder blank was adapted from Bales interaction recorder.

6. BARRON, MARGARET E., AND KRULEE, G. K. "Case Study of a Basic Skill Training Group." *The Journal of Social Issues*, 4:10-30; Spring 1948.
   Gives a description of a discussion training group in action. Discusses goals and difficulties in reaching these goals.

7. BASS, B. M. "An Analysis of the Leaderless Group Discussion." *Journal of Applied Psychology*, 33:527-33; December 1949.
   Describes experiment concerned with measurement of individual behavior in leaderless group discussion.

8. BENNE, KENNETH, AND MUNTYAN, BOZIDAR. *Human Relations in Curriculum Change.* Springfield, Illinois: State Superintendent of Public Instruction, 1949.

9. BENNE, K. D., AND SHEATS, PAUL. "Functional Roles of Group Members." *The Journal of Social Issues,* 4:41-49; Spring 1948.
   Gives stimulating analysis of healthy and non-healthy roles group members may play.

10. BISHOP, THELMA. "Group Work for Leaders of the Physically Handicapped." *Journal of Exceptional Children,* 16:49-61; November 1949.
    Considers group needs, leader characteristics, and training for group participation.

11. BRADFORD, L. P., BENNE, K. D., AND LIPPETT, RONALD. "The Promise of Group Dynamics for Education." *National Education Association Journal,* 37:350-52; September 1948.
    A report is given of what is said in a school staff committee meeting. An analysis is made of some typical unsaid thoughts by individuals on the committee. Some implications for effective group operations are suggested.

12. Columbia University, Teachers College. Horace Mann-Lincoln Institute of School Experimentation. *Guide to Study and Experimentation in Cooperative Planning in Education.* New York: Teachers College, Columbia University, 1947.
    Contains useful suggestions for planning.

13. CAYLE, GRACE L. *Group Experience and Democratic Values.* New York: The Woman's Press, 1947.
    Discusses the collective life of our times.

14. CUNNINGHAM, RUTH, AND ASSOCIATES. "Getting the Group Habit." *Educational Leadership,* 4:380-85; March 1947.
    Study, with parents, boys, and girls cooperating, of how groups originate and what makes them tick.

15. CUNNINGHAM, RUTH, AND ASSOCIATES. *Understanding Group Behavior of Boys and Girls.* New York: Bureau of Publications, Teachers College, Columbia University, 1951.
    This is an excellent study of learner groups in action. Among topics discussed are group interaction, group goals, group structure, group adjustment, organizing to study group living, parents as co-researchers, and techniques for studying group behavior.

16. CUNNINGHAM, RUTH, AND ROBERTS, MADELINE. "It Takes Experience." *Childhood Education,* 24:208-13, January 1948.
    Describes elementary-school role-playing and indicates leader characteristics as seen by nine- and ten-year-olds.

17. DEUTSCH, M., AND OTHERS. "Leadership in the Small Group." *Journal of Social Psychology*, 4:31-40; Spring 1948.
Analyzes leadership behavior, through a case study, with emphasis on the nature of the particular environment in which the leader perceives himself as functioning as well as on the characteristics of the leader himself.
18. Educator's Washington Dispatch. *Two Lessons of Group Dynamics.* Washington, D.C.: Educator's Washington Dispatch, 1948.
Gives useful suggestions for committee and conference work.
19. FRENCH, J. R. P., JR. "Retraining an Autocratic Leader." *Journal of Abnormal and Social Psychology*, 39:224-37, April 1944.
Gives good case-study picture of conversion from unsuccessful autocratic leadership to successful democratic leadership.
20. GORDON, THOMAS. "What Is Gained by Group Participation?" *Educational Leadership*, 7:220-26, January 1950.
Analyzes some "personal meanings" and values to be derived from group experience.
21. GRAMBS, JEAN. "Learning Group Skills in Teacher Education." *Educational Leadership*, 7:107-10; November 1949.
Points out some aspects of a teachers-in-training program that helps prospective teachers become proficient in group participation.
22. GRAMBS, JEAN D. "Training Teachers in Group Leadership." *California Journal of Secondary Education*, 24:365-67; October 1949.
Antidotes are proposed for authoritarian practices.
23. HEISLER, WALTER, AND OTHERS. "Group Dynamics: A Junior High—Class Experiments." *The Clearing House*, 24:151-54; November 1949.
Describes experiments that illustrate the use of group discussions and sociodramas for learning purposes.
24. HEMPHILL, JOHN K. "The Leader and His Group." *Educational Research Bulletin*, 28:225-29; December 7, 1949.
Emphasizes and analyzes the importance for leader roles of the characteristics of the social group that is to be led.
25. JENKINS, DAVID H. "Feedback and Group Self-Evaluation." *Journal of Social Issues*, 4:50-60; Spring 1948.
Analyzes types of information a group needs to improve its behavior and shows some procedures by which a group can become aware of its own difficulties, the reasons for these difficulties, and the connections that are necessary.

26. LEWIN, KURT. *The Research Center for Group Dynamics.* New York: Beacon House, 1947.

Pictures purposes and procedures of the center.

27. MIEL, ALICE. "It's Our World Again." *Educational Leadership,* 3:50-52; November 1945.

28. MIEL, ALICE. "A Group Studies Itself To Improve Itself." *Teachers College Record,* 49:31-43; October 1947.

Includes devices for describing what happens in a group, analyses of the data gathered by devices, and evaluation of experiences by group members.

29. National Education Association. *Interpersonal Perceptions of Teachers, Students, and Parents.* Washington, D.C.: Division of Adult Education, The Association, 1951.

Deals with the problem of working effectively together through a study of interpersonal perceptions.

30. NORFLECT, BOBBIE. "Interpersonal Relations and Group Productivity." *Journal of Social Issues,* 4:66-69; Spring 1948.

Analyzes data concerning ratings each group member got on (1) productivity and (2) choice as a leisure-time companion.

31. THELEN, HERBERT A. "Engineering Research in Curriculum Building." *Journal of Educational Research,* 41:577-96; April 1948.

Describes three distinguishing characteristics of the *art* of applying the basic scientific generalities to the solution of a particular social problem. Problems involved in such application are considered.

32. THELEN, HERBERT A. "Group Leaders Look at Frustration." *Educational Leadership,* 7:260-66; January 1950.

Five experts in group leadership analyze possible sources of frustration in group situations and define some roles of leaders in meeting frustration problems when they arise.

NOTE: Articles on group dynamics appear from time to time in:

Human Relations. Research Center for Group Dynamics, Cambridge, Mass.

Journal of Social Issues. 347 Madison Avenue, New York.

Educational Leadership. Association for Supervision and Curriculum Development. N.E.A., Washington, D.C.

Group Psychotherapy. Beacon, New York.

12

DEVELOPING READING FOR

PROBLEM ATTACK

Some problems to consider

What individual differences in reading abilities may be expected?

Who should determine reading goals?

What are important considerations about types of reading goals?

How may in-school reading goals be related to out-of-school reading behavior?

What changes in reading emphasis are probable with the increasing use of problem approaches?

Changes are needed in in-school and out-of-school reading. In our present school and community culture the importance of desirable reading attitudes and habits cannot be overemphasized. Not only is reading a key service process for learning while in school, but it also can provide a sound basis for continuous self-improvement after school is over.

In order to realize much more fully the potentialities that reading holds, teachers and prospective teachers must make significant changes in several respects. First, teachers and learners should determine and utilize large and objectively verifiable differences between individuals in ability to learn to read when they enter school and differences in level of reading achievement within any particular age, grade, or class group.

Second, success in a reading program should be determined largely on the basis of the actual reading behaviors of the student *when he is on his own* rather than almost exclusively on pencil-and-paper tests given on teacher-assigned material. This change will involve modifications in the reading goals of teachers and learners.

Third, many changes will be made in what is emphasized in reading with increasing use of the problem-process approach. These changes will involve such things as learning to read for many different purposes, learning the *uses* of reading while learning the *how* of reading, and helping learners play an increasing role in deciding what, when, and how to read.

Fourth, professional reading on the part of the teacher will assume increasing importance. Reading will become a key tool through which the teacher keeps professionally alive after he leaves his formal teacher-training. Teachers will set a good example for learners through functional professional reading.

Some self-diagnostic questions follow, after which the preceding four points will be developed in the remainder of the chapter.

EVALUATIVE QUESTIONS ON READING ABILITIES [1]

Attitudes and motivation

1. What is my present attitude and motivation toward improvement in reading skills?

2. To what extent is my non-recreational reading done with intrinsically purposeful goals in mind?

3. Do I have too great a tendency to study printed material simply to pass a test?

Types of reading skills used

4. Do I recognize and use a variety of different types of reading skills?

5. In what reading skills am I making a conscious effort to improve?

6. Do I have well-developed abilities to read at different speeds for different purposes?

7. Can I quickly isolate the parts of printed resources that have particular significance to the problem or problems I am studying?

8. In reading a chapter, do I usually make a preliminary survey of what the chapter contains?

---

[1] These questions are phrased primarily for individual diagnosis by the student in teacher-training courses where teaching and learning methods are studied. It is also suggested that high-school students can and should be trained to ask themselves similar questions.

9. Do I sometimes read a chapter summary before reading the chapter itself in order to get some orientation on what the chapter contains?

10. Do I sometimes read through the paragraph headings of a chapter before starting to read the chapter in detail?

11. Do I make use of work-type reading to help identify and solve the professional and/or personal problems I am now facing or am likely to face?

Using materials

12. Do I make sufficient use of such resources as the *Readers' Guide* and the *Education Index* for locating appropriate reading materials?

13. Am I well able to distinguish between primary sources and secondary materials?

14. Can I discriminate between statements of fact and statements of opinion or statements of motive?

15. Can I distinguish between statements of fact that are well oriented and statements of fact that are given out of context?

16. Am I sufficiently critical of what I read?

17. When I go to printed resources for specific purposes do I keep myself to the task or do I allow myself to become sidetracked by enticing and interesting material that is not relevant to the problems being attacked?

18. Do I have the abilities necessary to evaluate what is read and to appropriate parts of it in the organization framework that I have previously set up as a pattern for the particular study in which I am engaged?

19. Do I understand the function of each of the following? Which ones do I actually utilize when they are given in a book?

a) A detailed table of contents
b) Paragraph heads
c) Italics
d) Review questions and exercises at the ends of chapters or selections
e) Maps, charts, diagrams, and tables
f) Outlines
g) Summaries
h) The glossary
i) The index
j) The preface

Transfer of training

20. Am I reading in such a way that I shall be likely to continue reading after I leave school?

Evaluation, including diagnosis

21. Am I able to diagnose my own strengths and weaknesses in reading?

22. Do I periodically check back over my reading skills and abilities and then attempt to eliminate the weaknesses that become apparent?

23. Have I made sufficient use of standardized diagnostic reading tests and tests of ability to use the various parts of a book and the library efficiently?

24. Am I measuring my skill in reading and its use too much in terms of averages for groups and not enough in terms of my individual abilities and needs?

WHAT INDIVIDUAL DIFFERENCES IN READING ABILITIES MAY BE EXPECTED?

At any particular age or grade level a spread of from five to thirteen or more average grade levels in reading readiness or reading ability is to be expected. The farther along in school a particular group goes, the greater the spread in reading abilities, as well as in other abilities, is likely to be. In other words, the range of reading ability tends to increase as a particular group of students moves up through the grades. In general, the better the educational opportunities, the greater the spread is likely to be at any particular age or grade level. The practical implication of these points is that students on any specific age or grade level should not be expected to use material on the same difficulty level. Having a single text and giving uniform reading assignments may seem to be a simple way of handling a group. Actually, such a procedure is not only likely to be unsound insofar as the learning is concerned, but is also likely to breed disciplinary problems that will be upsetting to the teacher.

More realistic goals for individual learners are needed. The problem of what to expect of the individual learner is tied up with understanding the meaning of the term "a retarded reader." When teachers and administrators are asked what they understand to be

PURPOSEFUL READING LADDER

Reading is done to help in problem identification, selection, and solution with the learner assuming the major share of responsibility for keeping learning processes under way. The teacher gives suggestions and guidance as these are needed.

Reading is done to help identify problems and get possible solutions to problems with the teacher and student working together but with the teacher assuming primary responsibility for the process.

Reading is done to help identify problems and get possible solutions to problems considered of significance to the *group of learners* as a whole but of little or no significance to some in the group.

Reading is done to help get solutions to problems identified by the teacher and recognized by the learner as of some importance.

Reading is done after the teacher has attempted to explain its significance and then assigned it. The learner either does not understand or does not accept the teacher's explanation.

Some reading is done because the teacher assigned it, but only the teacher sees some intrinsic purpose in it.

Practically all reading is done without either the teacher or the learner seeing any particular purpose in the latter's doing the reading except to keep the teacher from punishing him or giving him a low mark.

READ UP ⟶

In my classes at what reading level on the ladder above do I operate? What can I do to move higher on the ladder?

the meaning of the term "a retarded reader," we get a picture of the kinds of concepts that are currently held. "A retarded reader is one whose reading ability is below that which he needs to carry on his schoolwork, to enjoy stories, to read about the world around him. Jack is in the ninth grade and cannot read ninth-grade books. He is retarded because he only reads like a sixth grader and cannot carry on ninth-grade work." Note that here the emphasis is laid on the pupil's inability to meet a prearranged school program of work, which has been almost exclusively laid out for him without consideration of his individual needs or training. No attention is given to the child's basic ability. What would be good ninth-grade material for Jack might be extremely boring for Mary, who is also in the ninth grade but who has average ninth-grade reading ability.

Let us look at another concept given by a teacher. "A retarded reader is one behind his grade norm in reading speed and comprehension. I gave Henry, who is in the twelfth grade, a standard reading test and he scored on the tenth-grade level. Obviously, he is retarded two grades in reading." If this definition were used, approximately 50 per cent of the students in our schools would be retarded at all times, since a grade norm simply represents the average achievement at a particular grade. Again, no attention is given to the innate ability of the individual learner. Are we going to expect all children to be Jack averages rather than expect of each according to his ability? Equally inadequate are such concepts as the following: "One who may be in the fourth grade, but has the reading ability of the average second grader." "One who does not read as well as the average member of his class." Each of the definitions given in this paragraph implies that every child should be up to average and that if he is above average, his reading progress is satisfactory. Psychologically these concepts are unsound.

Let us take the case of James, for example, a child in the eighth grade who has average ninth-grade reading ability. He is seriously retarded since his tested reading *capacity* is as great as that of the average twelfth grader. That child is most retarded in reading whose purposeful reading achievements are farthest below his reading capacities. There are thousands of youngsters at all levels with above-average reading ability who are seriously retarded from a psychological standpoint in their reading. We must expect much more of many above-average readers and much less of many below-average readers if reading for problem identification and solution and for appreciation is to be healthy.

Closely related to the needed revisions in expectations of reading abilities is the fact that reading improvement is most likely to come only if the teacher is willing to start working with each learner where he is rather than expecting him at any particular grade level to use certain materials simply because he is in a particular grade or has a certain chronological age. Standards are likely to be improved if expectations are tied up with the basic reading capacity of each individual learner.

Not only should we expect that different students in a class or grade will be operating at quite different levels in general or average reading ability, but we should also expect that a particular learner may be operating much higher in one type of reading ability, for example, the ability to get details, than he is in another type of reading ability, skimming, for example. This means essentially that in addition to having interindividual differences, we also have significant intraindividual differences in reading as well as in other learning abilities. It is sound to expect that a learner whose general reading level is at a particular point may have some reading skills, such as those involved in reading graphs and tables, which are considerably below or considerably above his average reading level.

WHO SHOULD DETERMINE READING GOALS?

In general, individual goals in reading should be determined largely by the learner with the necessary amount of guidance from a teacher. Under optimum conditions—conditions we would hope to try to approximate—motivation for reading should arise primarily from the learner's knowledge of his needs and from a realization of the use the particular reading will be to him. It is extremely important that care be taken that the reading is not done or assigned just to keep the pupils quiet or busy. Purposeful reading of a desirable sort takes place when the learner knows what he is trying to find in his use of printed materials.

Periodically, the individual learner should be encouraged and helped to reconsider his purposes and goals, and, with the help of the teacher, he should attempt to ascertain if any changes should be made, and to determine if progress is being made in the direction of the goals that have previously been set up.

WHAT ARE IMPORTANT CONSIDERATIONS
ABOUT TYPES OF READING GOALS?

The primary purpose in promoting improvement in functional reading is to make it of practical use to the learner in and out of school. In doing this, we will attempt to help him to help himself in solving his problems and to help him to develop a constant means of self-improvement. In the case of the slow learner, the functional use of reading is particularly important in helping him to live in this modern world. Being able to read the newspapers intelligently, the reader is in a position to keep abreast of things, read the latest developments concerning events of importance to him and the community. By reading intelligently, he will be a better judge of advertising schemes of dubious merit. If the learner can be brought to see the value of functional reading to him as an individual, his interest is likely to be aroused. A key goal in all reading training should be the development of reading activities that will establish a lifelong reading habit—compounded of reading for enjoyment and reading for help in identifying and solving problems.

In considering reading goals, it is important to remember that learning *how* to read is only one phase of an important syndrome of abilities necessary in desirable reading. Learning how to get appropriate reading materials, learning when particular reading materials are likely to be helpful, learning why reading is done, and learning at what speed to read for different purposes are but a few of the other fundamental jobs that are necessary in developing adequate reading abilities.

Reading should be recognized as a way of getting, vicariously, experiences that will help the learner to identify his own problems better and to discover some possible solutions to them. This, of course, is problem-solving reading. Reading for recreational purposes should, as the name implies, provide pleasure in the process to the learner involved. In a sense, the one is using reading for trucking purposes, and the other is using reading as a pleasure-car is used for recreational driving. It is particularly important to remember the great possibilities that are involved in using reading to help identify problems and to select appropriate ones for study. In the past, attention in reading has been restricted too much to the getting of answers or to the memorization of answers for test purposes. Reading will be more profitable if both teacher and learners systematically attempt to study and practice different types of reading abilities.

A skill closely related to reading itself is the ability to locate needed information. To learn where to look, how to use the libraries, indexes, geographical studies, summaries at the ends of chapters, and books of reference are extremely valuable abilities which, in many schools, have been considerably neglected and need much greater emphasis.

Another reading goal that has been given insufficient attention in many schools is critical reading, which in essence means critical thinking with reading as a tool for developing the thinking. Ordinarily, students should not be taught to accept an author's idea as the gospel truth but rather to read different authors and practice drawing conclusions from various approaches as such conclusions seem justified. An intelligently critical attitude toward all that is read or heard should be encouraged. This is not meant to imply that the learner knows more than the writer, but rather that the learner considers the meaning, significance and rationale back of what is said before he attempts to conclude that it is true under all circumstances and for all time. He also considers what it may mean to him as an individual.

And finally, the major goal, perhaps, for reading work while in school is to give practice in the types of reading situations and the types of reading skills that the teacher and learners anticipate will be needed when the learner leaves school. Not only should our goal be to improve reading and reading activity while the learner is in school, but we should be as much concerned about the amount and quality of the reading the learner is trained to do after he leaves school.

In order to improve in reading ability and in order to help him move toward the suggested reading goals the learner must see his own weaknesses in reading particular kinds of materials for specified purposes. He must see why it will profit him to improve. Unless the student sees the need for improvement, it is unlikely that very much improvement of a significant sort will take place. The best purposeful reading is done when the learner is motivated to read on his own instead of being forced to read a prescribed number of pages or books. Learners will tend to do desirable purposeful reading if they see that the problems being studied are of importance to them.

Marks are with us and will probably be with us for some time. However, marks should be de-emphasized in favor of developing more intrinsic motives for reading, motives that grow out of recognized needs and visualized problems. Desirably, reading should be intrinsic from the standpoint of the learner and not dependent upon external reward or merit that is not directly tied up with the values that may be gained from the reading itself. A related goal that tends to make reading more meaningful is to encourage the learner to clarify his reactions to what is read by writing them down. Ideas are likely to remain rather hazy and vague unless we incorporate them into our own thinking and push them to the extent of forcing ourselves to write down what the ideas mean. Otherwise, reading tends to become a relatively passive process without particularly desirable results and certainly is not likely to be very economical.

A key indication of the extent to which learners are improving in reading is the amount and type of reading done during a free-reading program. Here the learner is likely to do what he would do after he leaves school. The second important clue is to be had from checking on the extent to which the learner actually uses reading and enjoys reading when he is out of school and after he has graduated from school. This is the acid test of the quality of the reading program that the school has promoted for the particular learner.

Illustrations of how in-school goals may be tied up with out-of-school behavior will be given in the next section. Here the reading problems considered are largely ones related to preparation for leisure-time activities.

HOW MAY IN-SCHOOL READING GOALS BE RELATED TO OUT-OF-SCHOOL BEHAVIOR? [2]

Reading goals. Reading goals in most high-school English classes and in other classes concerned with reading improvement have characteristically been stated in terms of general objectives, which placed emphasis only upon the learning and reading to take place in school. In most listings of objectives, little or no attention has been given to the specific behavior changes that the teaching of

[2] Adapted from an article by the author that appeared in the March, 1950, issue of *The School Review.*

reading or literature is expected to produce after the learner leaves school.

One way of considering this problem is to visualize the situation in a particular high school in which every other youngster in a particular class had literature training and other types of reading training while the alternates had no such training. If we were to look at those two sets of individuals five years after they left school, what behavior differences would we expect to find between the group that had received reading training and the group that had had no specific reading training in the form of literature appreciation or other formalized reading experiences?

Obviously, if we are to be concerned with the effectiveness of reading training—whether it be in the English class or in other classes—it is important that we consider not only the changes in reading behavior that take place while the teacher is in charge and exerting pressures of various sorts, particularly marking and credit pressures, upon the reader. We must also be concerned with the changes in reading behavior that take place *after* the learner leaves school but that are largely a result of the reading training obtained while in school.

Spaulding,[3] after an extensive study designed to appraise "the social competence of boys and girls who are through with the secondary school" in New York State, concluded that "most boys and girls read almost solely for recreation, chiefly in magazines of mediocre or inferior fiction and in daily newspapers." He found that, while the boys and girls were reasonably well acquainted *on leaving school* with standard school selections, *they tended very largely to let books alone once they were out of school.* Less than 4 per cent "had read fiction that could properly be classed as superior.... The nature and quality of their magazine reading differed little from that of their reading in books." It should be added that the group reported on by Spaulding were the 80 per cent of high-school pupils who did not go on to college. Spaulding concluded that "left to their own devices, most of these young people cease to read serious books and articles or good fiction."

Leary, in an extensive summary of research findings relating to this problem, emphasizes "the fact that less than 2 per cent of the

[3] Francis T. Spaulding, *High School and Life,* The Regents Inquiry into the Character and Cost of Public Education in the State of New York (New York: McGraw-Hill Book Co., Inc., 1938), pp. 43-44.

130,000,000 people in this country are book readers." [4] This is certainly a serious indictment of the way in which we teach the reading of books—an activity to which a major portion of school time is now devoted.

This section is intended for the teacher and the learner who are interested in transferring the values of reading training to out-of-school behavior. Here an attempt is made to suggest some possible reading goals, in terms of out-of-school behavior, that might be considered of importance. To make the goals clearer, some of the measurement approaches that might be used to check on these behaviors are listed. Obviously, in most cases all these checks will not be used. However, it is strongly felt that, if the teacher and the learner realize the types of checks that might be made, they will be less likely to teach or to learn reading with the vague and highly generalized goals typified in the expression, "I am teaching (or learning) appreciation of literature." We will, through an analysis of the goals to be achieved, understand more clearly the changes in reading behavior we wish to attain.

The suggested goals and possible measurements are categorized under the following headings: book-reading, magazine-reading, newspaper-reading, and reference-reading. Other reading categories might, of course, be added to these four. Also, many additional goals and possible approaches to measurement might be included. What is given below is primarily for illustrative purposes. The goal in each case is followed by some possible measurements. [5]

SUGGESTED GOALS AND POSSIBLE MEASUREMENTS
RELATED TO BOOK-READING

Goal—Increased reading of nonfictional books

POSSIBLE MEASUREMENTS:

Percentage that nonfiction book sales are of total retail sales in community

Per capita number of nonfictional books circulated by local library (use checkout cards at library)

[4] Bernice E. Leary, "What Does Research Say about Reading?" *Journal of Educational Research,* XXXIX (February, 1946), 435.

[5] Obviously many of these goals may be community goals as well as possible school goals. No *direct* evaluation of the present school program is possible in some instances. However, each item does suggest a tangible goal for consideration.

Per capita sales of nonfictional books at local bookstores and other book outlets

Number of nonfictional books available in public libraries in community

Number of nonfictional books available in representative sample of homes

Number of nonfictional books borrowed from others per month by representative sample of groups whose reading is being measured

Number of nonfictional books read in last month in representative sample

Amount spent on new nonfictional books in public library per capita, per year

Number of nonfictional books received as Christmas or birthday presents in specified period among representative sample

Goal—Increased reading of fictional books

POSSIBLE MEASUREMENTS:

Number of bookstores, in relation to population of the community, selling fictional books

Per capita number of fictional books circulated by local library

Per capita number of sales of fictional books at local bookstores

Percentage of total city expenditures devoted to libraries

Number of fictional books borrowed from other people in certain designated period

Amount spent on new fictional books in public library per year, per capita

Number of fictional books read in last two weeks by representative sample of population

Goal—Increased number of books owned by representative cross-section of families

POSSIBLE MEASUREMENTS:

Make poll of books owned by random sample of population

Percentage that book sales are of total retail sales in community

Use survey to determine how many books have been purchased from all sources by representative sample of people in community

Goal—Increased quality of books read

POSSIBLE MEASUREMENTS:

Ratio of "acceptable" books to "questionable" books sold at bookstores

Ratio of "acceptable" books to "questionable" books drawn from library

Analyze library books circulated. Set up value system to rate quality, or sample borrower's cards for reading quality

Goal—Increased reading of classics

POSSIBLE MEASUREMENTS:

Get from nonschool members of representative families a list of books read in last two weeks and see how often classics are listed

Number of classics withdrawn from public library

Number of juvenile classics in public library

Number of juvenile classics withdrawn from public library

Goal—Increased reading of drama

POSSIBLE MEASUREMENTS:

Interview representative families regarding number of plays read in the last month

Number of drama books withdrawn from library in specified period

Goal—Increased reading of poetry

POSSIBLE MEASUREMENTS:

Make spot check of poetry read in last two weeks in representative families

Check with newsstands to see if there have been requests for poetry books or magazines

Number of poetry books withdrawn from library

Goal—Larger memberships in book clubs

POSSIBLE MEASUREMENTS:

Determine the number of memberships in each club, either by writing to publisher or by questioning representative sample of community

Goal—Increased use of books on gardening, on "fix it around the house," and on home decoration

POSSIBLE MEASUREMENTS:

Check number of such books owned by representative families
Determine sales of such books in community in specified time
Check library distribution of such books

Goal—Increased number of children and adults who spend money for books in a specified period

POSSIBLE MEASUREMENTS:

Check total sale of nonschool books in community
Make survey of total books purchased by representative families

SUGGESTED GOALS AND POSSIBLE MEASUREMENTS
RELATED TO MAGAZINE-READING

Goal—Increased use of "acceptable" magazines

POSSIBLE MEASUREMENTS:

Ratio of newsstand sale of "acceptable" magazines to "questionable" or "trash" types
Per capita newsstand sales of "acceptable" magazines
Make study, based on high-school students' interviews in the community, of magazine-reading habits
Use of "acceptable" magazines in local libraries
Use *Life* (Crossley) technique in interviewing to determine actual reading habits of magazine-readers
Measure use of *National Geographic Magazine, Better Homes and Gardens, etc.*
Number of subscriptions in community for each "acceptable" magazine
Number of subscriptions for each "acceptable" magazine given as presents

Goal—Decrease in use of "questionable" or "trash" magazines

POSSIBLE MEASUREMENTS:

Set up "experimental racks" in barber shops, doctors' offices, and dentists' offices, and keep a record of what magazines are read by patrons and how long each is read
Check sales of "questionable" magazines in community

Goal—Increased use of magazines rating those things consumers buy or use, such as Consumer Reports *and* Buying Guide, *and* Consumers' Research Bulletin, *etc.*

POSSIBLE MEASUREMENTS:

Check use made of resources in helping consumer to buy more intelligently; for example, check sale of sample of "good" and "poor" articles noted by resources

Check ratio of movie attendance at movies rated high by guides to attendance at movies rated low

Check sale of patent medicine rated useless or dangerous by guides

Check amount spent per capita on such magazine subscriptions in the public library

Check actual per capita use of such magazines as indicated by sample or reader use in public library

Check number of subscriptions of such magazines in the community

Goal—Increased filing of items from magazines for future use

POSSIBLE MEASUREMENTS:

Interview sample of homes to determine the number of files for magazine articles and the apparent extent of their use

Make survey to find number of articles clipped

Goal—Better ratio of "acceptable" comics to "unacceptable" comics

POSSIBLE MEASUREMENTS:

Check on types found in homes and compare on quality

Check types of magazines found in homes and rate on a quality index

Check types of comics given as gifts

Also see beginning of this section on *Increased use of "acceptable" magazines*

SUGGESTED GOALS AND POSSIBLE MEASUREMENTS
RELATED TO NEWSPAPER-READING

Goal—More regular newspaper readers

POSSIBLE MEASUREMENTS:

Check per capita local newspaper subscriptions

Percentage that sales of newspapers are of total retail sales in community

Per capita sales of all news dealers in community

Check per capita out-of-town newspaper subscriptions

Check increased newsstand sale of local newspapers

Check increased newsstand sales of out-of-town papers

Make survey to determine number of newspaper readers in community

Goal—Increased reading of editorials

POSSIBLE MEASUREMENT:

Poll of selected sample of families to find familiarity with selected recent editorials

Goal—Increased reading of sports pages

POSSIBLE MEASUREMENT:

Poll of selected sample to find knowledge of leader in each of these in appropriate seasons: American League, National League, local high-school league, local collegiate league, local softball league, etc.

Goal—Increased reading of news stories on local political activities

POSSIBLE MEASUREMENTS:

Take selected political news stories from local papers and determine familiarity of sample of readers with these stories

Take poll on single stories asking: "Did you read this?"

Goal—Increased ratio of "good" newspapers sold to "questionable" newspapers sold

POSSIBLE MEASUREMENT:

Check circulation figures of papers considered questionable from the point of view of the English teacher

SUGGESTED GOALS AND POSSIBLE MEASUREMENTS
RELATED TO USE OF REFERENCES

Goal—Increased use of Readers' Guide to Periodical Literature

POSSIBLE MEASUREMENTS:

Check on the familiarity with the setup of various guides by asking representative individuals in the community such questions as the following: "In what ways might a particular article be listed in the *Readers' Guide?*"

Set up systematic check on use of *Readers' Guide* in public library

Check on wear of certain references

Goal—Increased use of dictionary

POSSIBLE MEASUREMENTS:

Sales of dictionaries per capita

Number of dictionaries in homes in community

Check use of dictionary in public library

Take poll asking, "Have you used dictionary in last two weeks?"

Goal—Increased use of encylopedias, including children's encyclopedias and similar books

POSSIBLE MEASUREMENTS:

Check use of encyclopedias in public libraries

Check proportion of families that have encyclopedias

Check number of families to which encyclopedia yearly additions are being sent

Goal—Increased use of tables of contents, topical headings, indexes and other parts of books that are frequently unused

POSSIBLE MEASUREMENTS:

Determine by sample check of community the extent to which the members of families actually make use of such parts of the book as have been considered

By representative poll determine parts of books used in last two weeks

It is quite possible that sound questions may be raised about the desirability of one or more of the goals mentioned above. For example, some teachers of reading would certainly question whether it is sound to try to increase the reading of sports pages. This suggestive goal is included primarily to indicate some possible "uncommon" goals and also because the results of such reading certainly have some conversational value in many groups. On the other hand, it is quite possible to conclude, with a different set of values, that such a goal only gives impetus to an emphasis on sports which is believed to be already too great. In connection with this goal, as with many others, possible short-time values versus long-time values would need to be weighed carefully.

What is considered "acceptable," "unacceptable," "good," "poor," or "questionable" is obviously a matter that should involve the considered judgment of those persons most concerned. The terms have been used with the assumption that there are differences in the quality of different reading materials.

SOME USES OF GOALS AND MEASUREMENTS

As has already been implied, one way of getting away from vague and ill-defined reading goals is to force ourselves to state our goals in behavioral terms. Even if it does not seem feasible to do more than see clearly what our goals are in terms of specific prospective behavior changes, this process itself should be worth while. The goals and the measurements that have been stated can form the basis for a purposeful study of reading goals by teachers and learners.

It would also be possible for a teacher or, preferably, a group of teachers in a community who are interested in teaching reading as an aid to living, first, to develop a set of goals to which they can subscribe, then to set up specific measurements relating to the goals that could be applied in the community, and, finally, actually to make the measurements with the aid of students or student committees. Such a procedure would be of considerable aid in clarifying the meaning of specific goals to both learners and teachers. If interviews and other oral activities were used, learners would have opportunities to practice oral composition in realistic situations. A project of this kind would serve as a type of motivation to learners who are not too sure of the value of school for them. Finally, it could be of real value in helping the school serve the community in more direct and useful ways.

If a survey of this kind were made at a specified time each year, perhaps October or November, a file of useful information could be built up over a period of years that would give the school a rough basis for evaluating its strengths and weaknesses on the ultimate criterion—the behavior of the schools' products after they leave school.

WHAT CHANGES IN READING EMPHASIS ARE PROBABLE WITH INCREASING USE OF PROCESS APPROACHES?

The learner will functionally use reading as he learns how to read. In the first place, it is psychologically unsound to disassociate the *how* of reading from the *uses* of reading. Some teachers have actually gone so far in the past as to have pupils read textbooks backwards "just for the practice in how to read!" Many pupils never really find out that reading can be of service to them, since reading, as an end in itself, has been too much emphasized. John, a pupil in the seventh grade, came to his teacher excitedly one day and said, "Look at this book I picked up in the library today. It is the only book I have ever seen that I enjoyed. Gee, why didn't you tell me reading could be fun! This is not like the stuff we have in reading class at all. I just read that stuff so I won't get a bad mark." New vistas had accidentally opened up to John, vistas that had long remained closed because reading had been taught largely *as an end in itself.* The *how* of reading a particular kind of material needs to be tied up closely with the *why* of reading it.

In the second place, an individual is expected to read new kinds of materials as he progresses through school. This involves acquiring new reading skills and abilities. Some time ago there came to the attention of the writer a college student who was doing excellent work in social studies and English but who was doing very poorly in mathematics and science. Upon investigation it was found that he read all material, regardless of kind, at about the same rate. His speed in reading social studies material was about the same as his speed in reading "heavy" science. He had never been taught how to read science material or mathematics problems appropriately. He was like a car with only a high gear. The learner's reading rate must increasingly vary with the purposes he has in reading and with the difficulty of the particular material being read.

Third, new teaching and study methods related to the problem approach demand training if the student is to profit most from them. Learning how to identify problems using reading materials is quite a different skill from using reading materials to get possible solutions to problems. Reading to get a general orientation in particular types of material is quite a different skill from reading the same or similar material to find particular items of information.

Fourth, even if the elementary school does an excellent job of training its pupils in reading, many of those graduating from the sixth grade are still going to read less well than the average reader entering the seventh grade. The writer recently investigated the reading status of each of the seventh-grade groups in a "good" school system. The most representative seventh grade, made up of thirty-five pupils, produced the following results:

> 1 had average 11th-grade reading ability
> 1 had average 10th-grade reading ability
> 1 had average 9th-grade reading ability
> 3 had average 8th-grade reading ability
> 8 had average 7th-grade reading ability
> 6 had average 6th-grade reading ability
> 8 had average 5th-grade reading ability
> 6 had average 4th-grade reading ability
> 1 had average 3rd-grade reading ability

---

35 equals the total number in the class
9 equals the range of average reading grade
levels in the class

About half of the students entering the seventh grade are not likely to have average seventh-grade reading ability. There is great need for recognition of this fact. The high-school teacher may say that they *should* have, average seventh-grade reading ability, but we know, in view of individual capacity, they will not. Under these circumstances, it is the job of the high-school teacher to take each pupil where he is and help him to move along by means of appropriate resources and methods.

Learner purposes will play an increasing role in reading. In the problem approach the purposes of the individual learner play an increasing role in practically all areas of work. This tends to be particularly true in connection with reading. Instead of the teacher deciding *what* shall be read, *when* it shall be read, and *how* it shall be read, the learner begins increasingly to set up his own purposes and to practice deciding, in the light of those purposes, what it would be desirable to read and how particular types of reading materials should be handled. As Francis Bacon once said, "Some books are to be tasted, others are to be swallowed, and some few to be chewed and digested." The rate and kind of reading in a particular situation should depend primarily upon the purposes of the learner in using the material. In the problem situation, it is recognized that the teacher is unable to do a particularly good job of setting the problems that are most meaningful for all learners. Therefore, with learners assuming an increasing share in identifying their own problems, they also play an increasingly large role in setting up these problems and getting possible answers to them.

Teacher monopoly of some key steps in reading processes must be eliminated. If we examine the key steps of the reading process, at the present time, we find that a good number of these in most classrooms are largely or almost wholly practiced by the teacher. This in effect means that the teacher is getting practice in these processes rather than the learner. More specifically, in the problem approach we must give greater attention to seeing that each pupil has an increasingly large share in (1) thinking through what his most important present and probable future problems are, (2) selecting reading materials that will help in more intelligently facing these problems, (3) using these materials wisely, and (4) evaluating the worth of each experience in terms of its value to him.

One basic reason why few products of our schools make much intelligent use of reading materials for problem solving is that they have had little or no training in these four abilities. The teacher has tried to do it all in many classrooms. Readers have become soft, dependent individuals, who are lost with problems when the teacher is not there to make the assignment, to see that they do the assignment, to get the resources for them, to evaluate the worth of what has been done, and finally to give a mark. Pupils learn to do by doing and not by having the teacher decide entirely what should be studied, how it should be studied, what materials should be used, and how worth-while the experience was. We do not learn to ride a bicycle by having someone else who knows how to do it ride it for us. Nor do we learn these reading abilities by having someone else practice them for us.

In advocating that the learner be given increasing practice in these processes, we are definitely not advocating a laissez-faire approach. We are not suggesting that the learner be turned loose and left to shift for himself in practicing these processes. Rather, we are definitely proposing that the teacher give the learner an opportunity to practice these processes *with guidance.* Thus, if we say that the teacher should not monopolize these processes, we do not mean that we would go in the direction of entirely independent learner activity as has sometimes been the case where this point has been misinterpreted. Rather, the teacher and learner together will cooperate in working through these processes with the hope that the learner will gain additional facility in them as he gets the needed practice.

We teachers ourselves will develop more functional reading ability.[6] This point is of key importance to basic reading improvement related to the problem approach. The import of it is suggested by the statement that teachers will learn to use their own reading abilities in a fashion that will help them actually identify and solve reading and other professional problems they face.

Who is probably the most serious reading disability case in your school? When this question is asked, the teacher or administrator will invariably select some pupil for the "honor." Actually, *in many schools the most serious reading disability cases are among teachers and administrators themselves.* This is a serious indictment, but we believe there is evidence to indicate that it is true.

Practically all of the hundreds of articles and books on reading that have been published are concerned with the matter of pupil disability and pupil weaknesses in reading. In this fact there is the implied assumption that pupil reading disabilities are the only weak links in the reading situation in our schools. We challenge this assumption.

We have experimental evidence that indicates that one of the most serious reading problems in our schools concerns the lack of functional reading habits for attacking professional problems which characterize a large proportion of our teachers and administrators. Unless and until a teacher or administrator practices the efficient use of printed materials in getting help in meeting and solving his own professional problems, it is rather unlikely that he

[6] Throughout this book it is emphasized that the best teacher is a developing teacher, one who is systematically attempting to improve professionally. In this role the teacher is himself a student.

will effectively teach functional reading habits to his pupils. Practice is ever stronger than precept, and the teacher who never thinks, or does not consistently think, of using printed professional materials when he encounters a problem in his teaching, such as, "What tests or questionnaires might I use in helping these learners diagnose their needs?" or "What are possible ways of finding the most likely needs of this child?" is not likely to teach youngsters really to use reading of the functional problem-solving type.

Some time ago, with the cooperation of the administrators and eighty-five teachers in a city school system, we helped the faculty diagnose some of their reading abilities. We will not go into the details of the experiment in which the teachers participated willingly, but in general these are some of the significant results: 3 per cent of the twelfth-grade pupils read better than 100 per cent of the teachers and administrators tested, 15 per cent of the twelfth-grade pupils read better than 95 per cent of the teachers and administrators, 75 per cent of the twelfth-grade pupils actually read better than 15 per cent of the teachers and administrators. A more detailed analysis of the reading skills studied indicated that the faculty was relatively strongest in vocabulary and "poetry comprehension," and was relatively weakest in "selection of key words" and "use of the index." The foregoing results certainly indicate that the teachers and administrators themselves were lamentably weak in the *how* of reading.

Unfortunately, we believe that the darkest side of the picture has not yet been given. The study of the functional reading that these school men and women actually did during a typical month indicated that a fair amount of leisure-time reading was done. But little or no professional reading to help solve school problems was done by the typical teacher or administrator in this school system. *Even those teachers and administrators who scored quite high on the reading test, which indicates they knew quite well how to read, made little if any more professional use of this ability than did those who scored low. The crux of the matter is that many teachers and administrators know how to read but made extremely little use of this skill in identifying professional problems and in getting possible solutions to such problems.*

Why do teachers and school administrators not make more use of reading for professional purposes? The following possible causes are suggestive of changes that might be made to improve the situation:

1. Many school men have unfortunately been led by our colleges and universities to think that their professional growth naturally ends when the coveted degree is received. This philosophy tends to stunt professional growth.

2. Many administrators and teachers are hired largely on the basis of past credit-getting activities rather than upon probable self-education and growth on the job.

3. Many administrators have not expected the teachers with whom they work to continue to grow professionally while on the job.

4. Teachers and administrators have not been taught how to get the printed materials that will be of definite help in solving their day-by-day problems. We in teacher-training institutions have been seriously at fault in not promoting this ability.

5. In many cases, professional libraries of magazines, pamphlets, and books have not been made available by school boards and school administrators. Frequently, to spend a small amount of money periodically on professional materials for teachers and administrators is a very sound procedure even if this means slightly less money can be spent for learner materials.

How can professional reading be improved? Teachers and administrators, with the aid of their respective school boards, can increase teacher and administrator reading abilities in a variety of ways. Some of the procedures that have been used with success in certain school systems are briefly indicated below.

Set aside a small amount of money each month for professional materials. Such professional books and magazines would presumably be selected by a teacher committee, which will examine various possible materials that might be brought into the school.

Frequently, with teachers and librarians cooperating, it is possible to establish active professional libraries in each school. It is considered as important by the teachers and librarians that the teaching staff make use of the library as that the students make use of the library. Actually, improved teacher and administrator use of the professional library is likely to increase the desirable use of the library by the learners through example and through use of the ideas derived from study.

While this approach has to be handled carefully, some school systems have made salary increases partially contingent upon evidences of professional growth. One bit of evidence of this would be a consistent use of professional materials and a constant attempt to try out ideas that are obtained from such materials.

At faculty meetings and elsewhere, encouragement is given to the consideration of new ideas that have been gleaned from various sources. Such ideas may relate to methods, materials, goals, and evaluation as well as other types of problems that the staff is continually running into.

Sometimes the major job teachers have is to isolate the specific professional problems that are most pressing. After these have been identified in a specific and realistic fashion, teachers can help each other in getting and using resources that are of help on these problems.

In many school systems, the teacher either has a time set aside during the working day, or can at least plan some time each week to keep himself up on new practices and trends in his field. If this is done, the learners' reading is likely to be improved because the teacher is attempting to set a good example in using reading to solve his own problems as well as in suggesting that learners use reading to identify and solve their problems.

In general, it may be said that poor reading on the part of students is usually indicative of poor teaching at various levels rather than due to any intrinsic difficulties on the part of most of the students themselves. This throws the responsibility for improvement directly in the laps of the teachers involved in the training of the readers. One of the best indications of improved reading practices in a school is the consistent and continuous use of professional reading materials on the part of the teachers to help keep professionally alive.

OPERATING PRINCIPLES FOR DEVELOPING FUNCTIONAL READING FOR PROBLEM ATTACK

I. *Principles related to levels of prereading capacities and of expected reading abilities*

    A. In a group of six-year-olds entering school one should expect some who may not be ready to read for two, three, or even four years and others who already read as well as the average second or third grader.

B. The range of reading ability for a particular group is likely to increase as it moves through school. Thus, a range of nine or more average grade levels should not be unexpected in, for example, a tenth-grade history class.

C. The ranges of reading ability one is likely to find in any particular class or group accentuates the need for elimination of the single text for all and the substitution of varied reading resources. (Range of interest, need, purpose and motives also dictate such a change in resources.)

II. *Principles related to reading goals*

A. Individual differences in ability, need, purpose, and interest make individual reading goals imperative.

B. A retardation concept based on deviation from the average is psychologically unsound since it implies unrealistic goals for many learners, too high goals for some and too low goals for others. Retardation must be related to individual *capacity* and achievement.

C. The learner should have a major share in determining his reading goals. The teacher's role becomes one of giving guidance to the student as he sets up and revises his goals.

D. Many types of reading that are presently given little if any attention will be seen to be of paramount importance for functional reading.

E. Teachers and learners should give more attention to goals stated in behavorial terms.

III. *Principles related to teaching practices*

A. The *uses* of reading should be taught with, rather than after, the *how* of reading.

B. All teachers, particularly high-school and college instructors, should give attention to reading improvement since a student may read excellently in one field and very poorly in another.

C. Learner purpose must play an increasing role in teaching-learning reading situations.

D. The student must get more practice in many parts of reading operations that are now almost wholly practiced by the teacher.

IV. *Principles related to teacher reading*

    A. Many student difficulties in reading can be traced to reading disabilities in teachers and administrators.

    B. The teacher or administrator who makes little systematic use of reading for identifying and solving professional problems is setting a poor example for learners with whom he works.

    C. Systematic professional reading can provide an excellent basis for professional improvement and help the educator identify and solve his problems in a more satisfying fashion.

BIBLIOGRAPHY

1. ALTICK, RICHARD D. *Preface to Critical Reading.* New York: Henry Holt and Co., 1946.
   Designed to aid in teaching critical reading and thinking.
2. DEBOER, JOHN J. "Teaching Critical Reading." *Elementary English Review,* 23:251-54; October 1946. Also in the *Education Digest,* 12:33-36; November 1946.
   Gives a very useful analysis of some aspects of critical reading and thinking.
3. GANS, ROMA. *A Study of Critical Reading Comprehension in the Intermediate Grades.* New York: Bureau of Publications, Teachers College, Columbia University, 1940.
   Gives pattern, results, and implications of a very stimulating and significant study on critical reading.
4. GRAY, WILLIAM S. "Summary of Reading Investigations, July 1, 1947, to June 30, 1948." *Journal of Educational Research,* 42:401-37; February 1949.
   This summary is illustrative of others that form excellent starting points for investigations of reading problems.
5. Junior Town Meeting League. *Teaching Controversial Issues.* Columbus Ohio: The Junior Town Meeting League, 1948.
   This exploration of ways of teaching controversial issues indirectly gives some important clues to critical reading.
6. National Society for the Study of Education. *Reading in the the High School and College.* Forty-seventh Yearbook, Part II. Chicago: The University of Chicago Press, 1948.
   Contains some very useful discussions and bibliographies on reading problems with which teachers in the higher schools are now confronted.

7. Progressive Education Association. *Critical-Mindedness in the Reading of Fiction.* Evaluation of the Eight-Year Study. Columbus, Ohio: Progressive Education Association, 1938.
   This test is designed to check on some key aspects of reader reactions.
8. RUSSELL, DAVID H. "Education for Critical Thinking." *The School,* 30:1-7; November 1941.
   Some possibilities for teaching critical thinking and reading are examined.
9. SEMMELMEYER, MADELINE. "Extensional Methods in Dealing with Abstractions in Reading." *Elementary School Journal,* 50:28-36; September 1949.
   Offers suggestions for developing meaning. A junior high school class is used for illustrative purposes.
10. TRAXLER, ARTHUR E. *Ten Years of Research in Reading, Summary and Bibliography.* New York: Educational Records Bureau, 1941.
    Brings together an annotated bibliography and brief summary of most of the important studies of reading that were published between January 1, 1930, and January 1, 1940.
11. TRAXLER, ARTHUR E., AND TOWNSEND, AGATHA. *Another Five Years of Research in Reading.* New York: Educational Records Bureau, 1946.
    Summarizes and annotates research studies on reading published from January 1, 1940, to January 1, 1945.
12. WATSON, GOODWIN, AND GLASER, E. M. *Watson-Glaser Tests of Critical Thinking.* Yonkers, New York: World Book Co., 1943.
    In many respects these are test measures of certain types of important reading abilities. "Discrimination in Reasoning" contains these tests: (*a*) Generalizations, (*b*) Inferences, (*c*) Discrimination of Arguments, (*d*) Recognition of Assumptions. "Logical Reasoning" contains these tests: (*a*) General Logical Reasoning, (*b*) What Do You Think? (*c*) Survey of Opinions, (*d*) Applied Logical Reasoning.

Part Four

LABELED TEACHING METHODS AND
PROCESS-RELATED PROBLEMS

13

AN ANALYSIS OF "NAME" METHODS

Problems to consider

What are the "name" methods that are frequently mentioned in educational discussions?

What are the primary purposes each method is designed to serve?

What activities typically characterize each method?

From a psychological standpoint, what are the weaknesses or limitations of each method?

The basic purpose of this book has been to help the learner who is a teacher or prospective teacher to develop for use a basic understanding of methods based on sound psychological principles. No attempt has been made to spell out a specific method in such detail that little is left to the ingenuity or originality of the teacher.

It is felt, however, that the student of educational methods should be familiar with the purposes, characteristics, and apparent limitations of a variety of specific methods or approaches, each of which has been used in a significant number of classes or school systems. It is hoped that a study of the approaches and operating principles that have been suggested in the preceding chapters will form a sound basis upon which the learner may evaluate the purposes, characteristics, and limitations of each of the methods described.

It should be noted that some methods are almost "cookbook" approaches, giving an exact pattern to use in the teaching-learning situation. Others try to emphasize fundamental principles and procedures and let the teacher and learners work out such items as timing, curriculum, and evaluation.

In the following discussion, methods have been grouped according to what seems to be the primary purposes of the proponents of each method. Such an analysis of the primary purposes back of each method produced these three categories: (1) methods in which the primary goal is to convey subject matter, (2) methods designed to give the learners' purposes primary weight, and (3) method approaches designed to teach solutions to problems that the teacher or school has identified.

I. GOAL—TO CONVEY SUBJECT MATTER

Daily assignment method

The daily assignment method is the one with which most teachers and prospective teachers have the greatest familiarity. It is probably the method with which they had the greatest practice in both secondary and college teaching-learning situations. Of all methodological approaches it is the one that is perhaps the most hallowed by tradition and at the same time most criticized by educational experts.

Purpose. Perhaps the basic assumption underlying the purposes involved in using the daily assignment method is the theory that if the learner conscientiously studies small bits or fragments of information over a period of time, these fragments can be pulled together into larger wholes and eventually can be used when needed. A primary purpose of this approach is to have the student examine or "study" and *cover* a certain amount of subject matter within a conventionally organized field of knowledge. Typically, the goal of the teacher with this approach is to transmit, with explanations, to the learner the knowledge that he hopes will lead to more desirable behavior. Secondary purposes that typically characterize this approach are: (1) to give the learner mental exercise by the study of materials organized by an expert or scholar in the field; (2) to train the learner to follow directions and soak up ideas; (3) to have the learner understand and accept, but not critically examine, what the teacher and the text say; (4) to get everyone up to "a normative level." This level, presumably, represents the minimum information needed by the student to move to the next grade or subsequent class in the subject-matter area.

The paramount purpose of the teacher is to give to the learners information rather than to train them to develop ideas. The teacher's role is primarily one of assigning work and explaining assignments to the learners rather than helping them explore or practice finding out things for themselves.

Characteristics of the daily assignment approach. Since the pattern common to this approach is rather well known, relatively little space will be given to it. Basically, the teacher prescribes the amounts of subject matter that all the learners in the class or grade are expected to master by the next class period. The pattern typically involves the teacher's assigning a certain number of pages to be studied, study on these pages, recitation on these pages, more assignment, more study, more recitation or lecture. This cycle is repeated with tests being given periodically. The purpose of the tests is to enable the teacher to check up on the amounts of information the learner has acquired and to give him a basis for assigning a mark.

Class time is usually taken up by the teacher in quizzing individual class members to see if they have studied the assignment, in a lecture that explains or elaborates on the text, or in introducing and making a new assignment. Considerable time is frequently given to drill on specific facts or skills. Time is sometimes given for study during the class period, during which time the teacher does a certain amount of supervision.

The pattern of the course or class following this method is teacher-planned or text-planned without learner participation in planning. Teacher practices tend to encourage learning based on the atomistic stimulus-response school of thought and learning.

Weaknesses or limitations of the daily assignment method. In this approach the learner gets little if any guided practice in planning his own learning activities. The reverse of the coin—the learner does get practice in depending upon the teacher to get learning under way, to do the planning for the learning, to do the evaluating, to supply almost all the leadership. In addition to learning a certain amount of subject matter, the student will frequently be trained in learning to dislike the subject area, and such dislike may produce what some psychologists have called "affective expansion." This means that dislike of the subject may be transferred to the teacher, and/or the school and/or systematic learning in general.

The learner typically has no organizational, mental framework into which to put the ideas he is expected to study and hear from day to day. Thus, while he may be able to remember the fragmentary bits of information for test purposes, the likelihood that they will be retained and remembered in a meaningful fashion in a functional situation is not too great.

Closely related to this criticism is the fact that with the subject matter usually divorced from current realistic problems, the use of these facts and bits of information in such problems is not very likely. It would appear that the advocates of this approach are trying to make scholars in an informational field rather than trying to meet the needs of laymen with nonacademic problems to be faced from day to day.

An additional major weakness of this approach is that the ideas, patterns of thinking, readiness level, and purposes of the individual learner are virtually disregarded in the uniform assignments that are given from day to day. What is supposed to be good for one is supposed to be good for all. The standard that each is expected to meet is the standard that all—without regard to purpose, interest, and ability—are expected to meet.

The final major criticism of this subject-matter approach is that it tends to encourage the development of docile students. Critical thinking is discouraged and the student is supposed to accept what is said by the text or the teacher as always right. His job is to learn the information that has been analyzed, organized, and developed by someone else rather than to analyze critically the points of view that are expressed by different "authorities." [1]

Morrison Plan or the "mastery method" [2]

Purposes. In the Morrison approach the primary goal is to teach subject matter as was the case in the daily-assignment approach. However, the primary difference is that in the Morrison approach units rather than fragmentary parts are used.

The primary goal in this plan is to train the learner in and through "the mastery formula" which includes: pretest, teach, test, adapt procedures, teach, and retest. The cycle is to be repeated as often as necessary to insure learning of the material in the particular unit involved. In theory, it is emphasized that subject-matter mastery must be shown through actual change of behavior in desirable directions.

---

[1] It is recognized that some writers take a much more sympathetic view of the daily assignment approach than has been presented here. Differences in writer purposes are probably primarily responsible. The present writer believes teacher-learner planning and democratic assignment-making are extremely important.

[2] This method is important historically and because it represents essentially an approach that many teachers accept as desirable.

Characteristics of the Morrison Plan. The Morrison Plan uses the unit approach almost exclusively.

Five categories of procedures are identified. These categories are differentiated on the basis of the nature of the content to be taught and include: the science type, the appreciation type, the practical-arts type, the language-arts type, and the pure-practice type (involves drill).

"The teaching cycle" emphasized is supposed to include:

Exploration step designed to help students find out what they already know and what they need to know.

Presentation by the teacher of what he thinks are the main ideas of a unit.

Assimilation of information on the part of students.

Organization of information into a coherent unit whole.

Recitation in which students give oral or written essays on their findings in the particular unit being studied.

Each of the five steps in the teaching cycle just given is to be accompanied by the phases of the mastery formula, which includes pretest, teach, test, adapt procedures, teach, and retest.

Limitations or weaknesses in the approach. In its pure form it is seen that the Morrison Plan is too complicated for actual use. Some phases of it have been used successfully by teachers whose primary goal is the teaching of subject matter in large meaningful units.

It should be pointed out that the primary organization of the unit is done by the teacher with the learner having little share in diagnosing what his major problems are and in practicing activities connected with evaluation. In addition to the criticisms that have already been made of the general subject-matter approach, the basic question needs to be raised of whether simply learning the subject matter out of problem context is an economical way to change the behavior of learners outside of school.

The Dalton System [3]

Purposes. The primary goal in the Dalton System is to teach all the same subject-matter categories as in conventional divisions. Again, that which is to be studied is defined in detail by the teacher.

---

[3] Probably few schools now have a plan specifically labeled the Dalton System. However, basically similar approaches are used in many schools. For this reason, it is believed a discussion of it is important for the student of teaching and learning methods.

There is an attempt to provide for some freedom for self-development and cooperation in the "community life" (home room) situation.

A special attempt is made partially to meet individual differences of one type—speed of learning.

In the Dalton setup, students are encouraged to budget time, to work up to abilities, and to develop initiative and responsibility to get assigned subject-matter contracts completed.

Characteristics of the Dalton System. The curriculum includes conventional subject-matter divisions as has been previously mentioned. *Major subjects,* which are the only ones used as a basis for promotion, include English, history, math, science, foreign language, geography, and other academic subjects. *Minor subjects* not used as a basis for promotion, include gymnastics, art, music, domestic science, manual training, handiwork, and other special fields. In the typical schedule most of the afternoon is devoted to study in the minor fields. Actually, work in the minor field activities is quite similar to that of many other typical subject-matter school programs.

The basic feature of the Dalton System involves the use of learner *contracts.* A contract is a teacher-constructed set of assignments, almost always in a major subject, which the learner is supposed to complete in twenty days. The contract itself is subdivided into four weekly and twenty daily parts. The learner is supposed to complete ten contracts each year and is promoted at any time during the year when he gets the ten completed.

The contracts usually include (*a*) an introduction designed to bridge the new information to preceding contracts, (*b*) prescriptions covering what is to be solved and what is to be prepared, (*c*) specific references including texts and other books to be used. Contracts also indicate "departmental cuts." These refer to work done in one department that is acceptable for credit in another subject-matter field. For example, some work done in English literature may also give the student Social Studies credit.

The student prepares a budget showing what time he will allocate to each subject. He has regularly scheduled conferences with teachers, and extra conferences may be called by the teacher as he sees fit.

The learner is supposed to keep abreast on all of the subjects. To facilitate quick inspection of contract standing, the teacher keeps a "laboratory graph" for each of his students, and the learner keeps a "contract graph," which indicates the number of daily portions of the twenty in the contract that he has done.

Work is largely done in subject-matter *laboratories,* which replace classrooms. Each laboratory is designed to include the resources needed for a particular subject. Subject-matter teachers stay in their respective subject-matter laboratories.

Although exams are not greatly emphasized, they are given over contracts as these are finished.

Limitations or weaknesses of the Dalton System. In addition to the learner's not getting practice in planning—this practice is gotten by the teachers—the assumption is made in the Dalton System that all should go on the same track (sequence of contracts), regardless of basic abilities, individual purpose, and interests. This assumption seems quite questionable from a psychological standpoint.

While one of the goals of the Dalton approach is to meet individual differences in speed of work, actually there is probably considerable pressure put upon those who are below average to "keep up" with the contracts. This is likely to promote social and emotional difficulties if the learner is basically considerably below average in ability to learn. Although those who are considerably above average in ability may move ahead at the rate at which they are capable, there is a tendency for some or many of them simply to keep ahead of the average expectation. This tendency is aggravated by the fact that the learner has had little or no share in planning what the jobs or contracts would be which he is supposed to carry out. The contracts are arbitrarily handed to the student and he is expected to carry them out. Again, it is a case of autocratic imposition of learning goals, material, and procedures. It does not seem to be in line with psychological evidence concerning the nature of most desirable learning.

Core and common learnings approaches with subject-matter emphasis

Purposes. As with most subject-matter approaches the primary goal is to transmit to the learner a prescribed and specific body of subject matter. In the subject-matter type of the core and common learnings approaches an attempt is made to achieve better understanding and retention than is possible in the atomistic daily assignment plan by helping the learners to see and learn information as a part of larger patterns. The goal is to try to train learners into organizing parts or fragments or bits of information into meaningful wholes.

An attempt is made to meet some types of individual differences in ability level and purpose by having a variety in the types and amounts of information to be learned *within* a particular subject unit or large segment of subject matter. An additional purpose in the broad subject-matter unit is to make a different approach to the learner from that which he has probably had before in most of his school career.

Characteristics. The subject-matter units themselves are teacher-selected. The learner may or may not share in planning the activities within a particular unit. Basically, the subject matter is prescribed for the learners with some latitude about how much will be required within a particular unit.

Conventional subject-matter lines are broken down in this approach since units typically cut across such lines. The development of social skills and understandings may or may not be emphasized. Frequently, but not always, large blocks of time go with the use of this approach, and a unit usually covers the time of a whole class for several weeks.

Within each unit there are typically set up by the teachers so-called minimum essentials, which are considered particularly important in testing and marking. Each learner is supposed to master at least the "minimum essentials" of the subject matter.

Limitations or weaknesses of the core or common-learnings subject-matter approach.[4] Most of the objections already raised in connection with other subject-matter approaches apply here also. The teacher typically dominates activities, dominates planning, dominates organization, and dominates evaluation.

There is greater likelihood of understanding with this approach than with the daily assignment method, because the learner is more likely to see the relationship of bits of information. The likelihood of transfer of knowledge to actual use is questioned, particularly by advocates of the problem and problem-process approaches.

---

[4] Most descriptions of the approaches described in this chapter emphasize the merits of the methods. In this chapter we are trying to point up their limitations to help the student of methods get a balanced perspective on them. It is recognized that the methods discussed in the latter part of this chapter have been largely steps in the right direction.

Also, it is not probable that it is best for all in a particular class to work on the same unit for the same length of time during a particular four-, five-, or six-week period. The origin of this doubt is to be found in the spread of individual differences in maturity level, general ability, purpose, motivation, and general familiarity with the type of thing that is being studied.

II. GOAL—TO GIVE LEARNERS' PURPOSES PRIMARY WEIGHT

The activity approach

Purpose. The primary purposes of proponents of the activity curriculum or method are in striking contrast to the purposes of those whose primary goal is to teach subject matter. Actually, the major purpose of the activity curriculum is to de-emphasize bookishness and dead wood in curriculum construction and to emphasize overt doing on the part of the learner. An attempt is made to get away from a "mania for instruction" and to move toward what advocates call a natural type of learning. Student purposes and interests are given a key part in the planning of learning activities. The emphasis is upon seeing and hearing life rather than just reading about it. A strong attempt is made to unite in-school and out-of-school experiences.

Major recognition is given to individual differences through having learnings center around the student's self-expression and creativeness rather than around the covering of particular subject matter. Failure is largely eliminated through attempts to de-emphasize the necessity for "minimum standards" and to try to get desirable motivation and favorable attitudes through emphasis on the interests and needs of the individual learner.

Characteristics. The teacher's primary role is to determine the interests and purposes of individual learners in his classes and help the individual student select and study the most worth-while of these.

Where interests and purposes happen to be common to all students in a particular class, all carry on similar activities that are cooperatively planned with the teacher. Interests and purposes that are common to some of the class, but not to all, form the basis for grouping and for small-group work. Interests and purposes that are unique to a particular individual form the basis for strictly individual activity.

Although some critics of this method would say that there is no organization, proponents contend that the organization in this method is basically a developing individual learner organization—not a preplanned teacher organization imposed on the learner.

While the activity program in itself is not planned in advance, the teacher does plan ways of determining and guiding individual learners and groups of learners to identify their primary interests and purposes. The teacher also plans ways of helping the learner determine which of his interests and purposes it is best to follow in setting up study plans. In this approach the problem-solving method is much used since typically the interests and needs that learners bring up revolve around problems.

Limitations. Perhaps the most common criticism of this type of approach is that the learner may have major subject-matter gaps caused by the "haphazard" nature of his learning activities. Proponents of the activity approach claim that the desirable motivation and favorable attitudes that are developed will help the learner meet situations where such subject matter is needed later on by having him acquire the know-how for its acquisition at the time the information is needed. An attitude favorable for acquiring the needed subject matter at the appropriate time is also considered important by activity-approach advocates.

Another objection frequently given by administrators and also by teachers who like class activities to run smoothly is that this approach will not give a neatly prepatterned curriculum, which is characteristic of most of the other methods that have been described. To advocates of the activity approach this lack of a neat curriculum, externally imposed, is a most desirable feature. To critics this is supposed to lead to curriculum chaos. Critics say the lack of an imposed organization will produce no organization and lack of sequence in desirable learning experiences. Proponents believe that meaningful organization must spring from within the learner anyhow and hence the kind of activities that are encouraged do, in fact, support a dynamic developmental organization that has great significance to the individual learner. Where the truth lies probably depends to a large extent upon the ability of the teacher to help the learner develop his own meaningful organizational setup and thinking. In the hands of a poor teacher this approach is in great danger of degenerating into a "laissez-faire" technique which permits learners simply to do pretty much as they please.

This approach probably has, on the one hand, greater possibilities, and on the other hand, greater dangers than the other approaches discussed thus far.

In this approach relatively little attention is given to standard tests, one reason being that most of the presently available tests are primarily subject-matter tests and do not get at the types of learnings most emphasized in the activity approach.

Project method

Purposes. The project method is closely related to the activity approach insofar as purposes are concerned. The goal is to have "the whole-hearted purposes of the learner pursued to wholesome consummation in a social environment." An attempt is made to have the learner study in meaningful wholes that grow out of his own thinking and creative ability. In some respects this goal is similar to other types of unit goals.

Characteristics. Characteristics of the project method may perhaps best be indicated by listing the steps in a project. These typically are:

1. *Purposing.* Here the learners, preferably on their own initiative, set up particular goals which they as a group or as individuals wish to attain.

2. *Planning.* The procedures for achieving the purposes or goals that have been set up are assembled, considered, and one plan is selected as being most desirable. This plan is then refined in preparation for the next step in the project.

3. *Executing.* In this step the plan that has been selected and refined is put into action.

4. *Evaluating.* In this step the learners check up on the success of the plan that has been developed and carried out. In some cases unsatisfactory results may mean returning to step 2 (planning) or even step 1 (purposing) in an attempt to develop satisfactory proposals for procedure.

Kilpatrick, who has been one of the major advocates of the project method has described four types of projects:

1. The *producers'* project results in the production of something, such as a garden, a play-box, or a plan for health improvement in the community.

2. A *consumers'* project involves the use or appreciation of something that has already been made by someone else.

3. The *problem* project involves solving a problem.

4. The *drill* project involves the acquisition of a skill, such as learning how to use a library, how to use a book, or how to type-write.

Typically, in the project method, the goal is to base motivation on natural interests, and attempts are made to add new interests to old ones. The teacher tries to use the students' experiences and encourages freedom of expression of their own ideas. The project method tends to be somewhat more defined and to offer somewhat more clearly identifiable units of experience than was the case in the activity approach.

As in the activity approach an attempt is made to eliminate useless materials from the curriculum. Emphasis in the project approach is upon positive and successful achievement as a means of decreasing the amount of failure and the undesirable psychological concomitants that frequently accompany failure.

Limitations or weaknesses of the project method. Most of the limitations or weaknesses that have been discussed under the activity approach tend to apply to the project method also. Critics claim the work of the school tends to be chaotic, to lack organization, to tax the genius of the teacher beyond the ability of the typical instructor. It is claimed that the method does not offer the rigorous discussion through orderly procedures that is needed for disciplining the mind of the learner.

It is also claimed that there is an unwillingness on the part of some advocates to submit the approach to school experimentation. This unwillingness may be due to the lack of appropriate tests for checking on the types of learnings that are promoted in this type of method.

An additional criticism is that the project method has led to an overemotionalized attitude toward teaching on the part of some of its strongest supporters. This attitude, it is contended, does not result in needed continuous evaluation and improvement of teaching-learning situations.

Experience unit

Purposes. The primary purpose of the experience approach or the experience unit approach is to use direct experience in realistic problem situations, to encourage vividness and reality of learning activities. In the experience unit the learner is supposed to be the major origin of experience purposes. Ends that have value to the student are important since they are supposed to give unity to the experience.

In this approach subject matter is to be considered as a means to an end rather than the end itself. Social learnings involving cooperation and participation with other learners are given a paramount place in the experience unit approach.

The teacher's role is primarily that of a guide to the individual learner who is relatively free to project what he considers to be good. The primary goal is to tie up the mind and body processes into a single unit of learning activity.

Characteristics of the experience unit. The outstanding characteristic of the experience approach is the realism of the learning situations in which the student is encouraged to participate. Considerable attention is given to such activities as community cleanups, community surveys, and to participation in such community activities as traffic control, Red Cross drives, soil conservation, developing new industries, improving the local government, and improving race relations. Experience units within the school may involve such things as landscaping the school grounds, developing better student government, improving sanitation within and around the school, planning changes in the curriculum. The chief characteristic of the experience unit comes from the idea that pupils can best learn to live by practicing such living in real life activities in the pursuit of ends that they have helped to set up and that are of significance to them.

Limitations or weaknesses of this approach. The major limitations or weaknesses of this approach are very similar to those that have already been discussed in connection with the activity and project approaches.

III. GOAL: TO TEACH SOLUTIONS TO PROBLEMS THAT THE SCHOOL HAS IDENTIFIED

Core and common learnings approaches with problem emphasis

Purposes. Although there are some differences in core and common learnings programs with problem emphasis, the purposes, procedures, and difficulties involved in their use seem to be sufficiently similar to include both in the same discussion. Actually, a core or common learnings setup in one school may differ considerably in emphasis from that in another school. Differences tend to depend largely upon the particular combination of purposes that are given most attention.

The advocates of both core and common learnings approaches with problem emphasis assume that most present-day secondary schools are not doing a particularly good job in training youths as they need to be trained. There is serious concern with the apparent lack of transfer of training from in-school situations to out-of-school activities. The lack of serious concern on the part of the learner in the planning and carrying on of learning activities in the school is also decried.

Thus, the programs under discussion represent attempts to help students work on the problems that it is felt should be of real concern to all learners. These problems are typically set up by the teacher or teachers and within such problem areas learners may be given much or little choice in helping to decide which phases will be most emphasized by the group and which parts will be worked on most intensively by individual students. Since problems do not stay within conventional subject-matter lines, there tends to be a breaking down of such lines where core or common learnings approaches with problem emphasis are attempted.

One of the purposes some school leaders have had in starting such approaches has been to help secondary-school teachers avoid giving the student another dose of the same subject matter that he feels he has already had one or more times. In social studies, for example, the student may feel that he already has had American history in a similar form one or more times, and sometimes is reluctant to attack the subject aggressively an additional time unless it is approached in a different fashion. The core and common learnings approaches, which use problems as the organizational framework, while using similar material to that given in subject-matter areas, tend to present the student with a different study framework. This is designed to enlist more interest than a repeat of something that the student has already studied or at least feels that he has studied before.

Another major purpose of the common problem approach in most schools where it has been initiated is to help stabilize the students' day by giving larger blocks of time for study. The goal is to get away from a kaleidoscopic hodge-podge of departmental learnings where the students really just get started working on a particular problem or problem area and then the bell rings and he has to move to another subject. Since the core and common learnings setups disregard subject-matter boundaries, it is possible to assign larger blocks of time—two-hour blocks, for example—and under this arrangement the student can get started and continue planning and problem solution over a sufficiently long period of time. The larger time block also gives greater flexibility in teaching. Field trips and projects related to problems, for example, can be worked on for a long enough period of time to make them more profitable than they would otherwise be if only forty or fifty minutes were available.

It has been said that our best teaching at the present time, on the average, is probably in the elementary schools. If this is true, one reason probably is that a teacher stays with a group of students for a sufficient length of time to become acquainted with them, to understand their problems, and to give them guidance rather than simply dictate what should be learned. A larger time block on the high-school level can help teachers and learners reap some of the values that typically accrue only on the elementary-school level.

Another major purpose of these approaches is to help learners put the ideas that are studied in a functional problem context. In English, for example, reading, writing, speaking, and listening abilities are diagnosed in functional learning situations, plans for improvement are set up, and practice is actually given in these skills as the learner works on realistic problems, which may be largely centered in science, mathematics, or social studies. Instead of the typical pattern where the learner studies a text, discusses it in class, and eventually takes a test, we have the setting-up of problems, and attacks on these are made by the individual and by groups. Practice is given on the skills that are related to improved problem attack. Obviously, this concept of desirable learning is a more complex one than that typically involved in subject-matter acquisition, frequently for test purposes only.

Closely related to the idea of having subject matter learned in problem context is the goal of having resources acquired and used in a realistic situation. For example, when history is studied, it is not studied simply to pass a test, but rather to get help in understanding and having intelligent views on such questions as: What might we do about unemployment? and How should inflation difficulties be approached? If the learner's purpose in getting and using resources is to get help on problems, he is more likely to use resources for this purpose outside of school than if his purpose in school is primarily one of doing what the teacher told him to do, hoping to pass the inevitable examination.

Another purpose that most advocates of problem core and common learnings approaches have in mind is to promote the social adjustment of the learners. Attempts are made to achieve this through continuous practice in student-teacher planning, student-student planning, group diagnosis, and the operation of general democratic processes in the teaching-learning situation. A major purpose here is to help the learner practice the abilities necessary in getting along with peers and also to develop a sense of self-reliance and self-directing ability which is frequently noticeably absent in conventional learning products.

Since the core or common learnings setup gives the teacher an opportunity to get acquainted with his students through large time blocks and because of the nature of the activities typically carried on (teacher-pupil planning, for example) in many schools, the guidance function—both individual and group guidance—is closely tied up with these programs. As a matter of fact, one basis sometimes used in selecting a teacher for this type of program is his experience in guidance programs or his ability to give guidance. In many respects the best teacher in a core or common learnings setup is one who works with the students in a guidance framework which both permits and promotes such student-teacher relationships as are desirable and necessary for group guidance.

A final purpose sometimes prominent in these programs is that of encouraging in-service training for teachers. Since core and common learnings programs are frequently set up by two or more teachers and are sometimes taught by a pair of teachers, the programs themselves tend to promote closer relations among teachers and more teacher-teacher planning. This may be a secondary purpose of core or common learnings programs, but it is one that should be kept in mind since it may be significant in helping teachers to grow on the job.

Characteristics. As has been suggested in the preceding paragraph, the problem core consists of learning activities that are judged as basic for all students. These learning activities cut across traditional subject-matter lines since problems cut that way. Typically, a larger block of time is utilized, which permits uninterrupted attention and work on a given problem. In order to illustrate what may happen when these approaches are followed, a picture of some of the features of such operation is given below.

Before the course starts, the teacher or teachers may list the possible problem areas that could be explored by the class. Typically, these are derived from the teacher's own past experience, from the experiences of other core or common learnings teachers, from the diagnosed needs and problems of learners at the particular age level involved, or from a combination of these and other sources. The teacher, also, is likely to attempt to gather together a variety of resources that might be useful, at least as starters, for learners attacking some of the particular problem areas listed. Of course, if the teacher has not taught a core or common learnings course or class before, he is likely to study the available literature and perhaps will attempt to observe some classes of this sort in operation.

After the class has convened, the teacher is likely to try to have the students indicate which problem areas they keenly desire to explore and which problems hold no interest for them. There are several ways that this may be done. One is to use such tools as a learning problem check list on which the students identify the problems of most concern to them. These are then studied by the teacher and/or a group of students and out of them may come what seem to be the most common concerns of the members of the class. One difficulty here is in having the majority opinion governing decisions. This is likely to result in a minority of students whose choices are not given particularly strong weight.

After the problem area to be attacked first has been selected either by the teacher or by the teacher with the help of the students, student-teacher planning typically follows. Assignments may be of a definite day-to-day variety or they may be more elastic and of a more continuing sort. This depends largely on the teacher and the particular group of learners involved.

After it has been decided by the teacher or the group which problem area will be attacked first, the discussion frequently shifts to the question of how answers will be found for the problem or problem area being attacked. Typically, no single text is used; rather, many texts are examined to uncover material pertinent to the problem. Another characteristic that is different from typical subject-centered courses is that considerable use is made of the suggestions and ideas of fellow students and other human resources, such as other teachers, citizens in the community, parents, etc. Much use is, of course, made of the library, and such materials as the *Readers' Guide* and the *Education Index* become key tools in the learner's operation.

As has been suggested before, "assignments" or individual work plans are likely to vary in type, amount, and level of difficulty depending on the teacher and the individual learner. The scope and sequence of the learners' activities are dependent upon the needs of the situation rather than on particular logical organization such as one has in a textbook or syllabus. Much use is made of notebook records. Some teachers go so far as to say that the notebook tends to become the text. Here the learner keeps a record of his plans and achievements. Also, he will frequently list the difficulties he has run into and the needs he has recognized.

The record or notebook also forms the basis for systematic evaluation. Such an evaluation is typically a combination of teacher and learner activity and involves diagnosis of both planning and work accomplished. The primary purpose of the diagnosis is to set up procedures that can be more profitable to the learner. It should be noted that drill and laboratory exercise are de-emphasized. These might be used if the learner and teacher involved decide that such would be desirable to promote the identification or attack on particular problems.

Difficulties and limitations likely to be encountered in the core or common learnings program. It appears that most schools which have started a core or common learnings program seem to be pleased with the results and indeed there is evidence that its operation is more in harmony with psychological principles than the typical course approach. It should be recognized, however, that there are difficulties which are likely to be faced by those who attempt to use such a program. This is certainly not intended to imply that such a program should not be tried, but rather that the school system using it should be familiar with the challenges that must be met as plans are made and acted upon.

The adoption of core and common learnings approaches will sometimes result in a lack of self-confidence on the part of the teacher engendered by lack of familiarity with their purposes and procedures and by the broadness of the problems attacked. The teacher is likely to be working with problems that utilize material outside his own field of specialization. This will involve the need for teacher development. While in a sense this may be considered a difficulty, on the other hand it may be considered an advantage in that the teacher tends to have a broader outlook and to consider subject areas and materials as tools for attacking problems rather than as ends and goals in themselves.

The longer time block is likely to necessitate the use of varied approaches. In a time block of a hundred or a hundred and twenty minutes, it will probably be necessary for the teacher with the learners to plan at least two or three types of activities that will be carried on during the class period.

Teachers who have experimented with core and common learnings approaches report that a changed library setup and somewhat different library resources are typically needed. One reason for this is the greatly increased use of the library that is likely to result when learners are attacking problems as opposed to using texts to get information primarily to pass tests. Such a resource as the *Readers' Guide* may be greatly in demand, and, for some types of resources, some staggering of the hours when core or common learnings classes will use the library is usually desirable. Another help is for the teacher or a student committee to formulate partial bibliographies on certain problems or problem areas. While this keeps the learner using such materials from having practice in searching for resources, such practice can be gained under other circumstances and at other times or later on in the study of the problem. It should be emphasized that this core approach does demand a much more realistic use of the library than does a program that expects the learner simply to use the library to look up particular references that he has been asked to study for test purposes.

It should be recognized by those attempting to use the core or common learnings approaches that such a course or courses may become as "strait-jacketed" as conventional courses after a period of time. In fact, there is danger that a new group of teacher-selected problem areas may become, in effect, new subject-matter areas, which may become ends in themselves.

While most would agree that the purposes that have been suggested for core and common learnings approaches are excellent, the indicated method of trying to achieve these goals sometimes disregards the individual learner and tends to assume that all on a particular grade level will work effectively on the same problems at the same time. More specifically, the question may be raised, "How does the same for all at a particular grade level jibe with the objectively demonstrated fact that the spread of 'maturity levels' within a particular grade ordinarily overlaps the average mental maturity level of six to eleven average grade levels?" For example, in the tenth grade we expect, on the basis of objective testing, some learners with a maturity level corresponding to that of an *average* fourth or fifth grader and others whose maturity level is similar to that of *average* fifteenth or sixteenth graders. If one set of problems (basal problem core) is used for all, to which part of the range of individual variation will it be geared? Can *individual differences* in purposes, in interest, in motivation, in level of complexity of problem that can be attacked successfully, and in other variables in which individuals differ significantly, be disregarded successfully? Supporters of the core and common learnings approaches say that attention can and must be given to individual differences within the problem area that is being attacked at a particular time.

Another potential danger that needs to be recognized is that the learner may be denied practice in two key steps of the learning process, namely, problem identification and problem selection for systematic study. If these first two steps are done by the teacher for the learner, it is probable that he will not be able to do them very successfully outside the school. In a fairly fixed or stable culture this might not be a major disadvantage, if the student learned all the solutions to primary current problems while in school. However, in a dynamic, changing culture like ours, it would seem extremely important to give the learner as much practice as possible in identifying and selecting for study the problems he needs to face at a particular time. Unless he gets such practice in school, he is not likely to operate very successfully outside of school. There is perhaps nothing intrinsically at variance with this point of view in the core or common learnings approach, but it must be recognized that as this approach has operated in some school systems the teachers have brought to the courses a set list of problem areas which they "know" the learners will "select" before the end of the course.

A question related to that mentioned in the preceding paragraph raises the issue: Do the programs as carried on place too much emphasis upon learning or memorizing the solutions to current problems at the expense of learning the whole process needed by the student if he is to cope effectively with changing conditions that raise new problems? If it is necessary to have teacher-imposed content, most would agree that learning solutions to current problems is more desirable than memorizing a Greek or Latin text. However, should not a sound approach put more emphasis on helping the learner develop the total complex of processes involved in successfully identifying, selecting for study, and solving effectively current and *prospective problems?* If we are teaching for transfer values, the processes just indicated are of equal importance to learning solutions to current problems.

There is also the danger that fundamental motivation of an intrinsic sort may be neglected in the interest of putting over a preselected "content" of problems identified and selected without the ones most concerned, the learners, sharing in the process. It is quite possible that skillful teachers can put over such an undemocratic program or pseudo-democratic program with results much more satisfactory than those being attained at the present time. However, in the long run unless the learner participates in decisions concerning what, when, and how he is to study, the learning is likely to be for most learners predominantly extrinsically motivated and is not likely to be carried on in a systematic fashion after schools days are over.

Mention has already been made of the lack of teacher familiarity with the approach. A closely related difficulty is that of accustoming students to the approach. For example, some have the idea that if there is no text, there is really no work in the course. Others feel that if a course is not clearly prestructured and specifically organized by the teacher, then the learner has no idea of what he is to do. It should be recognized that any significant approach is likely to result in some upset on the part of the learner; this need not be a serious difficulty if properly approached. In some schools it has been found that where the core or common learnings approaches have worked quite well, some students complain of a lack of interest in classes conventionally taught. The issue seems to revolve around the question: Should the learner know why he is studying what he is told to study by the teacher in the conventional class, and should he have a share in planning such study activities?

Parental opposition to the new approach is usually to be expected. Such interest on the part of parents in how their schools are operating is desirable. Typically, through group explanations and individual contacts with parents, the support of most parents can be enlisted. Work reports that students take home periodically are also of aid in helping parents understand what is being attempted and what is being accomplished. The experience in some schools has been that after parents become familiar with core and common learnings approaches they later want similar procedures continued in other years in the education of their children.

A difficulty that is primarily an administrative one is that of getting time during the working school day for joint planning by teachers. This, of course, is particularly true where the common learnings or core approach is handled by more than one teacher. Communication between teachers and planning teaching programs so that instructors can go on the job and attack their courses with new points of view necessitate careful planning on the part of the administrator or the administrative committee that sets up the working schedule.

In the following paragraphs are given a few constructive suggestions that the writer feels should be kept in mind in initiating or developing a core or common learnings program. These suggestions are based upon what psychologists have found out about individual differences, motivation, the nature of the learning process, and transfer of training.

Instead of arbitrarily assigning a certain number of problems to each grade level, make suggestive lists only. These lists would include some relatively simple problems, some difficult ones, and all variations of complexity between these two extremes. These suggestions would be one resource used by the teacher and learners in identifying and selecting problems for individual or group study.

It is desirable to work on the assumption, which has been demonstrated objectively many times, that no two learners in a particular grade level will have exactly the same maturity. Teachers must expect intragrade range of maturity levels to extend over the average maturity level of several grades. Use of this point will make educators hesitate to set up any precut group of problems for all learners who happen to be in a particular grade.

Teachers, administrators, and curriculum planners should not take the easy road of monopolizing decisions regarding what will be studied by any learner or even any group of learners. The learner needs to participate in these decisions for at least two basic reasons: (1) to build up intrinsic motivation and zest for what is being done, and (2) to get practice in making such decisions as he will have to make for himself when the teacher is no longer in front of him.

Learning all the processes involved in problem identification, selection, and solution along with the concomitant service learnings that have already been discussed, namely, self-evaluation, purposeful reading, and democratic interpersonal relations, is of more long-time importance than learning the solutions to current problems identified by someone else. If the latter is emphasized, we have to try to cover all problems. This is obviously impossible. If the former is emphasized, we are interested in using problems as vehicles to get practice in meeting similar problems, rather than in memorizing solutions to all conceivable problems the learner may face.

The probable functional usefulness of knowledge and subject matter in identifying and solving personal and group problems should form the chief basis for deciding what subject matter to study. Rather than by clinging to the criterion of covering a certain amount of subject matter (number of problems or problem areas), what is studied should be determined by what appears to be for and to each learner, with appropriate guidance, the most needed learning experiences for him. The teacher and learner should together plan this with the teacher's greater experience being given considerable weight. This weight should not be all-determining, however.

A primary goal should be to accustom students to the habit of engaging voluntarily in (systematic) learning, rather than submitting involuntarily in certain periods to formal instruction.

BIBLIOGRAPHY

1. BURTON, W. H. *The Guidance of Learning Activities.* New York: D. Appleton-Century, 1944.
   Describes principles and practices in traditional method approaches, and in recent unitary organizational setups.
2. DOUGLASS, H. R., AND MILLS, H. H. *Teaching in High School.* New York: The Ronald Press Co., 1948.
   Contains many useful suggestions for the teacher who is primarily interested in teaching approaches in which subject matter and materials are selected and assigned by the teacher.
3. GILES, H. H. *Teacher-Pupil Planning.* New York: Harper and Bros., 1941.
   Methods and their relation to democracy are discussed. Ways of moving toward more democratic methods are described.

4. QUILLEN, I. J., AND HANNA, L. A. *Education for Social Competence.* Chicago: Scott, Foresman and Co., 1948.

  A worth-while book for all teachers and prospective teachers interested in contributing to the social education of students.

5. SMITH, B. O., STANLEY, W. O., AND SHORES, J. H. *Fundamentals of Curriculum Development.* Yonkers, New York: World Book Co., 1950.

  Pages 376-531 give a clear and comprehensive analysis of the chief characteristics, problems, practices, and criticisms of the subject curriculum, the activity curriculum, and the core curriculum.

6. STILES, L. J., AND DORSEY, M. F. *Democratic Teaching.* Philadelphia: J. B. Lippincott Co., 1950.

  Pages 15-109 and 235-554 suggest ways of developing democratic teaching procedures in secondary schools.

7. THUT, I. N., AND GERBERICH, J. R. *Foundations of Method for Secondary Schools.* New York: McGraw-Hill Book Co., Inc., 1949.

  Particularly useful in describing (1) daily-assignment method, (2) subject-matter unit method, and (3) experience unit method.

8. UMSTATTD, J. G. *Secondary School Teaching.* New York: Ginn and Co., 1944.

  Has useful discussions of pre-instructional problems, classroom procedures, associated activities of the teacher, and the unit idea. The unit idea is considered as most significant content and method approach.

14

PROCESS-RELATED PROBLEMS

Problems to consider

What is desirable discipline and how can it be developed?

How can we develop favorable attitudes and appreciations?

What cautions need to be observed in interpreting standard test results?

What are the possible uses and dangers of marking?

What difficulties confront the teacher who attempts to improve class interpersonal relations?

This chapter will consider five types of problems related to teaching-learning processes. The discussion is not intended to give either an exhaustive list of problems or all the possible approaches to the five selected. Rather, it is intended to reveal the range of problems the teacher faces and to suggest some sample ways of approaching them.

DISCIPLINE

What is discipline? In a very real sense everything that has been written in this book so far has been related to problems of discipline. A situation in which we have good discipline is one in which we have a set of conditions where desirable learning and development will take place for the individual learner. Promoting good discipline, in effect then, becomes a matter of promoting desirable teaching-learning situations.

The definition that has been given in the preceding paragraph differs radically, of course, from that which is commonly thought of by many parents and teachers. Unfortunately, to some parents and teachers, discipline is regarded simply as obedience to authority. A well-disciplined child is one who is docile, who does not question what the teacher or textbook says, and who follows all directions without question. Such a concept of discipline assumes an autocratic, authoritarian philosophy of education. Under this setup the job of the learner who is well disciplined is to follow the teacher's plan or course of study closely, to do what he is told down to minor particulars, and to give strict adherence to rules that have been laid down by someone else. This particular concept of discipline ties up closely with the subject-matter-oriented methods that have been discussed in the preceding chapter.

The modern concept of discipline regards it as a problem of growth from great dependence on the part of the learner to a learning situation where the student assumes the responsibility for getting and keeping his learning going. One aspect of the teacher's role under this concept of discipline is to help children get practice in self-control and to develop standards of individual values and activities that will be carried on regardless of whether the teacher or parent or someone else in authority happens to be around or not. The best way to get good discipline is probably to study all of the complex ramifications involved in promoting an effective teaching-learning situation.

How can desirable discipline be promoted? As has been suggested above the problem of developing desirable discipline is an extremely complex one and at this point we will only attempt to emphasize a few of the key aspects of good discipline. In general, the long-time goal of the teacher who is attempting to promote situations with desirable discipline potential is to build up an optimum degree of self-confidence and self-control in the learner. This means that the teacher is as much if not more concerned about the shy, timid, or dreamy child as he is about the aggressive child who tends to irritate him.

In considering discipline the teacher must remember that he is constantly faced with two behavior problems. One is the problem of what to do to take care of the immediate situation—this is the one to which the teacher typically gives relative overemphasis. The other problem is that of visualizing the long-time behavior patterns that the teacher is trying to develop in the learner. The learner must also be helped to recognize long-time needs and goals and also visualize the behaviors that are likely to help him achieve these goals. In other words, the teacher and the learner must both attempt not only to plan present behavior to meet day-to-day situations, but must also have a vision of the goals of his behavior in the future that will be most satisfactory. Teachers must help learners practice seeing both immediate and remote consequences, particularly the latter since these are more difficult to see.

It is also extremely important that both the teacher and the learner recognize that at any particular time multiple learnings are being practiced by the learner. For example, if the teacher assigns a certain number of pages for the student to study for the next class period, it is dangerous for the teacher to attempt to evaluate the behavior resulting from that assignment simply in terms of the amount of information the learner has apparently acquired from it. It is critically important, too, that the teacher and learner also attempt to assess the attitudinal changes and the internal long-time effects on learning that the particular situation has produced. In this particular situation the amount of subject matter learned may be regarded as a distinct asset. However, when we consider the number of liabilities also learned, which are related to the development of dependency and undesirable attitudes toward school, we may find that the net balance on the learning ledger is in the red column. This is frequently true of required literature reading and other required reading and study where the learner sees no particular purpose for doing the study except that the teacher has assigned it and, in order to keep out of trouble, he feels he is required to do what the teacher has told him to do.

It is well to keep in mind, too, that there is no specific formula for good discipline, just as there is no specific formula for good teaching. What is good procedure in one situation in one school might be extremely poor procedure in another situation in another classroom or school. The basic rules for developing desirable teaching-learning situations, which have already been indicated to some degree at the end of Chapters 3 through 12, tend to apply in general in all classes. However, it must be kept in mind that the teacher must consider each situation as a novel one and attempt to adjust to it with the help of the learners in the way that seems most feasible under the particular set of circumstances involved. It is desirable that the teacher attempt to foster the idea that the class is "our class," rather than the teacher's class. Shared experiences and cooperative planning will tend to promote this desirable attitude toward the classroom situation.

DEVELOPING FAVORABLE ATTITUDES AND APPRECIATIONS

In a very real sense what has already been written bears directly or indirectly upon attitudes and appreciations. All learning processes of the type so far discussed are accompanied by the development of favorable or unfavorable attitudes. Necessary for real appreciation of science, or art, or music, or reading, is a favorable attitude toward doing the processes associated with the subject. A student may know much poetry and hate poetry. Having learners share fundamentally in the development of course activities is one of the best ways of encouraging desirable attitudes toward that course and its learnings.

Attitudes and appreciations can be, in fact are, taught in all courses. Frequently the teacher is unconcerned or unaware of what kinds are developing.

To illustrate more specifically how a teacher may go about developing favorable attitudes and appreciations we will use reading, a skill that is used, or could be used, in most if not all subjects. To differentiate this from "work-type" reading we have called it free reading, the primary purpose of which is to develop desirable attitudes and appreciations toward the process. Similar approaches can be used in other processes if the teacher will adopt the suggestions.

In most schools and in most courses the vast potentialities of a free-reading program for developing desirable attitudes and appreciations are largely unrealized at the present time. This section will attempt to help the teacher, prospective teacher, administrator, or supervisor (1) to understand better the purposes, uses, and values of free reading, (2) to see more clearly what the teacher needs to do in preparing for a free-reading program if favorable attitudes and appreciations are to be developed, (3) to identify some of the methods of procuring appropriate resources, without undue expense to teachers, learners, or the school system, (4) to visualize some of the methods that may effectively be used in promoting the free-reading program, (5) to consider some of the records that should be kept in a free-reading program, and (6) to appreciate some of the ways a free-reading program may be used in effective evaluation.

Purposes and uses of free reading

One might appropriately say that the well-read man is one who has learned how to read effectively on his own initiative. Such a person must have developed desirable attitudes and appreciations. This implies what is, perhaps, the basic purpose of most free-reading programs: to help the learner assume a constantly increasing amount of initiative in getting and using reading materials that are appropriate to his interests and needs. Many students, if put in close proximity with suitable materials, will develop excellent reading tastes on their own, and undesirable attitudes built up toward reading through inefficient teaching practices can frequently be eliminated through placing appropriate materials in the classroom.

One of the most desirable trends in modern education is the emphasis on education of a continuing sort. A good free-reading program provides a means by which the alert teacher can develop growing independence in reading and the gradual assumption of a greater degree of responsibility on the part of the learner. Free-reading programs can well develop what may be called "self-starter" education, which continues to operate after the person has left school and the teacher is no longer at hand to initiate the learning.

Individual differences in interests, needs, and abilities have long been known by most teachers. How to provide for them in mass education, however, still remains much of a mystery to most of the teaching profession. The flexibility that can easily characterize a free-reading program provides opportunity for the English, social-science, or science teacher in the high school, as well as for teachers in other fields, to break away gradually from the lock step of using the same materials and methods with every pupil in a class, regardless of varying needs, abilities, and interests. Although the teacher may find it necessary to start at a relatively low level with certain readers, the free-reading program, because of its elasticity, provides an excellent means through which the tastes and attitudes of each learner can be gradually raised.

Urges and motives that sometimes lead to undesirable behavior traits can frequently be sublimated through the free-reading program, which provides a vicarious social outlet and a temporary escape from what may seem to be, from the standpoint of the learner, almost unbearable home conditions or an intolerable school situation. Of course, too much escaping is dangerous, but a certain amount, which can be procured through reading, is a good safety valve for many youngsters.

Another major, but still largely unexplored, possibility in a free-reading program is its use as an evaluative approach. The program can be of great help to the teacher through providing a functional index of ability. What the learner actually reads when he is largely on his own and when a great variety of reading material is provided is one of the best indications of his actual reading level. This evaluation may be facilitated if the teacher will learn the approximate difficulty level and the interest level of each book that is used in the free-reading program. The activities practiced indicate the level of functional appreciation at which the learner is operating.

By keeping a record of what is read and who reads it, the alert teacher can make an excellent appraisal of the types of materials that are most needed. When the opportunity for obtaining additional materials is presented, either through purchase or through tapping sources of reading materials already available in the community, the teacher can see that appropriate and useful books are acquired.

Under a free-reading setup, the quality and amount of reading, or even the lack of quality and amount of reading, will usually be a good index of the effectiveness or the lack of effectiveness of the reading instruction that has been given to the child in the past. If little free reading is done when the chance is given, all members of the school staff should take warning that something is seriously amiss. If a student knows how to read but does not use his skill because of the development of poor attitudes, his skill is of little value. The quality, quantity, and variety of materials that are actually read by a youngster without coercion are good indications of the basic effectiveness of his past reading training.

Teachers who use standardized objective tests can determine the age-difficulty level and age-interest level of most of the available materials. The average age-difficulty level may be determined by figuring the average reading age of the pupils who actually like a particular book or magazine over a period of time. An index of age-interest level is obtained in a similar fashion, by determining the average chronological age of those pupils who like the particular book or magazine that is under consideration. For example, the average reading age of pupils who like a book or magazine may be 12.5, while the average chronological age of the group may be 14.0.

The Preparation of the teacher

The intelligent teacher is, of course, concerned with the types of approaches that he should consider adopting in order to promote an effective free-reading program. The following paragraphs suggest some of these approaches, which have been effective in developing desirable attitudes and appreciations.

Approaches concerned with purposes and goals. The possible purposes and goals a learner may have in reading should be thoroughly studied by the teacher. For example, it is desirable to have a clear understanding of the fundamental difference between reading primarily for pleasure and reading primarily to get the answer to a problem or question. The former type of reading is recreational in nature, and the major consideration is the degree to which the reader enjoys the process of reading. In problem, or work-type, reading, the primary consideration is whether the end result of the reading is satisfactory. Closely related to a study of differences in the purposes of reading is an analysis of the possible motives and interests of the pupils and a familiarity with the ways and means of discovering individual interests and motives. Consideration should be given to the advisability of using some of the interest questionnaires and inventories now available, for means of discovering the mainsprings of action in each learner are basic to understanding him and his reading needs.

Careful consideration should be given also to ways of determining reasonable goals to be set up with the learner. Determining the goals will frequently involve planning how to check the reading level of the learner and also how to obtain some indication of the breadth or lack of breadth of his reading activities. Reasonable goals, involving improvement of both quantity and quality of reading, can best be set up if the teacher has planned for this activity beforehand.

In setting up reasonable reading goals, the teacher must remember that the child should always start at the reading, and interest, level at which he is likely to have some measure of success, regardless of how low that level is. With some learners this may mean starting almost exclusively with picture magazines and books.

A major goal of both teachers and learners should be to develop democratic methods of planning, working, and learning during the free-reading period. Democratic development of the program is fundamental to its efficient operation.

Another goal of the alert teacher is to examine his own free-reading activities to discover whether any changes in the type or range of his own reading should be made. The good teacher believes enough in what he is teaching to practice it himself. Attitudes and appreciations tend to be reflected in practice.

A reasonable and generally desirable goal of the teacher is to try to draw other teachers into the program through soliciting their advice and help. Any free-reading program is likely to be more successful if everyone who works with the learners is familiar with what is being attempted. Frequently, it is also possible to have several teachers, or even the whole teaching staff, develop the free-reading program on a cooperative basis. Librarians, administrators, and parents can often be of great assistance in such a program.

Approaches concerned with resources. Helping students learn how to get and to enjoy appropriate reading materials is a key factor in an effective free-reading program. Accomplishing this goal will generally involve a large amount of planning by the teacher before the class gathers for its first session. Several types of activities have been found helpful in planning for a free-reading program.

It is usually desirable for the teacher to familiarize himself with the grade levels of all available materials. Listing these resources, together with the average reading level to which each item is likely to have most appeal, is frequently a helpful approach. A comprehensive list should include the appropriate materials that are accessible in public libraries.

The high-school teacher should be willing to read many samples of books liked by high-school students, for if the teacher believes that it is beneath his dignity to sample learners' books, his students are not likely to read many of the books the teacher selects. Closely tied up with this willingness should be the ability to determine, with considerable accuracy, the reading difficulty level and maturity interest level of each book that is sampled. This evaluation should be noted for future classroom use.

Standard lists, which group books according to age level (or maturity level) and difficulty level, should be freely utilized by the teacher. These lists, together with the sampling suggested in the preceding paragraph, should help the teacher gather as good a supply of reading materials as time and the financial resources of the school will permit before the class first meets. Reading materials brought by the learners themselves should be continuously added to those already assembled.

If a choice of rooms is possible, the teacher should try to get a room with a good physical setup. The room should have many shelves, a blackboard, adequate lighting, and tables and chairs rather than rows of seats and desks. It should be relatively quiet, and the atmosphere should be informal.

Preparation concerned with methods. While an essential feature of an effective free-reading program is the large share that learners have in carrying it on, there still remains much planning that the wise teacher will do before the program is launched.

In the preplanning, the teacher will devise ways of developing democratic participation in the activities that are tied up with the free reading. It is not enough for a teacher to resolve to be democratic in his methods. Plans must be laid for developing in the learners such abilities as selecting interesting books, ordering reading materials, planning a balance of individual and group activities, deciding what records should be kept, and evaluating wisely the worth of various individual or group reading activities.

Since diagnosis of individuals in any group for teaching-learning purposes is important, the teacher should plan means by which each learner will be able to study himself and by which the teacher can get to know the children with whom he is to work. This will involve becoming familiar with tests, questionnaires, and inventories that can help in a study of the social, emotional, mental, and reading differences of individual pupils. Also, since interests are of paramount importance in developing desirable attitudes and appreciations in a free-reading program, the teacher may well make a study of the ways of measuring and developing interests.

Closely related to the need for diagnostic plans is the need for plans for evaluation. The teacher should make definite plans for helping each learner continuously to evaluate his progress under a reading program. The teacher will, of course, participate in the evaluation, which will involve such aspects as seeing whether the interests of the reader expand, whether interests improve in quality, and whether the student, of his own accord, reads more books of better quality. The teacher will do well to remember that the primary success of a reading program and all attitude and apprecia-tional programs is contained in the answer to the question: What does the student do in his spare time while away from the direct guidance of the school?

Another phase of the program is tied up with questions concerned with keeping records of the reading activities. Examples are: What types of records should the students be encouraged to keep? How should the problem be presented to the learners? What record of plans, procedures, information about learners, and other data would it be desirable for the teacher to keep? Generally speaking, the records kept by the learner should be brief but specific enough to give him a picture of what he has read and some concise evaluation of his reaction to various parts.

Collecting materials for a free-reading program

An effective free-reading program or other attitude or apprecia-tional program on any level or in any subject demands the gathering of a wealth of reading materials on a great variety of subjects and of many difficulty levels. This is the only way that individual differ-ences in abilities, interests, and needs can be met. For this reason, the problem of how to collect a sufficient supply of reading materials is important.

Enlisting cooperation of learners. A most important consideration in developing any free-reading program is enlisting the cooperation of the learners in selecting and obtaining materials. This procedure produces results in terms of additional materials for the classroom library and gives the learners much-needed practice and experience in locating resources—a skill that will prove invaluable after they leave school. Learners may be encouraged to select books and magazines through the use of annotated bibliographies.

Lists of free or inexpensive materials can be furnished to the students with the suggestion that each write for at least one type of material that looks interesting and valuable to him. Not only is this a worth-while experiment in the acquisition of resources, but it can, in many cases, be justified on the basis of functional letter-writing alone. When the materials arrive, the teacher can give the learners guided practice in evaluating the resources. Another letter-writing experience of worth is to have the learners who are mem-bers of the resource committee write to publishers, describing the types of materials for which the class is looking.

Students may frequently be encouraged to bring books from

home to share with other pupils. This exchange brings a greater variety of books into the classroom and may develop the desire to build up home libraries. Day-old newspapers brought from home into the classroom each day will frequently be of value, particularly to those pupils who see only one newspaper each day, or perhaps none at all.

In many schools in which the student buys or rents his books, a procedure can be set up that is less expensive than most present systems and also provides much greater variety of reading resources. For example, in an English class of thirty-five students in which each student is expected to buy or rent the same textbook or set of textbooks at a yearly cost of $1.50, each student can pay $1.25 into a pool from which the class, with the guidance of the teacher, acquires needed materials. In this arrangement every learner will not ordinarily get the same materials as every other learner. Rather, not more than four or five copies of any single book or magazine will be purchased by a particular class. The rest of the money will be spent on other books, magazines, newspapers, pamphlets, and even tests if they are needed. Variety in interest and difficulty level will be a major goal. The process of selecting, obtaining, classifying, and using the variety of material that can thus be procured can become an excellent learning experience. In using the money, the class should consider the possibility of purchasing many ten- and twenty-five-cent books rather than a few more expensive books. Buying from secondhand bookstores should be considered. The learners themselves should have a major share in starting or developing a good classroom library for free reading. (See Chapter 10 on getting, selecting, and using resources effectively for additional ideas.)

Pupils can frequently help the teacher build up a good variety of picture material. Picture-reading is an enjoyable experience to many children and will often lead to other types of reading. Those pictures that seem likely to be of most interest should probably be mounted.

Utilizing clubs and other organizations in the community. In most communities the members of civic clubs or other organizations are glad to help or sponsor worth-while projects. If the learners and teachers request an opportunity to explain to these organizations the need for more materials, the presentation of the problem will sometimes bring assistance in building up classroom libraries. In some communities the parent-teachers' association has taken this as a special project.

Some teachers maintain that it is impossible to get a sufficient variety of appropriate reading materials without added money outlay, but this assertion is often more of an alibi than a real reason for the lack of materials in the classroom. Experience has shown that, in practically every American community, a wealth of usable reading materials is to be found in old magazines in attics or storerooms. An alert teacher and his students can (1) prepare a list of appropriate magazines, such as *Life* and the *National Geographic Magazine;* (2) make a systematic collection of old copies; (3) cull the material, selecting only what seems to be of value and interest to the students in the grade level concerned; (4) classify according to subject; and (5) label and file the materials for future use. After the teacher has promoted a project like this for a few years, the problem will not be one of having insufficient material but rather one of finding a place for all the useful reading resources that have been gathered.

In some communities chambers of commerce are good sources for certain types of maps and descriptive materials. Sometimes they can also give information on sources of other useful reading matter.

Another procedure that works well in certain situations is for the teacher periodically to borrow groups of books from the public library for a certain length of time and to place them in the classroom. It may be argued that these books could just as well be used at the public library or drawn from the library by the students. While this statement is true, the books are much more likely to be read if they are available in the classroom.

Encouraging parents to give magazine subscriptions or books to their children as Christmas or birthday presents will help form a sound basis for favorable attitudes and appreciations. A good method of encouraging parents to do this is to send home lists of books or magazines that would be appropriate for specified age groups. These lists are of definite help to parents who would like to give their children useful gifts but who do not know what to get. It is well to be sure that the reading-difficulty level of the books or magazines on the list is low for the age group concerned.

Working with other educators. Lists of books compiled by educational experts can often be helpful in deciding what resources to acquire. For example, a list like Slater's [1] will aid the teacher who has difficulty with slow learners.

In many schools much can be done by an active teacher to help administrators and teachers see the inadvisability of following the policy of forcing each learner at any particular grade level to get and use the same books and magazines as every other student on the same grade level. The nature of individual differences, which has been demonstrated by psychologists, makes this practice unsound, but it still persists in too many schools.

Teachers can frequently encourage the promotion of a free-reading program through exchanging books and various reading resources with other teachers. The aid of these teachers and of their students can be solicited in discovering magazine and newspaper resources in the community. Thus, the other teachers are encouraged to talk about what is being done, and desirable changes may be produced in these teachers themselves.

Use of free-reading time

Location and place of use of reading resources. Experience has shown that there are great advantages to building up a comprehensive assortment of easily available reading materials. Having the resources close at hand tends to promote reading in the classroom and also the reading of more books in the central library. Appropriate reading in the classroom begets reading elsewhere.

Book jackets and other advertising materials put out by book companies may often be used to arouse interest. A classroom bulletin board that displays materials of this kind, plus student-drawn posters and cartoons depicting interesting scenes from books or magazines, will tend to develop wider reading interest.

Ordinarily the class will have a system by means of which the resources from the classroom library can be taken out overnight or longer. Those persons who are allowed to draw out the materials need not be restricted to students in the immediate classroom.

Procedures in working with individuals and groups. What procedures should be used in developing an effective free-reading program? This question is of primary concern to the classroom teacher. The program should be geared to developing democratic

[1] Russell Slater, *Books for Youth Who Dislike Reading,* Ohio Conference on Reading, Bulletin No. 2 (Columbus, Ohio: Ohio State University Press, 1941).

procedures, the students being trained to take more and more responsibility. Direct assignments are to be avoided in an appreciation and attitude developing program, particularly after it gets under way. It should be developed as a class program, not a teacher program.

The program may start with the students reading largely what they like to read. This method gives the teacher a picture of the functional reading level of each learner. As the reading plans develop for each individual, the teacher should attempt to give guidance, so that the variety of materials enjoyed may increase and the quality of what is enjoyed may improve. Since the teacher knows the reading level and tastes of each learner, he should be in a position to suggest at any time a piece of reading that any particular student will be likely to enjoy.

A free-reading program can, and should, be largely a creation of the learners themselves. Placing a student in charge of checking books, magazines, and newspapers in and out will help. This position can become one of honor, which is rotated among the students so that many of them will have the educational experience of doing this type of work. Enlisting the support of learners in drawing up a list of books and magazines that are suitable for Christmas and birthday presents and permitting the students to distribute the list will frequently encourage desirable reactions.

Occasional discussions held in large or small groups, or presentations on topics such as the following, will be helpful: "Things I Have Read and Liked, with Reasons," "The Field of Reading I Enjoy Most," "Dramatizing a Scene I Have Read," " 'Teaser' Report on a Book I Have Read and Liked." The effectiveness of the last type of report can be measured partially by the speaker's keeping a check on how many students read the book as a result of his "teaser" report. "Sales" talks for books constitute another avenue for arousing interest in reading. Allowing a student to tell part of a story in an attempt to influence his listeners to read the rest of it will often produce good results. Opportunity for oral reading of poetry is sometimes desirable.

Puppet shows frequently encourage free reading in the field of drama. Reading may also be tied up with, and develop from, seeing current movies. The scheduling of the latter often can be determined in advance by telephoning the local theater managers. For pupils who do not seem to be able to get interested in books, it may be advisable at first to encourage the use of magazines and newspapers almost exclusively. At times, painting, construction, etc., can be tied up with the other activities of the free-reading period.

The wise teacher will, of course, encourage many individual conferences to give the student an opportunity to talk over his likes, dislikes, plans, and problems. In these conferences the teacher can give guidance toward broader and deeper appreciation of the pleasure of reading.

Records to be kept

The student should be encouraged to keep a record of what he has read. A record of this kind will not only give him encouragement and a feeling of growth but will also serve as a basis for evaluation by the learner himself and by the teacher. Care should be taken, however, not to make the keeping of records so time-consuming that the student comes to dislike the process.

Sometimes it is worth while to have a sheet in the back of each book or magazine on which each person who uses it indicates his reaction to it in a sentence or two. This may motivate more reading and gives the prospective reader a picture of how other readers have felt about what he is considering reading.

The making of an appropriate book cover by the first reader can sometimes be used as a desirable type of motivation.

Some classes have found that using a large chart on which the name of each student appears is helpful. Under each name is placed a pocket in which that particular student places a record of the reading he has done since the previous summer.

It is well for the teacher also to keep some record of the leisure-time reading of each student. This type of record is more valuable if a brief indication of the reaction of the reader to each piece of material that he has read is also recorded. Sometimes a teacher's record of his own leisure-time reading serves as a stimulus both for him and for his students.

Effective evaluation

A free-reading program that is properly operated has several definite advantages from the standpoint of evaluation. At the present time, most teacher evaluation of reading is based either on assigned reading or on formal reading tests in a rather artificial setting. Evaluation in a free-reading situation can discover the intrinsic motivations for reading, the basic attitudes and appreciations that are operating.

Evaluation and functional use of reading. What the student does in a free-reading period, with a minimum of assignment or supervision, constitutes one of the finest means of evaluating the recreational-reading program of a school because it is an index of the probable carry-over value of formal reading instruction to out-of-school activities. Most schools and most teachers have been much more conscious of the problem of teaching the child how to read than they have been of the problem of teaching the student to want to read in recreational and problem-solving situations.

The kind of reading a student does in his free time is a good index of his self-motivated reading level. This reading level may be examined from the standpoint of sheer quantity—how much does he read? It may also be considered from the standpoint of types of reading done—does he read for many different purposes? It may be judged from the standpoint of difficulty of what is actually read—what is the top difficulty level and the average difficulty level of the free reading? Again, the reading may be analyzed with regard to the diversity of subjects used for enjoyment or other functional purposes—what is the variety of the reading? Attitudes toward reading can be examined in a fairly true-to-life situation—do attitudes reflect a general like or dislike for reading? Making a single estimate in each of these areas is of value; periodic checks on the same factors give a basis for estimating progress or lack of progress in reading uses. These areas are a few in which free reading can give a realistic setting for evaluative purposes.

Ability to select and obtain type of reading materials needed. In many of our classes, the selection and acquisition of reading materials usually have been functions over which the teacher, or at least someone besides the learner, has had a virtual monopoly. This method has had the unfortunate effect of producing school graduates who have had little or no practice or facility in selecting and obtaining reading materials on their own. The learner has been trained to depend on the teacher or on someone else to procure materials for him. A free-reading program tends to expose the weakness of this current practice to both teacher and student. Thus a good groundwork can be laid for helping the student see the necessity for him to develop abilities in selection and acquisition if he is to be able to procure and use reading materials appropriately when he leaves school.

Free reading and self-evaluation. A good reader, for most purposes, is a critical reader. The critical reader has the ability to evaluate his own reading skills and actual practices in a realistic situation. The free-reading program helps the student to appreciate this need and provides for him many and varied opportunities to practice self-evaluation related to reading.

For example, the teacher can encourage the student to give a brief evaluation of the apparent worth to him of each thing he reads, to ask, "Was my time well spent in doing this reading? Why?" The learner can keep a record showing what he has read, when he read it, and what his reaction was to it. After a period of time he can go back over his record and, with some guidance, determine what changes have taken place in his reading, by asking: "Did I develop new interests? Did my reading become more varied? Does my reading show a good balance between reading done for recreation and reading done to help me solve personal or probable occupational problems?"

Appreciation depends basically upon developing understanding and liking for the reading of science or literature, for painting, for music, or for whatever channel or means of communication is being used. Unless liking and favorable attitudes are developed toward the reading, painting, music, or other art the dynamic aspect of appreciation is missing.

THE CRITICAL INTERPRETATION OF STANDARD TEST RESULTS [2]

The skill of many teachers and administrators has been woefully weak in properly interpreting standardized test results. In most cases this has not been due to a lack of potential ability on the part of the educators but rather to a lack of appropriate preservice and in-service training in an understanding of the possible values and limitations of various types of tests. Largely because of this lack of

[2] A discussion of the type conventionally given in tests and measurements books has been consciously omitted here. For such material the reader is referred to H. H. Remmers and N. L. Gage, *Educational Measurement and Evaluation* (New York: Harper and Bros., 1943); H. A. Green and others, *Measurement and Evaluation in the Secondary School* (New York: Longmans, Green and Co., Inc., 1953); W. J. Micheels and M. Ray Karnes, *Measuring Educational Achievement* (New York: McGraw-Hill Book Co., Inc., 1950).

understanding, some educators have attributed too much importance to particular test results while others, disillusioned, have said in effect: Away with all standardized tests.

Where teachers and administrators use or plan to use standardized tests, it is important that care be taken in interpreting results. In the two chapters on evaluation some limitations of testing "assigned" to the learner have been noted. In the following paragraphs some additional cautions are indicated.

Some time ago the writer came in contact with a situation that illustrates the points that have just been made. The facts in the case are essentially as given below, disguised only enough so that the school system itself cannot be readily identified; they are followed by questions and comments that are designed to be thought-provoking.

A large school system gave a comprehensive standardized achievement test to all of its seventh-grade pupils and found that the median score of those taking the test was 9.2 or 1.5 grades above the median score of 7.7 of the groups on which the test was standardized. Self-satisfaction verging on smugness was the typical reaction of the teachers and administrators in the system.

It is quite possible that a very superior type of work is being done in this school system, *but* before this could be known with any great degree of certainty, we would need some additional information. The questions and comments given below suggest some of the areas that the thoughtful teacher and administrator should investigate and consider before drawing his conclusions about the effectiveness of a school system similar to the one used as an illustration.

What is the retention policy in the school? It is quite possible for a school system that is doing a relatively poor job to reach or even to exceed the test results of the school system under consideration by having a rigid policy of promotion. For example, the writer is familiar with a school system that takes great pride in its "standards." With very few exceptions, no learner is promoted until he has reached the "norm" score for his grade on the standardized achievement test, which is used as a primary basis for promotion. This means that a child in the fifth grade is not promoted to the sixth grade until he can make a score equivalent to 5.9 on the test. This policy has resulted in excessive retardation with about 50 per cent of the seventh-grade pupils retarded at least one year. Obviously, a comparison of the median score of this group with the group on which

the norms of the test were based is unsound. With excessive retention in grades even an inefficient school system may seem to have a
good seventh grade if only grade norms are considered.

How much elimination is there in the school system before the
seventh grade is reached? Some schools have a deliberate policy of
"weeding out" the weakest members of a particular age group; other
schools just fall into the habit. Consider each of two schools that
started out with 200 pupils entering the first grade. In school A
only 60 per cent, or 120 pupils, ever reached the seventh grade—
the others were eliminated in one way or another. In school B 95
per cent, or 190 pupils, entered the seventh grade. Since it usually
is the weaker learners who are eliminated in a school such as A,
it is obvious that school B with a lower median score than A might
still be doing a much better job of educating the children in its
community. The holding power of a school needs to be carefully
considered in interpreting test results. The twin evils of excessive elimination and excessive average retention-in-grade demand
thoughtful consideration and test makers and publishers should be
encouraged to give figures indicating the extent of the elimination
and more-than-one-year-retention-in-grade in the schools on which
the norms are based.

Did the teachers teach the test directly or indirectly? It may seem
undignified even to suggest that such an unprofessional practice
might be carried on. But in certain school systems the practice *is*
carried on by some teachers, and those who are trying to interpret
test results need to be aware of this possibility. Of course any time
a group of learners is taught a test the use of norms accompanying
the test becomes meaningless. Unfortunately some administrators
and supervisors have unwittingly encouraged this practice, partially
through a procedure suggested by the next question.

Are teachers given raises or promotions on the basis of test results?
Some superintendents, principals, and supervisors, casting about for
an objective basis for giving promotions in rank or salary increases,
have settled on the idea of giving these rewards to those who can
produce the best test results. The goal is admirable but this particular method has resulted in many unprofessional practices and generally should be eliminated in any place it exists.

Is the primary goal of the teachers to help the learners or to get
good test results? In some school systems it is unfortunately true
that in the struggle to have "my class" come out on top the teacher

has almost forgotten the primary purpose of education, to help the learner. In these schools test results have tended to become an end in themselves. When this occurs, "good" test results may be accompanied by poor education.

Has teacher emphasis been on improving the test results of those just below the median even at the expense of the highest and lowest learners? This question is closely related to the preceding ones. If a teacher knows that her group and her teaching are likely to be evaluated on the score of the middle learner (median score) of her group, she may gear her teaching to the level of the middle third of the group, feeling that the highest third will get fairly good scores anyhow and that the lowest third or at least the lowest fifth does not have much chance of bringing up the median score anyway. Those who are familiar with the percentile system can investigate this possibility by seeing how the 10th, 25th, and 90th percentiles of the group compare with the norms for each of these levels.

What is the length of the school term in the system under consideration as compared with the lengths of school terms of the schools on which the norms were based? What would a similar comparison of the annual amount spent per child show? The time spent with the child and the wherewithal for educating him should be considered in evaluating and interpreting the test results.

How many years has the test or another form of it been given in the school? Undue familiarity with a particular test will tend to produce artificially high results on that test. For example, the writer is familiar with a school which twice a year has used some form of the same test for five years. This means that most of the seventh graders in that school have had ten very similar tests and some repeats on the same test. Too great familiarity with a test will indicate the need for using a different test.

Are test results in certain learnings being achieved at the expense of other equally important learnings? The basic importance of this point cannot be overemphasized. The writer has known schools where it appeared that the teaching was so slanted by the standardized tests to be given that many learnings considered at least equally important by outstanding educators were at best neglected. In some schools it even appeared that some desirable attitudes and practices the learners already had were being eliminated to a significant degree. For this reason it is very significant for the interpreter of test results to consider the probable effect of the type of training being used on attitudes toward: acquiring more learning, teachers in general, schools, testing itself, specific subjects, such as art, music, speech. We would also need to consider whether the learner is developing the ability to use the learnings being acquired in practical situations. Is training being given so that there is likely to be much carry-over to out-of-school situations?

What effect is the method of teaching having on self-adjustment and social adjustment? This question is closely related to the preceding one, but it is so important that it is given separate consideration. What does it profit a school to overemphasize to students information that enables them to pass an achievement test if thereby the chances of a high degree of self- and social adjustment are decreased? Certainly interpretation of achievement test results should not neglect a consideration of learner adjustment. Personality or adjustment inventories or questionnaires, if properly approached by teachers and learners, will usually give some clues to the extent of maladjustment.

What are the primary motivators of the learners? Are secondary motivators and even undesirable motivators being used to a large degree? Threats, fear of punishment, marks, extrinsic rewards, and the like can produce what seem to be fairly good temporary results, but the net result is likely to be undesirable in the long run. To what extent is learning likely to go on without the immediate stimulation of the teacher? Are the learners being pushed too much for their own good? Is the motivation for the learning coming largely from inside of the learner or from the outside?

To what extent is it likely that good home teaching and much travel and other educational influences outside the control of the school have contributed to the high median score on the tests? Some schools take credit for doing a lot more than they are responsible for, particularly if it is something worth-while. Schools with learners coming from homes with good "educational opportunities" should give the home credit for many learnings that the pupils demonstrate.

What is tested by the test? What are the goals of a "good" school? How many goals of a "good" school are tested by the test in question? These questions are fairly self-explanatory. For example, does the test sample application as well as memorization? Does it contain many items that can be answered by intelligence alone? On what basis has the test been validated? What other tests are available for checking on other important goals of a "good" school?

Was the test given and scored in a standardized fashion? It has been found in some schools that "standardized" tests are given in a very unstandardized fashion either through lack of knowledge of good testing procedures or because the person giving or scoring the test has something to gain or to lose by good or poor performance showing up on the test. If lack of knowledge of good testing procedures is the difficulty, training in this is, of course, indicated. If tests are intentionally given or scored in an unstandardized fashion, then the reasons for having the whole testing program need to be carefully examined.

What is the potential ability of the learners as compared with those upon whom the tests were standardized? While this probably cannot be determined exactly, some clues to the answer can be obtained through the use of a good intelligence or mental test. The occupational level of the parents will frequently give a very rough indication of the answer also.

What are the actual living conditions in the community? Is the school teaching the things that are most needed in this community? These questions are ultimately the most important ones of all that have been raised. No school should be self-satisfied unless satisfactory answers can be given to the following questions suggested in part by Thorndike's *American Cities and States.*[3] What is the infant death rate? What is the general death rate? What is the per capita expenditure for recreation? How rare is poverty in the community? What is the excess of physicians, nurses, and teachers over male domestic servants? What is the per capita circulation of the better magazines in the community? What is the average real wage in the community? To use Thorndike's phraseology, what is "the general goodness of life for good people in the community in question, the per capita income of its residents, and their personal qualities of intelligence, morality and care for their families?"

[3] Thorndike, Edward L., *American Cities and States: Variation and Correlation in Institutions, Activities, and the Personal Qualities of the Residents* (New York: The New York Academy of Science, 1939).

MARKING—USES AND DANGERS

In most teaching-learning situations marking is an established part of the educational setup. Whether they like it or not most teachers must live with a marking system and make the best possible use of it until it can be modified or eliminated in favor of other procedures. This typically means that the teacher and learners must attempt to capitalize on the potential values of marks and to be aware of the potential difficulties and dangers inherent in most marking systems.

In the remainder of this section on marking we will attempt (1) to point out some legitimate purposes of marking and show how these purposes may be achieved, and (2) to emphasize some possible dangers to be avoided in the use of marks.

Purposes of marks

A first major use that can be made of marks is *to point up teaching and learning goals.* One of the major weaknesses of many teaching-learning situations is that the specific goals and purposes of the work are not clearly identified in the minds of the learners and sometimes even in the mind of the individual teacher. Working cooperatively with the learners, the teacher can help them set up both individual and group goals. Actually, of course, group goals are individual goals that are common to several members of a class. If this approach is used, the learners will understand the goals better and will also strive harder to achieve them, since the goals themselves are or have become to a greater degree a part of the learner's self. Social and emotional goals such as citizenship should preferably be stated in behavioral terms. This is also true of most other types of goals. In general, such phrases as "teaching international understanding" and "teaching appreciation" must be spelled out in specific terms in order that the teacher and the learner may actually visualize what the goal is.

A second major goal is *to provide desirable motivation* on the part of the learner. In a sense, one aspect of this was discussed in a preceding paragraph, namely, the setting up of specific goals and purposes that represent the tangible aims of the work in a teaching-learning situation. In general, punishment or the fear of failure is a relatively low-level motivator and should be avoided. Threat of failure seems to have little or no significant and desirable effect on educational growth. If weaknesses are pointed out, actual and specific ways of going about eliminating them should be designated.

It is unfortunate that marks have become primary motivators and frequently these extrinsic motivators have been substituted for a basic understanding of the goals of the work while the work is being carried on. It is also unfortunate, but sometimes true, that in some respects marks have been used by teachers to avoid facing adequately those basic motivational teaching problems that are involved in assignment-making, the getting and using of resources, and planning class procedures.

If marks are to be given, we must try to have them based on desirable teaching and learning practices. This will typically involve critical self-evaluation on the part of the learner, and reasoning, rather than memorization of texts for test purposes. The bases for marks should be clearly understood by the learner and should be developed as the student moves along in the work of a particular class or course. Thus our goal should be to de-emphasize the grade itself as a motive and to build up emphasis on intrinsic values that can be got by the learner from the work itself. It should be emphasized that marks are not necessary to insure proper motivation. The evidence is that adult education work frequently is much more vital and stimulating in situations where teachers cannot use marks as a crutch. If the work is thought useless the class will evaporate.

A third major purpose of marking may be *to help develop self-evaluative ability*. The problem of developing self-evaluative ability has already been discussed in considerable detail in the chapter on this subject. The goal in marking would be to try to make the marking a dual responsibility with the learner assuming a major role at least *during* the learning process. In this way we can gradually develop in the learner an increasing share of responsibility for identifying the specific goals and purposes, both short- and long-time, toward which he should work, and also help him analyze the procedures he is attempting to use in working toward these goals. One specific approach for developing self-evaluative ability in relation to marking is to discuss with the learners the suggested principles and possible criteria for grading. Then each student is encouraged to draw up a statement of the bases or criteria that he thinks would be most sound for grading himself. Each student then gives the instructor such a list and the instructor adds to or takes from it until mutually satisfactory bases for grading the individual student are established. Obviously, this makes grading a somewhat more difficult and complicated process than it commonly is, but it does help to promote the important ability of self-evaluation and does tend to help take care of individual differences to a degree.

A variation of the method suggested immediately above, which brings the learner into the process even more, is for the teacher and student jointly to set up the bases or principles for determining the latter's grade. Members of the class then determine general class policies, goals, and suggested principles on which the class should be operated and which provide a framework for determining the grade. Then the teacher and the learner each individually take the records of the student's work and, in the light of the principles previously agreed upon, each passes judgment on the quality of work and assigns a mark. After this is done the teacher and learner meet in conference and attempt to iron out or at least clarify points of difference. Obviously, in most school systems the teacher is responsible for finally assigning the mark, but this approach helps to get the learner in on the process and helps the learner to see that the teacher is attempting to mark on the basis of the achievement of goals that will help the individual student.

The fourth purpose of marking, which is related to the one discussed in the preceding paragraphs, is *to provide a basis for educational and vocational counseling.* For this purpose it is ordinarily desirable that the basis on which the mark or marks are arrived at be clearly determined and indicated on the record of the learner. Typically, it is important that the status of the learner with respect to particular groups be indicated. Also, progress of the learner in relation to what seems to be his individual ability is likely to be of some use in counseling and guidance. It is extremely important that the specific bases for judgment in arriving at the mark be indicated together with a listing of the specific strengths and weaknesses the learner has shown. The question is sometimes raised of whether the student should know his specific achievement level in relation to other learners. The same question is also raised frequently about intelligence test scores. This essentially is a guidance function. Over a period of time it is of paramount importance that the learner have an understanding of his potential abilities and his current achievement status in comparison to other learners. This understanding must be *developed* in the learner and cannot be successfully handed to the learner. This means that while the teacher or administrator typically should not *give* the student his intelligence tests scores or perhaps even his achievement level, it is desirable that gradually the learner become able to understand and use such information in deciding his future educational and vocational activities.

Marking may also be legitimately used as a basis for *deciding promotion, acceleration, or retention.*

Promotion should be considered primarily as a placement problem for getting the learner into the best possible future teaching-learning situation. It is just as important that we do not consider promotion as punishment for past performance or lack of achievement. To do this is to endanger future attitudes and learnings. In other words, the teacher should look *forward* rather than backward in considering promotion plans and decide where the learner is likely to move ahead most rapidly.

The learner should quite early become involved in promotion plans that affect him and typically should know in advance what is being considered about his future activities so that he may help to arrive at the decision on where it may be best to place him in the next semester or the next year. If the learner's record indicates the bases upon which marks have been reached, marks can be used in deciding whether the learner is likely to do well in a particular college or advanced class or school. Here again the learner should understand and appreciate the bases on which marks are assigned and thus be in a better position himself to make judgments on his future class and school connections.

A final important purpose that marks may serve is to *inform the parents of the learner of his school progress and goals.* If the parents are to be a really functioning part of the teaching-learning situation and if they are to support the schools properly, it is extremely important that they be informed of school goals and changes in these. One way of doing this is through the marking setup. Mark reports can be planned to aid parents in evaluating the work of the school and indirectly this will pave the way for the parents' giving support to the school, particularly financial support.

When changes are made in the technique of reporting to parents, it is usually desirable to pave the way by enlisting parent help in diagnosing the reporting problems and in setting up a more informative reporting system. Since many of the parents in some communities will not attend meetings for such a purpose, it is typically desirable to use the old type of reporting *with* the new marking system when changes have been effected. This provides the parent with a report of the type with which he is familiar and at the same time paves the way for the introduction of improved reporting.

Usually it is desirable to give some descriptive picture of what the school and the particular parents' child is doing. It is extremely important that an attempt be made to present at least some favorable aspect of the work as well as the real weaknesses of the student. The latter are described in order that the parent, teacher, and learner may work together in helping the student progress. It is important that the teacher attempt to explain the real situation to the parent so that he or she can cooperate in helping the learner move ahead. Usually, the parent is vitally interested in the welfare of the child and is willing and anxious to help the child achieve desirable educational goals if he understands them.

Typically, it is desirable to use the products of learner activities as one key part of reporting to parents. A continuing progress record of the work the learner has planned and carried through gives the parent some picture of what is happening in the school.

If marks are on the basis of individual progress in relation to ability, it is vitally essential that parents be educated to this procedure. Otherwise they are likely to assume that the mark indicates the status of the learner with respect to other learners. Frequently, it is desirable to supplement and support a standard reporting system by using personal notes to parents. So that these will not present too much of a time problem to the teacher the sending of reports can be staggered with so many going each week rather than all going on a particular day.

Parent-Teacher Association meetings at which school goals, procedures, and reporting approaches are discussed will help in promoting an understanding of what the school is trying to do.

Dangers involved in marking

In the following paragraphs will be stated some potential dangers in marking. These will be in the form of questions, and each question will be followed by a brief discussion.

How much relationship do marks have to really significant learnings? There is a very real danger that marks will put emphasis upon those learnings that are easily measured—memorization for example —and de-emphasize many significant learnings such as those involved in cooperation, general social development, emotional development, intellectual curiosity, and healthy attitudes toward continuing learning.

Do the marks tend to measure only favorable learnings and disregard unfavorable learnings, such as those that may be involved in undesirable attitudes toward subject, school, and teachers? Marks may even develop antisocial feelings of superiority and/or inferiority among learners. It is unfortunate that our tests, upon which marks typically are largely based, usually limit considerably the scope of learnings upon which a check is made.

Have marks tended to become an end in themselves rather than a means to superior development? This is unfortunately true in a large number of schools as can be proved by conversations typically heard around examination time. It must be recognized that marks may actually dull the intellectual curiosity of children and sidetrack them from desirable educational pursuits.

Do marks give teachers an extrinsic whip or crutch that may encourage poor teaching? Without marks the poor or incompetent teacher would probably have to get busy. Those who have taught in adult education classes where there are no marks have found this to be particularly true. If the work in the class does not have use and appeal to a class the class itself is likely to disappear. It is quite possible that, if our secondary schools were operated without the marking whip, a more careful study of sound learning and teaching procedure would be necessitated.

Do marks erect a barrier to development of desirable teacher-learner relationships? This question is closely related to that raised in the preceding paragraph. When a student knows that a particular teacher is going to give him a mark at the end of the semester or year, it is somewhat difficult for the learner to reveal his weaknesses to the teacher so that he may get help on them. The student's tendency is to cover up his weaknesses so that he will not be penalized when the judgment is reached on his mark.

How much does the effect of striving for marks result in such undesirable social or character traits as cheating, copying, and trying to beat the game? In a particular school, where Latin was taken by 75 per cent of the students because parents considered it an erudite subject and the mark of a scholar, it was found that cheating on examinations was extremely common. When the students were questioned about this situation most reported that they could see no particular value in their studying Latin but that they had to make a passing grade in order to move along in their work. Therefore, their adjustment to the undesirable teaching-learning situation that had been set up was to try to "beat the game" through cheating on examinations.

Marks in themselves are probably neither bad nor good. It is important that the teacher carefully study the positive values that can be obtained through the use of marks and also be clearly aware of the dangers that may attack the unwary in a teaching-learning situation.

Summary

In summary it should be emphasized that a marking system may either facilitate or hinder desirable learning. To avoid the pitfalls potentially involved in marking and to capitalize on some of the values of a reporting system requires continuous reappraisal and improvement of the system by the teachers and learners involved. Promotion policies must be based on desirable placement practices.

INTERPERSONAL DIFFICULTIES IN CLASS

To be realistic we must recognize that in most school situations the problem of improving interpersonal relations is beset with difficulties. None of these difficulties are so overwhelming as to preclude the strong possibility of making definite improvements along this line, if the teacher is alert and willing to study the possible ways of making improvements. Having a clear recognition of some of the probable difficulties that are likely to be faced makes the chances of work on interpersonal relations more productive. Some of these difficulties are centered largely in the learner and some in the teacher.

In the following paragraphs some difficulties or obstacles in improving interpersonal relations in classes have been identified, briefly discussed, and grouped under the following categories: Learner-centered difficulties, teacher-centered difficulties, and difficulties centered in the administrative or physical setup of the school.

Learner weaknesses that make good interpersonal relations in teaching-learning situations difficult

Learner weaknesses that probably originated with teachers. Initially, it should be recognized that most, if not all, of the difficulties that we have labeled learner-centered have actually been instilled in the learners by one or more previous teachers.

Perhaps the major obstacle to improved interpersonal relations in the school is the tradition well set in the minds of many students that the teacher should do practically all the talking in the classroom with the learner's role one of copying and memorizing what the teacher has said. Another way of stating this is that many learners assume that the teacher has the primary responsibility in the teaching-learning situation and that the student's role is a relatively passive one. The traditional classroom or lecture setup has helped foster this concept. One might approach this question by asking the learners when they come into a particular class how many are attempting to assume significant responsibilities for the development of the class. In the minds of many learners, this traditional outlook on class activity has resulted in a conflict between the desire on the part of the learner to acquire a considerable amount of responsibility, which he may recognize as desirable, as opposed to the well-established habits of dependence on the teacher or administration for what to do, when to do it, and how to do it.

Course pattern constructed without benefit of student ideas. Closely related to the traditional teacher-domination role has been the great emphasis upon a text curriculum or teacher preplanned schedule of work activities for learner groups. This tends to keep the learner from being an actual participant in planning his learning and is likely to quash active group participation. As long as the learner is trained to feel that "the gospel" comes almost entirely from the teacher and/or the textbook, it will be extremely difficult to help him develop desirable learner-learner relationships and optimum teacher-learner relationships.

Purpose of class activities. The well-set idea that the purpose of the class in many cases is for the teacher to quiz the learners and check up on the extent to which they have memorized a text has in many instances made the class a game in which the learner tries to beat the teacher in this checkup process. Closely related to this in the minds of learners is the concept that the class is primarily for marking purposes. This, together with the difficulties that have been presented above, has resulted in a lack of planning on the part of students for class discussion and a lack of information about what will be discussed in the class period. Coupled with these difficulties and resulting partially from them has been a lack of respect on the part of the individual learner for the ideas and suggestions of other learners. This has resulted in a lack of cooperation between other learners in class setups. Some teachers have even gone so far as to discourage one learner from working with other learners with the idea that such activity, if not actually dishonest, at least verges on the dishonest.

Marking systems may work against desirable relations. The testing and marking system that has grown up in many school systems tends to encourage the learner to express what he believes the teacher wants him to say or write rather than to give a real expression of his point of view or his beliefs. This not only tends to put discussions on a relatively superficial level, but it also tends to keep the learner from raising questions that are troubling him, since he may feel that either the teacher or the other learners may look down on him and rate him low in the class if he raises what may seem to them unimportant or insignificant questions.

Teacher-related difficulties, obstacles, or barriers in improving interpersonal relations

Lack of attention to interpersonal relations. Perhaps the major obstacle to improved interpersonal relations development has been the almost exclusive emphasis on the part of teachers in dealing with ideas in books tied with little or no concern with developing desirable interpersonal relations. The overwhelming goal in many classes has been the acquisition of subject matter. This has tended to result in too little attention's being given to the social relations that are being learned at the same time as the subject matter. It has also resulted in relatively little concern for, and attention to, human dynamics in situations in which the information and ideas being learned will presumably be used.

The past lack of attention on the part of the teacher to interpersonal relations has tended to produce similar inattention to communication on the part of learners. Many teachers have given little or no consideration to factors that improve interpersonal relations or to asking such diagnostic questions as these: In what ways do we get our perceptions of others? Why do our faculty meetings tend to break down? Would this type of learning or decision-making be best promoted in an individual, small-group, or large-group procedure or setup? In many cases, past success as a student in the dictatorial type of group operation tends to lead the teacher to use a similar approach. If the teacher has apparently been successful from his standpoint in "getting the job done quickly" through autocratic procedures, he is likely to challenge any suggestion for change in group operations, since that will entail a relearning of many behavior patterns of which he has grown very fond.

Covering information has been paramount. Closely related to this point has been the overwhelming desire on the part of the teacher to cover so much information. Emphasis, in such a situation, is placed on "covering subject matter" rather than on developing learners in the types of activities they most need to practice. This has resulted in the ignoring of basic individual and community social problems or the feeling that interpersonal relations are only in the province of social studies. Even many social studies teachers feel that it is more important to teach the subject matter than to pay any attention to the real individual or community problems. What has been said does not mean that the substantive learnings are not important. It simply means that, from a psychological standpoint, attention should be given to the interpersonal relations habits that are being developed while the substantive material is being learned, and it also means that for the substantive material to function after it is learned, attention must be given to the interpersonal relations situation in which it is to be used.

Teacher selection of discussion topics. Connected with the preceding points is the fact of almost exclusive instructor selection of what is to be discussed, together with a discouraging attitude toward learner discussion since "it takes too much time" and "there is so much to be covered." Only material assigned by the teacher is considered appropriate for discussion in many classes. This means in effect that the learner is disqualified insofar as introducing ideas that seem of considerable significance to him in a particular class is concerned.

Tradition overweighted. Acceptance of tradition as the chief basis for deciding what should be taught and how it should be taught constitutes one of the major obstacles in improving interpersonal relations. "This is the way it has been done, why change?" Even in cases where there has been a desire to move from instructor domination toward democratic teacher-learner relationships we have found that lack of teacher practice in teacher-learner cooperation has frequently resulted in a laissez-faire setup. This has tended to produce excessive bewilderment and lack of needed guidance in developing purposes, in identifying problems, and in setting up ways of going about solving these problems. Some mental upset is desirable for effective learning but an excessive amount is to be avoided.

Exclusive emphasis on individual work. A major difficulty is tied up with the teacher's point of view that out-of-class work should be strictly individual. The idea is even built up in the learner that he is cheating if he works something out in cooperation with other learners. Some teachers take the point of view that since learning is individual it cannot be made profitable, mutually profitable, through the interaction of learners.

Overdependence on text. The third major factor in the classroom triangle, the textbook, has to a large extent been responsible for insufficient emphasis on interpersonal relations. This has been particularly true when we have the archaic single textbook system, putting emphasis on memorization of ideas primarily for test purposes. This too frequently results in discussion coming from text and standard assignments instead of using varied resources and making the discussion a creative pooling of ideas from such resources. In fairness to the single-text approach one should point out that, when it was originally set up, objective evidences of individual differences in learning abilities were not readily available. Such is not the case at the present time, and it is very questionable whether one can defend a single-textbook approach except, perhaps, in a very small number of courses.

Significance of learner status and point of view neglected. Closely related to the point in the preceding paragraph is the idea, which many teachers hold, that only printed materials and the teacher's points of view are of significance. Emphasizing this aspect tends to lead learners to disregard or look down upon other students' points of view. Frequently, the latter can be of considerable significance to the developing learner.

The major difficulty is represented in the point of view of a large number of staff members that learners, at least up to the college level, are really unable to do critical thinking. This point of view, while not supported by experimental evidence, has had much to do with allowing the teaching process to be primarily an information-giving process.

Need for varied methods. Another difficulty, residing primarily in the teacher, has been the lack of recognition of the fact that methods which are very appropriate with one group of learners may be quite inappropriate for another group of students of similar age and grade level. This means that it is an essential part of the job of the teacher or any group leader to become attuned to the operational level upon which a class or group is ready to operate at the moment and then to attempt with the appropriate next steps gradually to raise the self-sufficiency and efficiency level of each member of the group.

Effects on learner insufficiently considered. There has been a relative lack of consideration of the probable effects of what is said on the learner himself. For example, too severe criticism of the learner before he is ready to accept such criticism may have a negative effect on his learning. Another way of stating this point would be to say that tactless direct beating-down of the ego of the individual before he is ready to "take it" may put him down permanently from a learning standpoint. In general, on this point we may say that there has been an inadequate recognition of the need for safeguarding the influence of each on the staff and in the student body. Each individual has a need to influence others and to recognize his influence if he is to be a part of a healthy communications setup in the teaching-learning situation.

Too great repetition of same communication patterns. Another major difficulty in improving interpersonal relations centers in the tendency on the part of many teachers to follow the same communication patterns in class activities. Unnecessary repetition of the same communication pattern tends to lead to duplication of the processes practiced just as much as unnecessary repetition of subject matter leads to the uneconomical use of time. The pattern for class activity that has been conventionally followed has been either to give lectures or to give oral quizzes in which the teacher asks questions and the students give or attempt to give the answers, with the student feeling that the answer is to a high degree for marking purposes rather than for learning purposes. Here the teacher tends to become a "whip" rather than a guide. The general questions and answers in such interpersonal relations situations tend to be limited to isolated details rather than to the development and solution of significant problems.

Many teachers have never experienced democratic teaching-learning situations. The teacher tends to ask questions that require merely factual information. This is likely to encourage memorization rather than thinking. Sometimes closely tied up with this is teacher avoidance of discussions on controversial issues, which usually are issues of real concern to the learner. The most difficult obstacle to overcome is probably related to the fact that many teachers are untrained in democratic processes in general, and in effective teacher-learner, teacher-teacher, and teacher-administrator relations in particular. This inexperience, of course, is reflected in a holding to relatively dictatorial procedures.

Lack of training on the part of teachers in taking the position of the other person and deciding what would seem to be appropriate from his standpoint is frequently apparent. If the teacher attempts to take the role of the learner, and the learner attempts to take the role of the teacher, an improvement in interpersonal relations will frequently result. We must attempt to get away from a feeling of insecurity and a fear on the part of the teacher that the class may "get away from him" if democratic procedures are followed.

Teacher training may be a source of difficulty. Teachers who have themselves been taught in teacher-training institutions that use relatively rigid and autocratic teaching procedures have great difficulty in visualizing what democratic procedure actually means. Even after rather clear-cut visualization of what such democratic interpersonal communications would be, the teacher still has the problem of developing skill in producing these relations. It is unfortunate that about the only type of teacher-learning situation in which many teachers have participated has been strongly teacher-dominated.

Professional shell. It is undesirable that teachers and other educators have frequently tended to build a professional shell, and have not built up effective communication channels with which to keep professionally alive. Other teachers, supervisors, administrators, students, and parents can provide good avenues of professional stimulation if appropriate channels are kept open. Periodically it is desirable for the teacher to seek new "faces" for new ideas.

Diagnosis neglected. Closely related to this difficulty is the almost complete professional concern and communication with the learners, forgetting that one teacher improved is as good as a hundred learners improved, and one administrator improved in point of view is probably as valuable for general improvement in learning as a thousand learners changed in a similar extent. Finally, to be mentioned is the lack of ability on the part of many teachers, administrators, and students to diagnose the quality and effectiveness of the communication channels that have been built up. Unless and until we are able to diagnose the strengths and weaknesses of such channels and to know effective procedures for improving them, it is extremely unlikely that great progress will be made in improving interpersonal relations.

BIBLIOGRAPHY

1. ALEXANDER, W. M., AND SAYLOR, J. G. *Secondary Education.* New York: Rinehart and Co., 1950.
   Discusses principles and practices related to secondary-school methods.
2. CARROLL, HERBERT A. *Mental Hygiene.* New York: Prentice Hall, Inc., 1951.
   Very useful to give student better understanding of the dynamics of adjustment that underlie many school problems.
3. COY, GENEVIEVE L. *Ways Toward Self-Discipline.* New York: The Dalton Schools, 1950.
   Describes discipline-related goals and methods for developing self-control, self-direction, and self-discipline.
4. HYMES, JAMES L., JR. *Discipline.* New York: Bureau of Publications, Teachers College, Columbia University, 1949.
   Contains a useful analysis of discipline problems.
5. KRETCH, DAVID, AND CRUTCHFIELD, RICHARD S. *Theory and Problems of Social Psychology,* 1948.
   Gives systematic, interpretative account of human behavior. Emphasis is given to interpersonal relations. Excellent basal material for graduate students and the more advanced undergraduate learners.
6. MORT, PAUL R., AND VINCENT, W. S. *Modern Educational Practice.* New York: McGraw-Hill Book Co., Inc., 1950.
   Attempts to give a guide to teaching by discussing twenty-one teaching procedures. Each procedure is described and illustrated, and the reasons for its use are indicated.
7. RIVLIN, H. N. *Teaching Adolescents in Secondary Schools.* New York: Appleton-Century-Crofts, 1948.
   Discusses a variety of method-related problems in such areas as planning, questioning, managing the classroom, studying, and evaluation.
8. SHEVIAKOV, G. V., AND REDL, FRITZ. *Discipline for Today's Children and Youth.* Washington, D.C.: Department of Super-

vision and Curriculum Development, National Education Association, 1944.

Analyzes discipline problems and suggests ways of meeting them through fostering growth in the person.

9. SWANSON, GUY E., NEWCOMB, T. M., HARTLEY, E. L., AND OTHERS. *Readings in Social Psychology.* New York: Henry Holt and Co. 1952.

Well portrays the empirical foundations upon which social psychology rests. Most useful for graduate students and advanced undergraduate students who want to build up a sound basis for understanding and dealing with school problems · involving interpersonal relations.

10. WILLIAMSON, E. G., AND FOLEY, J. P. *Counseling and Discipline.* New York: McGraw-Hill Book Co., Inc., 1949.

Emphasizes individualized methods of dealing with misbehavior.

Part Five

RESEARCH EVIDENCE

15

RESEARCH EVIDENCE ON

NEWER PRACTICES

THE educator may consider various kinds of evidence of the efficacy of particular approaches to teaching-learning situations. Some teachers are satisfied with evidence deduced from direct personal experiences. Others give considerable weight to the opinions of "authorities," frequently without considering how particular authorities arrived at their conclusions. Evidence accepted by some educators of the effectiveness of particular approaches may rest upon the way the procedures seem to fit into a theoretical framework of assumptions. These assumptions may or may not have been carefully and critically examined by the person using them.

One type of evidence relating to the effectiveness of different teaching and learning procedures, which, unfortunately, has been much neglected, is based on experimentation or research. It is with this that we are concerned in this chapter.

No attempt will be made to summarize all or even a large number of the researches that have been designed to test or improve the effectiveness of one or more aspects of what may generally be called the "newer practices" in education. A rather comprehensive and representative list of such researches is given at the end of this chapter. Here a brief picture will be given, however, of each of three types of studies: (1) a "matched pairs" study, (2) a developmental, process study, and (3) a summary evaluation of available research evidence.

Purposes

The study, launched in 1930, was designed to help get answers to questions such as the following: How can improvements be made in secondary schools without risking the students' chances of being admitted to college? In what areas is secondary education clearly inadequate? What can secondary schools do in the way of improvement if released from the usual subject and unit requirements for college admission? What new evaluative instruments are needed to test new teacher objectives? How well do high-school students who went to college from experimental schools succeed? Is the commonly made assumption sound that "the skill, knowledge, discipline, habit of mind, and understanding essential for success in a college depend upon the study in high school of certain subjects for certain periods of time"? Can secondary schools be trusted to use wisely their freedom from traditional college requirements? Is it possible to give more attention to the present concerns of all high-school pupils without sacrificing adequate preparation for those going on to college?

Procedures

At the request of the committee in charge of the study, most colleges and universities agreed to release a small number of representative secondary schools from the usual subject and unit requirements for college admission. Admission to college was to be based primarily upon two criteria: (1) an appropriate recommendation from the student's secondary-school principal, and (2) a carefully recorded history of the student's school life including results on tests and examinations of various types.

Thirty representative high schools were selected who were willing to experiment if freed from the usual college requirements. The schools started developing plans for changes in curriculum, organization, and procedure, in the fall of 1933. Patterns of change differed considerably from school to school. However, representatives of the thirty schools met annually for mutual stimulation in thinking and planning.

Two major principles guided the work of the thirty schools: "The first was that the general life of the school and methods of teaching should conform to what is now known about the ways in which human beings learn and grow." (1, p. 17.) "The second major principle which guided the work of the participating schools was that the high school in the United States should re-discover its chief reason for existence." (1, p. 18.) The Thirty Schools early became known as experimental schools. Much attention from the beginning was given to measuring, recording, and reporting the results of the work of the schools.

Considerable emphasis in the eight-year study was given to the development of testing instruments designed, by experts on the Evaluation Staff, to meet new teacher and administrator purposes. Two illustrations of the types of objectives for which instruments were designed are (1) the development of effective methods of thinking and (2) the inculcation of sound attitudes and the development of social sensitivity. It should be noted that these tests and evaluative devices were largely developed by outside experts and imposed on the learners, rather than growing out of the learners and the individual school's self-evaluative experiences as has been the case in the next major study discussed in this chapter. It should be noted that some tests were of the "home-grown" variety.

Results

Graduates of the Thirty Schools were studied to determine how they succeeded in college. A basis of comparison was established by "matching, with utmost care, each graduate from the thirty schools with another student in the same college who had taken the prescribed courses, had graduated from some high school not participating in the study, and had met the usual entrance requirements. They were matched on the basis of sex, age, race, scholastic aptitude scores, home and community background, interest, and probable future." (1, p. 109.) "In the comparison of the 1,475 matched pairs which were intensively studied, the College Follow-up Staff found that the graduates of the Thirty Schools

1. earned a slightly higher total grade average;
2. earned higher grade averages in all subject fields except foreign language;
3. specialized in the same academic fields as did the comparison students;
4. did not differ from the comparison group in the number of times they were placed on probation;

5. received slightly more academic honors in each year;

6. were more often judged to possess a high degree of intellectual curiosity and drive;

7. were more often judged to be precise, systematic, and objective in their thinking;

8. were more often judged to have developed clear or well-formulated ideas concerning the meaning of education—especially in the first two years in college;

9. more often demonstrated a high degree of resourcefulness in meeting new situations;

10. did not differ from the comparison group in ability to plan their time effectively;

11. had about the same problems of adjustment as the comparison group, but approached their solution with greater effectiveness;

12. participated somewhat more frequently, and more often enjoyed appreciative experiences, in the arts;

13. participated more in all organized student groups except religious and 'service' activities;

14. earned in each college year a high percentage of non-academic honors (officership in organizations, election to managerial societies, athletic insignia, leading roles in dramatic and musical presentations);

15. did not differ from the comparison group in the quality of adjustment to their contemporaries;

16. differed only slightly from the comparison group in the kinds of judgments about their schooling;

17. had a somewhat better orientation toward the choice of a vocation;

18. demonstrated a more active concern for what was going on in the world.

The College Follow-up Staff has this to say about these findings:

"Some of these differences were not large, but wherever reported, they were consistent for each class. It is apparent that when one finds even small margins of difference for a number of large groups, the probability greatly increases that the differences cannot be due to chance alone.

"It is quite obvious from these data that the Thirty Schools' graduates, as a group, have done a somewhat better job than the comparison group whether success is judged by college standards, by the students' contemporaries, or by the individual students." (1, pp. 111-112.)

"The graduates of the most experimental schools were strikingly more successful than their matchees. Differences in their favor were much greater than the differences between the total Thirty Schools and their comparison group. Conversely, there were no large or consistent differences between the least experimental graduates and their comparison group. For these students the differences were smaller and less consistent than for the total Thirty Schools and their comparison group."

The College Follow-up Staff comments on these facts as follows:

"If the proof of the pudding lies in these groups, and a good part of it does, then it follows that the colleges got from these most experimental schools a higher proportion of sound, effective college material than they did from the more conventional schools in similar environments. If colleges want students who have developed effective and objective habits of thinking, and who yet maintain a healthy orientation toward their fellows, then they will encourage the already obvious trend away from restrictions which tend to inhibit departures or deviations from the conventional curriculum patterns." (1, p. 113.)

THE SOUTHERN STUDY—A DEVELOPMENTAL, PROCESS STUDY

A very significant methodological study of quite a different sort from that already reported is represented by the Southern Association Study. Although only a very brief summary of some aspects of the study is reported here, the reader is referred to references numbered 10, 21, 31, and 36 at the end of the chapter for a more comprehensive picture of the origin and development of the study. In this study some thirty-three secondary schools were encouraged to make use of the scientific method in improving teaching-learning situations. Because emphasized goals and purposes were "individualized" in the schools, no conventional controlled experiment seemed feasible or desirable. Rather, most of the evidence regarding the outcomes of the developmental investigation is of the "case study" type.

Assumptions of initiators

Those who initiated the study in the thirty-three schools worked on the following assumptions:

1. Then-current programs of secondary education could and should be improved.

2. Educational improvement could be accomplished through programs designed better to serve the needs of youths. A school program should be particularized to provide for the common and individual needs of its students.

3. A continuous process of democratic cooperative problem-solving is needed.

4. The scientific method of problem-solving is the soundest method of promoting basic educational improvement.

Results of the study

Outcomes of the Southern Association Study have been categorized under two broad headings: (1) those distinguishing features that characterized the organization and procedures of the thirty-three secondary schools as they tried to implement the assumptions in local situations, and (2) those expressed in terms of pupils' learnings and accomplishments.

Features of school organization and practice

Distinguishing features that tended to characterize organization and practice were:

What was studied was particularized in terms of local students' needs. Thus, one major continuing problem was identifying needs (done cooperatively by teachers and students) and devising activities that would meet these needs.

Student activities became highly purposeful. Procedures became more directed to achieving specific and immediately purposeful ends. Relatively less emphasis was placed on conventional, intermediary purposes formerly used almost exclusively in the schools. This change characterized the work of both teachers and learners. Teacher concern and goals tended to shift from the teaching of subjects to a concern for the individual pupil.

To meet individual needs, the organization, curricula, and methods in the schools and classes became extremely flexible. School staffs and different teachers on the same staff found quite different procedures desirable in the various situations encountered.

Planned redirection in the work of teachers and students resulted in schools and classes becoming unconventional. One major aspect of this unconventionality was the frequency with which different parts of the community became, in effect, the school or classroom.

Schools were in a continuous process of flux or change. Teachers and students were "testing out, discarding, revising, testing out again, and changing the school program in whole or in part." Change resulted from continuous attempts in using the scientific method to find better ways of teaching and learning.

Individual teachers and school staffs continuously attempted to redefine the role or function of the school in society.

Student achievements

Most of those engaged in the study considered of greatest importance those learnings "that resulted from a more intimate, personal, and purposeful part in the educative process" on the part of the learner. Before considering these learnings, let us first consider the extent to which more conventional learnings, in subject matter, were acquired.

As has been already suggested, any centrally conducted, uniform testing program was inappropriate in this study in view of the purposes that have already been indicated. Since the goals and purposes of individual schools were different and those in charge of the study, including students in some phases, attempted to evaluate in terms of the objectives of the schools and students themselves, it was not felt that a uniform testing program was appropriate. It was recognized that an externally imposed testing program would, in effect, tend to set the objectives which it was believed important that the individual school be largely responsible for evolving to meet individual learner and community needs. Although there was not a central testing program, there was much standardized achievement testing done in individual schools where the need for it seemed to exist. In the *Southern Association Quarterly*, volume seven, pages 253-303, can be found a detailed analysis of test results. However, this is a brief summary of the results. "Of the 86 groups tested, 59, or more than two-thirds of them, were *at* or *above* the norms. 54 groups, well over one-half of them, *exceeded* the norms. Because the achievement tended to be higher in the larger groups tested, an analysis in terms of the number of pupils who were from groups that *equaled* or *exceeded* the norms revealed even higher achievement. More than *80 per cent* of the pupils tested were from groups that *equaled* or *exceeded* the norms on the tests." (10, p. 200.) In general, the investigators concluded that "use of the method of the study as an instrument of school improvement resulted in more learning of the informational and skill sort than is commonly achieved in a typical American high school. (Or, shall we be conservative and say just as much?) The truth is that those of us who have worked with standardized tests in the South are well aware that such achievement is not too common in Southern high schools." (10, p. 201.) ". . . reports from these studies (of high-school graduates in college) indicate that the graduates have done well in college. Their grades have been satisfactory, usually higher than those made by graduates of the same schools prior to entering the Study and often above the average of the grades given in the institutions where they attended. Furthermore, graduates have actively participated in college life; and although often critical of the colleges, they have made satisfactory adjustments to them." (10, p. 202.)

Learnings of a personal-social nature

It is recognized that how well learners are able to score on standard achievement tests and what grades they make in college is important. However, most of those concerned with the study were primarily interested in those learnings "directly related to the personal, social and intellectual development of students." These learnings involve such things as "a broadening of interests, the development of acceptable purposes, formation of good habits of work, learning careful planning, the assumption of responsibility, and the need for constant evaluation; and learnings with wide social implications—skill in democratic group procedures, habits of direct attack on social problems—were the kinds of learnings which many teachers sought." (10, p. 202.)

Those in charge of the study felt that the most appropriate data for judging learnings were those that revealed the origin and nature of the purposes with which learners engage in a school activity, plus the nature of the student's experiences as these purposes develop. A case illustration of the kind of learnings and data considered important in the study is the following, which is quoted from a teacher's report on work in a social studies class: "There was a tree located on the south side of the campus which some of the students decided was a menace to individuals and to cars parked nearby. They suggested that something be done about it. Some thought that the tree should be cut down and others thought that steps should be taken to save the tree. After discussion it was agreed that a tree expert should be consulted. This was done and his opinion was that the tree should be cut down because the cost of saving it would be too great. The teacher raised a question as to the legality of cutting down a tree on public property. The group sought advice from a law student and asked if he would visit the class and discuss the legal aspects of removing the tree. After presentation and discussion, the conclusion was reached that the responsible person should be interviewed concerning the removal of the tree. This individual was the school superintendent. He would have been responsible for any damage done by falling limbs. The students asked for and were granted an interview with the superintendent, who heard their suggestions, promised to have the tree removed, and made provision for this to be done. In the meantime, some of the students had considered the appearance of the campus and suggested that a new tree should be planted in place of the old one. A tree was secured, and plans were made for it to be planted and dedicated at a ceremony attended by the whole class, other students who were free at the time and the principal. One of the boys presided at the planting ceremony. A girl recited Joyce Kilmer's poem, 'Trees.' The chairman of the group made a short talk on conservation of our trees and dedicated the new tree to the boys of the school in the armed forces. The principal accepted the tree for the school, and the music group completed the ceremony by singing 'God Bless America.'

"The theory accepted here concerning the data that are necessary and appropriate for inferring learning of a personal-social nature postulates that (to the extent we can accept the statement as reporting the facts) the report just quoted *furnishes valid evidence that worthwhile learning took place*. Activities of the sort described, engaged in with reasons which were made clear, constitute 'purposeful practice,' which in turn means learning. The reader is warned that he must be willing to accept this theory if the data presented here are to be satisfying to him.

"Furthermore, the reader should not expect any efforts to quantify the data. Since such technological developments as the counting of outcomes seem to be the inevitable result of continued use of the scientific method, efforts in this direction would undoubtedly have been forthcoming had the Study been permitted to reach greater maturity. But, as the reader was cautioned in Chapter 3, (Reference 10) implications of the scientific method to 'new fields' must of necessity give primary attention to methodology.

"The theory of learning presented in the paragraphs above was implicit in the work of great numbers of the teachers and administrators participating in the Southern Study. This fact is evidenced by the further fact that a good part of their reporting, both formal and informal, not only described the activities of teachers, pupils, and patrons, but also carefully identified the nature of the purposes back of the activities and the means by which these purposes were determined. Published reports from the schools and articles from numerous teachers in the Study were often so characterized and, therefore, constitute data relating to the learnings of the children." (10, pp. 203-204.)

There is not room in this book to give a complete picture of the evidence of learnings of a personal-social nature. However, the reader is urged to study the reports given in references numbered 10 and 31 at the end of this chapter.

AN EVALUATION OF MODERN EDUCATION

Leonard, Eurich, and others, after an intensive study of 154 research investigations, concluded: "In practically every study and in almost every skill that has been considered, as the charts so strikingly show, children in schools following the newer practices are slightly, if not markedly superior to children in the more conventional schools. On an *a priori* basis one might expect children working in a modern program to do much better in the skills that are given more emphasis than formerly—skills such as work-study library, critical-thinking, health and the skills in personal-social relationships. But for them to excel also in the skills that form the 'stock-in-trade' of the conventional program and to which the newer programs devote less time is really an amazing accomplishment for which too much credit cannot be given to the more modern and efficient practices." (14, p. 280.)

The weight of evidence as documented in the literature is overwhelmingly in favor of newer practices. More and better studies need to be made, but present evidence should encourage the teacher to become familiar with and to experiment with newer practices.

BIBLIOGRAPHY

Representative research studies or summaries concerned with the relative effectiveness of traditional approaches and newer teaching-learning practices.

1. AIKEN, W. M. *The Story of the Eight-Year Study.* New York: Harper and Bros., 1942.
2. BRIGGS, T. H., AND OTHERS. *Laboratory Techniques of Teaching.* New York: Bureau of Publications, Teachers College, Columbia University, 1938.
3. CHAMBERLIN, D., *et al. Did They Succeed in College?* New York: Harper and Bros., 1942.
4. DAVEY, J. R., AND HILL, H. C. *Review of Six Unpublished Studies of the Morrison Plan.* Eighth Yearbook of the National Council for Social Studies. Cambridge, Massachusetts: The National Council for Social Studies, 1937. pp. 1-20.
5. DAVIS, P. R., AND MORGAN, M. *A Balanced Educational Program for Santa Monica.* Santa Monica, California: Board of Education, 1940.
6. DOLL, RONALD, "High School Pupils' Attitudes toward Teaching Procedures." *School Review*, 55:222-27; April 1947.
7. FINCH, FRANK, AND GILLENWATER, V. "Reading Achievement Then and Now." *Elementary School Journal*, 49: 446-54; April 1949.
8. HELBING, MARY E. "Evaluation of the Procedures of a Modern Elementary School in Terms of the Subsequent Adjustment of Its Pupils." *California Journal of Elementary Education*, 8:137-46; February 1940.
9. HOPKINS, L. T., AND MENDENHALL, J. E. *Achievement at Lincoln School.* New York: Bureau of Publications, Teachers College, Columbia University, 1934.
10. JENKINS, FRANK C., AND OTHERS. *Cooperative Study for the Improvement of Education.* Durham, North Carolina: Duke University Press, 1946.
11. JERSILD, A. T., AND OTHERS. "An Evaluation of Aspects of the Activity Program in the New York City Public Elementary Schools." *Journal of Experimental Education*, 8:166-207; December 1939.
12. JERSILD, A. T., *et al.* "A Further Comparison of Pupils in Activity and Non-Activity Schools." *Journal of Experimental Education*, 9:308; June 1941.
13. KIGHT, S. S., AND MICKELSON, J. M. "Problem vs. Subject." *The Clearing House*, 24:3-7; September 1949.

14. LEONARD, J. P., AND EURICH, A. C., editors. *An Evaluation of Modern Education*. New York: D. Appleton-Century, 1942.

15. LEWIN, K., *et al.* "Patterns of Aggressive Behavior in Experimentally Created 'Social Climates'." *Journal of Social Psychology*, Bulletin for the Society for the Psychological Study of Social Issues, 10: 269-98; May 1939.

16. LINDSAY, MARGARET. *A Comparative Study of Educational Achievement and Personality Development in Progressive and Traditional Schools*. Masters Thesis. State College, Pennsylvania: Pennsylvania State College, 1939.

17. LONGSTREET, R. J. "An Experiment with Social Attitudes." *School Review*, 43:202-8; March 1935.

18. MORRISON, J. CAYCE, *et al*. *The Activity Program; A Survey of the Curriculum Experiment with the Activity Program in the Elementary Schools of the City of New York*. Albany, New York: N.Y. State Education Department, 1941.

19. New York City Experiment. See Volume 12, page 282 of June, 1942, issue of *Review of Educational Research* for a list of articles on this six-year experiment based on 65,000 children in 69 elementary schools.

20. OBERHOLTZER, E. E. *An Integrated Curriculum in Practice*. New York: Bureau of Publications, Teachers College, Columbia University, 1937.

21. ORR, M. L. "Montevallo High School Experimental Program." *The Southern Association Quarterly*, 9:110-18; February 1945.

22. PISTOR, F. A. "Evaluating Newer School Practices by the Observational Method." *Sixteenth Yearbook of the Department of Elementary School Principals*. Washington, D.C.: National Education Association, 1937. pp. 377-89.

23. PROCTOR, WILLIAM M. *The Six-Four-Four Plan of School Organization in Pasadena, California*, Pasadena, California: Board of Education, 1933.

24. Progressive Education Association (Informal Committee on Evaluation of Newer Practices in Education). *New Methods vs. Old in American Education*. New York: Teachers College, Columbia University, 1941.

25. QUILLEN, I. JAMES, AND HANNA, LAVONE. *Education for Social Competence*. Chicago: Scott, Foresman and Company, 1948.

26. ROSANDER, A. C. "A Quantitative Study of Social Attitudes." *School Review*, 43:614-20; October 1935.

27. The Roslyn Elementary Schools. *A Report of a Study of the Instructional Program*. Roslyn, New York: Board of Education, 1938.

28. SCHWEBEL, M., AND ASCH, M. J. "Research Possibilities in Nondirective Teaching." *Journal of Educational Psychology,* 39:359-69. October 1948.

29. SMITH, B. O., STANLEY, W. O., AND SHORES, J. H. *Fundamentals of Curriculum Construction.* Yonkers, New York: World Book Company, 1950. pp. 582-614.

30. SMITH, EUGENE R. "Results of the Eight-Year Study." *Progressive Education,* 22:30-32, 43-44; October 1944.

31. *Southern Association Quarterly.* See the February and August, 1946, issues, Volume 10, for a picture of the purposes, methodology, outcomes, and implications of the Southern Study.

32. STANFORD, T. S. *The Effectiveness of the Activity-Unit Procedure vs. the Textbook-Recitation Method in Teaching.* Master's Thesis; abstract in the *Pennsylvania State College Studies in Education,* No. 22, 1940. pp. 59-60.

33. STEWART, DOROTHY H. "Children's Preferences in Types of Assignments." *Elementary School Journal,* 47:93-97; October 1946.

34. TATE, H. L. "An Evaluation of the Project Method." *Elementary School Journal,* 37:122-32; October 1936.

35. WALLACE W., CHREITZBERG, J., AND SIMS, V. M. *The Story of Holtville.* Deatsville, Alabama: Holtville High School, 1944.

36. WARD, W. E. "An Experimental Study of Two Methods of Teaching Chemistry in Senior High School." *Journal of Experimental Education,* 11:69-80; September 1942.

37. WASHBURNE, C. W., AND RATHS, L. E. "The High School Achievement of Children Trained under the Individual Technique." *Elementary School Journal,* 28:214-24; November 1927.

38. WATERS, EUGENE A. *A Study of the Application of an Educational Theory to Science Instruction.* New York: Bureau of Publications, Teachers College, Columbia University, 1942.

39. WILLIAMS, SIMON, AND LAURITS, JAMES D. "Scientists and Education." *The Scientific Monthly,* 72:282-88; May 1951.

40. WRIGHTSTONE, J. W. "Measuring the Attainment of Newer Educational Objectives." *Sixteenth Yearbook of the Department of Elementary School Principals.* Washington, D.C.: National Education Association, 1937. pp. 493-501.

41. WRIGHTSTONE, J. W. "Evaluation of Newer Instructional Practices." *Twelfth Yearbook of the National Department of Supervisors and Directors of Instruction.* Washington, D.C.: National Education Association, 1939. pp. 307-27.

Part Six

THE CHALLENGE OF THE FUTURE

16

SOME CHALLENGES THE

TEACHER FACES

In the preceding chapters of this book an attempt has been made to suggest some of the vast number of challenges that the alert teacher faces from day to day. In these final paragraphs we will point out some of the key challenges the professional teacher gladly accepts as a stimulating part of his occupation.

Too great emphasis cannot be given to the challenge of individual differences. It is unlikely that any teacher will ever be able to meet with complete success the immense challenge of differences in abilities, needs, attitudes, motivations, interests, and all the other dimensions of individual differences. However, the teacher with a healthy attitude welcomes such a challenge to his professional ability. Some evidence has been given in preceding chapters that it is unlikely that a teacher will make significant progress in meeting individual differences if he attempts to monopolize the learning processes as he has done in many classes in the past. It does appear extremely possible that immense, almost unlimited, progress can be made in meeting individual differences if the teacher is willing to try to train the learner in the many processes necessary to carry on learning without continuous specific direction on the teacher's part. Not only is such a step sound from a motivational standpoint but it is also imperative if we are to train students to continue systematic learning after they leave school. The challenge to the teacher then becomes primarily one of learning how effectively to guide students in the development of key learning processes, including such ones as identifying problems, evaluating work, doing purposeful reading, and other processes that have been discussed in preceding chapters.

The teacher also faces the challenge of being continuously alert to a developing, dynamic set of processes and relationships with which he is dealing. This is opposed to the cut and dried curriculum and course procedures upon which many instructors have depended in the past. It means that if the student is encouraged to be a working partner in teaching-learning situations no one can predict in advance with great accuracy exactly what the learner can or should be doing at any particular point in his developmental process. As a matter of fact, the teacher faces the challenge of helping each learner in the classroom develop his own course and his own curriculum in terms of his needs, abilities, interests, and all the other factors of significance in deciding what is most important for him to do. Some of these activities on the part of the learner will be common activities shared with one or more others in the class. It does mean, however, that it will be impossible for the teacher to lay out in advance exactly what he wants the learner to do during the course. To many teachers this challenge is particularly upsetting. But it would appear it must be faced if we are to recognize the essentially developmental and dynamic characteristics that characterize healthy process learnings.

It would seem also that the teacher faces a significant problem or challenge in trying to develop attitudes on the part of the student that will result in continuing systematic learning after the teacher is no longer with the learner. This means that instead of the instructor's attempting to put across or to cover a certain amount of subject matter during a course, one of his primary concerns will be helping learners to develop an attitude that will result in continued systematic learning after finishing a course and after graduating from formal education. To meet this challenge, the teacher will have to try to develop self-guidance, self-direction, and internal discipline on the part of the individual learner.

There are many other challenges that the teacher faces but perhaps none is more significant than the challenge to the teacher to continue his own systematic learning. Will the teacher believe enough in systematic learning to set an example for his students? If such an example is set, it will mean that the teacher will practice the learning processes characteristic of healthy learning activity in meeting his own professional problems. It will mean that the teacher will practice becoming more and more adept himself in such processes as problem identification, problem selection, problem solution, and the service learnings that have been discussed in preceding chapters. Meeting such a challenge successfully involves two major gains for the teacher and indirectly for the learner. In the first place, the teacher will gain self-satisfaction of the type he is trying to help learners gain by practicing what he preaches. In the second place, the continuous study on the part of the teacher will not only result in the improvement of his teaching and in his more effectively meeting challenging teaching-learning situations, but will also, in the long run, result in vastly improved learner behavior on the part of those with whom he comes in contact.

Teaching can and should be an exhilarating experience if we are willing to face the basic challenges that teaching-learning situations suggest.

AUTHOR INDEX

481

SUBJECT INDEX